From Solidarity to Schisms

126

Internationale Forschungen zur
Allgemeinen und
Vergleichenden Literaturwissenschaft

From Solidarity to Schisms
9/11 and After in Fiction and Film from Outside the US

Edited by Cara Cilano

Amsterdam - New York, NY 2009

Cover Image:
9/11, mixed media piece by Jean Tock

Cover design:
Pier Post

Le papier sur lequel le présent ouvrage est imprimé remplit les prescriptions de "ISO 9706:1994, Information et documentation - Papier pour documents - Prescriptions pour la permanence".

The paper on which this book is printed meets the requirements of " ISO 9706:1994, Information and documentation - Paper for documents - Requirements for permanence".

Die Reihe „Internationale Forschungen zur Allgemeinen und Vergleichenden Literaturwissenschaft" wird ab dem Jahr 2005 gemeinsam von Editions Rodopi, Amsterdam – New York und dem Weidler Buchverlag, Berlin herausgegeben. Die Veröffentlichungen in deutscher Sprache erscheinen im Weidler Buchverlag, alle anderen bei Editions Rodopi.

From 2005 onward, the series „Internationale Forschungen zur Allgemeinen und Vergleichenden Literaturwissenschaft" will appear as a joint publication by Editions Rodopi, Amsterdam – New York and Weidler Buchverlag, Berlin. The German editions will be published by Weidler Buchverlag, all other publications by Editions Rodopi.

ISBN: 978-90-420-2702-2
E-Book ISBN: 978-90-420-2703-9

Printed in The Netherlands

to Samuel and Sofia

for Joseph Kandefer, Sr.

Contents

Acknowledgements

I extend my gratitude and thanks to all the volume's contributors. They excited me with their ideas and proved themselves to be exemplary colleagues through the timely completion of their work. Two contributors deserve special recognition: Silvia Schultermandl and Magali Cornier Michael. To Silvia, my friend, I owe thanks for her organization of our 2008 MESEA panel, which is what prompted me to start thinking about my own contribution to this volume. Magali, old friend and mentor, provided me no end of good advice, support, and encouragement.

The University of North Carolina Wilmington provided me with leave time in the fall of 2008 during which I compiled much of this volume. I am grateful for their support of my research. Several of my UNCW colleagues in various departments helped me disseminate the call for contributions, and I thank them for their efforts. I want also to express my gratitude to Keith Newlin, professor and chair of the Department of English at UNCW, for his enthusiasm and time-saving indexing software.

Many thanks go to Lee Schweninger, intellectual companion and friend, who read my contributions with care and listened to my detailed recounting of the travails of manuscript preparation with patience and good humor.

There is, of course, no way to convey accurately my gratitude to my family. So, instead, I offer this work to our future and our past.

September 11, 2001

Ewa Lipska
translated by Margret Grebowicz

Poets secret agents holy rolling taxpayers
songwriters jewelers
will hang posters
detailing a crime.

Sometimes even poems. Sometimes even songs.

Jewelers will carefully polish the facts.
The appropriate shape. The appropriate shine.
The precise jewelry of catastrophe.

Naturally
everyone will surrender to the press.

And only my tailor
with whom I chat in a quiet
chain stitch
says
that the world has unraveled.

As the sewing machine
cackles.

11. Września 2001

Poeci wywiadowcy świątobliwi podatnicy
pieśniarze jubilerzy
ogłaszać będą
rysopisy zbrodni.

Czasami nawet wiersze. Czasami nawet pieśni.

Jubilerzy starannie będą szlifować fakty.
Odpowiedni kształt. Odpowiedni połysk.
Precyzyjna biżuteria katastrofy.

Naturalnie
wszyscy poddawać się będą do druku.

I tylko mój krawiec
z którym cicho rozmawiamy
ściegiem płaskim
mówi
że świat się spruł.

A maszyna do szycia
zjadliwie się śmieje.

Introduction: From Solidarity to Schisms

Cara Cilano

The early weeks of 2009 marked a time of nearly unparalleled exuberance in the United States and, perhaps, much of the rest of the world as Americans inaugurated their 44th president, Barack Obama. The event was historic, of course, because of Mr. Obama's mixed race heritage and his self-identification as an African American. From both within and beyond the US's borders, Mr. Obama's election signaled the liberatory potential of the longest running experiment in democracy. At the same time, Mr. Obama's election represented an end to the exploits of power that characterized George W. Bush's administration. Cars and lawns I see here in southeastern North Carolina still bear pro-Obama stickers and signs in these months after the election. One sticker I see regularly endorses the Obama/Biden ticket with the slogan: "Hope Over Fear." This optimism speaks directly to how deeply troubled ordinary American citizens have been with what the US government has perpetrated and tried to justify both in its domestic and foreign policies in the shadow of 9/11. Thus, the hope accompanying Mr. Obama into the Oval Office complements the historic import of the US's election of its first African American president.

And, yet, there's something peculiar about this overflow of optimism and celebration in the early weeks of 2009. The very infrastructure of the globalized economy is imploding. As nations around the world feel the effects of calamitous decline, they risk dismissing the importance of the situations in Iraq and Afghanistan, two immediate consequences of the US's response to the events of 11 September 2001. And if the Obama administration alters the US's "war on terror" in any way, it will certainly be by raising troop levels in Afghanistan, thereby perpetuating the country's image as military aggressor and, potentially, embroiling the US in an unending conflict.

The simultaneity of Americans' political and historical hope alongside the worldwide economy's downward plummet and the US's prolonged "war on terror" mirrors another moment similarly characterized by unfathomable vulnerability and the possibility of a better future: 11 September 2001. To identify this moment as one of possibility rather than solely of grief at first appears callous given the tremendous loss of life. Grief is compounded, after all, by fear, as Jacques Derrida explains: "[T]he wound remains open by our terror before the *future* and not only the past."[1] In other words, what is "tragic"

---

1 Giovanna Borradori, *Philosophy in a Time of Terror: Dialogues with Jürgen Habermas and*

about 9/11 is "not what is presently happening or what has happened in the past but the precursory signs of what threatens to happen."[2] This anticipation of future "traumatism" obstructs the "work of mourning" while it also works to justify the violations of democratic principles, civil liberties, and agreed-upon conceptualizations of justice that have emerged in the wake of September 2001.[3]

To succumb to the fear and anxiety that the anticipation of a future traumatism produces, however, is to fall away from the pursuit of precisely the ideals—democracy, civil liberties, justice—endangered by what Ghassan Hage has called "anthrax culture."[4] David Simpson, for one, conceptualizes an alternative to this traumatism: "[T]o a remarkable degree the sight of those falling towers, the fates of those who died, and the grief of those who survived elicited a worldwide outpouring of sympathy and response that was clearly announced and reported."[5] With this remarkable solidarity in mind, Simpson wonders, "Could this have been a utopian moment, an opening?" (166). Hindsight confirms for us, however, that the decisions of a US administration bent on univocal pronouncements and unilateral actions systematically dismantled whatever utopian potential the global response to 11 September 2001 offered.[6]

Much the same end result came about in the aftermath of the Abu Ghraib scandal, which Simpson identifies as potentially utopian.[7] The photographs taken in Abu Ghraib function, in Simpson's view, as a "stand in for all the images we are not seeing that might have similar effects—not only the other two hundred or so other Abu Ghraib photos withheld from publication but also the evidence of the horrible deaths and disfigurations happening on a daily basis in Iraq."[8] Indeed, rather than merely reproducing the sense of spectacle created by the images of the falling Towers, which so many commentators likened to a blockbuster action film, the Abu Ghraib photos prompted a response of "acceptance and difficult recognition" on the part of

---

Jacques Derrida (Chicago: University of Chicago Press, 2003), p. 96.

2 Ibid., pp. 96-97.

3 Ibid., p. 97.

4 Ghassan Hage, *Against Paranoid Nationalism: Searching for Hope in a Shrinking Society* (Annandale: Pluto, 2003), p. 45.

5 David Simpson, *9/11: The Culture of Commemoration* (Chicago: University of Chicago Press, 2006), p. 166.

6 See also Deems D. Morrione, 'When Signifiers Collide: Doubling, Semiotic Black Holes, and the Destructive Remainder of the American Un/Real', *Cultural Critique*, 63 (2006), 157-173 (p. 158).

7 Simpson, p. 169.

8 Ibid., p. 133.

ordinary Americans.[9] As Simpson asserts, these photos confuse an American viewing audience insofar as they prompt an identification with the "pranksters" that disallows the framing of the US as military hero/liberator or 9/11 victim.[10] Yet, again as we all now know, the US Defense Department's stance that the photos were the actions of a few undisciplined enlisted men and women and its decision to keep the majority of the photos hidden from public view resulted in the scandal itself fading from view. Thus, while the Abu Ghraib scandal was what Deems Morrione might refer to as a "fatal event," it, too, was stripped of its significance and utopian potential by the "semiotic black hole" that is "9/11" in dominant US discourses.[11] In other words, "9/11" as a designation functions monolithically, disallowing any diversion from its fear-based, militaristically-backed signifying power.

These US-hegemonic responses to 11 September 2001 and the Abu Ghraib photographs in the spring of 2004 exemplify the two key words of this collection's title: "solidarity" and "schisms." The movement from the first term to the second is well known to people the world over and has dealt a near fatal blow to the principles, such as justice, democracy, and civil liberties, the US claims to honor. As I have been discussing, however, Simpson identifies 9/11 itself and the Abu Ghraib photographs as potentially utopian because they could have pushed people all around the world into "radically refiguring the relations of the homeland to the foreigner."[12] And Simpson's not alone. It's important here to recognize along with these commentators that the possibility for reconfiguration extended (and perhaps continues to extend) beyond the sphere of American intervention/interference and influence to the wider world, for such a telescopic view allows us to consider how nations and peoples outside the US contend with 9/11 and its aftermath. The essays collected in this volume purport to do just that through examinations of fictive and filmic representations of 9/11 itself as well as of a post-9/11

---

9 Ibid., p. 133.

10 Ibid., p. 133.

11 Morrione, pp. 163, 164. Morrione uses the phrase "fatal event" to refer to "prodigious semiotic-discursive phenomena," such as the Enron scandal, and coins the phrase "semiotic black hole" with specific reference to the Twin Towers and the much-underplayed attack on the Pentagon. A "semiotic black hole" is, for Morrione, "a collision of a fatal event and a perfect object that not only results in the multiplication of banal discourses and events under one sign such as Princess Diana or JonBenet Ramsey but a restructuring of the geopolitical universe in which the event takes place" (163). With respect to the Abu Ghraib scandal, which Morrione does not discuss, the sheer force of 9/11 as an event marker worked to neutralize and then dissipate the most serious aspects of the US military's mismanagement of that prison and the larger war.

12 Simpson, p. 169.

world from non-US perspectives. The novels and films discussed in this volume span continents, time zones, and historical periods. Amidst such diversity, this introduction seeks to plot two points of commonality.

The first point of commonality derives from Homi K. Bhabha's assertion, made in the weeks immediately following 11 September 2001, that "the decision to *implement* and administer terror, whether it is done in the name of god or the state, is a *political* decision, not a civilizational or cultural practice."[13] Even as Bhabha makes this significant distinction, his comments point toward another question, necessarily subsequent to the events themselves. How have the events of that September day, as well as their aftermath, affected cultural practice? And how do these practices clear a space for a critique of political decisions and of the politicization of 9/11 itself? The essays that follow offer a myriad of answers to the first question, ranging from an unironic return to literary convention (Michael, Kempner) and a consideration of the role of aesthetics (Lehnguth) to deeply self-reflexive filmic experimentation in both documentary and narrative examples (Murray Levine, Schultermandl, Hicks). Several other essays take up critiques of the politic discourses swirling around 9/11 by placing works in dialogue with one another (Anselmi and Wilson, Cilano, O'Reilly, Durham), by analyzing the role of writer as public intellectual (Mendes, Sutherland and Swan), by marking the long shadow of the political shifts brought about by those events (Ahlberg), and, finally, by interrogating the possibility and need for mourning (Tancke).

The second point of commonality that holds the collected essays together elaborates upon the discussion with which I opened this introduction: the utopian potential of 11 September 2001. In order to perceive this potential, I contend, we must expand outward beyond the borders of the US. The breadth of this volume's scope—bringing together works from Canada, Australia, Great Britain, France, Germany, Israel, Iran, and Pakistan, and scholars from Europe, Australia, and North America—accomplishes this expansion and, in doing so, sometimes leaves the US far behind.[14] That is, the novels and films discussed in this volume frequently feature settings, characters, and issues at

---

13 Homi K. Bhabha, 'Terror and After....', *Parallax*, 8 (2002), 3-4 (p. 3).
For a counterview on the "clash of civilizations" issue, see: Bill Brown, 'The Dark Wood of Postmodernity (Space, Faith, Allegory)', *PMLA*, 120 (2005), 734-750.

14 Ann Keniston and Jeanne Follansbee Quinn's edited collection, *Literature after 9/11*, provides a solid grounding in primarily US-centered literary responses to 11 September; one essay in this volume deals with Ian McEwan and David Hare. Keniston and Quinn's introduction also provides an extremely useful overview of the publishing history of literary responses from immediately after 9/11 up to 2008. In this history, Keniston and Quinn trace formal experimentation and conventionality in both poetry and fiction.

best only tangentially related to anything American. This movement beyond the US traces how different peoples and cultures may represent and understand their post-9/11 worlds in non-US centered ways, thereby pointing toward possible reconfigurations of what this event means and how it may alter relations between groups and nations. In this volume, then, 9/11 thus truly functions as an aterritorial signifier but not one, however, that leaves territoriality itself behind.[15] Specificity of location still matters greatly as the essays here facilitate unique comparisons of different understandings of "homelands" and their inverse, the foreign. In a general sense, *From Solidarity to Schisms* investigates both political and cultural constructions of home, thus gesturing toward what it would mean to become unhomed. That is, these essays, collectively, contend with Theodor Adorno's imperative: "it is part of morality not to be at home in one's home."[16] Simpson takes up just this imperative in order to critique how post-9/11 discourses spin the obligation not to be at home in one's home around, now making it "important to assign morality exclusively to being at home in one's home."[17] *From Solidarity to Schisms* extends this critique as it traces how 9/11-centered discourses define "home" and speculates over what is at stake in being uncomfortable in one's home.

"Home" does indeed become a dangerous concept in politicized framings of 9/11. The above-cited quotation from Bhabha indicates the tendency of these framings to represent 9/11 as a civilizational or cultural conflict. Like Bhabha, David Palumbo-Liu seeks to forestall the conflation of the political with the civilizational as he critiques the "civilizational model" currently in use: "National interests seem indistinguishable from 'a way of life' and national policy seems synonymous with large, civilizational imperatives."[18] An "our way of life" explanation creates an unbridgeable chasm between the "modernized" West and the backwards East—a reduction of complexity and complicity into cardboard cutout stand-ins. For Michael Rothberg, such civilizational thinking "focus[es] on feeling ('terror') instead of a particular political tactic ('terrorism'), and [thus] draws our attention to the affective level of

---

15 See Morrione, p. 170.

16 Theodor Adorno, *Can One Live after Auschwitz ?*trans. by Rodney Livingstone et. Al, ed. by Rolf Tiedemann (Stanford: Stanford University Press, 2003), p. 41. See also Simpson, p. 159.

17 Simpson, p. 160.

18 David Palumbo-Liu, 'Multiculturalism Now: Civilization, National Identity, and Difference Before and After September 11', *boundary 2*, 29 (2002), 109-127 (p. 110).

politics […].”[19] Herein lie the potency of these politicized framings and the success of their conceptual vocabulary.

The irresistible force of what Morrione calls the Twin Towers’ “gravitational pull” accounts for the mass inculcation of this vocabulary, including such phrases as “Homeland Security.”[20] Donald Pease makes explicit the ideological work that the phrase “Homeland Security” does:

> The introduction of the signifier of the *homeland* to capture the experience of generalized trauma recalled themes from the national narrative that it significantly altered. The *homeland* was what the colonial settlers had abandoned in their quest for a newly found land. When it was figured within the *Homeland* Security Act, the *homeland* engendered an imaginary scenario wherein the national people were encouraged to consider themselves dislocated from their country of origin [the US] by foreign aggressors […].[21]

Through the production of the sense of dislocation, “Homeland Security” works to localize within national borders a militancy against the other, as Amy Kaplan notes.[22] At the same time, this localization obscures the degree to which post-9/11 US foreign policy extends the imperative of “Homeland Security” well beyond the homeland’s borders. According to Kaplan, “A relation exists between securing the homeland against the encroachment of foreign terrorists and enforcing national power abroad. The homeland may contract borders around a fixed space of nation and nativity, but it simultaneously also expands the capacity of the United States to move unilaterally across the borders of other nations.”[23] The domestically- and internationally-oriented impulses of “Homeland Security” construct a notion of “home” based on fear and containment of the folk and the foreigner alike that is meant to pass as comfort, inviolability, and stability.[24] Finally, as Kaplan and others contend, any notion of a homeland relies upon some place, some people that is identifiably “foreign” to the folk.[25] It’s this reliance on the “foreign” that marks the semantic fallout of “Homeland Security,” for, as several of the essays in this volume argue, this phrase influences the foreign

19 Michael Rothberg, ‘Seeing Terror, Feeling Art: Public and Private in Post-9/11 Literature’, in *Literature after 9/11*, ed. by Ann Keniston and Jeanne Follansbee Quinn (New York: Routledge, 2008), 123-142 (p. 124).

20 Morrione, p. 158.

21 Donald Pease, ‘9/11: When Was “American Studies after the New Americanists”?’, *boundary 2*, 33 (2006), 73-101 (p. 75). Emphasis in original.

22 Ann Kaplan, ‘Homeland Insecurities: Reflections on Language and Space’, *Radical History Review*, 85 (2003), 82-93 (p. 87).

23 Ibid., p. 87.

24 I follow Kaplan’s lead in calling “Americans” the “folk.” See Kaplan, p. 88.

25 Ibid., p. 86.

and domestic policies of many nations outside the US as well. The point here is that, post-9/11, the production of "home" entails a tightening of identifications intended to align people ideologically based on appeals to a manufactured sense of cultural nativity.

To follow Adorno's imperative—"it is part of morality not to be at home in one's home"—entails a loosening of these identifications that, despite the warnings issued by government agencies (such as the TSA in the USA) and the "protections" offered by immigration measures and (coerced) oaths of loyalty, point the way toward the future. That is, being uncomfortable in one's home is to live in a state of optimism. Although Derrida identifies the power the specter of a future traumatism holds over the post-9/11 world, as I mention above, he nonetheless theorizes alternatives that reflect this optimism. Instead of the paralysis brought about by the fear of a future traumatism, Derrida emphasizes the necessity of

> leav[ing] a perspective open to perfectibility in the name of the "political," democracy, international law, international institutions, and so on. Even if this "in the name of" is still merely an assertion and a purely verbal commitment. Even in its most cynical mode, such an assertion still lets resonate within it an invincible promise.[26]

Derrida's notion of a promise is invincible, in my understanding, precisely because it remains unrealizable, unattainable. It cannot be conquered because it is responsive to circumstances rather than complete in them. Further, this promise holds no guarantee, for it "risks and must always risk being perverted into a threat."[27] Threats may arise out of the very openness that characterizes Derrida's conceptualization of promise, an openness "to time, to what comes upon us, to what arrives or happens, to the event. To history, if you will, a history to be thought completely otherwise than from a teleological horizon, indeed from any horizon at all."[28] Derrida's promise is radical—it is undecidability itself—in that it refuses prescription and fulfillment; it is not a note to be paid in full to the one who possesses it. Rather, Derrida's promise, related as it is to democracy, is "the possibility of being contested, of contesting itself, of criticizing and indefinitely improving itself."[29] Unsettledness is necessary in this conceptual framework, for the work of democracy is always in process, always aware of the stultification brought about by reification. And this process makes possible more just futures through its own

---

26 Borradori, p. 114.
27 Ibid., p. 120.
28 Ibid., p. 120.
29 Ibid., p. 121.

self-reflexiveness and –critique.[30] Marco Abel characterizes this process as a slowing down of the "rapid speed of judgment—not to escape judgment but to examine the value of value itself."[31] To be uncomfortable in one's home is, then, to take the time to acknowledge what is at stake in the construction of "home"—both for oneself and, more urgently, for others—and to commit oneself to the endless reconstruction of "home" so as to move toward greater inclusiveness and shared dignity.

The Plan of the Book

The poem "September 11, 2001" by Polish writer Ewa Lipska that appears before this introduction metaphorizes the preceding discussion about constructions of "home" in a post-9/11 world. The tailor continues to stitch together pieces of fabric despite proclamations by jewelers, poets, tax payers, secret agents, and songwriters—as well as by himself—that the world has come apart. What sort of wholeness will result? How evident and durable the seams? Each of the following essays engage with such generalized questions, variously conceptualizing and challenging how select novels and films represent the purported rupture 9/11 enacts on the world outside the US.

From Solidarity to Schisms opens with Magali Cornier Michael's contribution, "Writing Fiction in the Post-9/11 World: Ian McEwan's *Saturday*." Michael focuses on the novel's implicit intertextuality with Virginia Woolf's *Mrs. Dalloway* in order to argue that McEwan's turn to domestic fiction unexpectedly allows for a critique of any neat divide between public and private spheres. Such a critique is necessary if we are to understand how post-9/11 discourses posit the domestic sphere both as vulnerable to future terrorist attacks and as separate from the effects of politics and history. Brandon Kempner's essay, "'Blow the World Back Together': Literary Nostalgia, 9/11, and Terrorism in Seamus Heaney, Chris Cleave, and Martin Amis," provides a compelling context for Michael's discussion of McEwan's novel as Kempner's piece expands to consider the preponderance of "literary nostalgia" in British post-9/11 literature. "Literary nostalgia," for Kempner, is a reliance on older literary techniques and texts that seeks to trace the continui-

---

30 See Borradori, p. 113. Derrida's idea of "futures" privileges multiplicity. Derrida gave this interview a few short weeks after 9/11, and so he could not then know that the Bush administration would unspool a doctrine reliant on a very different structure, one premised on the Christian revelation of the One.

31 Marco Abel, 'Don DeLillo's "In the Ruins of the Future": Literature, Images, and the Rhetoric of *Seeing* 9/11', *PMLA*, 118 (2005), 1236-1250 (p. 1237).

ty of Western history and culture straight through 9/11. While such a reliance does hold some potential if pursued along the lines of the type of humanism Edward Said espouses, Kempner argues that, in several British post-9/11 texts, the use of "literary nostalgia" represents a regressive turn to colonialist thinking, a consolidation of "home."

Ulrike Tancke's "Uses and Abuses of Trauma in Post-9/11 Fiction and Contemporary Culture" focuses on Arab-American Laila Halaby's *Once in a Promised Land* and British Pat Barker's *Double Vision* in order to examine how in each novel the purported rupture of 9/11 fails to cement an inclusive sense of collectivity for all peoples. Tancke identifies how, in these novels, characters employ traumatic stories to prevent any chance of working through trauma rather than to accomplish this working through. The result is a disjointed sense of unbelonging. Ana Cristina Mendes' essay, "'Artworks, Unlike Terrorists, Change Nothing': Salman Rushdie and September 11," similarly concerns itself with a sense of unbelonging as it examines Rushdie's pre- and post-9/11 fiction and essays. Noting Rushdie's long standing problematization of "home," Mendes argues that Rushdie's interest in the notion of the "post-frontier" is a more productive way to understand his apparent post-9/11 shift "right" than is the argument that 9/11 represents a radical rupture in Rushdie's work as writer and public intellectual.

From these essays dealing with British and anglophone texts, the collection moves to a focus on German film. Henrike Lehnguth's "Sleepers, Informants, and the Everyday: Theorizing Terror and Ambiguity in Benjamin Heisenberg's *Schläfer*" looks at how, when the state—here, Germany—transgresses its own laws, it imposes a system of internalized terror. Heisenberg's film, in Lehnguth's analysis, demonstrates what happens when "everyday" citizens recognize the infiltration of state surveillance into the private sphere. No distinction between spheres holds, which makes it imperative, Lehnguth concludes, to guard against this internalized use of terror as a force within a state system. Gavin Hicks looks at another German film in his essay, "My Friend the Terrorist: The Political Burden of September 11 in Elmar Fischer's *The Friend*." Through a careful reading of filmic technique, Hicks demonstrates how Fischer's film "directs" the audience's remembering of 9/11, thereby preventing the realization of what Judith Butler calls an ethics of "subjectivation" in its aftermath.

Alison J. Murray Levine enhances the collection's discussion of film by focusing on a French documentary in her essay, "Ghosts on the Skyline: Chris Marker's France after 9/11." Murray Levine contends that Marker's "video essay," *Chats Perchés/The Case of the Grinning Cat*, disrupts standard documentary conventions of text, sound, and image in order to expose the problems of collective action in "hyper-mediated" cultures. Carolyn Durham's essay, "Daring to Imagine: Frédéric Beigbeder's *Windows on the World* and Slimane Benaïssa's *La Dernière Nuit d'un damne*," moves us from French film to French fiction. Durham's analysis of these two novels concerns itself with the possibility of holding a cross-cultural dialogue that will challenge the myopia of a monocultural nationalist perspective. Both novels incorporate multilingualism, making characters and readers alike linguistically uncomfortable. Durham views this uncomfortableness as strategic in that it points toward the many ways languages make meaning in a single context.

Multilingual and multicultural approaches distinguish the subject of Silvia Schultermandl's essay, "Perspectival Adjustments and Hyper-Reality in *11'09"01*." Schultermandl focuses specifically on two of the eleven shorts in Alain Brigand's compilation film: those by Iranian director Samira Makhmalbaf and Israeli director Amos Gitaï. In these two shorts, Schultermandl explores what "9/11" means in localized contexts, a move that introduces shifts in perspective meant to dislodge the monolithic, US-centered status of the discourses that have emerged since that September day. My own essay, "Manipulative Fictions: Democratic Futures in Pakistan," also seeks to shift perspectives as it explores a Pakistani novel, Mohsin Hamid's *The Reluctant Fundamentalist*, and film, Shoaib Mansoor's *Khuda Kay Liye* (*In the Name of God*). Deeply concerned with the US internalization of a surveillance system accomplished through "war on terror" rhetoric, this essay contrasts the closing off of democratic spaces in the US with the imagined and hopeful openings of such spaces in Pakistan.

Two essays that speak to post-9/11 Canada also explore the place of democracy. Sharon Sutherland and Sarah Swan's "Margaret Atwood's *Oryx and Crake*: Canadian Post-9/11 Worries" posits Atwood's dystopian novel as one suitable and distinct way to convey Canadian concerns over the aftermath of 11 September. Like Atwood's character from the novel, Jimmy/Snowman, Canada is "an intimate outsider" of the US, meaning that it is affected by US foreign and domestic policy yet powerless to affect such policies. Atwood's dystopia functions as a way to imagine the worst possible outcomes of this unique relationship. William Anselmi and Sheena Wilson's essay, "From *Inch'Allah Dimanche* to *Sharia in Canada*: Empire Management, Gender Representations, and Communication Strategies in the Twenty-First Century," illustrates that some of those outcomes may be more fact than fiction. In their analysis of the documentary *Sharia in Canada*, Anselmi and Wilson illustrate how, post-9/11, the Canadian government has all but relinquished its commitment to multiculturalism, thereby impeding productive public discussions about what the institution of sharia might mean. This impeded discussion stands out all the more starkly through the contrast Anselmi and Wilson construct between the documentary and Yamina Benguigui's narrative film, *Inch'Allah Dimanche*, which, in these authors' view, painfully illustrates where the non-Muslim world might have been with respect to understanding Islam and Muslims had the anti-Muslim discourses fomenting around "9/11" not emerged.

From Solidarity to Schisms closes with two essays on Australian post-9/11 fiction. Sofia Ahlberg's "Within Oceanic Reach: The Effects of September 11 on a Drought-Stricken Nation" extends other discussions of public discourses in this volume to encompass what she terms "the unlikely marriage of two discourses, nature and terror, that conspire to wage war against the Other." Both discourses, in Ahlberg's view, share a preoccupation with loss that threatens to enact an homogenizing exclusivity. To counter this tendency, Ahlberg draws on Gayatri Spivak's notion of planetarity, which allows for the conceptualization of collectivity amidst (ecological) diversity. Finally, Nathanael O'Reilly's essay, "Government, Media, and Power: Terrorism in the Australian Novel since 9/11" examines the domestication of "control" in an Australian national context. With his focus on the media's role in terror discourses, O'Reilly questions the extent to which the media produces the very terroristic spectacle it claims to report. Once again, we see a construction of "home" brought about through questionable measures.

Bibliography

Abel, Marco, 'Don DeLillo's 'In the Ruins of the Future': Literature, Images, and the Rhetoric of *Seeing* 9/11', *PMLA*, 118 (2003), 1236-1250

Adorno, Theodor, *Can One Live after Auschwitz?*, trans. Rodney Livingstone et al., ed. Rolf Tiedemann (Stanford: Stanford University Press, 2003)

Bhabha, Homi K., 'Terror and After….', *Parallax*, 8 (2002), 3-4

Borradori, Giovanna, *Philosophy in a Time of Terror: Dialogues with Jürgen Habermas and Jacques* Derrida (Chicago: University of Chicago Press, 2003)

Brown, Bill, 'The Dark Wood of Postmodernity (Space, Faith, Allegory)', *PMLA*, 120 (2005), 734-750

Hage, Ghassan, *Against Paranoid Nationalism: Searching for Hope in a Shrinking Society*, (Annandale: Pluto, 2003)

Kaplan, Amy, 'Homeland Insecurities: Reflections on Language and Space', *Radical History Review*, 85 (2003), 82-93

Keniston, Ann, and Jeanne Follansbee Quinn, eds, *Literature after 9/11*, (New York: Routledge, 2008)

Morrione, Deems D., 'When Signifiers Collide: Doubling, Semiotic Black Holes, and the Destructive Remainder of the American Un/Real', *Cultural Critique*, 63 (2006), 157-173

Palumbo-Liu, David, 'Multiculturalism Now: Civilization, National Identity, and Difference Before and After September 11th', *boundary 2*, 29 (2002), 109-127

Pease, Donald E., '9/11: When Was "American Studies after the New Americanists"?', *boundary 2*, 33 (2006), 73-101

Rothberg, Michael, 'Seeing Terror, Feeling Art: Public and Private in Post-9/11 Literature', in *Literature after 9/11*, ed. by Ann Keniston and Jeanne Follansbee Quinn (New York: Routledge, 2008), pp.123-142

Simpson, David, *9/11: The Culture of Commemoration* (Chicago: University of Chicago Press, 2006)

Writing Fiction in the Post-9/11 World: Ian McEwan's *Saturday*

Magali Cornier Michael

Ian McEwan's 2005 novel *Saturday* takes up the challenge of representing the post-9/11 cultural climate from a British perspective by depicting possible strategies of ethical, political work for moving beyond violence and terror as well as the inevitable failures of such strategies in a culture that holds on to a colonial, binary, Eurocentric mindset out of fear in the face of violence and terror. The novel thus contributes to contemporary discussions of the post-9/11 world and explorations of the possibility of moving past violence in a world marked by global terrorism at the beginning of the twenty-first century.

Ian McEwan's novel *Saturday*, published in Britain in 2005, engages the difficulties of representing the uneasiness plaguing the consciousness of twenty-first century citizens of Western nations in the aftermath of the deadly September 11, 2001, terrorist use of planes as bombs in New York and Washington D.C. and subsequent bombings and threats across the globe, all of which have defied representation and understanding within the Western cultural imagination. Set in London, McEwan's text focuses specifically on the British perspective. Notwithstanding Tony Blair's official support of George Bush's War against Terror and the British public's sharing with Americans the role of spectator to what Douglas Kellner calls the "*global media spectacle*" created by the relentless media coverage of the attacks in the age of "the interconnected networked globe" as well as the resulting "insecurity and anxiety which the media fueled with hysteric coverage,"[1] the British perspective differs from its American counterpart in terms of Britain's geographical distance from the sites of the attacks, Britain's familiarity with terrorist (IRA) attacks on its own soil, and most crucially Britain's global position as an ex-colonial power. Indeed, the novel at times hints at a parallel between Britain after World War II and the United States following the 9/11 attacks, which positions the contemporary British perspective as possessing historical insight and distance to which Americans do not yet have access and also allows for a kind of self critical gaze informed as it were by the spectacle of official American responses to the terrorist attacks.

McEwan's *Saturday* engages in a sharp assessment of Britain's position and posturing as illuminated through the parallels between Britain's response

---

1 Douglas Kellner, 'September 11, Social Theory and Democratic Politics', *Theory, Culture and Society*, 19 (2002), 147-159 (p. 152).

to the loss of its position as global colonial power and the American response to the events of 9/11 as a means of participating in the complex intellectual process of trying not only to understand the terrorist attacks of 9/11 and their global repercussions but also to retain hope for humanity. Indeed, as Jeffory Clymer argues, while terrorism "is a form of action whose sheer outrageousness may awe us into silence," it "also compels us to attempt to regain our mental balance by groping toward a narrative structure in which the tragic events can be understood, even if they still make no sense to us."[2] In a discussion of McEwan's earlier novel, *Atonement*, Doryjane Birrer makes the claim that McEwan's fiction demonstrates "that 'the pull of simple narrative' has the power to lure us with the hope of imaginative possibilities" and with the possibility that narrative can help "shape a more livable future," a claim that I would argue describes what *Saturday* strives for perhaps even more aptly.[3]

Rather than latch on to what Kellner describes as a simplistic "binary model of inexorable conflict between the West and Islam" that "homogenize[s] complex civilizations and cover[s] over differences, hybridizations, contradictions and conflicts within these cultures,"[4] *Saturday* utilizes narrative strategies that seek to engage and represent the larger picture by focusing on the local and specific. Because narrative remains inextricable from all attempts to represent historical events, in the sense that constructing a history involves the creation of a story to (re)present past events, choosing a narrative form that can give voice to recent historical events in terms of human experience necessarily poses a challenge to contemporary writers. McEwan's novel makes an attempt to represent the contemporary uneasiness not by painting a broad picture of the world at large but by focusing on a day in the

---

2 Jeffory A. Clymer, *America's Culture of Terrorism: Violence, Capitalism, and the Written Word* (Chapel Hill: The University of North Carolina Press, 2003), p. 211.

3 Doryjane Birrer, '"What Are Novelists For?": Writing and Rewriting Reality from Woolf to McEwan', in *Woolf in the Real World*, ed. by Karen V. Kukil. (Clemson: Clemson University Press, 2005), 165-170 (p. 169).

4 Birrer, pp. 148-149. Similarly, Homi Bhabha points to "the futility of framing the [9/11] event in such a divided and polarized civilizational narrative," as "a 'clash of civilisations'" ('Terror and after…', *Parallax*, 8 (2002), 3-4); Gayatri Chakravorty Spivak rejects the view of the 9/11 events "as a battle between fundamentalism and democracy" ('Globalicities: Terror and Its Consequences', *The New Centennial Review*, 4 (2004), 73-94 (p. 74)); and Jean Baudrillard notes that the terrorism evidenced in the 9/11 events is "a clash neither of civilizations nor of religions, far beyond Islam and America, upon which one attempts to focus the conflict in order to give oneself the illusion of a visible confrontation, and solution, by the use of force" ('L'Esprit du Terrorisme', trans. by Michel Valentin, *The South Atlantic Quarterly*, 101 (Spring 2002), 403-415 (p. 406)).

life of one upper class London man and emphasizing the ways in which his domestic, quotidian life is infected by, remains inextricable from, and cannot escape the larger socio-political forces at work.

In a move that might initially appear counterintuitive for a text engaging large historical events and forces, McEwan's novel deliberately offers a contemporary version of a domestic narrative. Moreover, the novel overtly uses and molds for its own purposes some of the narrative strategies developed by Virginia Woolf in *Mrs. Dalloway*; however, while a few reviewers and critics note this parallel, none explore the significance or efficacy of this narrative borrowing.[5] That *Saturday* borrows narrative strategies traditionally associated with the realm of the domestic, with women's fiction, and with early twentieth century modernism rather than with large scale historical events may at first glance seem like an odd choice on McEwan's part, although Woolf's novel, like McEwan's, does locate its action historically following violent world events, World War I in Woolf's text, and explore the traumatic effects of that violence on the individual and cultural psyche. Arguably, Woolf's novel both uses and chips away at the conventions of domestic fiction by highlighting the absurdity and impossibility of any clear demarcation between the domestic and public sphere.

That McEwan chooses to mine Woolf's narrative form is intriguing in that it suggests ways in which certain narrative forms often not associated with depictions of large scale historical events and the public sphere have something to offer writers confronted with the formidable task of representing events deemed unrepresentable and human consciousness plagued by fears of unimaginable violence. Perhaps narrative forms that already implicitly undermine faith in objectivity, scientific reason, binary thinking, and control—such as Woolf's—are particularly useful in the task of representing creatively the post-9/11 world. Karen DeMeester's notion that Woolf's *Mrs. Dalloway* can at least in part be read as an attempt to represent a historical "trauma that sabotages faith in traditional value systems and the cultural order, undermines our sense of safety and stability, [and] erodes

---

5 For example, Michiko Kakutani notes in his review of the novel that McEwan's "'Saturday' reads like an up-to-the-moment, post-9/11 variation on Woolf's classic 1925 novel 'Mrs. Dalloway'" in which the reader is "given a day in the life of an upper-middle-class character who lives in London" and "treated to meditations about time and age and death, and finely honed musings about the waning of an era" as well as to "a series of mundane events […] punctuated by a violent and alarming event" ('A Hero with 9/11 Peripheral Vision', *The New York Times*, March 18, 2005, n.p.).

identity and self-esteem" in many ways functions as a fitting depiction of McEwan's own novel at a different but also traumatic historical junction.[6]

Focusing on one day in a man's life within the context of his mostly domestic routine, since it is a Saturday and thus not a work day, not only allows McEwan's text to take on the cultural trauma that appears overwhelming and too diffuse to engage otherwise but also shatters the illusion that the private domestic realm exists as separate and as a shelter from the public political sphere. Indeed, setting the novel on Saturday, February 15, 2003, which witnessed large-scale demonstrations worldwide against the coming American invasion of Iraq, further illustrates the impossibility of separating the private from the public sphere in that the marchers are out in public addressing world events on what is for many of them a day off and also allows the text to portray the interconnections between ordinary, privileged existence and the violence or threat of violence that hovers over it. Although the novel's central character, neurosurgeon Henry Perowne, notably does not attend the London march against the war, his regular path on his string of errands is interrupted by the march because streets have been closed and some marchers even gather in the square on which he lives, bringing global politics to his doorsteps: from his window he glimpses a "handcart" with "rubber masks of politicians—Bush and Blair in wobbling stacks."[7] The novel's use of such details demonstrates that the private and public spheres collide and overlap within the contemporary moment, thus undermining any true distinction between them. Moreover, McEwan's strategic use of a third person limited perspective allows the text to represent Perowne's actions and thoughts while simultaneously presenting and subtly criticizing Perowne as symptomatic of and complicit with the problems Western cultures and human beings face in the contemporary moment and the difficulties of moving past those problems.[8]

---

6 Karen DeMeester, 'Trauma, Post-Traumatic Stress Disorder, and Obstacles to Postwar Recovery in *Mrs. Dalloway*', in *Virginia Woolf and Trauma: Embodied Texts*, ed. by Suzette Henke and David Eberly (New York: Pace University Press, 2007), 77-93 (p. 78).

7 Ian McEwan, *Saturday* (New York: Anchor Books, 2006), pp. 59-60.

8 A good number of reviewers and critics have fallen into the trap of equating McEwan with the novel's central character, which is problematic on multiple levels. I agree with Molly Clark Hillard, who reminds readers of their "own capacity for misprision, for taking the newspaper interview for the novel, the man for his text, the narrator for the protagonist" (and, I would add, the author for the narrator and protagonist) and argues that "the entire third-person narration should be re-read ironically" and that "McEwan's 'voice,' inasmuch as we can or should determine it, is not, as others have argued, Perowne's" (""When Desert Armies Stand Ready to Fight": Re-Reading McEwan's *Saturday* and Arnold's "Dover Beach"', *Partial Answers*, 6 (2008), 181-206 (pp. 189-190)). Hillard's essay focuses specifically on Perowne's misreadings of his culture in general. Mark Currie further notes that,

Indeed, although the novel depicts its main character as a decent likeable man, the text makes clear the ways in which the private realm he so cherishes is built upon global inequities and Western (here British) upper class privileges from which he benefits—for example, in the form of his "silver Mercedes S 500 with cream upholstery," for which he can "afford" convenient "off-street parking."[9] As Jürgen Habermas notes in an October 2001 interview, "the globalization of markets, particularly the financial markets," has resulted in "a world society" that is increasingly "split up into winner, beneficiary, and loser countries."[10] Even after the loss of much of its global empire and the physical destruction it faced at the hands of Hitler's air force in the early 1940s, Britain has held on to its status as a "winner" country based on the status it garnered from its own history of global dominance as well its membership in the group of European nations that for the past few centuries have dominated the world culturally and economically and that currently has reasserted itself as a formidable political and economic power bloc with the formation of the European Union. Although raised in the lower British middle class and never having "imagined he would end up living in the sort of house that had a library,"[11] Perowne's professional success as a neurosurgeon and marriage to a woman who practices law and whose mother came from the upper class have allowed him a privileged class position (including a house with a "library") in a nation that has retained sharp class boundaries.

By substituting a male protagonist for Woolf's Mrs. Dalloway in a narrative that locates its action explicitly in the domestic realm while simultaneously invalidating any strict separation between the domestic and public spheres, McEwan's novel calls attention to the ways in which, at the beginning of the twenty-first century, upper class privileged men in the West are perhaps more dependent on and more apt to preserve the illusion of the private sphere as a refuge from the chaos and violence of world events precisely because they have lost a sense of control and power in the public sphere, particularly in the face of the amorphous threat of terrorism—and certainly making Perowne a brain surgeon further highlights the attempt at assuming/asserting absolute control. The loss of control and power for the British

---

within *Saturday*, much is located "at a level not represented by any fictional mind or within the scope of [the narrator's] omniscience" (*About Time: Narrative, Fiction and the Philosophy of Time* (Edinburgh, UK: Edinburgh University Press, 2007), p. 129).

9 McEwan, p. 74.

10 Giovanna Borradori, *Philosophy in a Time of Terror: Dialogues with Jürgen Habermas and Jacques Derrida* (Chicago: The University of Chicago Press, 2003), p. 32. Kellner also notes that "globalization relentlessly divides the world into haves and have-nots" (p. 153).

11 McEwan, p. 64.

upper class man remains inextricable from the loss of empire and subsequent loss of Britain's position as a global power. In a discussion of McEwan's earlier novels that predates the publication of *Saturday*, Rhiannon Davies argues that, in his fiction, "McEwan problematizes the growing self-consciousness as well as the general unease that is involved in establishing and maintaining a coherent male English identity in the latter half of the twentieth century" and that, "in McEwan's later writing, the English male stands naked—without a subject position, without the richness of tradition, and unadorned with the regalia of empire."[12] I would argue that *Saturday* takes this one step further, in that the events of 9/11 fully undermined any notion of the self as whole, unified, powerful or as having any control or agency and, consequently, have dealt a death blow to the overtly masculine thriller genre that arguably dominated late twentieth century fictional representations of global politics, marked in Britain perhaps most overtly by the popular James Bond stories but also often borrowed by many so-called serious or literary writers. As Davies notes, "James Bond is, in effect, the modern adult equivalent of a superhero there to save the day" and thus "caught the imagination of a nation steeped in a severe confidence crisis" following its dwindling status as a global power.[13] The events of 9/11 invalidated fantasies of the superhero, notwithstanding media attempts to represent New York firemen as heroes, and thoroughly and irreparably shattered all of the values on which the thriller genre depends, revealing instantaneously and definitively as myths ideals of macho masculinity, independence, and individualism, which is why writers like McEwan have been left to create or recreate alternative means of representing twenty-first century life and consciousness.

From the novel's first sentence, the domestic sphere represented within McEwan's *Saturday* functions less as a space within which to escape the post-9/11 world and the traumatic effects of the terrorist attacks than as a space within which to engage that world and those traumas on a human scale. The novel opens within the quintessential domestic space of the main character's bedroom. When Henry Perowne wakes up "Some hours before dawn" on Saturday, February 15, 2003, he stands at his bedroom window literally, and not just figuratively, "naked"[14] and thus implicitly vulnerable; and, although he looks out over London from the seemingly safe position of his extremely comfortable luxurious home, that position of safety is immediately

---

12 Rhiannon Davies, 'Enduring McEwan', in *Posting the Male: Masculinities in Post-war and Contemporary British Literature*, ed. by Daniel Lea and Berthold Schoene (New York: Rodopi, 2003), 105-123 (pp. 205-206, 121).

13 Ibid., p. 119.

14 McEwan, p. 1.

undercut with multiple subtle details. He notes, for example, "thirty feet below, the black arrowhead railings like a row of spears" as well as, across the square, a "façade [that] is a reconstruction, a pastiche," having taken "some hits from the Luftwaffe."[15] By demonstrating that his home requires protective railing and that his upper class neighborhood has been the site of previous destruction during World War II, Perowne's seemingly neutral observations (in the sense that the character does not pause to think about the implications of that which he observes in relation to the present state of the world) highlight from the novel's first pages the precarious position of his home and family in the face of a dangerous, potentially violent world.

Perowne also recalls how the previous evening in his bath, a space conventionally marked as domestic and private, he had listened "to the radio news. The stolid Mr. Blix has been addressing the UN again—there's a general impression that he's rather undermined the case for war,"[16] prefiguring the many times radio and television news coverage will intrude into his quotidian Saturday activities and bring world politics right into his home in the pages that follow. At one point later between games of squash, Perowne deliberately "shifts position so the [television] is no longer in view" and asks "Isn't it possible to enjoy an hour's recreation without this invasion, this infection from the public domain?"[17]; and the novel makes clear that the answer to that question is a resounding "no" and that Perowne's notion that "He has a right now and then—everyone has it—not to be disturbed by world events"[18] is both elitist and impossible given his essentially powerless position in the face of the pervasiveness of the media.

That the novel intends to confront the cultural trauma that haunts the West in the aftermath of 9/11 becomes particularly clear in this opening scene when Perowne (mis)interprets what he witnesses in the pre-dawn skies out of his window: he sees "fire in the sky [...] traveling along a route that he himself has taken many times in his life," clearly a plane "in the final approaches to Heathrow,"[19] and hears "a straining, choking banshee sound growing in volume—both a scream and a sustained shout, an impure, dirty noise that suggests unsustainable mechanical effort."[20] He immediately interprets the scene as a "nightmare," as a "spectacle [that] has the familiarity of a

---

15 Ibid., p. 2.
16 Ibid., p. 4.
17 Ibid., p. 109.
18 Ibid., p. 110.
19 Ibid., p. 13.
20 Ibid., p. 20.

recurring dream."[21] His view of the scene is clearly mediated by the memory of watching the hijacked planes run into the twin towers in New York City over and over again on television and the resulting cultural and personal trauma that has become part of daily life and consciousness. As E. Ann Kaplan explains, "The phenomenon of 9/11 was perhaps the supreme example of a catastrophe that was experienced globally via digital technologies (Internet, cell phone) as well as by television and radio," thus creating an instance of "mediated trauma."[22] Indeed, Perowne notes that the scene in front of him is "familiar" even if "It's already almost eighteen months since half the planet watched, and watched again, the unseen captives driven through the sky to slaughter" and that "airliners look different in the sky these days, predatory or doomed,"[23] making clear that he sees the present scene through the lens of his media mediated experience of the 9/11 events.

Standing alone at his bedroom window, Perowne is once again thrust in the role of helpless, passive spectator. Although the narrative describes him as "Horrified,"[24] he remains disturbingly calm and distanced from the spectacle in front of his eyes. This distancing or numbness may be a function of what Jacques Derrida describes, in an interview shortly after the events of 9/11, as one of the effects of "the repetition of the televised images," which creates a kind of "neutralizing, deadening, distancing of traumatism."[25] For a moment, Perowne wonders rather dispassionately if "there's something he should be doing" but then immediately talks himself into remaining passive: "By the time the emergency services have noted and passed on his call, whatever is to happen will be in the past."[26] He cannot imagine an active role for himself in the face of what he experiences as the repetition of the traumatic event and of his helpless position as spectator.

The passivity and distancing quality of the position of spectator created by the intense media presentation and (re)presentation of the 9/11 events to the point of saturation creates a particular kind of terror and anxiety. As Habermas argues, "The presence of cameras and of the media" transformed "the local event simultaneously into a global one and the whole world population

---

21 In a September 12 essay in *The Guardian*, McEwan himself noted that "the screen became the only reality" for viewers ('Beyond Belief', Wednesday September 12, 2001, 1-2).

22 McEwan, p. 14. E. Ann, *Trauma Culture: The Politics of Terror and Loss in Media and Literature* (New Brunswick: Rutgers University Press, 2005), p. 2.

23 McEwan, p. 15.

24 Ibid., p. 14.

25 Borradori, p. 87.

26 McEwan, p. 16.

into a benumbed witness."[27] Moreover, Perowne understands that what chiefly keeps him glued to the scene is "the horror of what he can't see. Catastrophe observed at a distance. Watching death on a large scale, but seeing no one die. No blood, no screams, no human figures at all.[28]" The terror at least in part thus stems from the inability to visualize, imagine, represent the direct effects of the violence upon material human bodies. In addition, the horror of his position as spectator, shared by so many across the globe on September 11, 2001, stems from what Barbara Kirshenblatt-Gimblett calls "the morally ambiguous activity of watching."[29] Watching events that one cannot stop from a distance not only produces terror and anxiety but also the recognition of an absence of agency.

Although Perowne learns later on the news that the scene he witnessed was merely that of a cargo plane with mechanical problems and that the plane landed safely, his immediate viewing of the scene as a terrorist attack highlights the ways in which the events of 9/11 have not only marked the psyche of twenty-first century citizens of the West but also function as a lens through which they subsequently view the world. That this is the case even for a Londoner whose city has experienced multiple terrorist attacks demonstrates that the 9/11 attacks have had a distinct resonance and effect; Perowne even notes ironically that, "As a Londoner, you could grow nostalgic for the IRA."[30] According to Derrida, what characterizes the trauma produced by the 9/11 events derives not only from the "transgression" against "a country [the United States] that, even in the eyes of its enemies and especially since the so-called 'end of the Cold War,' plays a virtually sovereign role among sovereign states" but also from "the threat of the worst *to come*" and thus "from the repetition to come—though worse."[31] Indeed, Perowne immediately imagines the worst when he spots the plane on fire in the dawn sky. Moreover, as the day progresses, he gets sucked up by the news reports about the event. That "His nerves, like tautened strings, vibrate obediently with each news 'release'"[32] indicates a certain sense of powerlessness in the face not only of

---

27 Borradori, p. 28.

28 McEwan, p. 15.

29 Barbara Kirshenblatt-Gimblett, 'Kodak Moments, Flashbulb Memories: Reflections on 9/11', *The Drama Review*, 47 (Spring 2003), 11-48 (p. 15). Her argument focuses specifically on photography, arguing that "Photography materialized the morally ambiguous activity of watching" (p. 15). Indeed, she notes that "Mayor Rudolf W. Giuliani issued an executive order banning amateur photographs of the World Trade Center ruins because, as his office explained, the site was a crime scene, not a tourist attraction" (p. 12).

30 McEwan, p. 34.

31 Borradori, pp. 94-96.

32 McEwan, p. 185.

world events but of the media that controls the information ordinary citizens receive.

Although clearly demonstrating that the traumatic present cultural and political climate hovers over the novel's opening scene, the narrative also uses this scene to depict how Perowne manages to live in the face of the constant threat of terror. In response to his own question—"And now, what days are these?"—Perowne answers, "Baffled and fearful, he mostly thinks when he takes time from his weekly round to consider."[33] The reference to "his weekly round" in his answer is striking, in that it suggests that one method of keeping fear at bay is to envelop oneself in the routines of everyday existence, which is reminiscent of the emphasis on routine and ritual in domestic narratives and helps to understand why McEwan uses aspects of the domestic novel to structure his own narrative. Indeed, the novel suggests that even global terrorism has been incorporated into daily routines, so that "International terror, security codes, preparations for war [...] represent the steady state, the weather."[34] As Perowne notes, his own son Theo daily "scans the paper for fresh developments the way he might a listings magazine."[35] Moreover, Perowne himself reluctantly acknowledges that "he's adapting" to the new political climate "the way patients eventually do to their sudden loss of sight or use of their limbs,"[36] the clinical analogy highlighting the way in which living with the fear of future terrorist attacks produces concrete physical and psychic effects as well as mechanisms of adaptation.

Part of the process of adaptation for Perowne includes a relentless observation of routines in his work and home life, both of which are depicted in the form of domestic rituals that have a soothing, sustaining effect. On the Saturday in question, his senses of self and security remain intimately tied to the material, physical rituals in which he engages and over which he has at least limited control. As he goes through the motions of shaving, for example, the narrative notes not only that "He feels incomplete without this morning rite, even on a day off," the shaving ritual thus playing a role in the construction of his sense of self, but also that he "likes" the material objects themselves—"the wooden bowl, the badger brush, the extravagantly disposable triple-bladed razor, with cleverly arched and ridged jungle-green handle"[37]—at least in part because they are familiar and at his disposal. Moreover, the energy he acquires to face the day arises from the concrete routine he

33 Ibid., p. 3.

34 Ibid., p. 32.

35 Ibid., p. 32.

36 Ibid., p. 33.

37 Ibid., p. 56.

has set out for himself, which includes playing squash with a colleague, visiting his elderly mother, and preparing for the evening's family meal, a plan that involves "cook[ing] a fish stew" and thus "A visit to the fishmonger's" to purchase "monkfish, clams, mussels, peeled prawns"; indeed, "It's this practical daylight list" of things to do and buy "that make him leave the bed"[38] and shake off the "apprehensions"[39] that threaten to paralyze him in the face of global terrorism, of which he is continually reminded by the ever present media intrusions into his everyday activities.

Later in the day, Perowne yearns "to get home" so he can engage in the rituals of dinner preparations for what will be a little party with the addition of his visiting daughter and father-in-law: "He needs to check that there's champagne in the fridge, and bring some red wine into the kitchen to warm. The cheese too needs to be softened in the centrally-heated air."[40] The detailed preparations for this meal echo those of Clarissa Dalloway for a larger party in Woolf's *Mrs. Dalloway*, thus clearly extending the parallels to Woolf's novel even while subtly making alterations to situate *Saturday* within its own cultural moment. That Perowne shops and cooks while his wife is engaged in the public work world highlights a shift in notions of the domestic sphere and its rituals, in that the conventional female gendering of the domestic is shaken and the domestic is more overtly revealed to be tied to the public sphere. Indeed, he in some sense replicates in spirit and even in some of his actions his own mother's devotion to the routines of housework. For instance, his description of his mother as drawing "her deepest satisfactions from a tray of well-roasted beef"[41] parallels his own feelings of deep "content"[42] as he cooks a fish stew for the family evening meal, following a ritual that includes adding "pinches of saffron, some bay leaves, orange-peel gratings, oregano, five anchovy fillets, two tins of peeled tomatoes" to "the softened onions and garlic."[43] However, the outside world intrudes more overtly than in the case of his mother into his domestic ritual within the kitchen, as he feels "the pull like gravity, of the approaching TV news" that will connect him "to a community of anxiety,"[44] highlighting the way in which media technologies have broken down the distinction between domestic and public spaces. Shots of "the United Nations building in New York" and of "Colin Powell getting into

---

38 Ibid., p. 55.
39 Ibid., p. 76.
40 Ibid., p. 173.
41 Ibid., p. 158.
42 Ibid., p. 182.
43 Ibid., p. 181.
44 Ibid., p. 180.

a black limousine" occupy the same space as his cleaning and chopping of culinary ingredients in his kitchen.[45]

McEwan's novel depicts the possibility of facing life in a political climate that threatens to engender paralysis as dependent on domestic ritual, especially for its upper class male protagonist whose identity and position of power is in crisis in a post-colonial Britain. Moreover, domestic ritual is redefined as encompassing much that occurs in the so-called public sphere, such as Perowne's rounds at the hospital and the rituals of the operating room with its orderly rows of "instruments arrayed."[46] Indeed, the novel depicts Perowne as completely *at home* within the operating room that has become so familiar to him and within which he has agency in his professional capacity as an expert neurosurgeon: "once busy within the enclosed world of his firm, the theatre and its ordered procedures, and absorbed by the vivid foreshortening of the operating microscope as he follows a corridor to a desired site, he experiences a superhuman capacity, more like a craving, for work."[47] Domestic rituals both at home and work thus function as palliatives in that they connect human beings to the material, physical world and allow human beings a degree of control over their immediate environment. However, these domestic rituals occur within the context of and not separate from the larger world, as represented in the novel by the constant intrusions of the T.V. and radio news and by Perowne's encounter with the detours erected to accommodate the march against the war and with the thugs who beat him after a slight traffic accident on his way to his squash game. Even at work, he must step out of his comfort zone and participate in the ever changing "hospital's Emergency plan" that now includes "words like 'catastrophe' and 'mass fatalities,' 'chemical and biological warfare' and 'major attack' [...] and lines of command that stretch up and out of the hospital, beyond the medical hierarchies, up through the distant reaches of the Civil Service to the Home Secretary's Office,"[48] thus invalidating or at least deflating the "superhuman capacity" and sense of control he feels in the sealed off microcosm of the operating room.

The novel also highlights throughout its pages what Perowne often forgets: the privileged position from and within which his domestic rituals are actualized—from his movements about town in his Mercedes to the club to which he belongs to play squash to his posh London home to the expensive seafood and champagne he will serve his dinner guests—that remains inex-

---

45 Ibid., p. 183.

46 Ibid., p. 258.

47 Ibid., p. 10.

48 Ibid., p. 10.

tricable from the politics of the public sphere. When Perowne does reference his elite status, he seems to do so with little self reflection as when he notes that the "three monkfish tails" he buys "cost a little more than his first car. Admittedly, a pile of junk."[49] In contrast, the novel as a whole depicts his elitism as symptomatic of the West's inability to understand global terrorism. Most often, Perowne seems content to wallow in the illusion that his elitist status will keep him safe, believing that drawing the "heavy curtains" that had "a way of clearly eliminating the square and the wintry world beyond it" would keep the dangers of the world at bay,[50] a belief that the novel's plot line and emphasis on details radically undermines. That he willingly chooses the domestic rituals in which he participates serves as a key indication of his privileged class position at the same time as it demonstrates that the political climate has made new choices necessary. Indeed, his routines are depicted in terms of rituals to which he is attached and which provide him with a sense of control rather than in terms of drudgery that cannot be escaped. Ironically, *Saturday* presents the British upper class male, in the figure of Perowne, as revaluing and clinging for safety and a sense of control to the kinds of domestic rituals that historically were sloughed off onto middle class professional men, women in general, and the lower classes across gender lines. The only control Perowne holds in the contemporary moment is located in his professional skills as a surgeon that depend on set practices or routines and in the class specific routines of his everyday life. In both cases, the control he wields is local and grounded in his interaction with the concrete material world.

The novel's emphasis on the palliative effects of domestic rituals also encompasses the realm of familial ties. Throughout the day, his need for human connection, particularly with members of his family, highlights the ritualistic aspects of long lasting human relationships as well as their necessity to constructing a sense of self and of security.[51] As he lies in bed with his wife Rosalind, for example, he is drawn to the "simple daily consolation" provided by the "ritual of affection, briefly settled in the eternal necessities of

---

49 Ibid., p. 128.

50 Ibid., pp. 185-6.

51 In an essay published a few days following 9/11, McEwan argues that the "snatched and anguished assertions of love" over cell phones by those trapped inside the World Trade Center towers to their loved ones could be read as a form of "defiance": "Love [...] set against the hatred of their murderers" ('Only love and then oblivion. Love was all they to set against their murders', *The Guardian*, Saturday September 15, 2001, 1-3). McEwan arguably develops this idea within *Saturday* to suggest that the rituals of love function as an antidote to terror and fear.

warmth, comfort, safety, crossing limbs to draw nearer [...] Not the single occasion, but its repetition through the years."[52] As the day proceeds, he telephones Rosalind at work on several occasions at times when he begins to feel off-balance and/or his ordinary routine has been shattered; what he needs from her is "the sound of her voice in an everyday exchange, the resumption of ordinary existence."[53] His early morning time in the kitchen, drinking coffee, watching the news, and talking with his eighteen year old musician son Theo also has the earmark of a comfortable familial ritual: "In the past months they have sat across this table and touched on all the issues."[54] Although visiting his elderly mother who no longer recognizes him is difficult for Perowne, he manages the experience through the observation of a set "routine": "Once they're established together, face to face, with their cups of dark brown tea, the tragedy of her situation will be obscured behind the banality of detail, of managing the suffocating minutes, of inattentive listening."[55] He can almost imagine that nothing has changed in those moments "when she's skilful in the long established routines."[56] The visits keep alive his connection with the "woman she once was"[57] and thus with his own past, through the memories the sight of her elicits as "a woman who gave her life to housework"[58] but also was a champion swimmer who won a "tiny silver medal" at the 1954 Middlesex "county championship."[59]

When his now grown daughter Daisy arrives for her visit, their greeting is marked by ritualistic actions created over the length of their familial relationship as father and daughter, which serve to reinforce their continued affective ties: "As they embrace, he makes a low, sighing, growling noise, the way he used to greet her when she was five"[60] and "she half rubbed, half patted his back, a familiar maternal gesture of hers."[61] Although he is slightly taken aback by the heated political debate into which they immediately launch even as he recognizes it as "one of their set-pieces,"[62] he nevertheless believes that "It's good, it's healthy to have one their old head-to-head arguments, it's

---

52 McEwan, p. 50.
53 Ibid., p. 100.
54 Ibid., pp. 34-35.
55 Ibid., p. 155.
56 Ibid., p. 168.
57 Ibid., p. 156.
58 Ibid., p. 157.
59 Ibid., p . 159.
60 Ibid., p. 186.
61 Ibid., p. 187.
62 Ibid., p. 191.

family life resumed,"[63] highlighting the vital role that family life and rituals play for Perowne. The security and sense of control that his familial life and position of privilege provide him reverberate in his acknowledgment of "how luxurious [it is], to work it all out at home in the kitchen, the geopolitical moves and military strategy, and not be held to account, by voters, newspapers, friends, history."[64] At the same time, the text hints at the limits of that security and control: for example, Perowne understands that "Most of her [Daisy's] life is a mystery to him now"[65] and senses that "their conversation is moving out of control."[66] Moreover, it never occurs to him that Daisy is pregnant, although he does note that she takes "Barely a sip"[67] of the champagne he serves her and ascertains that she seems "preoccupied" as well as "a little heavier perhaps, a little wiser around the eyes."[68] His jealous thoughts about the lovers he believes his daughter to have because of her "wanton"[69] poems also reveal not only his lack of control but his discomfort with that lack of control, reflected here in a classic patriarchal wish to control the daughter's sexuality.

McEwan's use in *Saturday* of a narrative form that focuses on the domestic also allows the text to represent terrorism through a displacement, in the form of the intrusion of violence into the home and into the individual psyche. Although unable to conceptualize terrorist violence on a large scale or his own complicity within the vast complex networks of global politics, Perowne is forced to face a graspable form of such violence and his own participation in inequitable systems when an intruder enters his home and holds his family hostage.[70] Although it remains dubious that Perowne himself ever really grasps the parallel between the home invasion and global terrorism, the reader is invited to ponder the parallels as a means of beginning to imagine

---

63 Ibid., p. 194.

64 Ibid., p. 198.

65 Ibid., p. 188.

66 Ibid., p. 195.

67 Ibid., p. 190.

68 Ibid., p. 188.

69 Ibid., p. 188.

70 Elaine Hadley similarly points out that "Baxter's attack is terrorism finally, almost relievedly, brought home to his thoughts," although she attributes this link to what she sees as the novel's "liberal aspirations" ('On a Darkling Plain: Victorian Liberalism and the Fantasy of Agency', *Victorian Studies*, 48 (2005), 92-102 (p. 96)). Lee Siegel, in his review of the novel, also notes that Baxter "poses to Henry [Perowne] the ethical challenge presented by poor, starving countries to the affluent West, and Henry treats him—unthinkingly, innocently—with a reflexive contempt not unlike the West's indifference to the Third World" ('The Imagination of Disaster', *The Nation*, April 11, 2005. n.p.).

even if not to ever fully comprehend terrorist acts and those who resort to such acts. As Gayatri Spivak argues, to end violence, "we must be able to imagine our opponent as a human being."[71] *Saturday* arguably presents the lower class British intruder, Baxter, as a substitute for the global terrorist as just such an attempt "to imagine our opponent as a human being" and thus as a gesture toward the dimension of the ethical. "The ethical," for Spivak, takes the form of "an interruption of the epistemological, which is the attempt to construct the other as object of knowledge"—belonging "to the domain of the law, which seeks to know the other"—and entails the attempt "to listen to the other as if it were a self, neither to punish nor to acquit" but rather to "resonate with the other."[72] Moreover, the novel also forces the reader to "resonate" with and "listen to" its problematic protagonist Perowne rather than merely denounce his position and reactions. Although some critics have labeled McEwan's novel a failure for seemingly endorsing the Western world view, I would argue that *Saturday* performs useful political critical work in its razor sharp depiction and implicit indictment of Perowne's inability to shed his privileged perspective as well as in its pointing readers toward the possibilities that imagining the other as human might bring. The novel clearly takes risks in this endeavor, for which it is panned by some reviewers and critics, but I would argue that taking risks is necessary if the text is to really attempt to represent what at this point in time in the West appears unrepresentable.

The scale of the home invasion that *Saturday* narrativizes makes it possible to represent, sheds light on the power dynamics at work, and functions as a means of illustrating the uneasiness that accompanies the recognition that home and privilege are no protection against unpredictable forms of violence. Notwithstanding the "three stout Banham locks, two black iron bolts [...], two steel security chains," and electronic house alarm system, which the novel makes clear create only the illusion of safety, Baxter gets in by holding a knife to Perowne's wife as she arrives home from work. Baxter is a lower class man with a neurological illness with whom Perowne interacted briefly earlier in the day as a result of a minor fender-bender on his way to his weekly squash game. The earlier scene enacts the mutually antagonistic but uneven power dynamics of class stratification in Britain. Before Perowne even

---

71 Gayatri Chakravorty Spivak, 'Terror: A Speech after 9/11', *Boundary 2*, 31 (2004), 81-111 (p. 93). Similarly, Daniel Sherman and Terry Nardin argue that "to imagine" "the terrorist's position" is "surely a necessary step" in any attempt to "dealing with terrorism" ('Introduction', in *Terror, Culture, Politics: Rethinking 9/11*, ed. Sherman and Nardin (Bloomington: Indiana University Press, 2006), p. 8.

72 Spivak, 'Terror', pp. 83, 87.

gets out of his car immediately following the accident, he is already suspicious of the three men in the other car, whom he had seen "hurrying out of a lap-dancing club,"[73] and adopts a position of superiority over them reminiscent of the British colonial stance—at another point in the novel, he feels a "distaste" that is "visceral" when he observes from his car "three figures in back burkhas,"[74] making the connection between his attitude toward those of other classes and races and Britain's colonial past even more explicit. Although Perowne acknowledges that, "As far as he's aware, lap-dancing is a lawful pursuit,"[75] the comment indicates that he looks down on the activity and the men who take part in it. Moreover, he takes one look at their "series-five BMW" and "associates [it] for no good reason with criminality, drug-dealing,"[76] thus demonstrating that he judges the men negatively before having even met or spoken with them. He also reads the traffic accident and by implication the three men as assaults on his way of life, which the text consistently marks as privileged: "His car will never be the same again. It's ruinously altered, and so is his Saturday. He'll never make his game" of squash.[77] Perowne's social position of privilege also surfaces in his unequivocal belief "that he's in the right" while he stands in front of his car "with hands on hips, in a pose of proprietorial outrage" while "he keeps the men, now advancing as a group, on the edge of vision."[78] At the same time as he asserts his superiority, however, he is also aware of the ways in which his actions are mediated by "A century of movies and half a century of television" and thus have the feel of "play-acting,"[79] thus undercutting his agency.

The narrative's undercutting of his dominant position continues as he watches the three men approach and begins to acknowledge that "he might be in some kind of danger" given that "the street is completely deserted,"[80] which again positions the men as criminals. In a stereotypic colonialist move, Perowne judges Baxter (the driver) as inferior by dehumanizing him through the attribution of animal characteristics: "The mouth is set bulbously, with the smoothly shaved shadow of a strong beard adding to the effect of a muzzle. The general simian air is compounded by sloping shoulders."[81] Once

---

[73] McEwan, p. 79.
[74] Ibid., p. 124.
[75] Ibid., p. 83.
[76] Ibid., p. 83.
[77] Ibid., p. 82.
[78] Ibid., p. 83.
[79] Ibid., p. 86.
[80] Ibid., p. 84.
[81] Ibid., p. 88.

they begin to beat him after he refuses to give them cash, Perowne again asserts his position of privilege, this time in his professional role of physician, when he diagnoses Baxter as ill with "Huntington's Disease" and insinuates that he could help Baxter, thus capitalizing on his knowledge of "this impulse of patients, this pursuit of the slenderest lead."[82] The ploy partly works in that Baxter does want knowledge about his condition and sends his two sidekicks away; but their exchange ends with Baxter accusing Perowne of "trying to fuck with me. In front of those two"[83] and bitter over Perowne's colonialist tactics of affecting to help others from a position of superiority. On one level, Perowne functions as a stand-in for the West; he views himself as a victim of the thugs (terrorists) at the same time as the narrative indicates the ways in which he participates in and is complicit with the power dynamics that underlie the antagonisms and acts of violence.

When Baxter appears with one of his sidekicks inside Perowne's home in the evening, however, the text complicates its presentation of Perowne. The home invasion scene depicts Perowne as fluctuating between thoughtful self-conscious surveyor of the events and angry self-righteous victim. Not only does Perowne admit to himself early in the scene that he is at least in part "responsible" for the home invasion in that he had earlier asserted his privileged position as a doctor when he "humiliated Baxter in the street in front of his sidekicks,"[84] but Perowne at times attempts, as Spivak urges, "to imagine [his] opponent as a human being"[85] even if he cannot in the end sustain it. For example, Perowne imagines that "All afternoon he [Baxter] must have dreamed of making this entrance,"[86] thus indicating that Perowne possesses the capacity for the kind of ethical move via the powers of the imagination for which Spivak calls. As the narrative notes, Perowne even "tries to see the room through Baxter's eyes," focusing on the wealth and privilege that characterizes it: "the two bottles of champagne, the gin and the bowls of lemon and ice, the belittlingly high ceiling and its mouldings, the Bridget Riley prints flanking the Hodgkin, the muted lamps, the cherry wood floor beneath the Persian rugs."[87] In this fleeting moment of Perowne's resonance with Baxter, McEwan seems to fictionally enact his belief, as asserted in an article written a few days after the events of 9/11 and published in *The Guardian*, that "Imagining what is like to be someone other than yourself is at the core

[82] Ibid., p. 98.
[83] Ibid., p. 99.
[84] Ibid., p. 218.
[85] Spivak, 'Terror', p. 93.
[86] McEwan, p. 213.
[87] Ibid., p. 213.

of our humanity" and "the essence of compassion."[88] More forcefully than Perowne's own musings, however, the text's imaginative rendering of the scene insists upon the way in which the two men's parallel and yet divergent activities of planning for the evening reflect the power dynamics between them and inherent in British culture at large and by extension globally. While Perowne spends time planning the upscale family gathering just getting underway with the aim of bolstering family ties and applauding the successes of his children, Baxter plans to undermine Perowne's sense of security and authority by entering his home by force.

Although the text sustains its critical edge in the rendering of the scene, the narrative indicates that Perowne ceases to be able to imagine Baxter's perspective when he shifts to a more intellectual reading of Baxter's actions as those of "a man who believes he has no future and is therefore free of consequences."[89] Such a reading participates in attempts to understand terrorism that parallel those of contemporary philosophers. Indeed, in post-9/11 comments, Derrida describes terrorism as a mostly symbolic gesture that tends to be a function of "forces that are apparently without any force of their own" and Habermas defines terrorism as "revolt directed against an enemy that cannot be defeated in any pragmatic sense."[90] Within the context of the novel, however, such an understanding works against the ethical imperative of attempting to imagine and "resonate with the other," as Spivak describes it,[91] because Perowne's rationalistic understanding of Baxter fills him with a fear that reaffirms the binary positioning of Baxter as monster and Perowne and his family as victims. Perowne shifts to viewing Baxter in terms of illness and inferiority. Moreover, his anger rises when Baxter eyes his daughter Daisy and then forces her to undress by holding a knife against her mother's neck; Baxter's sidekick Nigel's comment "You know what I'm thinking?"[92] insinuates rape. That Perowne can protect neither his wife nor daughter makes it impossible for him to resonate with or imagine Baxter as a self any longer, because Perowne feels his own sense of self as husband and father being violated within cultural structures of masculinity that depend on binary patriarchal and colonial models.

The scene does not end in a rape, however; rather Perowne and his son Theo in the end overpower Baxter and push him down the stairs so that he is injured to the extent of having to be carted to a hospital in an ambulance.

---

88 McEwan, 'Only love', p. 2.
89 McEwan, p. 217.
90 Borradori, pp. 95, 34
91 Spivak, 'Terror', p. 87.
92 McEwan, p. 225.

Although many critics fault the novel for the events that take place between Baxter's ordering Daisy to undress and his critical injury, I want to argue for an alternative reading of the scene that unfolds. Once Daisy undresses, "the weighted curve and compact swell of her [now naked] belly" makes clear that she is pregnant, which surprises everyone since she had not told her family and which changes the situation given the fact that in Western culture the pregnant woman tends not to be sexualized given the lasting influence of the dominant mother-madonna/whore binary. In response, Baxter shifts gears and, spotting Daisy's newly released book of poetry, orders her to read from it. Too nervous to read one of her poems, she instead recites from memory a poem her grandfather made her learn as a girl: Matthew Arnold's "Dover Beach." Baxter becomes so entranced with the poem that he makes her reread it and announces that "It's beautiful."[93] While Nigel tries to get him to follow through with the rape—"I'll take the knife while you do the business"[94]—Baxter answers, "I've changed my mind."[95] Critics have panned McEwan for what they see as a reactionary and implausible resolution to the crisis, which they interpret as McEwan's attempt to depict poetry as saving the day by transforming Baxter and leading him to ethical action.[96]

While the poetry reading scene does appear overly contrived and does veer a bit close to a kind of nostalgic gesture toward the power of literature, especially given the use of Arnold's incredibly famous and canonical poem, I would argue that the scene remains more complex than such a reading suggests. First of all, I would argue that it is not "Dover Beach" in and of itself that initially transforms Baxter and the situation at hand but rather the material reality of Daisy's pregnant body. Once she is undressed, Nigel says, "Jesus. In the club. She's all yours, mate,"[97] indicating that he sees she is pregnant but is not going to let that stop the rape. Baxter's response, "Shut up," followed by "Well, well. Look at that!" as he points to Daisy's book, which he then picks up and flips through,[98] demonstrates that unlike Nigel he responds to Daisy's pregnant body by deliberately desexualizing her and shifting his attention to her book of poetry.

---

93 Ibid., p. 230.

94 Ibid., p. 230.

95 Ibid., p. 231.

96 For example, Hadley criticizes McEwan for "offer[ing] up duct tape and plastic sheeting as a response to the unknown agents and unpredictable consequences of the new world order" in the guise of "fantasies of liberal agency" that hark back to Victorianism and are embodied in Arnold's "Dover Beach" that "saves the day" in the novel (pp. 97, 92).

97 McEwan, p. 227.

98 Ibid., p. 227.

Moreover, the text draws attention to a parallel between Baxter and Perowne when it depicts them as both believing that Daisy has written the poem she is reading and both transfixed by her reading of the poem, which creates a kind of imaginative resonance within each of them toward Daisy. Perowne "feels himself slipping through the words into the things they describe"[99] and Baxter's "elated" look by the end of the second reading suggests a similar effect.[100] At one point in the reading, the narrative announces that "it's through Baxter's ears that [Perowne] hears the sea's 'melancholy, long withdrawing roar,...,'"[101] indicating another moment in which Perowne finds himself resonating with and imagining Baxter as a self. Similarly, Baxter's awed response, "You wrote that [...] It's beautiful. You know that don't you"[102] suggests that he is resonating with Daisy through the words she reads; he then tells her to get dressed again to Nigel's incredulous annoyance. Arnold's poem thus does not function as the only trigger to the similar response of the two otherwise dissimilar men; rather, I am arguing that the trigger comes from the *reading* of the poem by the pregnant young woman. The sense of wonder that captures both men derives not solely from the poem itself but from the creative potential of the woman's body as well as mind with which they are faced as they view her naked pregnant body and listen to the poetry they believe she has created. That the text depicts both men as experiencing similar reactions highlights for the reader their common humanity and again hints at the potential inherent in resonating with another (Daisy) and alongside an other (Perowne and Baxter), even if Perowne immediately after again uses his privileged position as physician to lure Baxter upstairs to get evidence about a new drug trial for his illness. Once upstairs, he and his son Theo manage to push Baxter down the stairs and regain the upper hand, shattering any imaginative resonance with Baxter.

Once the ambulance and the police leave, Perowne further solidifies his sense of himself and family as victims and of Baxter as the violent and inferior home invader. Indeed, "the sight of the abrasion on [his wife] Rosalind's neck hardens him," and he rejects as "delusional folly" any "sympathy" he felt for Baxter.[103] Perowne distances himself from Baxter by othering him as a criminal to the extent of even beginning "to regret the care he routinely

---

99 Ibid., p. 218.

100 Ibid., p. 230. In slightly different terms, Hillard notes of this parallel that "the diseased man [Baxter] and the doctor [Perowne] share a moment of profound misprision" that creates an "uneasy community of shared misprision" (pp. 183, 185).

101 McEwan, p. 230.

102 Ibid., p. 231.

103 Ibid., p. 239.

gave Baxter after his fall" and almost wishing that he had "left him to die of hypoxia."[104] Moreover, his detailed memory of the medical care he gave Baxter, which included opening "his airway with a jaw thrust" and "improvis[ing] a collar out of towels," and the instructions he gives over the phone to the hospital registrar work to resituate him in a position of power as benevolent superior and further push Baxter in the position of inferior *other.*[105] After the ambulance and police have left, the family's attempt to redirect the evening back to its original design by sitting around a table to eat, drink, and toast Daisy's book inside their luxurious home rid of its lower class intruders both demonstrates an attempt "to survive" their "fear"[106] and further indicates the reconsolidation of positions of power and privilege. The novel thus forces the reader to see that holding on to and reconsolidating power is a survival mechanism for those in positions of power.

Perowne most fully reasserts his position of power, however, when he agrees to perform surgery on the critically injured Baxter, thus asserting a god-like power over Baxter. Although, "as a general rule, Perowne avoids operating on people he knows," he does not decline when his colleague calls him from the hospital for help with the surgery.[107] When his wife questions his decision, he asserts that he must "see this through" because, as he claims, "I'm responsible,"[108] which on the surface sounds like an admission of responsibility and an ethical basis for his actions; however, the text immediately begins chipping away at Perowne's expressed rationale. To begin with, Rosalind immediately expresses doubts over his stated good intentions, when she asks, "You're not thinking about doing something, about some kind of revenge are you?,"[109] a notion that Perowne rejects outright. Later that night, however, Perowne does admit that, by saving Baxter's life, he "also committed Baxter to his torture" and thus "Revenge enough," in the sense that Baxter will have to live through the degenerative disease afflicting him.[110] The text thus indicates that Perowne's motives remain mixed at best.

More forcefully, however, the text highlights the ways in which Perowne moves away from the kind of ethical action that would allow him to imagine and resonate with Baxter in his positioning of himself as Baxter's surgeon and thus wielding incredible power over Baxter: Baxter's life depends on

104 Ibid., p. 239.
105 Ibid., p. 239.
106 Ibid., p. 242.
107 Ibid., p. 242.
108 Ibid., p. 245.
109 Ibid., p. 246.
110 Ibid., p. 288.

successful surgery. Perowne can reassert his power once he gets to the hospital's "neurosurgical suite," because "he can control outcomes here, he has resources, controlled conditions"[111] and because his education and training have given him access to his position as neurosurgeon. On the operating table, Baxter is further dehumanized in that "All that's visible of him is the wide area of his head shaved to the rear of the vertex, the crown" and "the sense of a personality, an individual" virtually "disappears."[112] Indeed, the narrative describes the neurosurgery in detail for almost ten pages, emphasizing Baxter's passive and helpless state and his complete dependence on his surgeon's skills and benevolence, both of which give back to Perowne his sense of power—including power over Baxter.

In addition, rather than returning home after the surgery, Perowne sits by Baxter's bedside, thus suggesting a need to continue to dominate and control Baxter. Indeed, Perowne further asserts his position of superiority and power through descriptions of Baxter that parallel Perowne's earlier colonialist notions during his initial meeting with Baxter in the street following the car accident earlier in the day. Perowne notes that "Sleep has relaxed [Baxter's] jaw and softened the simian effect of a muzzle,"[113] thus highlighting Baxter's inferiority through animal-like characteristics. This colonial strategy, in which "the opponent is dehumanized," can also be read as deriving from "a Manichean posture dividing the world into forces of good and evil," according to Stephen Toope, and in the contemporary context is leading to an erosion of hard won "normative edifices of human rights."[114] Perowne sets himself up as a force of good in his decision to save Baxter's life with his surgical skills; however, Baxter is never consulted about having the man who pushed him down the stairs operating on him, thus highlighting Baxter's position of powerlessness within the medical establishment. Furthermore, Perowne's assumption of the colonist's benevolence reaches beyond his willingness to save Baxter's life when he decides that he will drop the charges against Baxter.

The novel ends not with the home invasion scene and not with Perowne operating on Baxter, however, but with Perowne again standing at his bedroom window, "feeling skinny and frail in his dressing gown"[115] and feeling

---

111 Ibid., p. 253.

112 Ibid., p. 255.

113 Ibid., p. 271.

114 Stephen J. Toope, 'Human Rights and the Use of Force after September 11th, 2001', in *Terror, Culture, Politics: Rethinking 9/11*, ed. by Daniel J. Sherman and Terry Nardin (Bloomington: Indiana University Press, 2006), 236-258 (pp. 243, 245).

115 McEwan, p. 284.

himself growing old as he approaches "fifty" and knows he will have to "give up squash and marathons" and watch his children move away from him.[116] His awareness of his lack of control and power surface in his acknowledgment of the uncertainties of what the future will bring at this particular historical juncture. Not only does he note that "London, his small part of it, lies wide open, impossible to defend, waiting for its bomb, like a hundred other cities"[117] and that a "war will start next month," but he also admits his "fear" over "the way consequences of an action leap away from your control and breed new events, new consequences, until you're led to a place you never dreamed of and would never choose—a knife to the throat."[118] His feelings of vulnerability derive from his inability to control the consequences of events and actions.

Rather than accept such a lack of control and power in the face of fear, however, Perowne reaffirms a contemporary version of the British colonial stance by deciding that he will persuade his family "not to pursue charges" against Baxter[119] on the basis of the man's illness, a decision that on the surface could certainly be construed as ethical. Instead of an ethical decision of the type Spivak discusses, however, Perowne's decision arguably smacks of colonial benevolence marked by condescension in its embrace of what Derrida describes as "a form of charity" from a position of "power" and thus "always as a kind of condescending concession."[120] Indeed, as a physician and within the medical establishment, Perowne "can exercise authority and shape events"[121] and thus regains power and his sense of self by choosing to act benevolently toward Baxter. By highlighting Perowne's actions and anticipated actions as rooted in a loss of power and control and in attempts to hold on to a kind of power historically grounded in and connected to Britain's colonial past, the novel offers a stark portrait of the difficulties Western citizens will have in making headway toward imagining and resonating with the *other*—including the *other* in the form of global terrorist —as a first step to ending violence.

On the level of the novel, the home invasion functions as a sort of micro version of a large scale terrorist act that exists on a human scale and thus can be represented. Moreover, the scale of the event allows both the novel's characters and readers access to the event—it becomes neither unimaginable nor

---

116 Ibid., p. 285.
117 Ibid., p. 286.
118 Ibid., p. 287.
119 Ibid., p. 287.
120 Borradori, p. 127.
121 McEwan, p. 288.

unrepresentable. That the event in the end fails on the level of the characters, in the sense that Perowne and his family members reassert their positions of dominance by the novel's end and that the status quo is left intact, to my mind does not indicate the novel's failure. Indeed, the novel's foregrounding of Perowne's attempts to imagine and resonate with Baxter provides for the reader a vision of the possible, even if in the end Perowne cannot sustain it. Moreover, that the novel presents Perowne as ultimately unable to give up his position of power illustrates the complexity of ending violence in a world in which positions of power have remained inequitable and in which so few incentives exist for those who hold power to let go of that power, especially given that selfhood and power have become virtually inextricable, particularly in the West, and that political and economic power remain intertwined.

McEwan's novel takes up the challenge of representing the post-9/11 cultural climate by depicting possible strategies for moving beyond violence and terror as well as the inevitable failures of such strategies in a culture that holds on to a colonial, binary, Eurocentric mindset out of fear in the face of violence and terror. Homi Bhabha asserts that "To confront the politics of terror, out of a sense of democratic solidarity rather than retaliation, gives us some faint hope for the future."[122] *Saturday* arguably does just that through its fictional representation, even if its characters ultimately cannot sustain the ethical, political work necessary so that hope for the future within the confines of the novel remains faint and the novel does not provide any concrete closure or answers. Like all representations, McEwan's novel is a construct, but it is a construct that strategically allows for an engagement with the cultural climate of its day and as such is, in John Frow's terms, "bound up with real structures of enunciative interests."[123] *Saturday* thus participates in and contributes to contemporary discussions of the post-9/11 world and explorations of the possibilities of moving past violence in a world marked by global terrorism on the scale of the events of 9/11 at the beginning of the twenty-first century.

---

[122] Bhabha, p. 4.

[123] John Frow, 'The Uses of Terror and the Limits of Cultural Studies', *Symploke*, 11 (2003), 69-76 (p. 75).

Bibliography

Baudrillard, Jean, 'L'Esprit du Terrorisme', trans. by Michel Valentin, *The South Atlantic Quarterly*, 101 (Spring 2002), 403-415

Bhabha, Homi K., 'Terror and after…', *Parallax*, 8 (2002), 3-4. (First published Sept. 28, 2001 in *The Chronicle of Higher Education*)

Birrer, Doryjane, '"What Are Novelists For?": Writing and Rewriting Reality from Woolf to McEwan', in *Woolf in the Real World*, ed. by Karen V. Kukil (Clemson: Clemson University Press, 2005), 165-170

Borradori, Giovanna, *Philosophy in a Time of Terror: Dialogues with Jürgen Habermas and Jacques Derrida* (Chicago: The University of Chicago Press, 2003)

Clymer, Jeffory A., *America's Culture of Terrorism: Violence, Capitalism, and the Written Word* (Chapel Hill: The University of North Carolina Press, 2003)

Currie, Mark, *About Time: Narrative, Fiction and the Philosophy of Time* (Edingurgh, UK: Edinburgh University Press, 2007)

Davies, Rhiannon, 'Enduring McEwan', in *Posting the Male: Masculinities in Post-war and Contemporary British Literature*, ed. by Daniel Lea and Berthold Schoene (New York: Rodopi, 2003), 105-123

DeMeester, Karen, 'Trauma, Post-Traumatic Stress Disorder, and Obstacles to Postwar Recovery in *Mrs. Dalloway*', in *Virginia Woolf and Trauma: Embodied Texts*, ed. by Suzette Henke and David Eberly (New York: Pace University Press, 2007), 77-93

Frow, John, 'The Uses of Terror and the Limits of Cultural Studies', *Symploke*, 11 (2003), 69-76

Hadley, Elaine, 'On a Darkling Plain: Victorian Liberalism and the Fantasy of Agency', *Victorian Studies*, 48 (2005), 92-102

Hillard, Molly Clark, "When Desert Armies Stand Ready to Fight": Re-Reading McEwan's *Saturday* and Arnold's "Dover Beach"', *Partial Answers*, 6 (2008), 181-206

Kaplan, E. Ann, *Trauma Culture: The Politics of Terror and Loss in Media and Literature* (New Brunswick: Rutgers University Press, 2005)

Kellner, Douglas, 'September 11, Social Theory and Democratic Politics', *Theory, Culture and Society*, 19 (2002), 147-159

Kirshenblatt-Gimblett, Barbara, 'Kodak Moments, Flashbulb Memories: Reflections on 9/11', *The Drama Review* 47 (Spring 2003), 11-48

McEwan, Ian, 'Beyond Belief', *The Guardian*, Wednesday September 12, 2001, 1-2

---, 'Only love and then oblivion. Love was all they to set against their murders', *The Guardian*, Saturday September 15, 2001, 1-3

---, *Saturday* (New York: Anchor Books, 2006)

Michiko Kakutani, 'A Hero with 9/11 Peripheral Vision', *The New York Times*, March 18, 2005

Sherman, Daniel J. and Terry Nardin, ed., *Terror, Culture, Politics: Rethinking 9/11* (Bloomington: Indiana University Press, 2006)

---, 'Introduction', in Sherman and Nardin, 1-11

Siegel, Lee, 'The Imagination of Disaster', *The Nation*, April 11, 2005

Spivak, Gayatri Chakravorty, 'Globalicities: Terror and Its Consequences', *The New Centennial Review* 4 (2004), 73-94

Spivak, Gayatri Chakravorty, 'Terror: A Speech after 9/11', *Boundary 2*, 31 (2004), 81-111

Toope, Stephen J., 'Human Rights and the Use of Force after September 11th, 2001', in Sherman and Nardin, 236-258

"Blow the World Back Together": Literary Nostalgia, 9/11, and Terrorism in Seamus Heaney, Chris Cleave, and Martin Amis

Brandon Kempner

This article deals with a broad range of British works that frame the events of 9/11 with an abrupt turn towards literary nostalgia. Such texts include Seamus Heaney's poem "Anything Can Happen" (2001), Ian McEwan's *Saturday* (2005), Chris Cleave's *Incendiary* (2005), David Llewellyn's *Eleven* (2006), and Martin Amis's essay/story collection *The Second Plane* (2008). Each of these turns to older (humanist) literary techniques—whether in the form of allusion, a reliance on epistolary form, or a return to the universalized Western subject—as a way of counteracting the idea of 9/11 as a permanent rupture in Western history and culture.

When it comes to 9/11 and the broader "War on Terror," the United Kingdom is second only to the United States in the production of literary texts. While novels like Salman Rushdie's *Shalimar the Clown* and Mohsin Hamid's *The Reluctant Fundamentalist* challenge orthodox interpretations of terrorism (Rushdie) and 9/11 (Hamid), a much broader range of British texts frame the events of 9/11 with an abrupt turn towards literary nostalgia.[1] These texts include Seamus Heaney's poem "Anything Can Happen," Ian McEwan's *Saturday*, Chris Cleave's *Incendiary*, David Llewellyn's *Eleven*, and Martin Amis's essay/story collection *The Second Plane*.[2] When closely examined, these texts appear remarkably similar in their textual, theoretical, and political approaches.[3] Each of them turns to older literary techniques—whether in the form of allusion, a reliance on epistolary form, or a return to the universalized Western subject—as a way of counteracting the idea of 9/11 as a permanent rupture in Western history and culture.

Rupture is one of the dominant theoretical and political ideas to emerge from the 9/11 attacks. From a theoretical perspective, thinkers such as Jean Baudrillard in *The Spirit of Terrorism*, Slavoj Žižek in *Welcome to the Desert of the Real*, and Jacques Derrida in *Philosophy in a Time of Terror* have all

---

1 Salman Rushdie, *Shalimar the Clown* (New York: Random House, 2005); Mohsin Hamid, *The Reluctant Fundamentalist* (New York: Harcourt, 2007).

2 Seamus Heaney, *Anything Can Happen* (Dublin: TownHouse, 2004); Ian McEwan, *Saturday* (New York: Anchor Books, 2005); Chris Cleave, *Incendiary* (New York: Anchor Books, 2005); David Llewellyn, *Eleven* (Brigend, Wales: Seren, 2006); Martin Amis, *The Second Plane: September 11: Terror and Boredom* (New York: Knopf, 2008).

3 Other significant British texts about 9/11 and its aftermath include David Hare, *Stuff Happens* (New York: Faber and Faber, Inc., 2004), a play that directly satirizes the Bush presidency and its cabinet, and Simon Armitage, *Out of the Blue*, (London: Enitharmon Press, 2008), in which his long poem "Out of the Blue" depicts 9/11 as a total rupture, concluding with the line "Everything changed. Nothing is safe."

explicitly argued that the 9/11 attacks completely reconfigure Western culture and subjectivity.[4] For instance, Baudrillard claims that "the whole play of history and power is disrupted by this event"; Derrida says "such an 'event' calls for philosophical response. Better, a response that calls into question, at their most fundamental level, the most deep-seated conceptual presuppositions in philosophical discourse." [5] The political claims of absolute change as a result of 9/11 are equally widespread; Fred Halliday, a writer explicitly referenced by McEwan in *Saturday*, identifies 9/11 as an "all-encompassing"event that forces fundamental change in "a multiplicity of life's levels, political, economic, cultural, and psychological."[6]

From a literary perspective, such a mantra of total rupture would imply that older modes of literary expression and Western identity are no longer relevant in a post-9/11 age. Indeed, these pronouncements of total change can be found in many authors' initial reactions to 9/11. Amis, in his essay "The Voice of the Lonely Crowd," writes that, as a result of 9/11, all writers need to abandon whatever they were working on and to begin writing all over again:

> The so-called work in progress had been reduced, overnight, to a blue streak of autistic babble. But then, too, a feeling of gangrenous futility had infected the whole corpus. The page headed "By the same author"—which, in the past, was smugly consulted as a staccato biography—could now be dismissed with a sigh and a shake of the head.[7]

Despite his insistence, Amis's call for total change is not born out by close examination of British literature written about 9/11 and terrorism. In the texts I discuss in this essay—Heaney's poem "Anything Can Happen," Cleave's epistolary novel *Incendiary,* and Amis's terrorism stories "In the Palace of the End" and "The Last Days of Muhammad Atta"—what emerges is not the "gangrenous futility" of past literature, but rather a re-statement of some traditionally Western modes of narration, interiority, and literary framing.[8]

Instead of presenting a post-9/11 world where Western thought is disrupted, each of these texts presents a world where Western interiority remains the best intellectual framework for understanding terrorism. By rewriting a

---

4 Jean Baudrillard, *The Spirit of Terrorism,* trans. by Chris Turner (New York: Verso, 2003); Slavoj Žižek, *Welcome to the Desert of the Real!*, (New York: Verso, 2002); Giovanna Borradori, *Philosophy in a Time of Terror: Dialogues with Jürgen Habermas and Jacques Derrida* (Chicago: University of Chicago Press, 2003).

5 Baudrillard, p. 4; Borradori, p. 100.

6 Fred Halliday, *Two Hours That Shook the World* (London: Saqi Books, 2002), p. 31.

7 Amis, p. 12.

8 Amis, pp. 11-20, 93-122.

Horace ode to apply to the 9/11 attacks, Heaney's "Anything Can Happen" reaffirms the power of Western literature as an interpretative frame. Cleave's *Incendiary* make use of epistolary form and the interiority this form implies to overcome the violence and alienation of terrorist attacks. Amis's two terrorism stories work by re-universalizing the classic Western subject, attributing interiority to two extreme Islamist characters. All of these texts demonstrate a profound nostalgia for the universality of Western reason and logic, concepts that have allegedly been devastated by the events of 9/11.

In many ways, these British texts operate within the theoretical space articulated by Edward Said's *Humanism and Democratic Criticism.*[9] In this text, Said calls for a return to humanism as an antidote to "prepackaged and reified representations of the world that usurp consciousness and preempt democratic critique."[10] At the same time, Said is careful to acknowledge the ways that Western humanism has been closely linked to "the experience of Eurocentrism and empire."[11] Heaney, Cleave, Amis, and other authors of these British 9/11 texts engage in both what Said sees as the liberating and colonizing aspects of humanism. By a return to interiority, these texts attempt to restore the consciousness that has allegedly been ruptured by the terrorist attacks of 9/11, and yet each flirts—or in the case of Amis, embraces—the colonialism and Eurocentrism that has traditionally been associated with humanism.

While American literary responses to 9/11 have garnered a great deal of critical attention, British literary responses, with the notable exception of Ian McEwan's *Saturday,* have been largely overlooked.[12] The literary nostalgia of these British texts is one reason; when compared to the major American novels about 9/11, such as Jonathan Safran Foer's *Extremely Loud & Incredibly Close*, which mixes prose and pictures, or Don DeLillo's fractured, postmodern *Falling Man*, these British texts are remarkably straightforward and

---

9 Edward Said, *Humanism and Democratic Criticism* (New York: Columbia University Press, 2004).

10 Ibid., p. 71.

11 Ibid., p. 11.

12 The collection *Literature after 9/11*, ed. by Ann Keniston and Jeanne Follansbee Quinn (New York: Routledge, 2008), contains roughly a dozen articles on American literary reactions 9/11 and only one article (by Rebecca Carpenter) on British literary reactions, focusing on Hare and McEwan. Except for brief mention of Amis in Robert Eaglestone, '"The Age of Reason is Over [...] an Age of Fury was Dawning": Contemporary Anglo-American Fiction and Terror', *Wasafiri*, 22.2 (2007), 19-22, which generally finds 9/11 literature unequal to the task of explaining terrorism and its aftermath, I am unaware of any extensive critical readings of Heaney, Amis, Cleave, or Llewellyn's British 9/11 texts.

non-experimental.[13] Heaney, Cleave, and Amis are all quite conservative in their style in these texts, offering mostly linear narratives that focus closely on the interiority of their characters. Despite the seemingly non-experimental nature of these texts, they do an enormous amount of work framing and interpreting terrorism and 9/11. While it would be possible to quickly dismiss these texts as a dangerous form of cultural reactionism, this turn towards literary nostalgia is a significant aspect of 9/11 literature that has not, as of yet, received the close critical study it deserves.

From Rupture to Continuity: The Western Subject after 9/11

In *Windows on the World,* a novel by French writer Frédéric Beigbeder, the narrator—a writer named Frédéric Beigbeder writing a 9/11 novel—remarks that:

> Writing the hyperrealist novel is made more difficult by reality itself. Since September 11, 2001, reality has not only outstripped fiction, it's destroying it. It's impossible to write about this subject, and yet impossible to write about anything else. Nothing else touches us.[14]

Beigbeder's text is a struggle to reconcile the traditions of the realist Western novel with the allegedly new world order inaugurated by 9/11. Beigbeder's novel moves back and forth between a man and his sons trapped in the World Trade Center and an author attempting to compose that story; in this way, the novel tries to be both realistic and metafictional simultaneously. Beigbeder's solution of combining these two narrative tactics is only one way that various authors have tried to create new ways of writing about 9/11. While the desire to create new narrative techniques is one important aspect of 9/11 literature, this is matched by an equally significant attempt to use older literary techniques and ideas to explain and control the trauma of 9/11.[15]

---

13 Jonathan Safran Foer, *Extremely Loud & Incredibly Close* (New York: Mariner Books, 2005); Don DeLillo, *Falling Man* (New York: Scribner, 2007).

14 Frédéric Beigbeder, *Windows on the World,* trans. by Frank Wynne (New York: Miramax Books, 2003), p. 8.

15 The essays contained in the volume *Literature after 9/11* largely attempt to map out these "new genres of testimony" (a phrase used by Nancy Miller in her essay about the *New York Times*' "Portraits of Grief"), and contain primarily readings of American attempts to recreate literature in the wake of 9/11. See particularly Charles Lewis, 'Real Planes and Imaginary Towers: Philip Roth's *The Plot Against America* as 9/11 Prosthetic Screen', *Literature after 9/11*, ed. by Ann Keniston and Jeanne Follansbee Quinn (New York: Routledge, 2008), 246-260, where he argues that Roth's employment of a "counterfactual historical" narrative provides an entirely new way of interrogating 9/11. Further examples can be found in the col-

Ann Keniston and Jeanne Follansbee Quinn, in their introduction to *Literature After 9/11*, elaborate on this point:

> while the initial experience of 9/11 seemed unprecedented and cataclysmic, the experience of incommensurability generated a culture-wide need for explanatory narratives, not simply as means of countering the trauma, but as a means for refusing incommensurability [...] We might say, then, that the history of literary representations of 9/11 can be characterized by the *transitions* from narratives of rupture to narratives of continuity.[16]

Keniston and Quinn provide the necessary framework as to why a literary nostalgia might exist (to "counter the trauma") without necessarily detailing the specifics of that operation. David Simpson sets up a similar framework in his book *9/11: The Culture of Commemoration*. He rejects the standard view that 9/11 is "an interruption of the deep rhythms of cultural time, a cataclysm simply erasing what was there rather than evolving from anything already in place, and threatening a yet more monstrous future."[17] Instead of total rupture, Simpson argues that "the deaths of 9/11 thus occurred within a culture of commemoration that was already primed to restore to sanctification and personalization in the cause of upholding the image of a flourishing civil society and a providential national destiny."[18] What emerges from close study, then, is not rupture with earlier ideological systems but a profound continuity.

When applied to the British literature of Heaney, Cleave, and Amis, what emerges is continuity with Western interiority, as expressed through older literary techniques. Žižek, in *Welcome to the Desert of the Real*, offers a pointed model for understanding this literary nostalgia. Žižek sees 9/11 as a failed moment, a chance when Western culture could have revolutionized itself but failed to do so: "on September 11, the USA was given the opportunity to realize what kind of world it was part of. It might have taken this opportunity—but did not; instead it opted to reassert its traditional ideological commitments."[19] Simply replacing the word "USA" with the phrase "British literature" creates a powerful, albeit critical, method for reading 9/11 fiction. A great deal of British (and American) fiction has used literature about 9/11

---

lection *Terror, Culture, Politics: Rethinking 9/11*, edited by Daniel Sherman and Terry Nardin (Bloomington: Indiana University Press, 2006).

16 Keniston and Quinn, p. 3.

17 David Simpson, *9/11: The Culture of Commemoration* (Chicago: University of Chicago Press, 2006), p. 4

18 Ibid., p. 31

19 Žižek, p. 47.

and terrorism as a means of restating older ideologies. Žižek's treatment of United States culture, though, does not necessarily indicate what the precise nature of the ideological commitments of British literature will be.

The work already done by various critics on McEwan's *Saturday* has mapped out the initial direction of these ideological commitments, although such readings have generally not noticed how widespread these commitments are throughout British 9/11 fiction. In *Saturday,* after a confrontation at an anti-Iraq war rally, the main character's family is threatened by a thug who attempts to kill them; the whole disaster, though, is improbably averted when Perowne's daughter reads "Dover Beach" aloud. Critic Rebecca Carpenter remarks that, "Metaphorically, however, it could not be more fitting for McEwan's project: British tradition (as embodied by Mathew Arnold's poem 'Dover Beach') saves the day, and thuggish terrorism is put down by the keepers of the British spirit of fair play."[20] More specifically, Elaine Hadley, in her essay "On a Darkling Plain: Victorian Liberalism and the Fantasy of Agency," sketches out how McEwan's reference to "Dover Beach" re-invokes the Victorian liberal subject:

> Arnold's poem, of course, is much more than a love poem, for it details his belief in the liberal subject's ability to seek out a private space of thoughtful emotion, of human intimacy, where subjects alienated in mind or body can become fully authentic and intentional in relation to themselves and to each other, in spite of the chaotic world without.[21]

Hadley's description of the subject—which she defines as "liberal," but could easily be defined as humanist or Western—as a fully realized interiority, which in turn leads to a rational understanding of the world, stands as the traditional ideological commitment of this strain of British 9/11 fiction.[22]

---

[20] Rebecca Carpenter, '"We're Not a Friggin' Girl Band": September 11, Masculinity, and the British-American Relationship in David Hare's *Stuff Happens* and Ian McEwan's *Saturday*', in *Literature after 9/11*, ed. by Ann Keniston and Jeanne Follansbee (New York: Routledge, 2008), 143-160 (p. 154).

[21] Elaine Hadley, 'On a Darkling Plain: Victorian Liberalism and the Fantasy of Agency', *Victorian Studies*, 48 (2005), 92-102 (p. 93).

[22] Other literary critics who have commented extensively on the role of "Dover Beach" in *Saturday* include Molly Clark Hillard, '"When Desert Armies Stand Ready to Fight": Re-Reading Ian McEwan's *Saturday* and Mathew Arnold's "Dover Beach"', *Partial Answers*, 6.1 (2008), 181-206. For specific readings of Ian McEwan's *Saturday* along the lines of the British-American special relationship, see Rebecca Carpenter. Richard Brown, 'Politics, the Domestic, and the Uncanny Effects of the Everyday in Ian McEwan's *Saturday*', *Critical Survey*, 20.1 (2008), 80-93, and Frances Ferguson, 'The Way We Love Now: Ian McEwan, *Saturday*, and Personal Affection in the Information Age', *Representations*, 100 (2007), 42-

Said's *Humanism and Democratic Criticism* provides one of the best models for understanding this resurrection of humanism in this strand of British 9/11 fiction. First, Said's description of the humanist subject closely parallels the subject represented in British 9/11 fiction and criticism. Said rejects what he identifies as the moves made by Michel Foucault and others to show that

> systems of thinking and perceiving transcended the power of individuals [...] and therefore had no power over them, only the choice either to use or be used by them. This of course flatly contradicts the core of humanistic thought, and hence the individual *cogito* was displaced, or demoted, to the status of illusory autonomy or fiction.[23]

Instead, Said argues that he is "unaffected by that theory's ideological antihumanism" and that the humanist thinking subject—when removed from "its abuses by the experience of Eurocentrism and empire"—can still stand as a viable base for human existence. The return to the interiority of humanism stands, for Said, as a counter-measure to other, dehumanizing theories of the 20th and 21st centuries.[24] The same model can easily be applied to British 9/11 fiction. In this fiction, terrorism and 9/11 are depicted as the ultimate act of "ideological antihumanism," since terrorism seems to strip individual humans/subjects of any control or power. To counter the perceived antihumanism of the terrorist attacks, each uses a commitment to traditional concepts of Western literature and subjectivity as a way of re-expressing the idea that the thinking self can make sense of the world. The specific texts of Heaney, Cleave, and Amis map out the nature of this return, where interiority operates as the ultimate form of counter-terrorism.

Second, Said stands as a powerful example of a significant theorist who has rejected the "9/11 as rupture" concept. Early in *Humanism and Democratic Criticism*, Said acknowledges that "Since September 11, terror and terrorism have been thrust into the public consciousness with amazing insistence."[25] After briefly mentioning some of the ways that those attacks have been analyzed and packaged for public consumption, Said discards these preexisting interpretations of terrorism, writing that "I do not want to spend any time going over these notions or to try to refute them because, quite frankly, they strike me as trivial and superficial. I just want to note their lingering

---

52, both provide readings that discuss how *Saturday* operates against a background of the rapidly changing 21st century.

23 Said, *Humanism*, pp. 9-10.

24 Ibid., pp. 10, 11.

25 Ibid., p. 8.

presence and move on."[26] *Humanism and Democratic* criticism, for the most part, does not engage either terrorism, 9/11, or the "meaning" of these events; part of Said's argument is that such events do not require a wholesale revision of humanist concepts. Even Said's earliest published comments on 9/11, from the September 16th, 2001, issue of *The Observer,* operate as a call to understand 9/11 rationally:

> What is most depressing, however, is how little time is spent trying to understand America's role in the world, and its direct involvement in the complex reality beyond the two coasts that have for so long kept the rest of the world extremely distant and virtually out of the average American's mind.[27]

9/11 does not operate, in Said's view, as a disruptive force for the humanist tradition, and the proper response to 9/11 is the need to "understand." This sentiment closely echoes what Said argues in *Humanism and Democratic Criticism,* where he claims that "the core of humanism is the secular notion that the historical world is made by men and women, and not by God, and that it can be understood rationally."[28] As I will argue below, Said's call for a return to the rational, thinking subject is echoed in each of these British 9/11 texts. While Heaney, Cleave, and Amis all significantly differ from Said in their particulars, they all occupy a similar theoretical space, where a return to rationality operates as a counter-measure to the allegedly world-shattering nature of 9/11.

Lastly, Said's insistence on the thinking, rational subject is tempered by his understanding of the historical ways that humanism has been linked to colonialism and nationalism. Said is quick to reject a nationalistic humanism:

> there can be no true humanism whose scope is limited to extolling patriotically the virtues of our culture, our language, our monuments. Humanism is the exertion of one's faculties in language in order to understand, reinterpret, and grapple with the products of language in history, other languages and other histories.[29]

By rejecting what he terms the "exclusivism" of much past humanist discourse—the way that such humanism "sees in the past only self-flattering narratives that deliberately filter out not just the achievements of other groups but in a sense even their fructifying presence"—Said is able to distinguish

---

26 Ibid., p. 8.

27 Edward Said, 'Islam and the West are Inadequate Banners', *The Observer*, 16 September 2001, p. 27.

28 Said, *Humanism*, p. 11.

29 Ibid., p. 28.

between a mode of humanism that embraces the challenges of multiculturalism and a traditionally exclusive mode of humanism that rejects everything but Western culture.[30] Indeed, for Said, humanism is not inherently or even primarily Western. Unlike Said, these British 9/11 texts are not as careful to distinguish between modes of humanism, and at critical moments each reflects the colonialism and exclusivism inherent in earlier modes of humanist thinking.

By viewing these British texts through the lens of Said, we can see how each deploys both the explanatory and colonizing power of humanism. As an emerging discourse about 9/11, these texts represent an intriguing series of case studies: each tries to use the notion of the rational thinking subject to explain and contain the events of 9/11, and, by doing so, to reject the idea of 9/11 as a cultural rupture. By stressing the power of the subject to make sense of terrorist events, they provide a meaningful alternative to pre-packaged ideas about 9/11, such as the "us versus them" model that has been so widely disseminated. At the same time, however, each of these texts invokes the exclusionary aspects of older models of humanism. It is the complex dual nature of these texts, ultimately, that makes them a significant and fascinating contribution to literature about 9/11.

Seamus Heaney and the Return to Western Poetry

Heaney's "Anything Can Happen," written directly "in the aftermath of the September 11 attacks," and later published in book form alongside Heaney's essay about the poem, is one of the clearest uses of literary nostalgia in British 9/11 literature.[31] Heaney adapted his poem from Horace's Ode I.34 because, in his words, "there was an uncanny correspondence between the words '*valet ima summis mutare ... deus*' (the god has power to change the highest things to/for the lowest) and the dreamy, deadly images of the Twin Towers of the World Trade Centre being struck and then crumbling out of sight."[32] Heaney's poem uses its continued faith in Horace's explanatory power to reframe and resituate the shock of 9/11. Heaney's poem is, in essence, about the return of Western literature and culture; instead of being irrelevant to the acts of 9/11, the poem presents Western literature as being the most appropriate frame for understanding those attacks.

---

30 Ibid., p. 51.

31 Heaney, p. 9.

32 Ibid., p. 18.

In *The Spirit of Terrorism*, Baudrillard argues that Western culture can no longer explain the world: "The West, in the position of God (divine omnipotence and absolute moral legitimacy), has become suicidal, and declared war on itself."[33] In contrast, Heaney's poem focuses on the continued universalism and moral legitimacy of Western literature. In his commentary on Horace's Ode I.34, Heaney writes:

> It was written a little over two thousand years ago by the Roman poet Horace, but it could have been written yesterday in Baghdad. In it, Horace expresses the shock he felt when Jupiter, the thunder-god, drove his chariot across the sky [...]. This time, however, the god had arrived so suddenly there was no time to prepare for his terrific sound and fury, and hence it seemed that the safety of the world itself had been put into question.[34]

Instead of noting the massive difference between Horace's Rome and 21st century Baghdad, Heaney's rhetorical strategy is to focus on the similarities. If we follow Heaney's logic, the shock discussed by Horace is equally applicable to Horace's own time, 9/11, and to the War in Iraq. This universalism—the ability of Horace to frame events he could not have possibly conceived of—operates to diminish the trauma of 9/11. Since older poems can interpret current events, no rupture in Western culture could have occurred, and thus one troubling aspect of 9/11 is contained.

"Anything Can Happen" is a poem that initially seems to offer the idea of rupture to its audience. With its repetition of the phrase "Anything Can Happen"—once in the title, twice in the poem itself—and its grim depiction of disastrous reversals, the poem captures a sense of total, disastrous change:

> [...] Well, just now
> He galloped his thunder-cart and his horses
>
> Across a clear blue sky. It shook the earth,
> And the clogged underneath, the River Styx,
> The winding streams, the Atlantic shore itself.
> Anything can happen, the tallest things
>
> Be overturned, those in high places daunted,
> Those overlook regarded.[35]

The explicit references to 9/11—"the Atlantic shore," the tallest things being the Twin Towers—culminate in the poem's final line, with its images of the

---

33 Baudrillard, p. 7.
34 Heaney, p. 15.
35 Ibid., lines 3-10.

billowing ash clouds after the Towers' collapse: "Smoke furl and boiling ashes darken day."[36] The literal content of the poem seems to be one of absolute change: "nothing resettles right."[37]

On close examination, though, "Anything Can Happen" is a poem about continuity and return. The use of Horace as the backbone of the poem undercuts its content of change: there is no event so unpredictable that cannot be properly analyzed by the great tradition of Western culture. The trauma of 9/11 is thus not new or unusual but already explained by Horace. As intellectually significant as the mere fact of adaptation is, the content of Heaney's poem, through the changes it makes to the original, equally emphasizes the idea of return. Heaney makes several substantial changes to Horace's original, and then reprints the original version in his collection, inviting readers to acknowledge and ponder these changes. The original poem is somewhat clearer than Heaney's, since Heaney removes the first stanza of the poem. In Horace's original, this is the actual lesson of the poem, a lesson of return:

> I have been a reluctant and infrequent worshipper of the gods, have steered my own course and gone with the usual madness, but now I am forced back on myself, compelled to turn my sails, and retrace the course I had forsaken.[38]

By removing that first stanza, Heaney shifts the concept of return from the explicit to the implicit. Nonetheless, by simply comparing Heaney's poem to Horace's poem, this act of return takes place on several levels. Not only do readers learn the "meaning" of the poem by consulting with Horace (that shock can be overcome by a return to tradition), that mere act of consulting Horace reemphasizes the act of returning to tradition. At the center of the poem, there is nostalgia for tradition and pre-existing explanations; returning to these is the comfort that the poem provides.

"Anything Can Happen" maps out a solution to the trauma of 9/11. Just as the narrator of Horace's original is comforted by a return to the familiar, so too are readers of the poem comforted by a return to Horace and Western literature. Everything not explicable by that framework is excluded from the poem; "Anything Can Happen" goes so far as to attribute the agency of the terrorist attacks to Zeus, not to Islamist terrorists. This substitution may seem odd (and inaccurate), but it restores Western narratives' power over 9/11 and terrorism and excludes any agency from non-Western individuals. Instead of placing the 9/11 attacks outside the Western meta-narrative of progress, his-

---

36 Ibid., line 16.

37 Ibid., line 15.

38 Ibid., p. 16.

tory, and literature, Heaney firmly resituates those attacks into a pre-existing frame. Western literature can explicate 9/11: it is a sudden reversal of fortune, just as Horace experienced and wrote about some 2000 years ago. Here, Heaney participates profoundly in what Said identifies as exclusivism; by eliminating all Islamic reference in his poem, Heaney provides "self-flattering narratives that deliberately filter out"[39] the presence and influence of other cultural groups. This sort of exclusivism reproduces the idea of Western humanism as a closed system that need not engage with other cultures or ideas.

Despite this exclusivism, many other authors echo Heaney's invocation of the continued power of Western art: McEwan with "Dover Beach" in *Saturday*, Amis with Philip Larkin's "Church Going" in "Terror and Boredom." Amis claims that the "serious house on serious earth" section of Larkin's poem "contains everything that can be decently and rationally said,"[40] and his faith in Larkin is revealing. In these texts, 9/11 does not force us to reconsider canonical Western poetry. There is a profound comfort in the idea that everything can be explained via Larkin and Horace, and that our frame of reference need not be expanded in the wake of 9/11. Of course, this lack of expansion is exactly what Said rails against in his various writings about humanism. Heaney's poem, then, is a fascinating example that attempts to use the explanatory power of humanism to frame 9/11 while at the same reinvoking and reinscribing some of the exclusionary and colonizing aspects of humanism. By doing so, "Anything Can Happen" is quite representative of the way these British 9/11 texts operate. This strand of literature uses humanism to both challenge prepackaged notions of 9/11 as a culture shattering trauma while re-enforcing traditionally exclusionary modes of humanism.

Terrorism, 9/11, and Epistolary Form in Chris Cleave's *Incendiary*

Heaney's poem can also be read as a return to interiority: the shock of 9/11 forces the poem's narrator to pause and reconsider the course of his life. This literary technique—of using a return to interiority to diminish or frame the shock of 9/11—is clearly seen in Chris Cleave's epistolary novel *Incendiary*. In this, his debut novel, Cleave uses the interiority provided by epistolary form as a way of containing and controlling the trauma of terrorism. *Incen-*

---

39 Said, *Humanism*, p. 51.
40 Amis, p. 90.

diary is written as a long rambling letter to Osama Bin Laden from a woman who has lost her son and husband in a major terrorist attack at a soccer game. By creating a British 9/11 and then returning to the interiority of the writing subject, Cleave's novel expresses nostalgia for a simpler, pre-9/11 world where the subject was free to create itself without interference from catastrophic outside events. The novel demonstrates a continued faith in the power of writing, expression, and interiority, and thus operates as a complement to Heaney's return to Western literature.

Epistolary form, long associated with the traditions of the British novel, is one of the most direct ways of representing interiority. Critic Elizabeth Campbell, for instance, argues that letters are a "mirror" where writers "not only seek themselves and/or another but attempt to change their lives to reflect the mirror image."[41] Or, as critic Linda Kauffman argues, every letter can be conceived of as an act of "self-creation, self-invention."[42] Epistolary critic Anne Bower elaborates, claiming:

> While letter writing, each individual [...] becomes responsible for his or her subjective reactions and reportings; as the solo occupier of the epistolary space, the letter writer can elaborate for both the internal and external reader one set of replies to particular issues or to others' actions.[43]

The key idea here is that the epistolary form provides a freedom for the writer, where he or she is not impacted by uncontrollable events such as terrorism. As such, the return to epistolary form in *Incendiary* (and other novels such as *Eleven*) operates as a desire for a return to the self-created subject, where the individual has the power to control his or her world.

The novel begins with her directly addressing Bin Laden: "Osama I just want you to give it a rest. AM I ALONE? I want to be the last mother in the world who ever has to write you a letter like this [...] I'm going to write you about the emptiness that was left when you took my boy away [...] I am a mother Osama I just want you to love my son. What could be more natural?"[44] Throughout the book, the narrator relies on the self-expression provided by letter writing to heal the wounds caused by the terrorist attacks, wounds further complicated by her personal situation (she was cheating on

---

41 Elizabeth Campbell, 'Re-visions, Re-flections, Re-creations: Epistolarity in Novels by Contemporary Women', *Twentieth Century Literature*, 41.3 (1995), 332-348 (p. 332).

42 Linda Kauffman, *Discourses of Desire: Gender, Genre, and Epistolary Fictions* (Ithaca: Cornell University Press, 1986), p. 25.

43 Anne Bower, *Epistolary Responses: The Letter in 20th-Century American Fiction and Criticism* (Tuscaloosa: University of Alabama Press, 1997), p. 5.

44 Cleave, pp. 3-4.

her husband at the moment of the attack). The narrative arc of *Incendiary* is what is critical here: after the world-shattering event of the attacks and her infidelity, it is epistolarity and interiority that can put her world back together. If *Incendiary* were following the model of rupture laid out by Baudrillard and others, the narrator would doubtless have to find some new means of expression; her return to epistolary form, and the self-creation that form implies, marks a nostalgia for a simpler world, where self-expression matters, where even a terrorist might read a letter from one of his victims.

Instead of focusing on the politics of Islamist terrorism, *Incendiary* focuses solely on its narrator, and that narrator reacts to Bin Laden in an apolitical (insofar as she is largely indifferent to politics), emotional fashion. The focus is not on Bin Laden or the global situation. Instead, the novel focuses on how the narrator's imagined relationship with Bin Laden changes her. As the novel progresses, she begins to feel that the power of expression and the power of love can overcome the boundaries between her and Bin Laden: "In my dream Osama I wrote you this letter and you read it and then you went off behind a rock where your men couldn't see you and you cried and you wished you hadn't killed my boy."[45] As a result of the terrorist attack, the narrator lost faith in the power of love and decency in the world. Using her letters to recreate her own subjectivity and interiority, she recaptures a belief in them. This is, of course, decidedly odd, as her revolution is entirely interior; by the end of the novel, no real changes have been made in the world situation. *Incendiary* is nostalgic because it presents the proper reaction to terrorism as an interior revolution, as an expression of the self, as a return to values that seemingly were threatened by terrorism. Instead of creating a new world, it restores the old.

The novel concludes with the narrator's plea to Bin Laden to "get it done with love that's my whole point. Love is not surrender Osama love is furious and brave and loud [...] Come to me Osama. Come to me and we will blow the world back together WITH INCREDIBLE NOISE AND FURY."[46] The novel uses its epistolary form to "blow the world back together"; the narrator's desire for return is so strong that she even forgives Bin Laden. At the point of this forgiveness, *Incendiary* takes a strange turn when the narrator discovers that the British government had information about the attack but declined to act so they could continue their undercover work on terrorism; the narrator then shifts her sense of responsibility from Bin Laden to the government: "AT THE VERY HIGHEST LEVEL. That was the moment Osama.

---

45 Ibid., p. 209.

46 Ibid., p. 237.

When he said those words I stopped blaming you for my husband and my boy and I started blaming Terence Butcher [a British official]. He murdered them."[47] The narrator's justified rage at the British government is offset by her forgiveness towards Bin Laden. The narrator has become so dependent on her letters to Bin Laden, and the imagined relationship that this creates, that she refuses to give them up. Regardless of where the real blame might lie, she would rather blame her own government and continue her (imagined) relationship with Bin Laden; for her the interior of the letter-writing space is everything and more important than any exterior political reality she might face. Indeed, to return to Bower's concept of epistolarity, she has truly become the "sole-occupier" of her epistolary space, or, in Žižek's terms, she has refused to acknowledge "what kind of world" she is part of.

Incendiary presents a world where letter-writing (however improbably) retains its power to heal the subject, even in the face of devastating events such as terrorist attacks. The epistolary form is, by its very nature, nostalgic; in the 21st century, the very idea of drafting 200+ pages of letters is completely anachronistic. Nonetheless, *Incendiary* is an outstanding example of a commitment to the traditional idea that the subject—whether letter-writing or otherwise—can make sense of the world if she tries hard enough. Instead of being outdated or insignificant in a world full of terrorist attacks, the narrator's speaking voice remains at the center of the novel. Cleave's use of the subject, as a human being struggling to makes sense of her world, is perhaps closest to Said's, although the narrator's engagement with Bin Laden remains entirely imaginary and one-sided. Despite this one-sidedness, the narrator is able to resist the ready-made interpretations of terrorism, such as the ones the British government (in the novel, at least), are disseminating. Cleave is not alone in stressing the power of interiority and its perceived ability to self-reflect, explain, and heal. Llewellyn's *Eleven*, also in epistolary form, and McEwan's *Saturday* both use the closely observed interiority of their characters as a way of framing 9/11, and someone like Amis takes the next step, that of attributing the interior subject to actual Islamist characters. By reasserting the power of the rational subject, these authors contain terrorism within the framework provided by traditional Western narratives.

---

47 Ibid., p. 185.

The Subject versus Islam: The 9/11 Stories of Martin Amis

Since Martin Amis is well known for his experimental novels, and given his initial comments about 9/11 being an "apotheosis of the postmodern,"[48] we might expect Amis to approach 9/11 fiction through the lens of experimental postmodern thought, à la Derrida or Baudrillard.[49] Instead, the stories and essays included in *The Second Plane* show Amis evolving a very intellectually conservative approach towards the issues of 9/11 and terrorism. Amis brands what he terms "Islamism" a death cult: "we may compare radical Islam with the thanatoid political movements we know most about, namely Bolshevism and Nazism (to each of which Islamism is indebted)."[50] Amis's pointed attacks on Islam are supplemented by his celebration of the rational, Western subject, in whom he finds the antidote to the death-obsessed Islamic extremist: "Our moral advantage, still vast and obvious, is not a liability, and we should strengthen and expand it. Like our dependence on reason, it is a strategic strength, and it shores up our legitimacy."[51] In the two pieces of fiction included amongst the essays of *The Second Plane*, Amis contrasts interiority—the thinking, rational Western subject—against what he sees as the insanity and monotony of Islamist extremism. Since Amis's embrace of the traditional ideological commitments of Western interiority is explicit in his essays, his use of that interiority in his stories is not surprising. In both "In the Palace of the End" and "The Last Days of Muhammad Atta," Amis forces Western subjectivity onto extreme versions of Islamist characters; by doing so, he goes a step farther than Heaney or Cleave in advocating the universalism of Western thought. Amis's move here is intensely colonial; by imposing what he sees as the "truth" of the Western experience onto Islamist characters, he violently excludes the possibilities of other cultural or intellectual perspectives. From Said's perspective, the role of interiority and humanism is "not to consolidate and affirm one tradition over all the others"[52]; Amis's stories, however, are powerful examples where one tradition is affirmed over all other possible modes of being.

---

48 Amis, p. 5.

49 Interestingly, Amis began writing 9/11 literature in this direction; his abandoned story "The Unknown Known," discussed extensively in "Terror and Boredom," seemed to have been a postmodern satire of terrorism, involving a disaffected terrorist struggling to invent the next "paradigm-shift." See Martin Amis, 'The Unknown Known', *Granta*, 100 (2007), 153-163, which prints the completed sections of this abandoned novel.

50 Amis, p. 200.

51 Ibid., p. 73.

52 Said, *Humanism*, p. 49.

The first of Amis's terrorism stories, "In the Palace of the End," takes place in an Iraq-like country and is told from the point of view of one of the many stand-ins for Nadir the Next, a Saddam Hussein-like dictator.[53] These doubles, who appear for Nadir in public, give speeches, and eventually end up doubling Nadir's every action, down to his sexual perversions, have all retreated to a bunker as Nadir's regime collapses around them. Denied any existence of their own, they exist in a totalizing system where our unnamed narrator struggles to maintain some sense of individuality: "entering the doubles' commissary is, as I say, a depersonalizing experience. It is to enter a hall of mirrors."[54] As the story continues, the demands placed upon the doubles grow increasingly absurd: the doubles must mirror Nadir exactly, down to being physically scarred and reproducing his sexual proclivities in bed. The story ends with Nadir's death; the doubles are then killed in exactly the same fashion as Nadir.

The literary nostalgia of this story is found in its technique; Amis's story invests his nameless double with a melancholic, self-reflective interiority: "This is when I have to deal with my humanity, and answer the questions put to me by my wizened soul."[55] The narrator, who is completely alienated from the regime, over the course of the story emerges from an Islamist "totality" (as a pure double), to a differentiated, thinking individual. There is nothing in Amis's story to indicate where the narrator has learned his ideas about the "soul" or "humanity." These values are, in the story, simply universal. By locating the Western subject in the least likely place, Amis reaffirms the transcendent value of the subject. The story closes by rearticulating this same point, showing the double fully embracing his humanity:

> When you have been hurt yourself, there awakens a part of you that doesn't want to hurt anyone. When you love something as intimately fragile as your own body, you don't want to hurt anyone. That's what I'm saying to myself, now, in the changing room. Please let me not have to hurt anyone.[56]

The key phrase here is "there awakens a part of you"; by highlighting what the story (and by extension Amis) finds as a universal part of the human experience, the story reestablishes the universality of the subject. Even in this

---

53 The "The Palace of the End" is the name of one of Hussein's own torture chambers. See Con Coughlin, *Saddam: His Rise and Fall* (New York: Harper Collins, 2002), p. 42: "One of the most notorious torture chambers was located at the aptly named 'Palace of the End' (Qasr al-Niyahan)."

54 Amis, p. 34.

55 Ibid., p. 40.

56 Ibid., p. 46.

character—a man who has been a double of a horrific dictator, and himself a perpetrator of horrible deeds—human goodness wins out in the end. By presenting this sort of universal goodness, Amis defuses the idea of Islam as a totalizing system. Islam (in Amis's conception) may attempt to control everything, but a universal, rational, kind subject emerges even in the worst of situations. As Amis makes clear in the various essays of *The Second Plane*, he associates this "universal, rational, kind" subject exclusively with the West and its inherent moral superiority.

"The Last Days of Muhammad Atta" achieves this even more fully. The story depicts Muhammad Atta, the ringleader of the 9/11 attacks, and shows his final epiphany, where he realizes he loves life. Instead of representing Atta as a crazed Islamist zealot, Amis depicts Atta as a lost soul, alienated and disconnected from the terrorists around him: "he wasn't like the others."[57] The whole story unfolds as if inside Atta's thoughts (although they are narrated via the third person), and Atta comes across as a human being struggling to find his place in the world. Even though the story can end only with death, Amis still gives Atta his epiphany:

> How very gravely he had underestimated life. His own he had hated, and had wished away; but see how long it was taking to absent itself—and with what helpless grief was he watching it go, imperturbable in its beauty and power. Even as his flesh fried and his blood boiled, there was life, kissing its fingertips.[58]

Atta's final epiphany, just as he is about to crash into the Twin Towers, is a profound return of the subject. Even the most dedicated terrorist is unable to resist "the beauty and power" of life. Amis's essays clearly find this embrace of the "beauty and power" of life to be the "moral advantage, still vast and obvious" of Western culture.[59] He uses the interiority—these epiphanies—of his characters to show that this "moral advantage" can transform the most hardened individuals.

In Amis, terrorism is contained within the framework of the thinking, feeling interiority of the subject. Not even Atta is allowed to escape without his humanist epiphany. By attributing a revelation to so unlikely a character, Amis essentially eliminates the idea of Islamist difference: deep down, such characters are humanist subjects. While this may initially seem generous, it is ultimately a way of containing everything within a Western framework. The concept of interiority used by Amis is essentially the humanist, liberal sub-

---

57 Ibid., p. 94.
58 Ibid., p. 121.
59 Ibid., p. 73.

ject; by attributing this to Atta, he controls Atta, he colonizes him. As such, Amis is probably the most extreme version of what Heaney and Cleave (and McEwan, Llewellyn, Armitage, etc.) are attempting to accomplish.

Here, we see an embrace of humanism at its most exclusive and colonial, as Amis employs a model of humanism that designates all non-Western experience as false. Amis can be viewed, in Said's phrase, as one of the "many negative examples [of humanism] afforded us not only by our history but by the general tenor of modern experience all over the world."[60] Despite the colonial tone of Amis's stories, he is representative of how numerous British 9/11 texts try to demonstrate the continued relevance of the liberal, humanist subject and its power to make sense of the world. Amis's explicit colonialism does not necessarily invalidate all possible attempts of humanism to explain terrorism and the events of 9/11. Rather, he maps out one possible extreme of the use of humanism to understand terrorism, and by doing so he helps to define and articulate the space all of these British 9/11 texts operate within.

Conclusion

In Mohsin Hamid's *The Reluctant Fundamentalist*, the novel's unnamed narrator, an Americanized Pakistani who becomes de-Americanized as a result of the 9/11 attacks, reflects on the surge of American nostalgia in the wake of 9/11:

> Possibly this was due to my state of mind, but it seemed to me that America, too, was increasingly giving itself over to a dangerous nostalgia at the time. There was something undeniably retro about the flags and uniforms, about generals addressing cameras in war rooms, and newspaper headlines featuring such words as duty and honor. I had always thought of America as a nation that looked forward; for the first time I was struck by its determination to look *back*.[61]

If American culture returned to patriotism as its traditional ideological commitment, then the strain of British literature (represented by Heaney, Cleave, and Amis) returns to a nostalgic view of interiority and the rational self. Instead of 9/11 rendering these concepts outdated or irrelevant, they emerge as even more vital, as a way of controlling and containing terrorism: Zeus crashed into the towers, Osama Bin Laden reads your letters, and Muhammad

60 Said, *Humanism*, p. 50.

61 Hamid, pp. 114-115.

Atta has revelations about the beauty and meaning of life. Any perceived rupture in Western culture is contained by these representations.

Each of these texts invokes the power of humanism to explain the events of Islamist terrorism and 9/11, and while none of these texts necessarily rise to the level of humanism as described by Said, they each engage in a method of understanding terrorism that is likely to continue. Nostalgia for the rational thinking subject, and its ability to make sense of the world, is a powerful and unavoidable aspect of much 9/11 literature. While this nostalgia, by reconnecting to the exclusionary and colonial aspects of traditional humanism, can be dangerous, it can also provide a viable alternative to the pre-packaged idea of 9/11 as a total rupture. While it may be possible, even desirable, to argue for the continued validity of humanism along the lines laid out by Said, we cannot ignore the dangerous ways that these texts, particularly Amis, exclude all possibilities of non-Western experience and subjectivity. Nonetheless, texts such as "Anything Can Happen," *Saturday*, *Incendiary,* and the Amis stories all embrace a mode of nostalgia which re-articulates older, humanist ideas about interiority and the explanatory power of literature. As such, they chart a trajectory of British 9/11 literature that is likely to continue. Whether these authors (in future works) or their successors will rise to the model of forward-looking humanism described by Said, or whether they will sink to older and exclusionary forms of humanism is something that will doubtless unfold in the near future.

Bibliography

Amis, Martin, *The Second Plane: September 11: Terror and Boredom* (New York: Knopf, 2008)

---, 'The Unknown Known', *Granta*, 100 (2007), 153-163

Armitage, Simon, *Out of the Blue*, (London: Enitharmon Press, 2008)

Beigbeder, Frédéric, *Windows on the World*, trans. by Frank Wynne (New York: Miramax Books, 2004)

Baudrillard, Jean, *The Spirit of Terrorism,* trans. by Chris Turner (New York: Verso, 2003)

Borradori, Giovanna, *Philosophy in a Time of Terror: Dialogues with Jürgen Habermas and Jacques Derrida* (Chicago: University of Chicago Press: 2003)

Bower, Anne, *Epistolary Responses: The Letter in 20th-Century American Fiction and Criticism* (Tuscaloosa: University of Alabama Press, 1997)

Brown, Richard, 'Politics, the Domestic, and the Uncanny Effects of the Everyday in Ian McEwan's *Saturday*', *Critical Survey*, 20.1 (2008), 80-93

Campbell, Elizabeth, 'Re-visions, Re-flections, Re-creations: Epistolarity in Novels by Contemporary Women', *Twentieth Century Literature*, 41 (1995), 332-348

Carpenter, Rebecca, '"We're Not a Friggin' Girl Band": September 11, Masculinity, and the British-American Relationship in David Hare's *Stuff Happens* and Ian McEwan's *Saturday*', in *Literature after 9/11*, ed. by Ann Keniston and Jeanne Follansbee (New York: Routledge, 2008), 143-160

Cleave, Chris, *Incendiary* (New York: Anchor Books, 2005)

Coughlin, Con, *Saddam: His Rise and Fall* (New York: Harper Collins, 2002)

DeLillo, Don, *Falling Man* (New York: Scribner, 2007)

Eaglestone, Robert, '"The Age of Reason is Over [...] an Age of Fury was Dawning": Contemporary Anglo-American Fiction and Terror', *Wasafiri*, 22 (2007), 19-22

Ferguson, Frances, 'The Way We Love Now: Ian McEwan, *Saturday*, and Personal Affection in the Information Age', *Representations*, 100 (2007), 42-52

Foer, Jonathan Safran, *Extremely Loud & Incredibly Close* (New York: Mariner Books, 2005)

Hadley, Elaine, 'On a Darkling Plain: Victorian Liberalism and the Fantasy of Agency', *Victorian Studies*, 48 (2005), 92-102

Halliday, Fred, *Two Hours That Shook the World* (London: Saqi Books, 2002)
Hamid, Mohsin, *The Reluctant Fundamentalist* (New York: Harcourt, 2007)
Hare, David, *Stuff Happens* (New York: Faber and Faber, Inc., 2004)
Heaney, Seamus, *Anything Can Happen* (Dublin: TownHouse, 2004)
Hillard, Molly Clark, '"When Desert Armies Stand Ready to Fight": Re-Reading Ian McEwan's *Saturday* and Mathew Arnold's "Dover Beach"', *Partial Answers*, 6 (2008), 181-206
Kauffman, Linda, *Discourses of Desire: Gender, Genre, and Epistolary Fictions* (Ithaca: Cornell University Press, 1986)
Keniston, Ann and Jeanne Follansbee Quinn, eds., *Literature after 9/11* (New York: Routledge, 2008)
Lewis, Charles, 'Real Planes and Imaginary Towers: Philip Roth's *The Plot Against America* as 9/11 Prosthetic Screen', in *Literature after 9/11*, ed. by Ann Keniston and Jeanne Follansbee (New York: Routledge, 2008), 246-261
Llewellyn, David, *Eleven* (Brigend, Wales: Seren, 2006)
McEwan, Ian, *Saturday* (New York: Anchor Books, 2005)
Rushdie, Salman, *Shalimar the Clown* (New York: Random House, 2005)
Said, Edward, *Humanism and Democratic Criticism* (New York: Columbia University Press, 2004)
---, 'Islam and the West are Inadequate Banners', *The Observer*, 16 September 2001, 27
Sherman, Daniel J. and Terry Nardin, eds., *Terror, Culture, Politics: Rethinking 9/11* (Bloomington: Indiana University Press, 2006)
Simpson, David, *9/11: The Culture of Commemoration* (Chicago: University of Chicago Press, 2006)
Wallace, Elizabeth, 'Postcolonial Melancholia in Ian McEwan's *Saturday*', *Studies in the Novel*, 39 (2007), 465-480
Žižek, Slavoj, *Welcome to the Desert of the Real!* (New York: Verso, 2002)

Uses and Abuses of Trauma in Post-9/11 Fiction and Contemporary Culture

Ulrike Tancke

The terrorist attacks on the World Trade Center on 11 September 2001 are frequently said to have generated a sense of collective trauma. Taking familiar visual representations of 9/11 as its thematic cue, this essay investigates in how far the notion of trauma can be a useful concept in relation to the fictional representations of 9/11 in Laila Halaby's *Once in a Promised Land* (2007) and Pat Barker's *Double Vision* (2003). With their portrayals of characters whose lives are touched by the events of 9/11, but are ultimately marred by traumatic experiences much closer to home, both novels critically comment on and rewrite the contemporary understanding of trauma. As they acknowledge the material reality of genuine trauma, they reveal how ubiquitous catchphrases such as "9/11" potentially conceal the unpredictably traumatizing potentials of everyday violence and guilt.

The above book covers of three recent publications – Ian McEwan's *Saturday* (2005), Laila Halaby's *Once in a Promised Land* (2007) and Joanna Bourke's *Fear* (2005) – evoke a shared set of associations. In spite of the very different nature of these books, presumably anyone over a certain age would immediately associate with these pictures the images of the 9/11 destruction of the World Trade Center. Only one of the books will be a focus of this essay – Laila Halaby's *Once in a Promised Land* – but all three of the cover images are proof of the strong and widespread cultural presence that

9/11 commands. Two of these books are novels – *Saturday*[1] and *Once in a Promised Land* –whereas Joanna Bourke's book is an academic study of fear as a cultural concept.[2] Apparently, not only in fictional but even in non-fictional and allegedly non-emotional contexts, allusions to 9/11 are used to visualize an archetypal anxiety. Pictures like these conjure up a host of related images of the attacks and their aftermath: planes crashing into the towers, clouds of smoke, bodies falling from the sky, and the devastation of "Ground Zero." Significantly, these are images that capture the events of 9/11 from a remote bystander's perspective, safely removed from the material reality of debris, smoke, and dead bodies. In fact, the quasi-aesthetic quality of these images has frequently been commented on.[3] At the same time, the eerie beauty of large-scale destruction is inseparably bound up with its remoteness: it can only be appreciated from the safe distance created and upheld by the photographer's lens.

The book covers that allude to these images play on this fascination with the horrific. Obviously, before 11 September 2001, they would have had none of these disturbing and eerily evocative qualities. Pre-9/11, we would simply have seen something that looks like a comet against a nightly city skyline, the shadow of a plane on the surface of a swimming pool, and a plane against a blue sky. These images hold an undeniable grasp on our imagination now, and this is one of the reasons why 9/11 is generally considered an event that has violently disrupted our perceptions of the world and has left an indelible mark on our collective consciousness. For instance, Marianne Hirsch speaks of the "monumental, irrevocable change that we, as a culture, feel we have experienced";[4] Susan Coates invokes "the emotional

---

1 The novel tells the story of London neurosurgeon Henry Perowne who, in the general climate of fear post-9/11 and on a day of protests against the war in Iraq, is caught up in disturbing incidents that violently disrupt his contented middle-class existence.

2 Bourke delineates the various dimensions of fear in the course of the 20th century; her final chapter explores the diffuse anxieties that 9/11 has given rise to.

3 For instance, Peter Conrad comments on the aestheticization of 9/11, pointing out its function as sublimating pain: "The temptation to see that day in artistic terms – as a narrative, a scripted scenario, or a film in which the special effects were real – is understandable, because it pacifies the raw, enraged pain: the aesthetic is the anaesthetic. [...] Ian McEwan thought that the towers collapsed with a 'malign majesty'; Martin Amis thrilled to the 'opulently evil' flames. A terrible beauty was being born. How can we forgive ourselves for feeling, along with our terror, so fiercely elated?" Peter Conrad, 'The Presumption of Art', *The Observer*, 8 September 2002.

4 Marianne Hirsch, 'The Day Time Stopped', *The Chronicle Review*, 25 January 2002.

challenge of a radically altered world";[5] and a recent *Observer* article refers to 9/11 as "that great reordering of Western life."[6] Such is the typical turn of phrase that can be encountered in academia and popular culture alike. 9/11 is considered the collective trauma of post-millennial humanity, dividing our cultural frame of reference into "before" and "after."

Significantly, trauma has been the focus of considerable interest long before 9/11. For the purposes of my argument, trauma can be very broadly defined as an experience that is, in Susannah Radstone's definition, "understood to be elusive and impossible to grasp" and that "elude[s] sense making and the assignment of meaning [and that hence] cannot be integrated into memory, but neither can [...] be forgotten."[7] Trauma studies, influenced by Sigmund Freud's work on trauma as the root of psychoses,[8] has seen a massive boost in the past thirty or so years,[9] in particular with the analysis of Holocaust testimonials, the accounts of victims of sexual abuse, and of veterans of the Vietnam and Gulf wars. Long before 9/11, the twentieth century had been dubbed the "century of trauma."[10]

Parallel to this concern with trauma in the culture at large, trauma had become a topical issue in literary studies well before 11 September 2001. For instance, a great number of recent novels deal with characters whose senses of self and of the world are called in question by disruptive events and can be classified as trauma novels – Philip Tew goes so far as to argue that what he calls a "traumatological" aesthetic dominates contemporary writing: "much recent fiction senses and articulates a sense of collective wound and injury as

---

5 Susan Coates, 'Introduction: Trauma and Human Bonds', in *September 11: Trauma and Human Bonds*, ed. by Susan Coates, Jane L. Rosenthal and Daniel S. Schechter (Hillsdale and London: The Atlantic Press, 2003), 1-14 (p. 13).

6 Peter Beaumont, 'America Hails Cricket Fan's Novel that Met 9/11 Challenge', *The Observer*, 25 May 2008 (review of Joseph O'Neill's novel *Netherland* (2008)).

7 Susannah Radstone, 'The War of the Fathers: Trauma, Fantasy, and September 11', in *Trauma At Home: After 9/11*, ed. by Judith Greenberg (Lincoln and London: University of Nebraska Press, 2003), 117-23 (p. 117).

8 For a comprehensive outline of the Freudian understanding of trauma, see Anthony Storr, *Freud: A Very Short Introduction* (Oxford: Oxford University Press, 2001), especially pp. 17-28.

9 Prolific theorists in the field are Cathy Caruth, who has conceptualised trauma from a post-structuralist angle, and Dori Laub and Shoshana Felman, who draw especially on the accounts of Holocaust survivors.

10 See Radstone, p. 117.

part of its essential narrative sensibility."[11] Tew argues that this has replaced the postmodern critique of subjectivity and meaning.[12]

That said, critical opinion has been notoriously divided on the scope and appropriateness of the notion of trauma. Apart from the oft-voiced criticism that the term may be applied too liberally, there is a central dilemma at the heart of trauma studies itself that renders any proposition of trauma as the pivot of subjectivity inherently problematic. As Roger Luckhurst has pointed out:

> The idea of a "traumatic subject" is peculiarly paradoxical: trauma is, after all, held to dis-aggregate or shatter subjectivity; trauma is that which cannot be processed by the psyche yet lodges within the self as a foreign body [...]. To organise an identity around trauma, then, is to premise it on exactly that which escapes the subject, on an absence or a gap.[13]

At the heart of any exploration of trauma is the central conflict whether trauma erases the subject or, in fact, creates a new, albeit fragmented and precarious subjectivity. The widespread application of the term to the events of 9/11 and the controversy surrounding it exemplify this dilemma. On the one hand, the notion of trauma has been embraced as a means of accounting for the complex interaction of individual and collective responses to 9/11 and has been credited with producing a new subjectivity based on a collapse of history and memory, time and space.[14] On the other hand, 9/11 and its aftermath seem to have instigated a "process that weaves events into preexisting fantasy scenes"[15] long anticipated in Hollywood movies. From this vantage point, the idea of trauma alone fails to adequately capture the collective impact of 9/11, as the events are already involved in prefigured processes of signification. Where these approaches converge, however, is in their emphasis on the hermeneutic functions of trauma: rather than foreclosing the possibility of meaning, 9/11 has triggered and is implied in multifaceted processes of meaning-making.

A closer look at the 9/11 allusion on the book covers which have started my analysis adds a further twist to this argument. Their use also hints at the ambiguous dimensions of the contemporary concern with trauma, of which

---

11 Philip Tew, *The Contemporary British Novel*, 2nd edn (London: Continuum, 2007), p. xviii.

12 "[M]uch recent fiction is of a traumatological rather than a postmodern bent, abjuring both the latter's abandonment of certainty and meaning, and its deconstructive dissolution of identities" (Tew, p. 191).

13 Roger Luckhurst, 'Traumaculture', *New Formations*, 50 (2003), 28-47 (p. 28).

14 See E. Ann Kaplan, *Trauma Culture: The Politics of Terror and Loss in Media and Literature* (New Brunswick: Rutgers University Press, 2005), pp. 1, 4.

15 Radstone, p. 120.

9/11 is a prime example. On a very basic level, the appearance of these pictures on a book cover is, quite simply, a marketing ploy: it draws on potential customers' associations and fears. Obviously, this is possible only because these pictures merely hint at the actual attacks and their effects; it is the images' remoteness and detachment that makes them so titillating. However, one might also argue that this gives them an exploitative edge, as they use traumatic scenes – and, by extension, the traumatic memories of individuals – for a particular effect. In other words, these cover pictures point to the fact that trauma is not simply a primary emotional state, but that it can be instrumentalized. Kirby Farrell says just this in his study of trauma in 1990s culture: "People not only suffer trauma; they use it, and the idea of it, for all sorts of ends, good and ill. The trope can be ideologically manipulated, reinforced, and exploited."[16] It functions "as a strategic fiction that a complex, stressful society is using to account for a world that seems threateningly out of control."[17]

It is this latter understanding of trauma – its function as a hermeneutic tool that can be consciously employed – that provides the most useful framework for a discussion of representations of 9/11 in literary works. Taking the events of 9/11 as a thematic cue, the novels that this essay examines engage in processes of signification in which they shift the relevance and scope of traumatic experience in unexpected and uncomfortable directions, questioning our presupposed perceptions of the world and offering a disturbing vision of traumatized selves. Beyond this, the novels urge a set of questions at the interface of literary and cultural studies: what are the ideological functions of the concern with trauma, what purpose does it serve? How can trauma be adequately conceptualized, and what is its ethical dimension? More specifically, does 9/11 really point to a collective condition that is defined by trauma? How can fiction approach and respond to the ubiquitous concern with trauma?

I will investigate these questions by looking at two novels, one by an Arab-American and one by a British writer, Laila Halaby's *Once in a Promised Land* (2007), whose cover I have discussed, and Pat Barker's *Double Vision* (2003). I have chosen these two novels because they use the events of 9/11 as a pivotal reference point. Yet while both start from 9/11, they let it fade into the background and draw our attention to something else: the uncontrollability of human actions and the human psyche, the random eruption

---

16 Kirby Farrell, *Post-traumatic Culture: Injury and Interpretation in the Nineties* (Baltimore and London: The Johns Hopkins University Press, 1998), p. 21.

17 Farrell, p. 3.

of violence into everyday lives, and the destructive nature of coincidence. In their own ways, each novel moves beyond contemporary trauma discourse. Each juxtaposes the idea of collective trauma with individual experience and hence plays with the detachment that underpins the pictures I have drawn on. Their protagonists are not simply representatives of a traumatized generation but are also capable of inflicting trauma themselves.

Once in a Promised Land tells the story of an Arab-American couple living in Tucson, Arizona – Jordanian Jassim and Palestinian-born Salwa Haddad – whose marriage unravels as they face traumatic experiences of various kinds. At first glance, the novel is centrally concerned with the effects of September 11 and the anti-Muslim climate developing in its aftermath. Both Jassim and Salwa are exposed to increasing prejudice in their everyday encounters with ordinary Americans. These vicious assaults culminate in Jassim's victimization in a smear campaign that ultimately costs him his job. While the life-changing impact of the 9/11 attacks on the protagonists' lives is undeniable, the novel, from the start, self-consciously draws attention to the fact that Salwa and Jassim's story is more complex than a straightforward succession of cause and effect:[18]

> Our main characters are Salwa and Jassim. We really come to know them only after the World Trade Center buildings have been flattened by planes flown by Arabs, by Muslims. Salwa and Jassim are both Arabs. Both Muslims. But of course they have nothing to do with what happened to the World Trade Center.
>
> Nothing and everything.[19]

Thus it would clearly be an oversimplification to read the novel as an account of the post-9/11 victimization of Muslims in the West. While 9/11 undoubtedly comes to overshadow the protagonists' lives (in a literal sense, this is what the novel's cover picture alludes to), it is just as obvious that an exclusive focus on this aspect of their lives would be reductive, as their story is both implied in and develops independently of 9/11.

---

18 This makes it notoriously difficult to adequately summarize the events of the novel. Summaries such as Katrina Tuy De Los Reyes's – "their seemingly idyllic life in Tucson, Arizona begins to unravel as they face the repercussions of 9/11 in unexpected ways" – suggest a direct connection between diverse events, which does not do justice to the novel's complexities (Katrina Tuy De Los Reyes, '*Once in a Promised Land* by Laila Halaby', *About.com.ContemporaryLiterature* <http://contemporarylit.about.com/od/fiction/fr/onceInA.htm> [accessed 20 September 2008].

19 Laila Halaby, *Once in a Promised Land* (Boston: Beacon Press, 2007), pp. vii-viii.

After the prologue from which the above quotation is taken, the novel proper starts with a depiction of Salwa and Jassim's early morning routines. It is utterly poignant that Jassim's daily ritual of getting up early and going to a fitness center for a quiet swim is depicted as part of his desire for balance ("Jassim did not believe in God, but he did believe in Balance. At five o'clock, with the day still veiled, Jassim found Balance"[20]). After all, the harmonious equilibrium that he strives for is already being undercut, without his knowledge, by "the Lie" that Salwa builds up around herself: in spite of her husband's reluctance to start a family, she has stopped taking her contraceptive pill. Crucially, her actions are described as a not fully conscious impulse rather than a deliberate decision:

> Salwa's Lie covered a glorious underbelly. It was not *I didn't take my birth control pill* but instead a much more colorful *For a few years now I've felt that I've been missing something in my life.* [...]. *I think having a child will fill that void. I am going to try to get pregnant, even though Jassim says he doesn't want a child.*
>
> But even Salwa didn't look at it that way, couldn't see its truth, could see only a vague hint of red as she succumbed to the frantic desire struggling within her.[21]

Salwa's lie is thoroughly ambiguous: in spite of the betrayal that it implies towards her husband, it also has an intrinsic, mysterious allure. It has cast a powerful spell on her, although she is aware that it drives a wedge between herself and her husband: "Salwa could feel the Lie between them, the Lie that only she could see, that kept trying to hold her hand, to remind her of its beauty and silvery color."[22] Although she constantly promises herself that she will soon confess her pregnancy to Jassim, she even conceals from him her eventual miscarriage a few weeks later.

Yet at the core of the couple's failure to communicate is more than a relationship going awry. As the novel gradually recounts how and why Jassim and Salwa came to live in the States – Jassim studied hydrology in the US in order to eventually be able to help his home country improve its water supply and met Salwa by chance on a lecture trip to Amman – the shaky foundations of their relationship are revealed. Their rushed marriage and return to America is the result of Salwa's naïve dream of an easy life in the States and Jassim's subconscious unease about his future in a foreign country.[23] Its mis-

---

20 Ibid., p. 3.

21 Ibid., p. 10.

22 Ibid., p. 27.

23 As he proposed to Salwa, "he was succumbing to the pressure of his impending return to the States and to his job, which was squeezing his throat, forcing unplanned words off his tongue" (Halaby, p. 68).

guided hastiness is hinted at by one of the novel's various subplots, in which Salwa's former Jordanian boyfriend Hassan tries to contact her in the wake of his own half-hearted marriage and hence casts doubt on Salwa and Jassim's decision. At the root of their growing insecurity is their trauma of lost origins and severed connections to their home. Both Salwa and Jassim have deluded themselves as to the possibility of simply ignoring the tangled threads that their life in-between culture entails. The narrator draws on the image of threads to comment on the attachment to geographical and cultural origins:

> [W]hile place of birth does not alter genetic material, it does stitch itself under the skin and stay attached by virtue of invisible threads, so that if that person leaves that place for somewhere else [...] there is always an uncomfortable tugging as the [...] threads are pulled taut. And if the person returns to her place of birth, especially after a great deal of time has elapsed, quite often the threads have knotted or tangled somewhere between here and there, there and here, causing the person countless awkward moments. Sometimes the knot of crossed threads becomes so thick that it creates a painful and constant yanking no matter where the person finds herself.[24]

In spite of the apparent benefit and easy prosperity that life in America entailed for Salwa and Jassim, their status in-between cultures comes, first and foremost, with insecurity and pain.

For Salwa, it is only the loss of her unborn baby that initiates a slow process of reassessing the choices she has made. As her friend Randa massages her to ease the physical pain of her miscarriage, she feels:

> [f]ingers stuffed with centuries of wisdom, knots of history and meaning, somehow accidentally transported to this desert world where life comes in Large, Extra Large, and Enormous, where it is served on plastic trays now, now, now, where synthetic pads can absorb the blood of one lifetime. Those fingers kneaded out what Salwa had been avoiding for close to three years now: that she was not happy in her life.[25]

The glaring contrast between the sterile artificiality of American life with the messiness and brutality of the miscarriage makes Salwa realize that the life "she had custom-ordered according to her specifications"[26] has left her empty and unfulfilled. Her thoughts suggest that the very idea of "custom-order[ing]" a life entails a degree of guilt. The attempt to shape and fashion life according to one's personal plans and desires has the potential to inflict hurt on others: "she needed to change the direction of her life. [...] [I]f Jassim was not ready to have a family, [...] maybe she would turn this into an

[24] Ibid., p. 49.

[25] Ibid., p. 91.

[26] Ibid., p. 99.

American story and leave."[27] The reassuringly harmless guise of her possible decision ("story") veils its destructive potential. What is more, the use of the modifier "American" to denote a possible break-up suggests a simplicity and neat categorization with the help of which Salwa is able to delude herself about the pain that such a decision would inflict on both Jassim and herself. In a sense, the idea of simplicity and neatness misinterprets the entire concept of storytelling: after all, stories have the potential to be manipulative, to mould people and events according to the narrator's own desires. Storytelling implies an underlying violence that has the potential to be traumatic. The unrefined and brutal corporeality of the miscarriage during which this realization occurs underscores the physical immediacy and inescapability that constitutes trauma.

Just as Salwa has indulged in her vision of her perfect life in the States, Jassim, too, is unable to face up to the realities of his life. This is most glaringly obvious when he accidentally hits a teenage boy with his car and kills him. Jassim is initially aware of the life-changing nature of the accident, as "pleading-for-help words like *How do I undo this situation?* and *Will my life be the same after this?*"[28] race through his brain and relate his experience to the universal human experience of guilt and the need for redemption. And yet, Jassim, too, resorts to storytelling as a way of ameliorating the destructive impact of the event. He presents to Salwa an airbrushed version of the accident, in which he omits the fact that the boy has died: "Careful to walk around the truth, leave it safely protected by a white picket fence. [...] The version she [Salwa] heard was a simple accident with a couple of kids and a happy American ending."[29] Jassim's storytelling carries similar associations as Salwa's. His neat and uncomplicated account of events does not allow the physical reality of the accident – the boy's death – to hit home. Again, this airbrushed and sterilized version is dubbed "American." While it is alluring because of its simplicity, the "American" story denies Jassim the possibility of fully accepting and hence perhaps coming to terms with the consequences of his actions. At the same time, his lack of openness towards his wife deepens the rift between them. Ironically, his inability to tell Salwa about the boy's death is partly due to the fact that, coincidentally, she confesses her secret pregnancy and miscarriage on the same night, the momentousness of which makes Jassim unable to relate his own traumatic and guilt-ridden secret. Caught in an increasingly tangled web of half-truths, omissions, silence

---

27 Ibid., p. 92.

28 Ibid., p.124.

29 Ibid., p. 139.

and fateful coincidences, both start seemingly random affairs with people that they have met by chance – Jake, a drug-dealing teenage co-worker at Salwa's bank and Penny, a waitress in Denny's restaurant, where Jassim spends aimless and out-of-character early morning hours after the accident.

At the same time, both Salwa and Jassim delude themselves about the facile possibility of coming to terms with and atoning for their actions by articulating them. They have internalized the contemporary Western belief in the power of talking to ameliorate trauma, the popularized version of the Freudian "talking cure": Salwa believes that "she had been purged of guilt and was ready to resume the guise of her checklist life"[30] after coming clear to Jassim, and Jassim is drawn to the platitudinous formula delivered by Penny that "you should make peace with those you've hurt."[31] Instead of recreating their lost connection, both are eventually forced to realize that their marriage is based on illusion, self-delusion, and misguided motivations intricately entangled with their sense of unbelonging to US culture and loss of origins. Jassim comes to understand that

> [h]e loved Salwa because in her he saw home, which made her both more precious and a source of resentment. [...]. He had married Salwa because he had wished to protect and nurture her. Because he needed her. Quite possibly she had married him for need as well.[32]

Their hasty marriage was, first and foremost, a response to their feelings of loss and an expression of their need to belong, and it has intensified those feelings in turn.

It is highly ironic that Jassim's personal traumas – the death of the teenage boy and his inability to relate his innermost concerns to Salwa – though completely unrelated to 9/11, cause him to be unwittingly sucked into the climate of general anti-Muslim suspicion. Haunted by the recurring mental image of the dying boy and paralyzed by the disintegration of his marriage, Jassim's routine behaviours change, making his overly suspicious fellow citizens feel that "not everything was in its place, was as it should be."[33] A cluster of random and entirely innocent observations made by co-workers, swimming pool personnel, etc., trigger an FBI investigation whose repercussions cause Jassim to lose his job, with which his American identity and sense of purpose had been bound up.

---

30 Ibid., p. 145.
31 Ibid., p. 168.
32 Ibid., p. 325.
33 Ibid., p. 173.

In another sense, however, there is a parallel between these personal and collective traumas. The rise of anti-Muslim sentiment can certainly be seen as a narrative that mainstream US culture reverted to after 9/11 in an attempt to deal with the trauma of the attacks. Where both Salwa and Jassim have relied on (ironically, "American") stories, so too does mainstream US discourse. Just as Salwa and Jassim draw on stories that ultimately deny their genuine experience and feelings, the large-scale narrative of anti-Muslim suspicion displaces Muslims in US culture and society.

Given the multiply interrelated events in the novel, it is impossible to determine whether the novel plots the events of 9/11 against the backdrop of the gradual unravelling of Salwa and Jassim's relationship, or vice versa. While the forces that contribute to their growing distance from each other – lack of communication, dishonesty, sense of rootlessness, disenchantment with their American life, and plain coincidence – are unrelated to the attacks on the World Trade Center, 9/11 impacts on them in complex and indirect ways, heightening their sense of being outsiders in the US. Ironically, the attacks initially offer the possibility of connection and togetherness, if only momentarily: as they confront anti-Muslim prejudice for the first time on a shopping trip to the local mall, "[f]or the tiniest amount of time, the Lie was distracted by the War on Terror. For that slice of an afternoon, Salwa and Jassim were how they had once been: together."[34] However, the various forces that pull them apart prove that the traumas in their personal lives have a destructive potential that goes beyond the violent impact of 9/11. It is not the repercussions from 9/11 as such that causes Salwa and Jassim's life to disintegrate. The traumatizing proportions of the events in the novel are the result of coincidence and only vaguely connected events, and of the propensity of human beings to follow base instincts and their capacity to inflict pain on each other. Hence *Once in a Promised Land* critically and self-consciously explores the contemporary fascination with trauma: we tend to sweepingly apply ubiquitous and simplistic categories such as "9/11," while the traumatizing potentials of violence and guilt inherent in human relationships are impossible to measure and predict.

Pat Barker's *Double Vision*, too, critically comments on the trauma discourse as it portrays a life determined by trauma. The novel centers on journalist Stephen Sharkey, who is taking an extended period of sabbatical leave to write a book about his experiences as a war reporter. More importantly, he needs to recover from the cumulative experiences of atrocities in various war

---

[34] Ibid., p. 32.

zones, as well as a series of personal disasters: the break-up of his marriage, and his friend and colleague Ben Frobisher's death during a placement in Afghanistan. In this novel, too, 11 September 2001 provides the key structural event in which personal and collective traumas blur and intersect. In retrospect, Stephen muses on the ambivalent global status of 9/11:

> 11 September. Not a date anybody was likely to forget and many people had far worse personal reasons for remembering it than he had. On that day, having any kind of personal crisis seemed selfish, and yet of course they happened. People fell in love, or out of love, or down flights of badly lit stairs, got jobs, lost jobs, had heart attacks and babies, stared at the shadow on an X-ray, or the second blue line on a pregnancy-testing kit.[35]

In Stephen's particular case, 9/11 also marked the end of his marriage: incidentally posted in New York on the day of the attacks, he phones his wife to let her know he is unharmed, only to discover from a voice in the background that she is in bed with another man. Of course, the simultaneity of collective and personal tragedy that Stephen's story exemplifies is a somewhat trivial observation but also an intensely meaningful one if we consider its further-reaching implications. Obviously, the true scale of the event transcends human understanding. As Stephen is aware, the constant repetition of the images of the planes crashing into the World Trade Center reduces their impact to an easily recognizable and hence eerily familiar picture:

> The television screen domesticated the roar and tumult, the dust, the debris, the cries, the thud of bodies hitting the ground, reduced all this to silent images, played and replayed, and played again in a vain attempt to make the day's events credible.[36]

Stephen's observations recall Jean Baudrillard's famous dictum that "the Gulf War did not take place."[37] What Baudrillard means, of course, is not that there was no actual war, but that the seemingly illusory nature of contemporary warfare reduces war to its televised representation. Pat Barker plays with this postmodern cliché: to some extent, Stephen means exactly what Baudrillard means: namely, that the images cannot really express individual catastrophes, but can merely point to unseen human suffering. Yet Stephen also has something else to say: in contrast to allegedly global atrocities, personal, small-scale experiences of suffering, violence and guilt have

---

35 Pat Barker, *Double Vision* (London: Penguin, 2004), p. 96.

36 Ibid., pp. 96-97.

37 The phrase is taken from a series of three essays Baudrillard wrote before, during and after the 1991 Gulf War 1991 ("The Gulf War will not take place", "The Gulf War: is it really taking place?", "The Gulf War did not take place"). See Jean Baudrillard, *The Gulf War Did Not Take Place*, trans. Paul Patton (Sydney: Power Publications, 1995).

infinitely greater significance. Because they occur in contexts in which people are in positions to make decisions and unable to fully detach themselves, such events introduce an obvious ethical dimension, and it is this nexus that forces individuals to take a moral stand.

The connection is exemplified when Stephen reminisces about his own personally disastrous experience of 9/11. Having witnessed the collective catastrophe of the day itself, he has eventually retreated to his hotel room to fantasize about his wife – ironically, only minutes before he finds out about her adultery:

> He closed his eyes and for a moment almost drifted off himself, but then the remembered thud of a body hitting the ground jolted him awake. To shut the sound out, he focused on her breasts and was rewarded by a stir of lust. Sometimes when you're so saturated in death that you can't soak up any more, only sex helps.[38]

Of course, this is anything but a retreat into a cozy and sheltered relationship –Stephen's choice of words indicates as much. By playing on the link of sexuality and death, Stephen acknowledges the destructive implications of traumatic events – yet in a different and more disturbing way than we would probably expect. As in *Once in a Promised Land*, trauma lies elsewhere, not simply within the easily recognizable and undeniably momentous 9/11 attacks.

The subsequent events in the novel take up on the violent dimension of personal lives, as the link between eroticism, sex and death is explored in Stephen's relationship with Justine. 18-year-old Justine works as an au pair for Stephen's brother and his wife. Her odd jobs around the house also involve making deliveries to Stephen's cottage. From their first meeting, Stephen is in thrall to her budding and surprisingly bold sexuality, and they embark on a passionate affair. Strikingly, the scene of their very first sexual encounter is suffused with images of death. Driving Justine home from his brother's house, Stephen hits an animal with his car. Stephen and Justine get out of the car to look for it, and as they stroll through the forest undergrowth by the side of the road, both are intensely aware of each other's sexual presence. The erotic tension is violently resolved only when Justine catches her neck on a barbed wire fence:

> [Stephen] could only stare and stare at the red tear in the white skin. He wanted to put his hand over it. He wanted to touch it with his fingertips. It was as if his mind had been torn, a

---

[38] Barker, p. 97.

> rent made in the fabric of his daily self and through this rent, slowly, all previous inhibitions and restraint dissolved into the night air. He reached out for her and kissed her.[39]

Of course, the "red tear in the white skin" along Justine's neck aligns her sexuality with death, as do Stephen's remarks on his altered, almost brutalised state of mind. Significantly, he does eventually discover the badly mutilated carcass of the animal he hit, so that death physically intrudes into the intimacy of the kissing.

The specter of death that their first sexual encounter has opened up is pushed to the extreme when Stephen's fantasy of Justine merges with his mental image of a raped and murdered girl that he and Ben discovered by chance while posted in Bosnia. A short while after their first kiss, standing opposite Justine as they say goodbye, "[s]omething stirred in him, something nameless and irrational and a lot less healthy than lust. He smelled the stairwell in Sarajevo, and dragged cold air into his lungs. Her mouth was slightly open."[40] It is not even entirely clear which girl the final sentence refers to – Justine making an (unconsciously) erotic gesture, or the Bosnian girl expressing her agony? In both scenes, a sexual quality is attributed to death; the blurring of the two scenes reveals a disturbing merging of lust and suffering. And the image is even more complex than that: as Stephen recounts, perversely, he and Ben behaved with almost chivalric decency in war-torn Sarajevo, as they covered the girl's naked body and returned it to a more natural position. In bed with Justine, in the peace of the English countryside, however, Stephen recognizes the potentially destructive nature of sexual desire and is overwhelmed by the violence that intrudes with the Sarajevo image. In a situation that should be tender and intimate, the image of the Bosnian girl returns, unwanted. Thus establishing an obvious parallel to the thudding bodies that intrude on Stephen's fantasies of his wife in the evening of 9/11, the image makes a more general statement on the nature of traumatic experience: it is the unwitting intrusion of the mutilated body that constitutes genuine trauma. Far from being a mental state that can be analyzed and accessed, the traumatic nature of Stephen's experience lies with this intrusive body. It resists being explained, categorized, and untangled in its complexity.

The parallel between Justine and the Bosnian girl is brought to a head with the novel's violent denouement, when Justine's employers' house is burgled and she is beaten to the point of losing consciousness. Stephen, who can see the burglars from the distance of his cottage, but is too far away to get to the house in time to stop them, fears that Justine might be raped. Even

---

39 Ibid., pp. 90-91.

40 Ibid., p. 94.

after he has overwhelmed the burglars and been reassured that Justine has not been sexually assaulted, in his imagination the burglary merges with his memories of the war crimes he has witnessed and allows for another intrusion of the violated body:

> So many raped and tortured girls – he needed no imagination to picture what might be happening to Justine. It would not have surprised him to find her lying like a broken doll at the foot of the stairs, her skirt bunched up around her waist, her eyes staring. Years of impacted rage had gone into the blow he'd aimed at the back of the burglar's head. He'd meant it to kill.[41]

What Stephen acts out is not revenge but a primeval act of defence. He comes to understand that he himself – in spite of his revulsion at the crimes he has witnessed – would be capable of the utmost degree of brutality, perpetuating a cycle of rage and violence that implicates not the actual perpetrators, but erupts randomly and disproportionately.

At first glance, the novel's ending does not seem to fit the violence and destruction of the preceding action. Stephen takes Justine away to a small seaside town for a few days to recover, and the novel's final scene begins like a rather clichéd "love conquers all" scenario:

> He climbed in beside her and for a moment they said and did nothing, lying side by side, fingers intertwined. The moonlight found the whites of her eyes. For a moment he saw the girl in the stairwell in Sarajevo, but she'd lost her power. This moment in this bed banished her, not for ever, perhaps, but for long enough.[42]

This is a positive image in that the human bond that Stephen and Justine have created is able to overwhelm Stephen's traumatic memory.[43] And yet, the passage also makes it clear that things are not as easy as that: tenderness and intimacy can only push to the sidelines the traumatizing image of the Bosnian girl for a moment. This is no "working through" or "getting closure," but simply forgetting. Thus the scene points to an uncomfortable truth about traumatic experience: repression may be the only way of surviving and living

---

41 Ibid., p. 250.

42 Ibid., p. 302.

43 As such, it is an example of Ian McEwan's observation shortly after the 9/11 attacks that the universal human capacity for love is the only thing that could be set against the devastation and loss of the attacks: "There was really only one thing […] to say, those three words that all the terrible art, the worst pop songs and movies, the most seductive lies, can somehow never cheapen. I love you" (Ian McEwan, 'Only Love and Then Oblivion', *The Guardian*, 15 September 2001).

with trauma. There is no such thing as the proverbial "talking cure," only the mental capacity to forget.

Thus *Double Vision*, too, questions and rewrites the contemporary understanding of trauma. It is this stance that *Double Vision* and *Once in a Promised Land* have in common, in spite of the different angles from which they approach the subject. What links them is their acknowledgement of trauma as a physical reality that makes any form of detachment impossible.

Indeed, this is where the implications of the pictures discussed at the beginning of this essay dovetail with the novels' explorations of trauma: both deliberately evoke the familiar, easily recognizable images of 11 September and play with our fascination with the horrific. The invocations of 9/11, in the pictures as, initially, in the novels, do not as such make a statement on trauma: rather, they count on their distant perspective for their emotional effect. What makes them so alluring is their very remoteness.

Yet, as I have shown, the novels go further than offering a commentary on the inadequacy of the ubiquitous images of 9/11. Their point is to draw attention to the seductively simplistic nature of the immediate associations, "common knowledge," and assumed collectivities that are generally called up by allusions to 9/11. Rather than accepting a vague notion of "collective trauma," the novels take trauma back to its genuinely debilitating dimensions. They explore the unsettling truth that trauma, once it has come close to home, makes us unable to act, disrupts normalcy, even makes us animals or repulses us. In so doing, the novels function as sobering reminders that trauma forbids detachment, and that its physical and emotional immediacy makes it a subject that can be creatively used, but just as easily abused.

Bibliography

I am very grateful to Anja Müller-Wood and Cara Cilano for their helpful comments and suggestions at various stages in the preparation of this essay.

Barker, Pat, *Double Vision* (London: Penguin, 2004)

Baudrillard, Jean, *The Gulf War Did Not Take Place*, trans. Paul Patton (Sydney: Power Publications, 1995)

Beaumont, Peter, 'America Hails Cricket Fan's Novel that Met 9/11 Challenge', *The Observer*, 25 May 2008

Bourke, Joanna, *Fear: A Cultural History* (London: Virago Press, 2005)

Caruth, Cathy, *Unclaimed Experience: Trauma, Narrative and History* (Baltimore and London: The Johns Hopkins University Press, 1996)

Coates, Susan, 'Introduction: Trauma and Human Bonds', in *September 11: Trauma and Human Bonds*, eds Susan Coates, Jane L. Rosenthal and Daniel S. Schechter (Hillsdale and London: The Atlantic Press, 2003), 1-14

Conrad, Peter, 'The Presumption of Art', *The Observer.* 8 September 2002

Farrell, Kirby, *Post-traumatic Culture: Injury and Interpretation in the Nineties* (Baltimore and London: The Johns Hopkins University Press, 1998)

Felman, Shoshana and Dori Laub, *Testimony: Crises of Witnessing in Literature, Psychoanalysis, and History* (New York and London: Routledge, 1992)

Halaby, Laila, *Once in a Promised Land* (Boston: Beacon Press, 2007)

Hirsch, Marianne, 'The Day Time Stopped', *The Chronicle Review* 25 January 2002

Kaplan, E. Ann, *Trauma Culture: The Politics of Terror and Loss in Media and Literature* (New Brunswick: Rutgers University Press, 2005)

Luckhurst, Roger, 'Traumaculture', *New Formations*, 50 (2003), 28-47

McEwan, Ian, 'Only Love and then Oblivion', *The Guardian*, 15 September 2001

----, *Saturday* (London: Vintage, 2006)

Radstone, Susannah, 'The War of the Fathers: trauma, Fantasy, and September 11', in *Trauma at Home: After 9/11*, ed. Judith Greenberg (Lincoln and London: University of Nebraska Press, 2003), 117-23

Storr, Anthony, *Freud: A Very Short Introduction* (Oxford: Oxford University Press, 2001)

Tew, Philip, *The Contemporary British Novel*, 2nd edn. (London: Continuum, 2007)

Tuy De Los Reyes, Katrina, 'Once in a Promised Land by Laila Halaby', *About.com. Contemporary Literature* <http://contemporarylit.about.com/od/fiction/fr/onceInA.htm> [accessed 20 September 2008]

"Artworks, Unlike Terrorists, Change Nothing": Salman Rushdie and September 11

Ana Cristina Mendes

This essay sets out to demonstrate that rather than being an instance of fission, Rushdie's most recent literary journalism as well as his latest novels, in particular *Shalimar the Clown* (2005), are the ultimate product of fusion, in the way that they result from the synthetic encounter–not disintegration–of contradictory states of affiliation. Any critical engagement with the global brand "Rushdie" must explore its manifold reverberations. In this sense, my concern is with teasing out a interrelated set of elements that have contributed to shape the discursive predicament in which the writer has been trapped for a couple of decades, and not with attaching a one-dimensional label for his post-fatwa and post-9/11 politics. The purpose of addressing the writer's shifting positions as a public intellectual is not to appraise what might be called Rushdie's "American turn," nor to ascertain the inconsistencies of his ideological standing with reference to the cultural authority and military power of the US, in general, and to the aftermath of September 11, 2001, in particular. Rather, a focal intention is to undermine the idea that the writer manifests, or did indeed manifest, a clear-cut pro-US government position in support of the "war on terror."

> The truth is that there is no whale. We live in a world without hiding places; the missiles have made sure of that.
>
> Salman Rushdie[1]

> Rushdie in his Manhattan retreat is no longer a Third World writer but a bard of the grim one world we all, in a state of some dread, inhabit.
>
> John Updike[2]

Salman Rushdie's aptitude to apprehend experience from an array of transient positionings is rooted in the belief that the creative writer should identify himself or herself with a cosmopolitan ideal and steer clear of any explicit parochial agenda. In reality, his defence of Indian writing in English in the (infamous) introduction to the co-edited anthology *The Vintage Book of*

---

1 Salman Rushdie, 'Outside the Whale', in *Imaginary Homelands: Essays and Criticism, 1981-1991* (London: Granta, 1991), 87-101 (p. 99).

2 John Updike, 'Paradises Lost: Rushdie's *Shalimar the Clown*' *The New Yorker*, 5 September 2005 <http://www.newyorker.com/archive/2005/09/05/050905crbo_ books?currentPage=all> [accessed 18 June 2007].

Indian Writing (1997) is based on the conviction that "parochialism is perhaps the main vice of the vernacular literatures."[3] His call to detachment thus testifies to the inoperability and even outmodedness of the concept that "home" constitutes a biding filial connection which subjects are expected to experience in relation to a homeland. Viewed from his perspective, the post-independence generation of Indian writers of English had–and, one might add, still has–been garnering an unprecedented visibility since the 1980s because it had been "too good to fall into the trap of writing nationalistically."[4] Likewise, Edward Said–to whom Rushdie himself dedicates an eponymous essay in *Step Across This Line*, his compilation of non-fictional work published in 2002–censures anti-colonial nationalist models such as Frantz Fanon's, underscoring that fetishized allegiances of "[n]ationality, nationalism, nativism" might be just as constraining to the individual as colonialism.[5] In this way, Said's secular ideal is, at its core, both a form of exilic displacement and an adversarial critical exercise grounded in opposition to what the Palestinian critic perceives to be the near-dogmatic tenets of national alliances. Along the lines of Said's secularism, in the essay "Notes on Writing and the Nation" (1997) Rushdie updates the argument presented in the foreword to *The Vintage Book of Indian Writing*, dubbing the sort of parochialism entailed in "writing nationalistically"[6] as "New Behalfism." The writer expresses his contempt for "behalfies" thus:

> Beware the writer who sets himself or herself up as the voice of a nation. This includes nations of race, gender, sexual orientation, elective affinity. This is the New Behalfism. Beware behalfies! [...] Seeing literature as inescapably political, it substitutes political values for literary ones. It is the murderer of thought. Beware![7]

According to Said, the attention of contemporary secular criticism is engaged by the twin "temptations" of vertical *filiation*, wherein critical consciousness is inextricably connected "by birth, nationality, profession" to a stable place of origin, and horizontal *affiliation*, in which new-fangled critical solidarities are formed "by social and political conviction, economic and historical circumstances, voluntary effort and willed deliberation."[8] Not unre-

---

3 Rushdie, 'Introduction', in *The Vintage Book of Indian Writing: 1947-1997*, ed. by Salman Rushdie and Elizabeth West (London: Vintage, 1997), ix-xxii (p. xv).

4 Ibid., p. xv.

5 Edward Said, *Culture and Imperialism* (London: Vintage, 1993), p. 277.

6 Rushdie, 'Introduction', p. xv.

7 Rushdie, 'Notes on Writing and the Nation', in *Step Across This Line: Collected Non-Fiction 1992-2002* (London: Vintage, 2003), 64-8 (p. 66).

8 Said, *The World, the Text, and the Critic* (Cambridge, Massachusetts: Harvard University Press, 1983), pp. 24-5.

latedly, a review written by Randy Boyagoda of *Step Across This Line* underscores the "dizzying" outcome of the "contradictory affiliations" resulting from the author's self-pledged multipositionality.[9] "Over the course of the collection," Boyagoda notes, Rushdie presents himself as "a Muslim, Indian, New Yorker, Briton, European, American, trans-nationalist, post-nationalist, internationalist, immigrant, exile, emigrant, migrant."[10] The reviewer recognizes that such apparent changeability of political positioning–visible for the most part regarding the 9/11 attacks and their aftermath in US foreign policy–is defensible in Rushdie's fictional writing, where his characters exhibit hybrid selves, and are thus far from lending themselves to unitary categorization. Boyagoda considers nonetheless that in a *cultural critic* this multipositionality results in an unavoidable inconsistency, and hence turns this anthology of essays and newspaper columns into a sort of "postmodern chutney," most likely to cause "an unfortunate indigestion" to its reader.[11]

Alternatively, what this essay sets out to demonstrate is that rather than being an instance of fission, Rushdie's most recent literary journalism as well as his latest novels, in particular *Shalimar the Clown* (2005), are the ultimate product of fusion, in the way that they result from the synthetic encounter–not disintegration–of contradictory states of affiliation. In an interview with the British newspaper *The Telegraph*, the writer comments precisely on how individuals are being pigeonholed into circumscribed categories: "People are being invited to define themselves increasingly narrowly […]. They're either Muslim, or Christian, or British, American, or whatever. […] The truth, of course, is that we're not just one thing, or another; we're all these little clouds of contradictions."[12] On the one hand, Boyagoda seems to confirm the trend Rushdie discerns whereby individuals are being narrowly catalogued and, on the other hand, bypasses two prerequisites of Rushdie criticism in the 21st century: an Indian-born British citizen, New York resident, secular humanist Muslim, postcolonial writer, global literary celebrity, and transnational polemicist must of necessity experience some degree of paradoxical geopolitical ties. The reviewer sidesteps these by underlining not the fault-lines within the writer's affiliations, but rather by emphasizing the fact that they seem to *threaten* his integrity as cultural commentator.

---

9 Randy Boyagoda, 'Postmodern Chutney', *First Things: A Monthly Journal of Religion and Public Life*, 1 February 2003, 47-49 (p. 48).

10 Ibid., p. 48.

11 Ibid., p. 49.

12 John Preston, 'Salman Rushdie: Provoking People Is In My DNA', *The Telegraph*, 29 December 2008 <http://www.telegraph.co.uk/culture/books/4015303/Salman-Rushdie-provoking-people-is-in-my-DNA.html> [accessed 29 December 2008].

Any critical engagement with the global brand "Rushdie" must explore its manifold reverberations. In this sense, my concern is with teasing out a interrelated set of elements that have contributed to shape the discursive predicament in which the writer has been trapped for a couple of decades, and not with attaching a one-dimensional label for his post-fatwa and post-9/11 politics. The purpose of addressing the writer's shifting positions as a public intellectual is not to appraise what might be called Rushdie's "American turn," nor to ascertain the inconsistencies of his ideological standing with reference to the cultural authority and military power of the US, in general, and to the aftermath of September 11, 2001, in particular. Rather, a focal intention is to undermine the idea that the writer manifests, or did indeed manifest, a clear-cut pro-US government position in support of the "war on terror."

Even if throughout Rushdie's career he has always favored the unencumbered subject in his work, the writer's conceptualization of "home" and the broader interrelated idea of geopolitical space have subtly changed. In Rushdie's earlier writings, migrancy constituted "a *political* act with political implications."[13] Conversely, in the essay "Step Across this Line" (delivered at Yale University in February 2002 as *The Tanner Lectures on Human Values* and which provide the title for the collection and comprise its last part), the writer espouses a "new thesis of the post-frontier."[14] In view of this, de-territorialization–in which stable frames of reference have been diluted by "the emergence, in the age of mass migration, mass displacement, globalized finances, and industries, of this new, permeable post-frontier"–has resulted in the transcending of formerly given territorial boundaries. Ensuing from the escalating import of mobile capital, instant communication, and global travel in flexible capitalist societies, the permeability of frontiers is hence "the distinguishing feature of our times."[15] At a post-panoptical juncture dominated by the shifting dynamics of the internet and large-scale travel across the globe, many of Rushdie's later essays included in *Step Across This Line* thus set the stage for the writer's fictional manifesto.

Such manifesto is in line with the extant circulation of the post-national paradigm, with recent novels by Rushdie such as *The Ground Beneath Her Feet* (1999) and *Fury* (2001) reminding us of the intensifying inadequacy of

---

13 Anshuman A. Mondal, '*The Ground Beneath Her Feet* and *Fury*: The Reinvention of Location', in *The Cambridge Companion to Salman Rushdie*, ed. by Abdulrazak Gurnah (Cambridge: Cambridge University Press, 2007), 169-183 (p. 180).

14 Rushdie, 'Step Across This Line', in *Step Across This Line: Collected Non-Fiction 1992-2002* (London: Vintage, 2003), 405-42 (p. 425).

15 Ibid., p. 425.

institutional borders as boundary markers. *Shalimar the Clown*, postulating likewise a new age of the post-frontier, where "[e]verywhere was now a part of everywhere else. Russia, America, London, Kashmir,"[16] highlights the way transnational terrorist networks and fundamentalist movements have assisted in the weakening of territorial borders. As a result of this glocal interconnectedness, "[o]ur lives, our stories, flowed into one another's, were no longer our own, individual, discrete. This unsettled people. There were collisions and explosions. The world was no longer calm."[17] As Yumna Siddiqi notes about this development in Rushdie's last but one novel, *Shalimar the Clown* unequivocally articulates a cosmopolitan standpoint in the framework of post-9/11 terrorist and counter-terrorist practices–instead of "present[ing] private individual destinies as allegories of the situation of the nation, the novel symbolically maps geopolitics in relation to its protagonists' lives."[18]

Ultimately, Rushdie's de-territorialized exilic narratives bear out Zygmunt Bauman's analysis of the ongoing liquefaction of modernity–what Bauman dubs "liquid modernity"–wherein fluid and seamless power structures are displacing those once perceived as fixed and stable. Rushdie's recent work rehearses this melting of previously "solid" modernity into liquid modernity: whereas his earlier writing dealt predominantly with the individual's relation to the materiality of territorial figurations, now it is the non-physicality of the globe and the ultimate discarding of frontiers that appeal to him.[19] If, as the author argues, in "our deepest natures, we are frontier-crossing beings,"[20] then it seems that what used to be considered a political act–such as the traversing of borders–is turned into an innate one,[21] which might lead to an emptying of the potential transgressiveness of migrancy. Said's concept of "wordliness," understood as the intellectual's critical engagement with contemporary politics, implies an eradication of the strictures

---

16 Rushdie, *Shalimar the Clown* (London: Jonathan Cape, 2005), p. 37.

17 Ibid., p. 37.

18 Yumna Siddiqi, '"Power Smashes Into Private Lives": Violence, Globalization and Cosmopolitanism in Salman Rushdie's *Shalimar the Clown*,' *South Asia Research*, 27 (2007), 293-309 (p. 294).

19 In an interview with W.L. Webb in 1988, Rushdie manifested apprehension over the dangers implied in the idea of an international literature "for the same reason [he] would worry about speaking Esperanto," that is, "you can lose any real sense of a relationship with a language, or a relationship with a place if you find yourself appealing to this international body" (Webb, W. L., 'Salman Rushdie: *Satanic Verses*', in *Conversations With Salman Rushdie*, ed. by Michael R. Reder (Jackson: University of Mississippi Press, 2000), 87-100, (p. 94)).

20 Rushdie, 'Step Across This Line', p. 408.

21 Mondal, p. 180.

involved in "[n]ationality, nationalism, nativism."[22] Rushdie embodies, to a certain extent, wordliness in his professed anti-nationalist politics of non-alignment, as well as in his own uncompromisingly secular cosmopolitanism of which the voluntary exile in Britain and later in the US is part and parcel. Yet, by proposing his thesis of a post-frontier world, he has taken Said's model of wordliness to the extreme, potentially draining away the emancipatory potential of the crossing of borders, national or otherwise.

The reconfiguration of Rushdie's cultural geography has led critics to focus on the apparent shift of political positioning in the writer's non-fiction. In this respect, Anshuman Mondal argues that such change betrays, "in effect if not intent, [...] an endorsement of the status quo."[23] It should follow, then, that the writer's texts have of late betrayed an opposition to Said's understanding of the public role of the exilic intellectual as "outsider, 'amateur,' and disturber of the status quo."[24] Mondal interrogates the political significance of Rushdie's stance, and proceeds to conclude that, "[a]t best it has none, save for a residual rhetorical value that attempts to outmanoeuvre the politics of fear promoted by the US administration's 'war on terror', for which the permeability of borders represents a national security threat."[25] Has Rushdie indeed abandoned an earlier Saidean aspiration of speaking truth to power? Has his pen lost the ability to be provocative and incendiary, exciting debates, as both the front and back covers of the Vintage edition of *Step Across This Line* would lead us to believe?[26] If we follow Mondal's argument, the writer's latest work is non-adversarial. In fact, according to this critic, Rushdie as public intellectual seems to represent an updated, post-9/11, "war on terror" version of the professionalized and co-opted intellectual class of the cold war period that Said condemns in 1983: "The result [of this contemporary criticism] has been the regulated, not to say calculated, irrelevance of criticism, except as an adornment to what the powers of modern industrial society transact: the hegemony of militarism and a new cold war, the depoliticization of the citizenry, the overall compliance of the intellectual class to which critics belong."[27] While in the 1980s Rushdie's writings, in particular his travelogue *The Jaguar Smile* (1987), the novel *The Satanic Verses* (1988), and the essays assembled in *Imaginary Homelands* (1991), reflected a dis-

---

22 Said, *Culture and Imperialism*, p. 277.

23 Mondal, p. 182.

24 Said, *Representations of the Intellectual: The 1993 Reith Lectures* (London: Vintage, 1994), p. x.

25 Mondal, p. 181.

26 Both the 2003 and 2007 editions use the same image of the pencil-cum-match.

27 Said, *The World, The Text, and The Critic*, p. 25.

tinctive left-liberal political standing, the articles collected in his most recent anthology of non-fiction work have been, for the most part, the object of (mostly left-wing) disapproval and unprecedented controversy. Indeed, Rushdie's engagement as elite transnational intellectual with questions arising from the events of September 11 appeared, in the words of Sabina and Simona Sawnhney, "to join, rather than interrupt, the chorus on the street," and was perceived to be "surprisingly indistinguishable, in [...] tone and argument, from many mainstream [US] media responses."[28]

In an attempt to address the question of whether or not Sabina and Simona Sawnhney's statements have stood the test of time, the remainder of this essay focuses on the development and transformation in Rushdie's positioning from the pre-9/11 novel *Fury* to his post-9/11 non-fiction and novel *Shalimar the Clown*. What is inescapable is that September 11 acted as a conceptual turning point for the writer. In fact, Mita Banerjee argues, with reference to *Fury* and Hanif Kureishi's *Gabriel's Gift* (2001), that this traumatic event "could well be considered not only the ground zero of American literature and the American nation, but also the ground zero of the very paradigm of postcolonial studies."[29] Shortly after 9/11, Rushdie declared in an interview given to British journalist Sue Ellicott that because of this event we "need a new picture of the world," if only because "all the things we thought were true, turned out not to be"; September 11, he adds, "was a new fictional moment."[30] This reasoning is consistent with an earlier one voiced during the series of lectures given at Yale in 2002: "Like every writer in the world I am trying to find a way of writing after 11 September 2001, a day that has become something like a borderline. Not only because the attacks were a kind of invasion, but because we all crossed a frontier that day, an invisible boundary between the imaginable and the unimaginable, and it turned out to be the unimaginable that was real."[31]

---

28 Sabina Sawhney, and Simona Sawhney, 'Reading Rushdie after September 11, 2001', *Twentieth Century Literature*, 47 (2001), 431-44 (p. 433).

29 Mita Banerjee, 'Postethnicity and Postcommunism in Hanif Kureishi's *Gabriel's Gift* and Salman Rushdie's *Fury*', in *Reconstructing Hybridity: Post-Colonial Studies in Transition*, ed. by Joel Kuortti and Jopi Nyman (Amsterdam and New York: Rodopi, 2007), 309-24 (p. 309).Banerjee clarifies that "[e]ven as, due to the time lag of the publication process, these two novels cannot be literal reactions to September 11, they nevertheless react to a political climate out of which September 11 arose. For how else could these two texts not predict September 11 itself but the reactions to it?" (p. 313).

30 Quoted in Willard Manus, 'A Talk With Salman Rushdie', *Lively Arts*, November/December 2002 <http://www.livelyarts.com/books/2002/0211/ salman_rushdie.htm> [accessed 18 June 2007].

31 Rushdie, 'Step Across This Line', pp. 436-437.

The perceived turnabout in Rushdie's political affiliations can be traced back to one of his newspaper pieces written prior to the traumatic events of September 11. In the column "Globalization" (1999), first published in the *New York Times* where he was a regular commentator, Rushdie sustains the "authority of the United States" as "the best current guarantor," in the face of "tyranny, bigotry, intolerance, fanaticism," of the universal value of "freedom."[32] This standing sharply differs from his earlier critique of US foreign policy and the war in Nicaragua penned in *The Jaguar Smile.* In this travelogue of Rushdie's three-week stay in that South American country in 1986, the writer compares the US government, at the time under the Reagan administration, with "the bandit posing as the sheriff."[33] More than a decade later, while disapproving of the facile debunking of "the spread of American culture"–"[s]neakers, burgers, blue jeans and music videos aren't the enemy," he writes–Rushdie seems to support the role of the US as "world policeman."[34] The author contends that instead of seeing the US as the oppressor, we should "keep our eyes on the prize" since "[o]ut there are real tyrants to defeat."[35] These are the foes, not the dissemination of American culture we tend to slight "with our cultural hats on" whilst "shelter[ing] under the *pax Americana.*"[36]

From a position Rushdie might well characterize as "sanctimonious moral relativism," and regard as representative of "a *bien-pensant* anti-American onslaught,"[37] Priyamvada Gopal states that the writer's knighthood, granted by the Queen Elizabeth II in 2007, is "a reward for abandoning the anti-establishment stance he once espoused."[38] Gopal's article was published in the *Guardian* and is included in the media attack on Rushdie coming from British left-wing critics in the aftermath of the award. Gopal contrasts what she perceives to be Rushdie's current right-wing aligned political positioning with his prior critique of "tyrannical forces in both west and non-west," a recognition of these forces "as twinned," and a pronouncement of "a plague

---

32 Rushdie, 'Globalization', in *Step Across This Line: Collected Non-Fiction 1992-2002* (London: Vintage, 2003), 296-98 (p. 297).

33 Rushdie, *The Jaguar Smile: A Nicaraguan Journey* (London, Picador, 1987), p. 40.

34 Rushdie, 'Globalization', p. 296.

35 Ibid., p. 298.

36 Ibid., pp. 296-98.

37 Rushdie, 'The Attacks on America', in *Step Across This Line: Collected Non-Fiction 1992-2002* (London: Vintage, 2003), 391-93 (p. 392).

38 Gopal, Priyamvada, 'Sir Salman's Long Journey', *The Guardian*, 18 June 2007 <http://books.guardian.co.uk/comment/story/0,,2105445,00.html> [accessed 18 June 2007].

on both their houses."[39] Now Gopal sees Rushdie as the unthinking spokesperson for US political, military and cultural domination:

> Driven underground and into despair by zealotry, Rushdie finally emerged blinking into New York sunshine shortly before the towers came tumbling down. Those formidable literary powers would now be deployed not against, but in the service of, an American regime that had declared its own fundamentalist monopoly on the meanings of "freedom" and "liberation."[40]

Similarly, Stephen Morton posits that Rushdie's "recent fiction and essays seem to suggest a resignation to, and even at times a tacit approval for, America's unilateralist foreign policy in the early twenty-first century, and in particular the Bush administration's war on terrorism."[41]

Such interpretations of the writer's post-9/11 work as apologetic for the North American project of worldwide hegemony are irrespective of, for instance, the critique of the US government's rhetoric on the war against terror that Rushdie offers in an interview with François Armanet and Gilles Anquetil to the French *Le Nouvel Observateur* in 2006. Here, the writer argues that the word "freedom" acquires different senses whether employed by the former US President George W. Bush or by the writer himself, in the same way that it evinced dissimilar meanings when the Ayatollah Khomeni or John Stuart Mill used it.[42] Looking at these apparent paradoxes in Rushdie's politics, Timothy Brennan writes that "the evolution of Rushdie's public persona is more clearly understandable in the framework of professional pressures than diasporic insights (his need, that is, to find a space in the op-ed columns of the New York establishment, which considers itself at war)."[43] In fact, it is within these contradictions that one must critically scrutinize the writer's role as a public intellectual. Regardless of Rushdie's current self-positioning as a New Yorker and as an "American" writer, he has certainly not turned into an uncritical, flag-waving enthusiast of the US administration under Bush, which he portrays as a "hard-line, ideologue right-wing regime."[44] On the contrary, he posits that "it is America's duty not to abuse its

---

39 Ibid.

40 Ibid.

41 Stephen Morton, *Salman Rushdie: Fictions of Postcolonial Modernity* (Basingstoke and New York: Palgrave, 2008), p. 117.

42 Quoted in François Armanet and Gilles Anquetil, 'Mes Lumières', *Le Nouvel Observateur*, 21 December 2006 < http://hebdo.nouvelobs.com/p2198/articles/a327856.html> [accessed 20 August 2008].

43 Timothy Brennan, *Wars of Position: The Cultural Politics of Left and Right* (New York: Columbia UP, 2006), p. 92.

44 Rushdie, 'A Grand Coalition?', in *Step Across This Line: Collected Non-Fiction 1992-2002* (London: Vintage, 2003), 359-61 (p. 361).

pre-eminence, and our right to criticize such abuses when they happen"; in fact, in a note added to the article afterwards, he asserts that "[i]n spite of all Bush's attempts to turn the USA into a pariah state, however, it remains the case that American culture isn't the enemy. Globalization isn't the problem; the inequitable distribution of resources is."[45]

Post-9/11 Rushdie sharply criticized any endeavours by the intellectual left to draw simplistic connections between US foreign policy and the terrorist attacks in New York. In the article "Anti-Americanism," published in February 2002, he manifests his indignation at the anti-American offensive brought about by a left-liberal faction. In the militaristic aftermath of September 11, this is, according to the writer, "an ideological enemy [of America] that may turn out to be harder to defeat than militant Islam,"[46] Rushdie notes that one of "the most unpleasant consequences of the terrorists' attacks on the United States" has been, as the writer puts it in another article, "the savaging of America by sections of the left."[47] At this point, one should recall that, in the words of the narrator in the novel *Fury*, anti-Americanism buttresses US-centered exercise of global power in the way that it was "Americanism in disguise, conceding, as it did, that America was the only game in town and the matter of America the only business at hand."[48] Commenting on the US-led conflict in Afghanistan, an ongoing military operation which began on 7 October 2001, Rushdie argues that "America did [...] what had to be done, and did it well."[49] He adopts a liberal defence of the invasion, dubbed "Operation Enduring Freedom" in response to the September 11 attacks, justifying it in entirely humanitarian terms. As one knows with hindsight, he was proven mistaken. "Great power and great wealth are perhaps never popular," the writer points out, but proceeds to stress that "more than ever, we need the United States to exercise its power and economic might responsibly."[50]

Even considering that this newspaper piece was penned within months after the 9/11 attacks, and well before the Abu Ghraib prisoner abuse scandal in 2005 and the massive civilian casualties in Iraq–and that Rushdie has withdrawn to some extent his support to the United States government's so-called "war on terrorism"–Abdulrazak Gurnah notes the writer took part in protests

---

45 Rushdie, 'Globalization', p. 298.

46 Rushdie, 'Anti-Americanism', in *Step Across This Line: Collected Non-Fiction 1992-2002* (London: Vintage, 2003), 398-400 (p. 398).

47 Rushdie, 'The Attacks on America', p. 392.

48 Rushdie, *Fury* (London: Vintage, 2002), p. 87.

49 Rushdie, 'Anti-Americanism', p. 399.

50 Ibid., p. 400.

against the detention center at Guantanamo Bay in 2005, where suspects classified by the United States as "enemy combatants" are held[51]–a few questions are still in order. What to make of this accolade of the present-day geopolitical pre-eminence of America? Should we take the writer's words at face value? As Sabina and Simona Sawhney note, "Rushdie is certainly not the first writer to present us with a set of political writings incongruent with the general trajectory of his work."[52] Indeed, entertaining the expectation that the writer should be an unequivocal supporter of a predetermined political agenda might well be one of the pitfalls of reading Rushdie as "political event."[53] Still, how are we to interpret this noticeable and pronounced inner dialectic between the author's political and literary sensibilities? Even conceding that such distinction between the literary and the political is artificial–in the sense that Rushdie offers critiques of the status quo, openly and through literary subversion–how is the reader to balance, on the one hand, the vilification of an increasing anti-American sentiment and, on the other hand, the scathing critique in *Fury* of American strategies for legitimizing an imperialist project? It should be noted that in this novel, published just within a week of 9/11, its New York-based protagonist Malik Solanka, can be heard pondering:

> Might this new Rome actually be more provincial than its provinces; might these new Romans have forgotten what and how to value, or had they never known? Were all empires so undeserving, or was this one particularly crass? [...] Who demolished the City on the Hill and put in its place a row of electric chairs, those dealers in death's democracy, where everyone, the innocent, the mentally deficient, the guilty, could come to die side by side? Who paved Paradise and put up a parking lot? Who settled for George W. Gush's boredom and Al Bore's gush?[54]

Yet, a month after the terrorist attacks, in a newspaper article the writer seems to call forth a "secret war" against those who had assaulted his new adopted home:

> They broke our city. I'm among the newest of New Yorkers, but even people who have never set foot in Manhattan have felt her wounds deeply, because New York in our time is the beating heart of the visible world [...] To this bright capital of the visible, the forces of

51 Abdulrazak Gurnah, 'Introduction', in *The Cambridge Companion to Salman Rushdie*, ed. by Abdulrazak Gurnah (Cambridge: Cambridge University Press, 2007), 1-8 (p. 7).

52 Sawhney and Sawhney, p. 437.

53 Kate Muir, 'Exclusive Interview With Salman Rushdie', *The Times*, 4 April 2008 <http://entertainment.timesonline.co.uk/tol/arts_and_entertainment/books/article3681048.ece> [accessed 4 April 2008]

54 Rushdie, *Fury*, pp. 86-7.

invisibility have dealt a dreadful blow. […] Yes, we must send our shadow warriors against theirs, and hope that ours prevail.[55]

Rushdie's texts not only reflect anxieties which result from the vexed positionality of the US in "cultural globalization and its military-political sidekick, intervention,"[56] but also ponder over the cultural significance of 9/11. In this respect, the theorist of visual representation, W. J. T. Mitchell, reads the devastation of the World Trade Center on September 11 as "a new and virulent form of iconoclasm"[57] or "iconoclash."[58] Mitchell contends that "the moral imperative is to offend the images themselves"–such as those of the twin towers of New York–"to treat them as if they were human agents, or at least living agents of evil, and to punish them accordingly."[59] Thus, the "real target [of the 9/11 attacks] was a globally recognizable icon, and the aim was not merely to destroy it but to stage its destruction as media spectacle"; iconoclasm was accordingly "rendered as an icon in its own right."[60] Mitchell's reading echoes the description of the collapsing of the towers in Mohsin Hamid's 9/11 novel, *The Reluctant Fundamentalist*, whose protagonist Changez depicts the instant of the attack thus: "my thoughts were not with the victims of the attack […] no, I was caught up in the *symbolism* of it all, the fact that someone had so visibly brought America to her knees."[61] Interestingly, Rushdie anticipates both Hamid's literary portrayal and Mitchell's theorisation when he digresses in the essay "Step Across This Line" on 9/11 as artistic text, on the symbolic relevance of the destruction of the towers, and on the responsibilities of a novelist after these harrowing events:

> Murder was not the point. The creation of a meaning was the point. The terrorists of September 11, and the planners of that day's events, behaved like perverted, but in another way brilliantly transgressive, performance artists: hideously innovative, shockingly successful, using a low-tech attack to strike at the very heart of our high-tech world. In dreams begin irresponsibilities, too.[62]
>
> In the aftermath of horror, of the iconoclastically transgressive image-making of the terrorists, do artists and writers still have the right to insist on the supreme, unfettered freedoms of art? Is it time, instead of endlessly pushing the envelope, stepping into forbidden territory

---

55 Rushdie, 'The Attacks on America', pp. 391-2.

56 Rushdie, 'Globalization', p. 296.

57 W. J. T. Mitchell, *What Do Pictures Want?: The Lives and Loves of Images* (Chicago: University of Chicago Press, 2005), p. 13.

58 Ibid., p. 11.

59 Ibid., p. 15.

60 Ibid., pp. 13-14.

61 Mohsin Hamid, *The Reluctant Fundamentalist* (Orlando: Harcourt, 2007), p. 73.

62 Rushdie, 'Step Across This Line', p. 436.

> and generally causing trouble, to start discovering what frontiers might be necessary to art, rather than an affront to it?[63]

Rushdie's declared answer to the above question was in the negative mode, although he provocatively goes on to assert that "Artworks, unlike terrorists, change nothing,"[64] seeming to downplay–again baffling the reader–the transgressive potential of art. Here, he emphasizes instead the political ineffectualness of artistic creation,[65] while prior to the events of September 11 his defence of art was far from muted. In fact, the debate about artistic political responsibility is often interwoven within Rushdie's fictional narratives. For example, in *The Satanic Verses* the poet Baal presents a writer's work as possessing the symbolic power "[t]o name the unnamable, to point at frauds, to take sides, start arguments, shape the world and stop it from going to sleep."[66] Similarly, in the novel *Haroun and the Sea of Stories* (1990), the author has one of the characters, the sceptical son Haroun Khalifa, question ironically his storytelling father Rashid about the usefulness of "*stories that aren't even true*."[67] While Rushdie's fiction and his critical writing should not be correlated in any simplistic or reductive fashion, in the lecture "Is Nothing Sacred" (1990), in memory of Herbert Read, the writer states that the novel claims "*the right to be the stage upon which the great debates of society can be conducted*,"[68] and cautions in the essay "Outside the Whale" (1984) that if "writers leave the business of making pictures of the world to

---

63 Ibid., p. 440.

64 Ibid., p. 441.

65 Rushdie seems to reiterate W. H. Auden's despondency regarding the apparent uselessness of poetry in the elegy dedicated to W. B. Yeats (1939): "You were silly like us; your gift survived it all: / The parish of rich women, physical decay, / Yourself. Mad Ireland hurt you into poetry. / Now Ireland has her madness and her weather still, / *For poetry makes nothing happen*: it survives / In the valley of its making where executives / Would never want to tamper, flows on south / From ranches of isolation and the busy griefs, / Raw towns that we believe and die in; it survives, / A way of happening, a mouth" (emphasis added). Auden refutes the idea that "poetry makes nothing happen" later in the poem. In fact, poetry's effectiveness in bringing about change is stressed in the last verses: "Follow, poet, follow right / To the bottom of the night, / With your unconstraining voice / Still persuade us to rejoice. / With the farming of a verse / Make a vineyard of the curse, / Sing of human unsuccess / In a rapture of distress. / In the deserts of the heart / Let the healing fountains start, / In the prison of his days / Teach the free man how to praise."

66 Rushdie, *The Satanic Verses* (New York and London: Viking, 1989), p. 97.

67 Rushdie, *Haroun and the Sea of Stories* (London: Granta, 1991), p. 22.

68 Rushdie, 'Is Nothing Sacred?' in *Imaginary Homelands: Essays and Criticism, 1981-1991* (London: Granta, 1991), 415-29 (p. 420).

politicians, it will be one of history's great and most abject abdications."[69] Furthermore, in the 1997 essay "Notes on Writing and the Nation" he notes:

> In the aftermath of Empire, in the age of super-power, under the "footprint" of the partisan simplifications beamed down to us from satellites, we can no longer easily agree on *what is the case*, let alone what it might mean. Literature steps into this ring. Historians, media moguls, politicians do not care for the intruder, but the intruder is a stubborn sort. In this ambiguous atmosphere, upon this trampled earth, in these muddy waters, there is work for him to do.[70]

In an interview given in 2002 to Dave Weich, Rushdie confides that reading *Fury* has changed to the extent of becoming nostalgic after September 11. The author felt, while he was structuring the novel, "a sense of urgency about getting it down," as if he had been motivated by "some kind of prescience or foreknowledge" that the world would "change fast" (and in fact it would alter dramatically within a year from the time he finished writing it).[71] Referring to the "sense of infinite possibility" brought about by economic boom as a bubble that was inevitably "going to burst," Rushdie notes that even though he "didn't foresee calamity," he "did see that these moments in a city, or in a society, are usually pretty brief."[72] As the writer puts it, the novel is a response to the climate out of which 9/11 arose as well:

> [...] if I want to capture *this* moment, I better do it fast because any second now it isn't going to be here to capture. I think September 11 in a way underlined and dramatized that change [...]. I always thought the book, if I did it right, could at some later point— which we're already at, as it turns out—be a kind of evocation of an age. In the way, to be vain, that you look at the Jazz Age through Fitzgerald. [...] Sometimes literature is the way in which the past can really be captured and held, in such a way that we're able to enter it. I hoped the book would be that. I still hope the book will be that; it's just shocking how rapidly the future has arrived.[73]

Despite his intention that *Fury* might be truly evocative of a zeitgeist, upon the release of *The Enchantress of Florence* (2008), Rushdie argued in an interview at the City Arts & Lectures in San Francisco that so-called post-

---

69 Rushdie, 'Outside the Whale', in *Imaginary Homelands: Essays and Criticism, 1981-1991* (London: Granta, 1991), 87-101 (p. 100).

70 Rushdie, 'Notes on Writing and the Nation', pp. 66-67.

71 Dave Weich, 'Salman Rushdie, Out and About', *Powells.com*, 25 September 2002 <http://www.powells.com/authors/rushdie.html> [accessed 18 June 2007].

72 Ibid.

73 Ibid.

9/11 fiction–that has become a highly marketable commodity[74]–has yet to inaugurate new ways of representing aesthetically the attacks and their after-effects. Perhaps because one is too close to the events themselves, the writer feels that September 11 still needs to "return and be assimilated as art."[75] Thus, the traumatic events of that particular day, as well as their aftermath, have yet to be fundamentally rethought and significantly worked into the fabric of fiction and therefore affect cultural practice in a truly groundbreaking fashion. "Maybe another generation has to look at it from a greater distance," the writer argues, so that fresh ways of extracting meaning and rendering aesthetically this unique zeitgeist can be successfully forged.[76]

Like some post-9/11 literature, the novel *Shalimar the Clown* delves into the making of geopolitical strife, global terrorism, and Islamic militancy, and apparently fits into the conventional "clash of civilizations" plot line. Nonetheless, in initially upholding, yet ultimately undermining the "hyperdiscourse" that contributes to set up the dichotomy West/Islam,[77] Rushdie fashions a novel that subverts the reader's expectations–which influenced heavily the reception of the novel–of what a 9/11 literary text is/should be like. What at first appears to be the political assassination of the Jewish American Max Ophuls, head of US anti-terrorism operations, by the Muslim Kashmiri-born fundamentalist Shalimar–formerly a tightrope walker and, by a calculated turn of fate, Max's chauffeur–reveals itself in due course as passionately personal. Max is "America's best loved, then most scandalous Ambassador to India"[78] because he is romantically involved with Shalimar's wife Boonyi Kaul in Kashmir. Still, when India Ophuls, the illegitimate offspring of the ambassador's affair with Boony, discovers her father dead on her doorstep, assassinated by his Kashmiri chauffeur, she and the police suppose at once that the murder is terrorism-related and not the result of a personal quest for vengeance. Later on the police conclude that Max's death is not politically-motivated, even if Shalimar is indeed trained to be a terrorist:

74 September 11 is a central trope in several bestsellers, such as Ian McEwan's *Saturday* (2005), Jonathan Safran Foer's *Extremely Loud and Incredibly Close* (2005), Jay McInerney's *The Good Life* (2006), Ken Kalfus's *A Disorder Peculiar to the Country* (2006), John Updike's *Terrorist* (2006), and Don DeLillo's *Falling Man* (2007).

75 Quoted in Michael Krasny, 'A Conversation With Salman Rushdie', *FORA.tv*, 18 June 2008 < http://fora.tv/2008/06/18/A_Conversation_with_Salman_Rushdie> [accessed 28 May 2009], 10:43-12:50.

76 Ibid.

77 Armando Salvatore, 'The Problem of the Ingraining of Civilizing Traditions into Social Governance', in *Muslim Traditions and Modern Techniques of Power*, ed. by Armando Salvatore (Hamburg: LIT, 2001), 9-44 (p. 9).

78 Rushdie, *Shalimar the Clown*, p. 5.

> The crime, which had at first looked political, turned out to be a personal matter, insofar as anything was personal any more. The assassin was a professional, but the consequences of U.S. policy choices in South Asia, and their echoes in the labyrinthine chambers of the paranoiac jihadi mind, these and other related geopolitical variables receded from the analysis, could with a high percentage of probability be eliminated from the equation. The picture had simplified, becoming a familiar image: the cuckolded and now avenged husband, the disgraced and now very nearly decapitated philanderer, locked in a final embrace. The motive, too, turned out to be conventional. *Cherchez la femme.*[79]

Shalimar's quest is to take vengeance on Boonyi and Max. Siddiqi contends that Rushdie's depiction of *jihadist* violence in the novel is not apolitical but rather "a gendered politics of wounded masculinity."[80] According to this critic, the motif of dishonoured manhood attains political significance given that it is allegorical of the exploitative geopolitical effects of American neo-imperialism on the Indian subcontinent and Kashmir in particular. While Max stands for western economic and political influence, Shalimar personifies a kind of postcolonial grievance against such global power–he is "propelled by a rage against a US-dominated global order, which is responsible for the political and commercial seduction of Boonyi/India/Kashmir."[81] By the same token, Boonyi's later dependence on drugs and food, when Max takes her as his mistress after seducing her, degrade her body, making it in her own words hideous and monstrous,[82] which Siddiqi again reads allegorically as "globalized concubinage, one which destroys the national romance," that is, "as criticism of post-era liberalization, consumerism and cupidity: The East is seduced by the Western promise of limitless wares."[83] Alternatively, the narrative can be read as *purportedly* avoiding any causal engagement with the transformation of the title character Shalimar to *mujahideen*, while *ostensibly* failing to contextualize how American neo-imperialism and the current globalized Islamic terrorist movements (with their iron mullahs and fundamentalist messages) are both actors playing out their roles within the same scenario.[84] In this way, besides disconcerting some of the beliefs haunting post-9/11 debates about terrorism, *Shalimar the Clown* confronts the reader with her prejudgements about a post-fatwa, post-September 11 novel penned by an author notorious for his experience with Islamic fundamental-

---

79 Rushdie, *Shalimar the Clown*, p. 338.

80 Siddiqi, p. 303.

81 Ibid, p. 304.

82 Rushdie, *Shalimar the Clown*, p. 205.

83 Sidiqqi, p. 305.

84 Interestingly, Sidiqqi herself fears that such reading runs "the risk of being crude" (p. 304).

ism and also for his most recent fiery public statements, as a polemicist, after the 9/11 attacks and the 7/7 London underground bombings.

Concerns about Rushdie's political conflicting affiliations have at times implied that his work as (postcolonial) author should serve political goals. Understanding the writer's work as a "political event" accounts for the critics' stupefaction at Rushdie's perceived endorsement of the values of the western establishment. This tendency is manifest in Sabina and Simona Sawhney's foreword to the special issue of *Twentieth Century Literature* devoted to "Reading Rushdie after September 11, 2001." The editors' introduction discloses their bafflement in the face of the writer's "shift in [political] approach": "Part of the perplexity arises from a sudden onrush of doubt: did we misread the earlier texts, overlook the clues that would explain this surprising volte-face? Were those who had always dismissed Rushdie as another panderer to Western tastes for the colonial exotic right after all?"[85] As if aware of the "chronic ambivalence"[86] and "contradictory affiliations"[87] critics notice in Rushdie's current positioning, it seems that he is most recently defending a conceptual detachment between writing and political commitments. In this respect, Morton finds evidence in the 1999 novel *Fury* of the author's progressive "withdrawal from the political."[88] A recent interview, published in *The Times* to promote *The Enchantress of Florence*, reflects precisely this intended distancing. Although the writer is metonymically referred to as "walking political symbol," he is portrayed in the opening remarks of the interview as being, nearly twenty years after the fatwa, "tired of politics" and not willing "to talk about current affairs." As a forceful defender of the political responsibilities of the writer, he now presents himself as an unlikely proponent of an apolitical vision. He justifies his position in the following statements:

> I'm feeling less political than I used to […]. I've spent so much of my life talking about these issues which take on the times we live in very directly. I've had enough of that for a bit. […] I feel I have been damaged as a writer by the way people perceive my work *as part of a political event*. It is seen as a political entity rather than an artistic one. When *Midnight's Children* and *Shame* were published, people responded quite differently to my writing. Then there was a real shift in tone, when they said: 'Oh that was what he was really trying to do!' I am still a fiction writer underneath all that mess.[89]

85 Sawhney and Sawhney, p. 435.
86 Mondal, p. 174.
87 Boyagoda, p. 48.
88 Morton, p. 117.
89 Quoted in Muir, emphasis added.

During an interview, Rushdie confesses that the experience of the fatwa did not affect his writing, but had transformed "the kind of writer people thought [he] was";[90] in his own words, "[p]eople began to think of me as non-fictional. People asked me to comment on events, and for a while I fell into that trap. As if I were to become a rent-a-quote. So I decided I've got to go back to why I started writing in the first place." References to the fatwa during interviews, inevitable as they may be, provoke weariness in the writer, as worded in an interview with John Preston: "All I'm hoping is that I can say to people [on the 20th anniversary of the religious edict], 'Look, you've had 20 years of talking about this stuff, please can I have the rest of my life?' […] The whole thing has been an albatross around my neck in so many ways. […] All I want is to be seen as someone who writes books."[91] Not unrelatedly, the writer remarks in the lecture "Step Across This Line" that the transgressive qualities of his work–its unwavering "crossing of borders, of language, geography and culture" and its "lowering of the intolerable frontiers created by the world's many different kinds of thought policemen"–are part of "the literary project that was *given* to [him] by the circumstances of [his] life, *rather than chosen* by [him] for intellectual or 'artistic' reasons."[92]

Still, in "Outside the Whale" Rushdie argues that artists have an unavoidable political power, and therefore should make "as big a fuss, as noisy a complaint about the world as is humanly possible."[93] In this 1984 essay–whose title derives from George Orwell's "Inside the Whale" (1940)–he claims that "there can be no easy escapes from history, from hullabaloo, from terrible, unquiet fuss"[94] given that "we are all irradiated by history, we are radioactive with history and politics."[95] Arguing that "politically

90 Quoted in John Freeman, 'Hay Festival: Rushdie's Return to Magical Thinking', 26 May 2008 < http://blogs.guardian.co.uk/books/2008/05/hay_festival_rushdies_return_t.html> [accessed 17 November 2008]. In an earlier interview, the writer had already commented on the construction of "Rushdie" as public figure: "I think the worst damage that the fatwa did to me was […] [that] it gave people a very false sense of who I was and what my writing was like and what kind of reading experience it might be to open a book of mine. Attacks on my personality were also violent — and the great, famous thing about mud is that it sticks. Some of it did in some parts of the world, and I've been trying since to clean it off and to get people to see who's really here" (quoted in Vijaya Nagarajan, 'Salman Rushdie on Bombay, Rock N' Roll, and *The Satanic Verses*,' *Whole Earth Review*, Fall 1999, < http://wholeearth.com/issue/98/article/90/salman.rushdie.on.bombay.rock.n'.roll.and.the.satanic.verses> [accessed 14 May 2007]).

91 Preston.

92 Rushdie, 'Step Across This Line', p. 434, emphasis added.

93 Rushdie, 'Outside the Whale', p. 99.

94 Ibid., p. 101.

95 Ibid., p. 100.

committed art can actually prove more durable than messages from the stomach of the fish,"[96] he objects thus to Orwell's contention that the artist should recede into "the whale's belly," and concentrate on his or her own inner existence as subject matter.[97] If, as he notes in 2002, "[t]he journey creates us" and "[w]e become the frontiers we cross,"[98] what are we to make of this further tension of political multipositionality originating from one regarded by many as a cultural critic and, more relevant still, as a *political* writer? Frederic Jameson has famously elaborated on the significance of third world literature as national allegory. Third-world texts, he notes, "necessarily project a political dimension in the form of national allegory" in the way that "the story of the individual destiny is always an allegory of the embattled situation of the public third-world culture and society.[99] Notwithstanding the limitations of Jameson's theorizing, which have been extensively pointed out by Aijaz Ahmad and others, his argument might assist us in comprehending, at least in part, the phenomenon of reading Rushdie's work as political. Even if Rushdie has professed of late his detachment from politics, the persistent ambivalence of his standing remains and, to the reader's puzzlement, despite all the rationalisation he provides in the course of the interview given to Kate Muir from *The Times*, he does not altogether close the door on politics. "[N]ever say never," he states after a pause, and we can almost see him grinning.

---

[96] Ibid., p. 96.

[97] Ibid., 'Outside the Whale', p. 95.

[98] Rushdie, 'Step Across This Line', p. 410.

[99] Frederic Jameson, 'Third World Literature and National Allegory', *Social Text*, 15 (1986), pp. 69-88 (p. 69).

Bibliography

Armanet, François, and Gilles Anquetil, 'Mes Lumières', *Le Nouvel Observateur*, 21 December 2006 < http://hebdo.nouvelobs.com/p2198/articles/a327856.html> [accessed 20 August 2008]

Banerjee, Mita, 'Postethnicity and Postcommunism in Hanif Kureishi's *Gabriel's Gift* and Salman Rushdie's *Fury*', in *Reconstructing Hybridity: Post-Colonial Studies in Transition*, ed. by Joel Kuortti and Jopi Nyman (Amsterdam and New York: Rodopi, 2007), 309-24

Boyagoda, Randy, 'Postmodern Chutney', *First Things: A Monthly Journal of Religion and Public Life*, 1 February 2003, 47-49

Brennan. Timothy, *Wars of Position: The Cultural Politics of Left and Right* (New York: Columbia UP, 2006)

Dalmia, Shikha, 'The Iconoclast', *Reason*, August/September 2005 <http://www.reason.com/news/show/33120.html> [accessed 20 August 2008]

Freeman, John, 'Hay Festival: Rushdie's Return to Magical Thinking', 26 May 2008 < http://blogs.guardian.co.uk/books/2008/05/hay_festival_rushdies_return_t.html> [accessed 17 November 2008]

Gopal, Priyamvada, 'Sir Salman's Long Journey', *The Guardian*, 18 June 2007 <http://books.guardian.co.uk/comment/story/0,,2105445,00.html> [accessed 18 June 2007]

Gurnah, Abdulrazak, 'Introduction', in *The Cambridge Companion to Salman Rushdie*, ed. by Abdulrazak Gurnah (Cambridge: Cambridge University Press, 2007), 1-8

Hamid, Mohsin, *The Reluctant Fundamentalist* (Orlando: Harcourt, 2007)

Krasny, Michael, 'A Conversation With Salman Rushdie', *FORA.tv*, 18 June 2008 < http://fora.tv/2008/06/18/A_Conversation_with_Salman_Rushdie> [accessed 28 May 2009]

Jameson, Frederic, 'Third World Literature and National Allegory', *Social Text*, 15 (1986), 69-88

Manus, Willard, 'A Talk With Salman Rushdie', *Lively Arts*, November/December 2002 <http://www.lively-arts.com/books/2002/0211/salman_rushdie.htm> [accessed 18 June 2007]

Mitchell, W. J. T., *What Do Pictures Want?: The Lives and Loves of Images* (Chicago: University of Chicago Press, 2005)

Mondal, Anshuman A., '*The Ground Beneath Her Feet* and *Fury*: The Reinvention of Location', in *The Cambridge Companion to Salman Rushdie*, ed. by Abdulrazak Gurnah (Cambridge: Cambridge University Press, 2007), 169-183

Morton, Stephen, *Salman Rushdie: Fictions of Postcolonial Modernity* (Basingstoke and New York: Palgrave, 2008)

Muir, Kate, 'Exclusive Interview With Salman Rushdie', *The Times*, 4 April 2008, < <http://entertainment.timesonline.co.uk/tol/arts_and_entertainment/books/article3681048.ece> [accessed 4 April 2008]

Nagarajan, Vijaya, 'Salman Rushdie on Bombay, Rock N' Roll, and *The Satanic Verses*,' *Whole Earth Review*, Fall 1999 <http://wholeearth.com/issue/98/article/90/salman.rushdie.on.bombay.rock.n'.roll.and.the.satanic.verses> [accessed 14 May 2007]

Preston, John, 'Salman Rushdie: Provoking People Is In My DNA', *The Telegraph*, 29 December 2008 <http://www.telegraph.co.uk/culture/books/4015303/Salman-Rushdie-provoking-people-is-in-my-DNA.html> [accessed 29 December 2008]

Rushdie, Salman, 'Is Nothing Sacred?' in *Imaginary Homelands: Essays and Criticism, 1981-1991* (London: Granta, 1991), 415-29

---, 'Outside the Whale', in *Imaginary Homelands: Essays and Criticism, 1981-1991* (London: Granta, 1991), 87-101

---, *The Jaguar Smile: A Nicaraguan Journey* (London, Picador, 1987)

---, *The Satanic Verses* (New York and London: Viking, 1989)

---, *Haroun and the Sea of Stories* (London: Granta, 1991)

---, 'Introduction', in *The Vintage Book of Indian Writing: 1947-1997*, ed. by Salman Rushdie and Elizabeth West (London: Vintage, 1997), ix-xxii

---, *Fury* (London: Vintage, 2002)

---, 'Anti-Americanism', in *Step Across This Line: Collected Non-Fiction 1992-2002* (London: Vintage, 2003), 398-400

---, 'The Attacks on America', in *Step Across This Line: Collected Non-Fiction 1992-2002* (London: Vintage, 2003), 391-93

---, 'A Grand Coalition?', in *Step Across This Line: Collected Non-Fiction 1992-2002* (London: Vintage, 2003), 359-61

---, 'Globalization', in *Step Across This Line: Collected Non-Fiction 1992-2002* (London: Vintage, 2003), 296-98

---, 'Notes on Writing and the Nation', in *Step Across This Line: Collected Non-Fiction 1992-2002* (London: Vintage, 2003), 64-8

---, 'Step Across This Line', in *Step Across This Line: Collected Non-Fiction 1992-2002* (London: Vintage, 2003), 405-42

---, *Shalimar the Clown* (London: Jonathan Cape, 2005)

Said, Edward, *The World, the Text, and the Critic* (Cambridge, Massachusetts: Harvard University Press, 1983)

---, *Culture and Imperialism* (London: Vintage, 1993)

---, *Representations of the Intellectual: The 1993 Reith Lectures* (London: Vintage, 1994)

Salvatore, Armando, 'The Problem of the Ingraining of Civilizing Traditions into Social Governance', in *Muslim Traditions and Modern Techniques of Power*, ed. by Armando Salvatore (Hamburg: LIT, 2001), 9-44

Sawhney, Sabina, and Simona Sawhney, 'Reading Rushdie after September 11, 2001' *Twentieth Century Literature*, 47 (2001), 431-44

Siddiqi, Yumna, '"Power Smashes Into Private Lives": Violence, Globalization and Cosmopolitanism in Salman Rushdie's *Shalimar the Clown*', *South Asia Research*, 27 (2007), 293-309

Updike, John, 'Paradises Lost: Rushdie's *Shalimar the Clown*' *The New Yorker*, 5 September 2005, <http://www.newyorker.com/archive/2005/09/05/050905crbo_books?currentPage=all> [accessed 18 June 2007]

Webb, W. L., 'Salman Rushdie: *Satanic Verses*', in *Conversations With Salman Rushdie*, ed. by Michael R. Reder (Jackson: University of Mississippi Press, 2000), 87-100

Weich, Dave, 'Salman Rushdie, Out and About', *Powells.com*, 25 September 2002 <http://www.powells.com/authors/rushdie.html> [accessed 18 June 2007]

Sleepers, Informants, and the Everyday: Theorizing Terror and Ambiguity in Benjamin Heisenberg's *Schläfer*

Henrike Lehnguth

This paper analyzes how Benjamin Heisenberg's 2005 feature film debut *Schläfer* (translatable as *Sleeper* or *Sleepers*) theorizes terror. I argue that, in contrast to the majority of post-9/11 feature and documentary films that explore violence and terror and largely establish clear boundaries between terrorizer and terrorized, *Schläfer* describes terror not as an external threat but a force within the system itself. My article examines this film representation of terror as ambiguity at the crossroads of a post-9/11 fear of Islamist militant violence, police profiling of Arabs and Muslims, and state informant culture.

Since 2001, the attacks of September 11th, as well as the consequences of subsequent domestic and international policies for individuals and everyday life, have found their way into a range of feature and documentary films. These include American films staging the day itself such as Oliver Stone's *World Trade Center* (2006) to works on unlawful incarceration, extradition, and torture of Arabs and Muslims such as Gavin Hood's *Rendition* (2007), film explorations of the roots of terrorism such as Joseph Castelo's *The War Within* (2005), and more broadly conceived pieces on the culture of fear as David Fincher's *Panic Room* (2002) and vigilantism as Neil Jordan's *The Brave One* (2007).[1] In their exploration of violence and terror, these films have largely established clear boundaries between terrorizer and terrorized. They cast terror as external to what defines the United States as a system so that even a film like *Rendition*, which pictures the US government-sanctioned kidnapping of a permanent resident of Arab descent to a secret prison in Egypt for torture, contains terror in a few "bad apples" who are defeated through the civic courage of one American CIA officer.

This paper focuses on Benjamin Heisenberg's 2005 feature film debut *Schläfer* (translatable as *Sleeper* or *Sleepers*), which differs from these dicho-

---

1 The link between film representations and the September attacks in films that address more broadly conceived issues such as the culture of fear and vigilantism is, for instance, explored by Jonathan Markovitz in 'Reel Terror Post 9/11', in *Film and Television After 9/11*, ed. by Wheeler Winston Dixon (Carbondale: Southern Illinois University Press, 2004), 201-225. See also Biana Nielsen, 'Home Invasion and Hollywood Cinema: David Fincher's *Panic Room*', in *The Selling of 9/11: How a National Tragedy Became a Commodity*, ed. by Dana Heller (New York, NY: Palgrave Macmillan, 2005), 233-253. And lastly, see David Halbfinger, 'Unease in the Air and Revenge on the Screen', *The New York Times*, August 26, 2007 (late edition), 13.

tomous and individualized frameworks by consistently pointing to the ambiguous qualities of terror.[2] The film, which was part of the 2005 official film selection at the Cannes Film Festival under the category "Un Certain Regard," represents terror with the paradox that it encapsulates as a concept that refers as much to the anxiety felt as to the anxiety induced.[3] Even if we understand terror as intense fear only, this fear rests on ambiguity. Terror, in this definition, is founded on an *anticipation* of pain in the widest and most personal sense of what constitutes pain, an anticipation that is arbitrary and unpredictable as to when and how pain may or may not be inflicted.

Schläfer explores the link between terror and ambiguity at the crossroads of a post-9/11 fear of Islamist militant violence, police profiling of Arabs and Muslims, and state informant culture. The film, as I argue in this paper, positions terror not as an external threat but a force within the system itself that viewers are implicated in. In what follows I will first provide background to policing and security practices in post-9/11 Germany, where *Schläfer* takes place. I will then illustrate how the film deploys ambiguity in order to construct one of its lead characters, Farid Madani, a scientist of Algerian descent (played by Mehdi Nebbou), as a *potential* Islamist militant. The film here mobilizes viewers' assumptions about Arabs and Muslims as a possible threat to expose these assumptions as complicit with questionable and oppressive state security measures. I thereafter analyze in depth these state measures that monitor diverse facets of everyday life in order to illustrate that terror as a force internal to the system is ultimately located in state security practices that dissolve legal distinctions between public and private realms with impunity.

While *Schläfer's* understanding of terror as an ambiguous and internal force is translatable to other national and transnational arenas, including the United States, the film situates the September 11, 200, attacks and their aftermath within a specifically German context. The Federal Government of Germany, with Chancellor Gerhard Schröder, as spokesperson was quick to frame the event "not only as an attack against the United States of America [but] a declaration of war against the entire civilized world" that Germany sees itself a part of.[4] The attacks resonated with Germans all the more after it became known that key al-Qaeda operatives, including the three hijacker-

---

2 *Schläfer*, dir. by Benjamin Heisenberg, on DVD (juicy film, 2005).

3 The *Merriam-Webster Online* dictionary defines terror as "a state of intense fear" as well as "one that inspires fear" and "violent and destructive acts." Available at http://www.merriam-webster.com/dictionary/terror [accessed October 22, 2008].

4 My translation. See Hendrik Meyer, *Terror und Innere Sicherheit: Wander und Kontinuität staatlicher Terrorismusbekämpfung* (Münster: Schüling Verlag 2006), p. 49.

pilots Mohammed Atta, Marwan al-Shehhi, and Ziad Jarrah and middleman Ramzi Binalshibh had resided and studied in Hamburg, Germany. In response to the attacks and efforts to apprehend 9/11 conspirators, Germany's Federal Government passed Security Packet I and II, which allowed for greater state intrusion into the privacy of citizens and residents. Measures reintroduced police profiling practices, which had been controversially deployed against leftist militants and sympathizers in the 1970s and 1980s, and eased legal restrictions on the deportations of unwanted and suspect non-citizens.[5] Police profiling as it has been practiced against militants in Germany works initially with a large pool of persons of interest that share certain characteristics and then reduces the pool step by step by introducing more and more variables that are said to define members of the suspect group in question. One such variable is monetary transfer, where cash rental and utilities payments are deemed suspect because of their elusiveness to monitoring practices. The example of monetary transfer illustrates that the "grid search" (*Rasterfahndung*), as the profiling is referred to in German, penalizes individuals who defy traceability but have, when they pay cash, not broken the law or conspire to do so. With variables such as "country of origin with predominantly Muslim population," "Muslim" and "male," which, based on the profiles of the 9/11 conspirators, were used in post-9/11 counter-terrorism efforts in Germany, this police practice randomly criminalizes persons on the grounds of their identity and faith, antagonizes minority communities in Germany, and breaches legal prohibitions by the European Union against discrimination. Between 2001 and 2003 the German state utilized these variables to collect electronic data of approximately over eight million people.[6]

The grid profiling practices point to how the political climate after 9/11 has made greater state intrusion politically feasible. While privacy laws are still under greater constitutional protection in Germany than in several other industrialized countries, including the United States, privacy rights continue to be under attack. After a legal complaint was filed with the German Su-

---

5 See Meyer. Also see publication by the German Ministry of Interior, 'Nach dem 11. September 2001' <http://www.bmi.bund.de/Internet/Content/Common/Anlagen/Broschueren/2004/Nach__dem__11__September__2001__Massnahmen__Id__25583__de,templateId=raw,property=publicationFile.pdf/Nach_dem_11_September_2001_Massnahmen_Id_25583_de.pdf> [accessed 22 October 2008].

6 For this and more on the grid search, its legality, and effectiveness, in a European context, see paper by James Goldston, Executive Director of the Open Society Justice Initiative, 'Ethnic Profiling and Counter-Terrorism Trends, Dangers, and Alternatives,' in *Anti-Racism and Diversity Intergroup, European Parliament*, Brussels, 6 June 2006 <http://www.soros.org/initiatives/osji/articles_publications/articles/counterterrorism_20060606/goldston_20060606.pdf> [accessed 3 December 2008].

preme Court against the most recent post-9/11 legislative act, the so-called BKA-law, which took effect on January 1, 2009, may be short-lived. The law increases the capacities of Germany's *Bundeskriminalamt* (German Federal Police Office) and lifts some of the previous restrictions on surveillance of private phone calls and computer data in criminal investigations.[7] Critics have charged that the law legalizes the surveillance without concrete grounds, a practice that *Schläfer* effectively problematizes.

In Heisenberg's film the consequences of security policies for the private arena are presented in interplay with the threat of a terrorist strike and terrorist affiliations that are implicit in the film title and premise of the film's opening scene. The title *Schläfer* is translatable as sleeper or sleepers, a term for yet undetected Islamist militants. The title instills a frame of fear and suspicion against characters and their actions in its reference to religious and political radicalism. Sleepers, still dormant in conspiratorial cells, wait, as we may assume from the title, for their moment to strike. What we come to know in the film we thus observe a priori through a prism of paranoia and distrust against Muslims. The film thereby establishes preset structures that mark the parameters of our ability to know the characters and situations.

Schläfer opens with a scene in a park, where Ms. Wasser of the German secret service works on persuading scientist Johannes Merveldt (played by Bastian Trost) to become a state informant and report on his still-to-be-colleague of Arab origin Farid Madani. Their conversation in what is clearly a first encounter between the two unfolds as follows:

> Johannes: Why do you observe him [Madani]?
> Wasser: Uh, let's not discuss this now, otherwise you'll be biased.
> Johannes: I already am.
> Wasser: No, no, no. The person can very well be completely harmless. And if you consider him so, convince us. [8]

Johannes asks Wasser for concrete answers to why the secret service is interested in Farid. Wasser, however, remains purposefully ambiguous about the agency's investigation. By not addressing concrete motifs for why Farid is observed under the premise that Johannes would be prejudiced, she constructs any practice, belief, and interest Farid holds as potential national security threat, only to clarify that these practices, beliefs, and interests may after

7 See Michael Naumann, 'Jeder ist verdächtig', *Die Zeit*, 23 April 2009 <http://www.zeit.de/2009/18/BKA-Gesetz> [accessed 17 May 2009]. Also see Heribert Prantl, 'Gegen den Sicherheitsstaat,' *Die Süddeutsche Zeitung*, 23 April 2009 <http://www.sueddeutsche.de/politik/454/466039/text/> [accessed 17 May 2009].

8 I translated all *Schläfer* film quotes from German into English.

all be completely harmless. She, in other words, implies that Farid's entire life world must be scrutinized although neither Johannes nor the viewer know what to specifically look for. If this moment constructs Farid as suspicious, what constitutes his suspiciousness rests entirely on Johannes' and the viewer's unanchored preconceptions about and prejudice against Farid's identity as a single male Arab and Muslim scientist in Germany.

As viewers, we are set up to evaluate Farid's every action as those of a potential "sleeper," without knowing *what* constitutes relevant information. Alongside Johannes we are given clues that ambiguously speak for *and* against Farid *at the same time.* In one scene the camera rests on Farid's face as he destroys his colleagues or rather their avatars in the virtual war zone of the *Vietcong* computer game. Farid later explains to Johannes over a glass of wine at a restaurant that "*Vietcong* is no ego shooter. It's a strategic game. The strategy determines [the outcome]. It is like urban warfare." To emphasize his point about the strategic nature of the game, Farid draws a game plan onto a napkin. We may wonder why Farid is so serious about a game – *Vietcong* – that has clear anti-American and anti-capitalist overtones and ask ourselves how informed he is about urban warfare and to what end. At the same time, however, his colleagues clearly share his passion for *Vietcong* or they would not be playing with him in the first place. In the conversation with Johannes, Farid is completely open about how *Vietcong* – a possible simulation of actual urban warfare – is best won. His openness assuages the viewer's initial suspicion aroused about him. In the meantime both Johannes and Farid enjoy an alcoholic drink; we may read Farid's beverage choice as an embrace of secularism, a signal against his potential involvement with a militant Islamist group. And then again, what does the consumption of alcohol really signify, if there is evidence that at least one of the key September 11 conspirators, long after his radicalization and his trip to a training camp in Afghanistan, enjoyed his occasional beer with peers at the aviation school in Florida?[9] Viewers, in short, observe and assess Farid's ideas and actions with the knowledge that the secret service is seeking information on him. Individually taken, all of his ideas and actions are ambiguous in that they offer no interpretative certainty about Farid's character and intentions. Taken together, they likewise do not form any cohesive image of Farid as a threat. The opening scene as much as the film title *Schläfer* (*Sleeper* or *Sleepers*), however, make impending violence likely, even while it is uncertain when, how,

---

9 I am referring to the hijacker-pilot of United Airlines flight 93, Ziad Jarrah, who, according to his flight instructor in Florida, Arne Kruithof, drank alcohol in moderation. See Jere Longman, *Among the Heroes: United Flight 93 and the Passengers and Crew Who Fought Back* (New York, NY: HarperCollins, 2002), p. 92.

and why this may occur. Cast as a potential suspect, Farid thus at first adds to the film's overall terror that the ambiguous clues, which speak to nothing concrete, feed.

The terror of terrorism with its inherent reliance on ambiguity, as these film moments assert, has no system or profile that we as viewers can rely on. Alongside other critical voices, the film thereby exposes the premise of a stable terrorist profile as shortsighted. While these limits coincide less with efforts of German authorities to expand police profiling to all European Union members, despite the fact that the grid search has produced no results in the fight against terrorism, they match current critical surveillance theories. Kristie Ball, for instance, specifies four elements relevant to thinking about surveillance, including "re-presentation," "meaning," "manipulation," and "intermediary," all of which address the inherent data dependence on context. She illustrates how different cultural and historical frameworks that investigators bring to the data – and intelligence like all information needs to be interpreted – shape the results as much as the particularities and limits of specific technologies that produce the data in the first place.[10] This ambiguity of data paired with an acknowledgement that surveilling practices have become omnipresent has shifted the focus of surveillance scholars to issues of governmentality, issues that pay particular attention to how states and institutions produce, interpret, and use information to administer and regulate people, objects, and ideas.[11]

It is this link between surveillance and governmentality that Heisenberg's *Schläfer* is concerned with, when it ultimately identifies state practices involving the monitoring and profiling of people as a form of terror and a greater menace to personal well-being than terrorist activities committed by non-state actors. The film alludes to the state's problematic intrusiveness into the privacy of citizens and residents first in the park scene, where Wasser and Johannes meet. The film opens, in fact, with a shot inside the park – focused on trees and grass and then on a girl playing ball. This glimpse onto nothing and no one in particular captures the idea of the everyday as banal, which is enhanced by the screaming voices of playing children, who are in the park

---

10 See Kristie Ball, 'Organization, Surveillance and the Body: Towards a Politics of Resistance', in *Theorizing Surveillance: The Panopticon and Beyond*, ed. by David Lyon (Cullompton, Devon, UK: Culmcott House, 2006), 296-317 (pp. 300-301).

11 The issue of governmentality that Michel Foucault addresses in his later work is, for instance, for surveillance studies highlighted by Kevin Haggerty in 'Tear Down the Walls: On Demolishing the Panopticon', in *Theorizing Surveillance: The Panopticon and Beyond*, ed. by David Lyon (Cullompton, Devon, UK: Culmcott House, 2006) 23-45.

but not part of what we see in the frame. The sound of children as a background noise continues even after Johannes and Wasser enter the frame and walk close enough to the camera (the viewer's perspective) that we can overhear their conversation. The choice of the public park as initial meeting spot highlights the private and leisurely lives of people, who are potentially endangered by a terrorism that does not distinguish between the civilian and military wings of a given society. The park as meeting spot, however, also points to the state's entanglement with its citizens' most private matters. The state, as embodied by Wasser, is present at banal and clearly harmless activities like children at play and is, as we later see, thoroughly informed about its people's private engagements.

The park scene alone already hints at the significance of the everyday to the film's exploration of terror. That the everyday and private arena are key to *Schläfer*'s framework of terror is, however, not only emphasized through the choice of mundane public spaces like the park but also highlighted through consistent representations of routines in a number of recurrent settings, which include, among others, a gym, the laboratory that Johannes and Farid work in, and a go-cart race track. The scene where Farid plays *Vietcong* with his colleagues, which I described above, is such a scene that is matched with others, including some, where Johannes plays computer games alone at home. His preference for virtual car races that are not group efforts but solitary pleasures characterize Johannes, in juxtaposition to Farid, as an ambitious loner with an eye on the fast lane to success. Computer gaming, however, serves not only as a reference point for a comparison of Johannes' and Farid's characters. It also illustrates how terror rests not necessarily in extraordinary moments alone but lurks within the structure of the everyday. In the scene described above, Farid outdoes his colleagues in *Vietcong.* In a later episode he once again fights his colleagues in the *Vietcong* virtual war zone. During a break, his computer, on which he saved the game and valuable research, disappears from his station while four of his colleagues are present in the room. The disappearance of Farid's computer occurs in the space that, as we know from the earlier gaming scene, Farid frequents when he is at work. His colleagues react to the vanished computer with such calm that what appears to be a theft could be a prank. This possibility of a prank is dispelled when, later in the film, Farid tells Johannes that he has become subject to the grid search profiling. Farid then comments that "what happened with my computer was also no coincidence." The circumstances surrounding the computer's disappearance are initially as ambiguous as Farid's beliefs and practices, upon which Wasser casts suspicion in the opening scene. As the film progresses, the stolen computer emerges as the target of one of the many questionable strategies that the state employs in its fight for stability and security. These strategies include, in this case, theft, since the authorities do not properly identify themselves as they are required to do. A state that transgresses its own binding laws and secures "evidence" without legitimacy and criminal charges spreads terror. Terror, as these scenes set in recurrent habitual spaces point to, is not necessarily defined by spectacle. Instead, it resides in the *sum* of small acts such as the computer's disappearance that *together* make it a persistent force to be reckoned with. The theft of the computer, in other words, does not terrify as a singular act but as a pattern that points to a recurrent transgression of the law that protects the rights of citizens and residents.

Implicit in Farid's statement that his computer's disappearance "was no coincidence" is that, while he strongly suspects the police as culprits, he lacks concrete proof. The film, in other words, makes it clear *that* the state knows about its citizens and residents but is unclear about what actions are state-sponsored. *What* the state knows for *what* purpose thereby remains ambiguous. It is this ambiguity about state power, in turn, that induces terror. The state's purposeful ambiguity is a dynamic that the film further highlights in a scene where Johannes and Wasser meet for a second time. Johannes here angrily confronts Wasser with a stack of letters in hand and notes that these were unlawfully opened. Wasser denies her agency's involvement stating: "We get your phone bills directly from the *Telekom* [a phone company], Mr. Merveldt. This was the post office or someone else, as obvious as this was done." Since Johannes first suspects his grandmother's caretaker to be the one opening the letters and only later the state, it remains unclear who in the end committed the transgression and for what purpose. Johannes' letters are ripped open, which Wasser does not view as befitting state practices. She thereby implies that the state leaves no traces when monitoring persons of interest. The comment suggests that even if the state did not open Johannes' letters, he may still be observed. And the state could likewise have opened his letters, not to investigate Johannes, but to make its presence known. The answer to the question of who opened his letters is lastly irrelevant to the question of whether the state observes him, just as Farid's choices and actions *simultaneously* speak for and against him as a threat. The social space that Johannes and others inhabit is, as this scene illustrates, to a degree structured through what Michel Foucault describes as panopticism, where the public performance of individuals is disciplined by the awareness that one *could* be under (state) scrutiny, even when that is not the case.[12]

This framework of constant potential (state) surveillance points to ongoing and widespread data accumulation. Close to the end of the film Farid tells Johannes that he has become subject to police interrogation, not because he committed any legal transgressions but because he fits the sleeper profile created by the state that pre-marks him as guilty. He describes how the secret service has contacted people from all walks of his life, including Professor Behringer, who oversees the laboratory they work in. Farid mentions, "They have all kinds of documents about me, old passports, students IDs; they know everything about my parents, where I studied; they even called my ex-girlfriends and Behringer." Disperse data, as Farid's comment suggests, is compiled into a cohesive whole, a "surveillant assemblage," as sociologists Kevin Haggerty and Richard Ericson refer to it, that, under the premise of the sleeper profile, serves to confirm that Farid is a threat.[13] Data is not only assembled on Farid alone but on seemingly all persons in contact with him, including informants. When Johannes confronts Wasser about the opened letters in the incident that I just mentioned, she retorts "You were in his apartment, right?" Their exchange paired with the letter incident as such demonstrates how Johannes' own life, entangled with Farid's, has come under scrutiny and similarly subject to interpretation. Once a person of interest to the state – as suspect, informant or otherwise – Johannes is, as the film suggests, like Farid, no longer protected by privacy laws.

Wasser tells Johannes in a later encounter that the secret service "requires simply the truth." With her emphasis on "simply" and "truth" she implies that intelligence is straightforward, measurable, and objective, a notion that the film itself and surveillance theories debunk. The film highlights the unstable and subjective qualities of information through Johannes, who, in spite of his initial refusal to cooperate with the state, turns informant after Farid outdoes him romantically. Both initially compete over the affection of Beate, a woman they meet in a restaurant. Throughout the film Beate is instrumental to

---

12 See Michel Foucault, 'Truth and Power' and 'Panopticism' in *The Foucault Reader*, ed. by Paul Rabinow (New York, NY: Pantheon Books, 1984) 51-75 and 206-213. With this paper I am not proposing that one particular surveillance model such as panopticism explains all dynamics of the film or surveillance as such. As Haggerty (see above) outlines in his article, panopticism as a model comes with serious limitations, one of which is theorizing surveillance in an age of technologies like databases, webcams, etc. My paper therefore draws from different models to best address how state control, intelligence-gathering, and terror are imagined in Heisenberg's film.

13 See Kevin D. Haggerty and Richard V. Ericson, 'The Surveillant Assemblage', *British Journal of Sociology*, 51 (2000), 605-622.

Johannes and Farid's ability to relate to each other. Once the friendship between Beate, Johannes, and Farid is off-balance, when Farid and Beate become involved, despite Johannes' own romantic aspirations, Johannes consents to work as a state informant. Johannes' sudden willingness to inform therefore suggests that potentially incriminating intelligence is produced by and filtered through the informants' rather subjective rationales and desires. When Johannes reports intelligence, he, in fact, not only interprets Farid's life but actively constructs a reality that best fits with his (Johannes') own longings. On one occasion, he, for instance, answers Wasser's question whether Farid and Beate's romance is serious with a curt "no," which does not correspond to their lovestruck interaction in the two scenes that directly precede Johannes and Wasser's conversation.

It is significant that Wasser's question about Beate and Farid's relationship is directly preceded by her disclosure that Beate's last sexual partner was from Iran. This rhetorical move establishes a link between the Iranian ex and Farid not only as persons of interest to the state in the post-9/11 cultural climate of sleeper profiles, but as a "type" of man Beate is interested in. It subtly draws on an Orientalist legacy that makes the notion of Iranians and Algerians as being of similar backgrounds possible in the first place. In the light of Beate's sexual past, Wasser, who is, as we can assume, thoroughly informed about Johannes, seems to thereby purposefully suggest that Beate's relationship with Farid may flourish. She, in other words, implicitly hints at how Johannes' heterosexuality and by extension masculinity "failed" vis-à-vis Farid's, who, after all, may be a threat to the nation-state, while Johannes is idly standing by. The notion of failure is unacceptable to someone like Johannes, whose interest in virtual car races characterize him, as I already mentioned, throughout the film as distinctly competitive in juxtaposition to Farid, whose virtual war games, as Farid himself points out, depend on not losing sight of fellow players in his team. By capitalizing on Johannes' desires, Wasser's rhetorical strategy thereby aligns Johannes' personal incentives closely with the state's surveillance objectives.

Schläfer, in fact, visually imagines this alignment or transfer of subjective "truths" into "official" state reality. By the moment that Johannes dismisses Farid's and Beate's relationship with his "no," the camera has moved so far down his body that his head is no longer part of the frame. Johannes is headless and thereby becomes visually someone who is missing his central organ to think things through. The missing head as the body's most distinguishing marker de-individualizes him. Headless, he is just a cipher within the state intelligence machine. Disconnected from Johannes' head and by extension his individuality, his "no" to Beate and Farid's relationship becomes abstracted and part of the intelligence machine. It is Johannes' subjective desire, emplotted in his "no," that turns into an "official" state reality that is grounded on the state's implicit goal to unmask Farid as the sleeper it wants him to be.

It should be noted at this point that *Schläfer* presents a somewhat traditional image of state surveillance. While Farid mentions the grid search, which strongly relies on computer database searches, technology is largely absent from the policing practices that are represented in the film. This particular strategy, on one hand, amplifies ambiguities about state power, when viewers are left in the dark about the state's technological capabilities. The film thereby shifts the attention away from the mechanics to the ethics and human cost of surveillance that implicate us all. On the other hand, the absence of technology in policing maybe outdated, as criminologist Maria Los illustrates, when she outlines the transition from the surveillance "file" to the "data double" of the information age. While the data double is compiled through an integration of the data traces that we now rampantly leave with credit card records, among many other electronic data bits, the file evokes the centralization of information, all housed in one material place, such as was common in the surveillance culture of the Eastern bloc. The ways in which *Schläfer* relies exclusively on informants and not on technology to present state surveillance, in other words, clearly draws from impressions of East Germany's recent past, especially its state security apparatus, where having a file was rampant.[14]

While the electronic traces that we leave point to how surveillance has become widespread but dispersed and remind us that the state is far from the only stakeholder in the accumulation and management of data, the information flow was never unidirectional, even under the premise of the "file." As *Schläfer* director Benjamin Heisenberg notes, the *exchange* of information constitutes a critical appeal for recruits like Johannes to become informants.[15]

---

14 In October 1989, the East German *Staatssicherheitsdienst* (state security service) had 91,000 full-time employees for a population of 16.4 million people. It is estimated that they additionally employed about 600,000 "unofficial collaborators" in the course of the German Democratic Republic's history. In comparison, under the Nazi regime, about 45,000 people were employed with the *Geheime Staatspolizei* (secret state police), while the population of the "German Empire" during the 1930s ranged between 60 and 80 million (this range is due to annexations of territories in 1938 and 1939). For Maria Los's exploration of the "file" and the "data double," see 'Looking Into the Future: Surveillance, Globalization and the Totalitarian Potential', in *Theorizing Surveillance: The Panopticon and Beyond*, ed. by David Lyon (Cullompton, Devon, UK: Culmcott House, 2006), 69-94.

15 Ulrich Kriest, 'Beobachtungspuzzle: Benjamin Heisenberg über Schläfer', *FilmDienst*, September (2006), 14-15.

In exchange for his cooperation with the secret service, Johannes gathers, as I earlier hinted at, insights on Beate. He learns from Wasser that Beate's mother died of cancer, that she (Beate) was in therapy and previously dated a man from Iran. The disclosure of Beate's personal details points once again, like the theft of Farid's computer, to the state's more general careless and casual oversight of the laws that regulate it in the first place. Once these laws are breached the nation-state executes its monopoly on violence without the regulatory system that serves to protect citizens and residents from the arbitrary and unlawful enforcement of power. The illegal disclosure of information sustains the disciplining power that Foucault attributes to panopticism, when people must fear that personal choices are not only recorded but revealed to others at will. Disclosure of personal information, in other words, ultimately inhibits free exchange between people and nourishes a culture of fear that no longer corresponds to the democratic ideals that the state is nominally based on. This prospect of an intrusive state power without checks and balances, and instable, malleable intelligence is therefore, indeed, terrible and terrifying.

This brings me back to ambiguity which in its very definition defies clear categories of meaning. As the state transgresses the laws that regulate it, ambiguity works purposefully in line with unrestricted state power. This is most disturbingly put in a scene close to the end of the film, after Johannes has witnessed Farid's arrest in the empty and dark entrance area outside of his [Farid's] apartment building. Johannes, who spent the evening of a bomb attack in Munich with Farid, holds the key to Farid's alibi. The film is hereby explicit about Farid's non-involvement in the bombing. Following Farid's arrest, Wasser visits Johannes at his home to verify the alibi. By this point in the film Johannes has quit informing for the secret service after his advances to Beate (momentarily) appeared to gain ground.

> Wasser: Your friend says that you were in the night club at 2 a.m. on the night of the 25th to the 26th. But, no one remembers you there.
> Johannes: Why do you suspect him? [pause]
> Wasser: Now, were you with him in the night club or not? Mr. Merveldt, I depend on you. I understand that you want to protect him. [pause] Well, if you continue to remain silent, I'll take that as a no. [pause] Well. [pause] Goodbye, Mr. Merveldt.

In this crucial scene, Johannes betrays Farid with his silence. Silence neither affirms nor contests but defies the certainty of words. Johannes' silence is not accompanied by any gesture. His features are hardly visible as he disappears in the shade of the unlit room. He literally sinks into a darkness that figuratively speaks to his ethical shortcomings. I discussed earlier how Wasser maintains that the secret service leaves no traces. In this scene of betrayal, Johannes' disappearance into the shade furthermore speaks to this traceless state surveillance. His invisibility, paired with his silence, transforms him into the undetectable but disciplining presence that Foucault's idea of panopticism evokes. Akin to the scene where Johannes "loses" his head, here he once again blends in with the dehumanized intelligence apparatus that invades all private space in the name of security and thereby actively contributes to the terror Farid faces.

Although Farid clearly endures the most severe consequences of state surveillance, he is not alone in being affected by the terror-inducing practices. With the scene of betrayal, *Schläfer*, instead, demonstrates a more general state encroachment on the privacy and everyday lives of citizens and residents. If the state is, like Wasser, present at mundane everyday activities in the opening park scene, its practices and ways of knowing have literally invaded Johannes' most private and secluded space by the end of the film – namely his home that even his friends never get to see. The film thereby evolves from more communal and carefree visions of the state in the public sun-lit park to the "heart of darkness" of surveillance in Johannes' unlit domestic space. It slowly transitions from the opening scene, where Johannes has a voice with multi-layered opinions, to one where he is voiceless and his silence subject to Wasser's interpretation. While Johannes feeds this culture of terror as a state informant, he is also himself terrified by the mechanisms that take increasing control of his own private arrangements. Even prior to the scene of betrayal, he, on one occasion, turns nervously around in a parking garage, stops, and lets a suspected pursuer pass him. This moment indicates that towards the end of *Schläfer*, Johannes believes he is being tailed and is nervous, if not outright fearful, about this very prospect. The development of Johannes as a character illustrates how the conceptual boundaries between practices that terrorize others and terrify oneself ambiguously blur. These practices coincide with the state's increasing control of domestic space beyond the shared public arena.

The film passages that I have referenced demonstrate how *Schläfer* identifies terror above all in state practices that pervade the entire social fabric and individuals' everyday lives. It is banal actions and average people that contribute to terror as a paradigm that structures social relationships and everyday routines. The film's vision of terror as a force *within* the system emphasizes the ethical responsibilities each one of us shoulders vis-à-vis a politics of terror, paranoia, and fear that shape post-9/11 interactions. This ethical imperative resonates with earlier films from the New German Cinema of the late 1960s/70s and early 1980s that put social violence, state terror, and terrorism committed by non-state actors into perspective. In Volker Schlöndorff and Margarethe von Trotta's *Die Verlorene Ehre der Katharina Blum* (*The Lost Honor of Katharina Blum* – 1975) the state as represented through police detectives cooperates with the press in a smear campaign against Katharina, a woman they *suspect* to be a sympathizer of leftist terrorism. The powerlessness Katharina experiences in the face of state power mirrors Farid's inability to stop the forces that are in place to find him guilty. The ways in which Farid's everyday routines and choices take on new meaning through the sleeper prism resonates with how the state and press paint Katharina as terrorist sympathizer by willfully interpreting her alleged sexual practices as an indication of her questionable character. Rainer Werner Fassbinder's *Katzelmacher* (1969) highlights how social control is exercised through gossip and social expectations. It is these informal mechanisms that the state mobilizes in *Schläfer*, for instance, when Wasser willingly shares information – "gossip" – about Beate with Johannes. Wasser's personable Bavarian accent defines her relationship with Johannes by default in the somewhat informal terms that gossip is a part of.

In conclusion, I would like to therefore emphasize that *Schläfer* modifies the skepticism about state power voiced by the New German Cinema for a post-9/11 framework, where the relationship of terror and ambiguity oftentimes problematically draws from contemporary discourses on immigration, the social integration of migrants, and Islam. In the light of the range of films that mobilize simplistic theories of terror *Schläfer's* more complex perspective is instructive in that it reminds us of what stakes are involved when a politics of security overshadows fundamental ethics. This brings me back to the controversial legislative act that I alluded to in the beginning of my paper: the law that increases the capacities of the *Bundeskriminalamt* (German Federal Police Office) in Germany. The Minister of Interior Wolfgang Schäuble, who advocates the law, snidely dismissed any concerns about the law as "all that chatter about the surveillance state." Journalist Kai Biermann warns in a recent commentary that a law that does not define terrorism and enables the police to observe persons of interest for up to three days without any court's knowledge is just that: testimony to a surveillance state. He criticizes those who believe that "[n]othing will happen to me, when I am scrutinized; I have after all nothing to hide." And from Heisenberg's *Schläfer* we know that Biermann's concerns are not just "chatter" but well warranted.[16]

---

[16] For Wolfgang Schäuble and Kai Biermann, see Biermann's commentary 'Schäubles Betafehler,' *Die Zeit*, 3 December 2008 <http://www.zeit.de/online/2008/49/bka-gesetz-kommentar> [accessed 10 December 2008]. My translation.

Bibliography

Ball, Kristie, 'Organization, Surveillance and the Body: Towards a Politics of Resistance', in *Theorizing Surveillance: The Panopticon and Beyond*, ed. by David Lyon (Cullompton, Devon, UK: Culmcott House, 2006), 296-317

Biermann, Kai, 'Schäubles Betafehler', *Die Zeit*, 3 December 2008 <http://www.zeit.de/online/2008/49/bka-gesetz-kommentar> [accessed 10 December 2008]

Foucault, Michel, *The Foucault Reader*, ed. by Paul Rabinow (New York, NY: Pantheon Books, 1984)

German Ministry of Interior, 'Nach dem 11. September 2001: Maßnahmen gegen den Terror: Dokumentation aus dem Bundesministerium des Innern', 27 June 2004 <http://www.bmi.bund.de/cae/servlet/ contentblob/139934/publicationFile/15200/Nach_dem_11_September_2001_Massnahmen_Id_95066_de.pdf> [accessed 22 October 2008]

Goldston, James, 'Ethnic Profiling and Counter-Terrorism Trends, Dangers, and Alternatives', Brussels, 6 June 2006 <http://www.soros.org/ initiatives/osji/articles_publications/articles/counterterrorism_20060606/goldston_20060606.pdf> [accessed 3 December 2008]

Haggerty, Kevin, 'Tear Down the Walls: On Demolishing the Panopticon', in *Theorizing Surveillance: The Panopticon and Beyond*, ed. by David Lyon (Cullompton, Devon, UK: Culmcott House, 2006), 23-45

Haggerty, Kevin D. and Richard V. Ericson, 'The Surveillant Assemblage', *British Journal of Sociology*, 51 (2000), 605-622

Halbfinger, David, 'Unease in the Air and Revenge on the Screen', *The New York Times*, August 26, 2007 (late edition), 13

Kriest, Ulrich, 'Beobachtungspuzzle: Benjamin Heisenberg über Schläfer', *FilmDienst*, September (2006), 14-15

Longman, Jere, *Among the Heroes: United Flight 93 and the Passengers and Crew Who Fought Back* (New York, NY: HarperCollins, 2002)

Los, Maria, 'Looking Into the Future: Surveillance, Globalization and the Totalitarian Potential', in *Theorizing Surveillance: The Panopticon and Beyond*, ed. by David Lyon (Cullompton, Devon, UK: Culmcott House, 2006), 69-94

Markovitz, Jonathan, 'Reel Terror Post 9/11', in *Film and Television After 9/11*, ed. by Wheeler Winston Dixon (Carbondale: Southern Illinois University Press, 2004), 201-225

Meyer, Hendrik, *Terror und Innere Sicherheit: Wander und Kontinuität staatlicher Terrorismusbekämpfung* (Münster: Schüling Verlag 2006)

Naumann, Michael, 'Jeder ist verdächtig', *Die Zeit*, 23 April 2009 <http://www.zeit.de/2009/18/BKA-Gesetz> [accessed 17 May 2009]

Nielsen, Biana, 'Home Invasion and Hollywood Cinema: David Fincher's *Panic Room*', in *The Selling of 9/11: How a National Tragedy Became a Commodity*, ed. by Dana Heller (New York, NY: Palgrave Macmillan, 2005), 233-253

Prantl, Heribert. 'Gegen den Sicherheitsstaat', *Die Süddeutsche Zeitung*, 23 April 2009 <http://www.sueddeutsche.de/politik/454/466039/text/> [accessed 17 May 2009]

Schläfer, dir. by Benjamin Heisenberg, on DVD (juicy film, 2005)

My Roommate the Terrorist: The Political Burden of September 11 in Elmar Fischer's *The Friend*

Gavin Hicks

German film director Elmar Fischer has stated that he wished to portray a terrorist with a human face. But his German-language narrative film *Foreign Friend* (original title *Fremder Freund*) of 2003 provides a representation of the Islamic Other which is nothing but problematic. This representation, anchored in both the details of the Hamburg terror cell and the larger contemporary German discourse on immigration, employs a filmic syntax fashioned through the signification-heavy symbolism of September 11 not as a work of mourning, but rather as an instrumentalization of the traumatic weight of the terrorist attacks to the detriment of the Muslim immigrant in Germany. Fischer's construction of the Islamic Other is accomplished through many structural elements of filmmaking: through temporal and narrative devices, but also through a spatial configuration of essentialism enabled not only by the embodied presence but also the absence of the pro-filmic Islamic figure. The temporal sequencing of the film, in the mode of a modern detective story, condemns the Islamic Other from the very first scene by linking his actions to the Hamburg terror cell, while the narrative structures place the Islamic Other in the juridical position of defendant with identity politics on trial. Here the neo-Hegelian dialectics of Judith Butler can serve to explicate this ethically violent form of intersubjectivity. The absence of the embodied Islamic Other manufactures images of a static, unworldly Islamic threat (more the stuff of horror movies) which remind one of Siegfried Kracauer's considerations of the mass ornament and its modern social implications. Compounded with Germany's relatively recent self-declared status as an immigration state and the subsequent migrations of, amongst others, Turkish workers and their families from the 1960s through the 70s, *Foreign Friend* casts suspicion not only on the faceless Muslims beyond Germany's border, but also on Germany's current Muslim population. This political reading of a German film shall explore how structural elements filtered through the over-determined semiotics of September 11 are used to visually and thematically construct an Islamic Other who is arguably even more threatening by virtue of a dynamic, humanistic portrayal. Fischer demonstrates that September 11 as an essentializing tool is unfortunately quite easy to use; if the nameless brown Muslim is framed in opposition to September 11, the Muslim can only lose.

German film director Elmar Fischer has attempted to portray an Islamic terrorist with a human face. But his German language narrative film *The Friend*[1] (original title *Fremder Freund*) of 2003 provides a representation of a Muslim immigrant which is nothing but problematic and furthermore seems a example of what Slavoj Žižek has labeled Western European "right-populism with a human face."[2] This representation, anchored in both the his-

---

[1] Fischer's film was later released in the USA (April 2005) under the English title.

[2] Slavoj Žižek, *The Universal Exception: Selected Writings, II*, ed. by Rex Butler and Scott Stephens (London: Continuum, 2006), p. 301.

torical details of the Hamburg terror cell[3] and the immediate post-9/11 German discourse on immigration, employs a filmic syntax fashioned through the signification-heavy symbolism of September 11. The result is not a work of mourning but rather a channeling and limitation of memory and trauma positioning the Muslim opposite 9/11. The construction of the Islamic other is accomplished through many structural elements of filmmaking: through temporal and narrative devices and through a spatial configuration of essentialism enabled not only by the embodied presence but also the absence of the pro-filmic Muslim figure.[4] The non-chronological sequencing of the film, in the mode of a modern detective story, condemns the Muslim character Yunes from the very first scene by linking his actions to the Hamburg terror cell, while the narrative structures place Yunes as Muslim in the juridical position of defendant with identity politics on trial. Here the neo-Hegelian dialectics of Judith Butler, namely the intersubjective relationship between an "I" (subject) and a "you" (object) which determines a subject's identity not by subjugation but subjectivation, can serve to explicate this form of ethical violence. In regards to the construction of the other via embodied presence and absence, both strategies are contingent upon camera and thematic techniques, but the absence of the embodied Islamic other manufactures images of a static, unworldly Islamic threat (more the stuff of horror movies) which remind one of Siegfried Kracauer's considerations of the mass ornament and its social implications.

Compounded with Germany's relatively recent self-declared status as an immigration state, *The Friend* casts suspicion not only on the faceless Muslims beyond Germany's borders but also on Germany's current Muslim population. The figure of Yunes is the reification of the integration failure that is the Hamburg terror cell. Like Hamburg leader Mohammed Atta, Yunes is a bright student of urban planning interested in helping the Third World. Like cell member Ziad Jarrah, Yunes is a young, fun-loving man who

---

3 The "Hamburg terror cell" formed in 1999 at the *Technische Universität Hamburg-Harburg* under the leadership of Mohammed Atta. Its nineteen members, in coordination with al-Qaeda, played key roles in the organization of the September 11 attacks. The pilots of American Airlines Flight 11 (North Tower of the WTC), United Airlines Flight 175 (South Tower), and United Airlines Flight 93 (crash in Somerset County, PA) were all members of the cell.

4 The presence and absence of the *pro-filmic* Muslim figure refers to the thematic and visual construction of the Muslim existing within the fictive world of the film. While the term 'pro-filmic' does not strictly exclude extra- or post-filmic referents, the term does attempt to focus on characters within the film's plot and isolates such characters from a reality outside the film's narrative and the cinema itself for the sake of formulistic analysis.

occasionally drinks beer and goes to parties.[5] Like cell member Said Bahaji, Yunes is an industrious student who loves Formula 1 racing.[6] In a word, Yunes is the model of integration gone horribly wrong. This political reading shall explore how structural elements filtered through the over-determined semiotics of September 11 are used to visually and thematically construct an Islamic other who is arguably even more threatening by virtue of a dynamic, humanistic portrayal. The terrorist, as the German language title suggests, could not only be the easily recognizable fundamentalist but also a friend. Fischer demonstrates how September 11 can function as an essentializing tool. If the nameless brown Muslim is framed in opposition to September 11, the Muslim can only lose.

This film analysis begins not with the film proper but rather with the packaging of *The Friend* DVD, for the cover art of the DVD provides the leitmotiv for the entire film and this subsequent analysis. The image of the front jacket of the DVD is that now ubiquitous iconic image of public history – that of the World Trade Center in flames. The spectacular explosion of the WTC is framed by two human faces: that of a young white male and a young brown male. The caption underneath the faces reads: "We were friends. Weren't we?" (Wir waren Freunde. Waren wir das?) While there are many such dualistic visual framing devices in the film itself which serve to construct alterity, both postcolonially and phenomenologically considered, this is the defining image, the visual referent supporting all filmic signification in *The Friend.* The image of the WTC is only used once not in the film itself, but only on the aforementioned DVD jacket. The historical sequence of events – the toppling of the towers after the plane crashes – however, begins the films. Approximately two and a half minutes of seemingly original footage from various unspecified locations in Manhattan on September 11 provide glimpses of the minutes directly after the attacks: a grainy shot of a city street, pedestrians running in slow motion from an unseen terror, then a fade to black; an establishing shot (equally grainy in quality) of the Manhattan skyline, clouds of dust and smoke billowing up and through the skyscrapers, hiding the destruction of the towers, another fade to black. The image of the planes hitting the towers is not included in the montage, and its absence from the opening sequence serves to challenge the viewer's memory by presenting unfamiliar perspectives of a familiar event in public history. The viewer is

5 Dominik Cziesche, 'Allah, die Liebe und der Tod', *Der Spiegel*, 26 (2004), 48-50 (p. 48).

6 Klaus Brinkbäumer et al., 'Attas Truppe', *Der Spiegel*, 6 (2006), 74-85 (p. 83).

compelled to remember the trauma of that day, and this directed remembering, according to Susannah Radstone's description of trauma theory, recalls "the impact of catastrophic events" which "blocks free association, that creative process through which experience, memory, and fantasy are woven into the texture of a life – or a culture."[7] This trauma-montage establishes a filter which limits free association and mediates the subsequent storyline.

The plot that follows the 9/11 footage is fairly straightforward. Chris (full name Christian), a young university student in Berlin, meets Yunes, a German-speaking student from Yemen, who is searching for an apartment. Yunes moves in with Chris, and a friendship quickly develops. The plot spends much time on their respective love lives – Chris with his longtime girlfriend Julia, and Yunes courting, wooing, and losing the blonde Nora. Although the friendship of Chris and Yunes seems strong, Julia and Nora begin to wonder about Yunes when he voices his "extreme" political views on the Palestinian conflict, Turkish Kemalism, and the atrocities in Sudan. When Chris and Julia return to Berlin from a trip to Yunes' home country of Yemen, Yunes (who stays in Berlin) has changed; he now wears a full beard, owns a prayer rug, spends time with the "Islam-Group" and refuses to eat pork. Tensions rise between Chris and Yunes, but after a nervous breakdown, Yunes shaves his beard and seemingly purges radical Islam from his body. Soon after, however, Yunes mysteriously leaves Germany on short notice to make an "apprenticeship" in Pakistan. His return months later to Berlin is occasion for a party at the apartment, but the next day, September 8, 2001, Yunes disappears for the last time. Three days later, Chris and Julia rush home to watch the television coverage of the terrorist attacks in the USA. Terrified by the fact that the terrorists were linked to Hamburg, Julia suspects the worse, and Chris goes on the case like a good detective, collecting clues throughout Berlin which all but directly indicate Yunes' role as a "sleeper agent" (*Schläfer*) of al-Qaeda.

It is necessary to note that this storyline is told not in the linear fashion just detailed above but rather in long sequences of flash-forwards and flashbacks beginning one and a half years before and ending on September 17, 2001 – September 11 functioning as the zero hour of the film. Each sequence is marked by a time description displayed in text briefly over the respective filmic image. The sequences of narrative establishment and contextualization are broadly defined temporally: "1½ years before, March 2000," "6 months before, March 2001," "3 months before, June 2001" etc. The sequences cor-

7 Susannah Radstone, 'The War of the Fathers: Trauma, Fantasy, and September 11', *Signs*, 28 (2002), 457-459 (p. 457).

relating to the days directly before and after September 11 – the scenes in which Chris searches the city for clues – give the time by date and place: "Berlin, 7 September, 2001," "8 September, 2001, University," "11 September, 2001, Chris' apartment" etc. The time indicators (the actual superimposition of text) are accompanied by either a fade to black before a new sequence or a freeze of the respective frame of no more than several seconds.

There are two structural observations to be made here. The nonlinear development of the plot allows 1) the quick identification of Yunes as the subject completion of the German language title (*fremder Freund* = foreign friend) and 2) an efficacious representation of the radicalization of Yunes over a short period of pro- and post-filmic time. The identification of Yunes is established within the first two sequences after the opening 9/11 montage. The first short sequence begins with a drunken Chris laughing hysterically at the wheel of a stopped car. He has crashed the car into a fence. A concerned Yunes sits in the passenger seat. As diagetic police sirens grow louder, Yunes insists on switching places with Chris in order to deal with the police since Chris is driving sans license. Half of the German language title of the film (Yunes = *Freund* / friend) is now established without additional context. The frame freezes, fades to black, and an establishing shot of Chris' apartment complex fills the frame. The time indicator "Berlin, 7 September 2001" appears over the image. In this short sequence, Chris and Julia clean a filthy apartment, the aftermath of Yunes' return party. When they try to find Yunes, they discover he is gone. Only his immaculately clean room is evidence of his recent presence. This is the first sequence in the film in which shots are accompanied by an extra-diagetic music that can only be described as eerie (dissonant synthesizer tones and feedback reminiscent of horror films). Now the second half of the German title is established (Yunes = *fremd* / strange, foreign).

Regarding the depiction of Yunes' radicalization, a series of framing devices or oppositional pairs – similar to the stark duality of the DVD cover – chart Yunes' rather startling conversion from friend to the Occident to intolerant foreigner of the Orient. The oppositional pairs are interspersed throughout the film via the non-chronological narrative construct. For example, during Yunes' first date with Nora, Yunes states that he is a fan of Formula 1 racing; later we learn that "Formula 1 is *haram*…forbidden."[8] When Yunes moves in, he tells Chris that he has "no problem" with pork; later in the same kitchen Yunes gives Chris an angry sermon about the dangers of pork's impurities. In an early film sequence, Yunes hears a racist comment on the

---

[8] *Fremder Freund*, dir. Elmar Fischer, on DVD (Naked Eye Filmproduktion, 2003).

street and becomes enraged; towards the end of the film, Yunes is calm despite similar racist comments and walks away (at peace with his decision to assist the al-Qaeda network). Such visual and narrative frames provide easily identifiable benchmarks to plot a rather fantastic conversion almost void of nuance and with no topoi of identity politics between the passive and the aggressive, the secular and the fundamental, and between the friend and the foreigner. Consequently, Yunes exemplifies a metaphor often used in contemporary German migration discourse, that of "parallel worlds." Yunes is not in the a-cultural limbo of "betweenness" which Leslie Adelson regards so critically as an ontologically skeptical trope "designed to keep discrete worlds apart as much as it pretends to bring them together."[9] It is the dual, and not dialectical, nature of these oppositions which eliminates the possibility of "betweenness" and positions Yunes in a perpetual either/or constellation with clearly defined borders. Such subject positioning seems congruent with a post-9/11, post-multicultural world in which, as B. Venkat Mani describes it, "invisible frontiers" become visible again, and "lines dividing human races" reacquire their "traditional qualifications: national, religious, racial, ethnic, linguistic."[10] The dualisms in the film have merely refined those traditional qualifications and given them negative or positive cultural values.

In addition to these dualisms, there are many narrative devices which transform Yunes from the Muslim to the Islamist. However, within the confines of this paper it is sufficient to analyze a single take in which Yunes is positioned in diametrical opposition to the secular, Western European characters of the film. A medium close shot frames the two couples, Chris and Julia, Yunes and Nora. The four are lying on their backs, their heads resting on pillows. The camera is directly over them as if looking down from the ceiling. Chris and Nora appear to be sleeping, eyes closed. Julia's eyes are open but sleepy. All are quiet except for Yunes who speaks of the Israeli-Palestinian conflict, that people there are beaten randomly on the street by the police, women are raped, children are killed and no one does anything ("Keiner macht was!").[11] When Yunes states that the Palestinian conflict can be compared with the Holocaust ("Man kann das mit dem Holocaust vergleichen"),[12] the three German characters awaken and stir in discomfort. Yunes repeats this comparison, but before he finishes this sentence, Julia interrupts, insisting that he cannot make such a comparison. The conversation breaks

---

9 Leslie A. Adelson, 'Against Between: A Manifesto', *Unpacking Europe*, ed. by Salah and Iftikar Dadi (Rotterdam: NAi Publishers, 2001), 244-255 (p. 246).

10 B. Venkat Mani, *Cosmopolitan Claims*, (Iowa City: University of Iowa Press, 2007) p. 2.

11 *Fremder Freund*.

12 Ibid.

down into argument. Nora has the last word of the scene: "Yunes, why do you have such an extreme attitude?" ("Yunes, warum hast du so 'ne extreme Haltung?")[13]

Eyes play a subtle but important role in this scene. Yunes is the only character to keep his eyes open and alert during the entire take. This is noteworthy because of previous scenes of the couples in youthful play. They have just had a fun day of flirting and frolicking at the beach in winter, throwing snowballs and petting. There seems to be nothing remotely political or controversial in this play at all. It is good-natured, neutral, and structurally serves as comic relief in order to break narrative tension. In the scene at hand the viewer can logically assume that the end of their day has come. The couples are tired and have finally settled down to rest, yet Yunes, fueled by "extreme" political opinions, is wide-eyed and speaking with conviction. The others seem initially disinterested or ready for sleep, but Julia and Nora are brought to full attention by the mere word "Holocaust," arguably the most historically loaded word in the German language. Even more so than the image of the WTC in flames, the word "Holocaust" restricts free association in the German context and, out of the mouth of the Muslim Yunes, serves to radicalize his views par excellance. The pro-filmic German characters may not sympathize with Yunes after he has broken this taboo, namely the utterance of the unspeakable Nazi past. In the postwar German context, already Yunes' chosen conversational subject of Palestine is nearing uncomfortable ground upon which the German must tread carefully. In such banal, friendly circumstances like the one framed in this scene, the complexities of German/Israeli foreign policy and the Israeli-Palestinian conflict are to be avoided absolutely. Yunes, however, does not possess such social tact. The political has ruptured the environment of friendship and young love. Once again, Yunes is proved at once friend and familiar, foe and foreign.

A less obvious, but nevertheless essentializing narrative device of the film concerns the identity construction of the Islamic other, and here Judith Butler's ethics by way of a reconsidered dialectic in *Giving an Account of Oneself* (2005) shall be used to analyze the film's identity politics. To summarize Butler's theory briefly, Butler proposes an ethic of moral accountability by emphasizing the second-person perspective of an intersubjective dyad. Before the Hegelian and reflexive "I" of lord and bondsmen dialectic, there is a "you," Butler claims, who asks the subject to give an account of itself. However, Butler expands her dialectic beyond the "I" and the "you." She also incorporates the social and the historically circumstantial, i.e. the conditions

---

13 Ibid.

of the self's own emergence which must not only be taken into account in the personal narration but also demand as a matter of necessity that the self become a social theorist.[14] Contextual sociality, then, prevents the subject's complete ownership of personal narration. Furthermore, the "I" only gives account when it is asked for, and that account, nor sooner than it is recognized as "mine," as it were, is relinquished, forfeited to the demanding "you." Therefore, the "I" cannot have complete subjective mastery over narrative. This lack leaves one opaque to oneself because of the intersubjective construct of identity. The opacity to oneself is always anchored in contextual sociality and intersubjectivity. As in Hegelian dialectic, both a subject and an object/other must be present in order to acknowledge and be acknowledged. But if it is "precisely by virtue of one's relations to others that one is opaque to oneself, and if those relations to others are the venue for one's ethical responsibility" then it is "by virtue of the subject's opacity to itself that it incurs and sustains some of its most important ethical bonds."[15] Because of the opacity to oneself, both the "I" and the "you" are dependent upon each for identity formation and accordingly held responsible by the "ethical bonds" between them. The relationship between the "I" and "you" should be one of subjectivation, i.e. a reciprocal acknowledgement of the subject-status of the other, and not of subjugation, the unilateral definition and repression and of the other's identity.

It is Yunes who is asked to give account of himself; to narrate his accountability. The oppositional "you" takes various names in the film, but it is Yunes' singular role to play the narrating-I, the one who must explain or justify. Though Butler imagines this dialectic of accountability as an avoidance of ethical violence and the foundation of hope, here in praxis the sacrifice of the narrating-I is great while the "you" fulfills a role that is juridical and punitive, the very sort of accountability Butler tries to avoid. Chris, Julia and Nora ask Yunes to narrate, to account for his existence, and Yunes must scramble to give an account that at once narrates his subjectivity and also the non-personal social milieu of his emergence and continued existence, after which he must surrender that account to those who have asked for it. Yunes is asked why he speaks such good German, what he studies, why he has such extreme opinions, why he is suddenly so religious, where he is, and who he is. Yunes answers these questions and accounts for himself not in the service

---

14 Judith Butler, *Giving an Account of Oneself* (New York: Fordham University Press, 2005) pp. 7-8.

15 Ibid., p. 20.

of intersubjective moral responsibility but in his own defense and in the fear that his account could prove him guilty.

Butler intends such a scenario, which she questionably defines as Nietzschean, to be the departure for her ethics; that "accountability" should not "follow only upon an accusation or, minimally, an allegation, one made by someone in a position to deal out punishment if causality can be established."[16] The accusatory identity formation in the film presents two conclusions in light of Butler's theory of accountability. One could interpret the artistic representation of Yunes as a subjugated and not subjectivated "I" (at least not subjectivated in any satisfactory manner) and ergo claim that a Butlerian ethic of accountability vis-à-vis opacity to oneself is exactly what is needed to prevent such bullying by the juridical-you. One could also claim that Butler's dialectic cannot escape the event horizon of a social power differential without utopian beings who exist in absolute awareness of both subjective and objective opacity. In either case, Yunes is seemingly not aware of his intersubjective relationship to the other. He does not ask; he is asked. To further complicate matters, Yunes answers questions and accusations often in the struggle to narrate the social conditions of his emergence of which he has no control, but even more problematically, he often narrates this social using the pronoun "we." As the plot develops and Yunes' account narrates more of the social and less of the self, the "I" disappears and is replaced with the faceless Islamic "we." Chris, on the other hand, is never questioned, is never called forth to account for himself. Even Yunes himself does not ask but rather gives Chris his own identity narration. In their last conversation before Yunes disappears forever, Yunes tells Chris, "You are good just the way you are" ("Du bist so gut wie du bist").[17]

One of the most manifest constructions of Islamic otherness in the film is not, however, achieved through oppositional pairs – through a duality contingent on the visual presence of Yunes as Muslim – or through a punitive process of identity accusation. Rather the construction of Islamic otherness is achieved through the Islamic other as absence. This is demonstrated in the sequence which depicts the events on the day before the WTC attacks.

The sequence begins in still frame. A long shot shows Chris in mid-stride on steps outside a building. The eerie extra-diagetic music (previously described) darkly underscores the otherwise banal mise-én-scene of a university building. In the lower right hand corner of the frame, the time "10 September

---

16 Ibid., p. 11.

17 *Fremder Freund.*

2001, Universität" is superimposed over the image. The camera, handheld and digital, pans right and follows Chris as he finds a small office and asks for the directions to the "Islam Group,"[18] which he learns is on the second floor. There is a cut to a medium long shot framing Chris as he mounts steps into a poorly lit hallway. Another cut finds Chris in that dark hallway. The camera tracks backwards as Chris, in frontal view, walks down the hall. The eerie music continues. Chris flips a light switch without breaking stride. The camera tracks backward and around a corner, positioning Chris in half profile. He looks ahead, then down and to the right. A medium point-of-view shot frames the hallway floor; in center frame is a pile of unorganized sandals of various shades of blue and black. The music grows suddenly louder and intensifies to a dissonant, dramatic chord. The shot pans up and left to a closed door. A small picture enters the frame. A photo of the Kaaba in Mecca hangs on the door, Muslims in white bowed in prayer all around it. The eerie, intensified music persists. Chris in a medium close shot wears an expression of fatigue and worry. He looks down without much movement and then looks up again. A cut to another point-of-view shot finds a small wooden picture frame hanging on the wall near the door. Written on a small tab of paper in the middle of this frame is "Islam AG" (Islam Group). The camera pans up and right to find another sign, this time a sheet of paper tapped to the wall: "Islam Group disbanded, 10. Aug. 2001 ("Islam AG aufgelöst").[19] The frame freezes as Chris stares at the photo apprehensively.

No other scene or sequence in the film, not even the subsequent sequence of Chris and Julia on the day of the attacks, so manifestly frames Islam as a dehumanized, invisible threat. The fact of the group's disbandment a month before the attacks in tandem with the quiet assumption of Yunes' complicity is only one of many clues Chris collects which points to a sinister affiliation with the network of al-Qaeda. Even stronger than this clue, however, are the voiceless images in this sequence. The undifferentiated pile of sandals seems to depict a custom so strange (that of removing shoes before entering a room) that only suspenseful horror music can highlight its foreignness, all the while reducing Muslims to a dark, threatening, unclean mass in a synecdoche of "othering" (the sandal or foot equals the whole). The picture of the black cube of the Kaaba – itself geometric and surrounded by geometrical patterns of barely discernable and therefore faceless Muslim pilgrims in prayer – constructs an image of mass idol worship. One is reminded of Siegfried Kracau-

---

18 In the German, the "Islam AG" *(*Arbeitsgruppe). Although the term seems fairly innocuous, the context of 9/11 suggests an allusion to Hamburg terror cell leader Mohammed Atta, who gave the same name to his Islam group at the Technische Universität Hamburg-Harburg.

19 *Fremder Freund.*

er's description of ballet dancers in formation, that the mass ornament they create with their bodies and movements is not only an "end in itself," but also takes place "in a vacuum," in a "linear system that no longer has any erotic meaning but at best points to the locus of the erotic."[20] Most importantly, Kracauer identifies the bearer of this ornament not as the individual dancer, but the mass, for "whenever the people form figures, the latter do not hover in midair but arise out of a community."[21] In the arrangement of this ornament only the mass is employed, only "as parts of a mass, not as individuals who believe themselves to be formed from within, do people become fractions of a figure."[22] We may substitute the ornament of ballet with the Kaaba and the erotic with the religious. In this small photo of worship around the Kaaba, shown only for a few seconds, the purpose of this worship is primarily visual, formational, and is no longer religious. In its clean geometry, it can only signify a site of religion, but even this site of religion is not the function of the ornament. The Muslim formation is, in the end, an end in itself and accordingly serves to conjure a dehumanizing nature of Islam, here presented as an anti-individualistic belief system which organizes itself in mass patterns where the individual is nothing more than a necessary and simultaneously devalued piece of the grand geometry.

The otherness in this sequence, then, reaches far beyond the particularity of Yunes. Such broad essentialism is only possible when no embodied other is present upon which to focus. Even the "Islam AG" – a religious organization with headquarters in a secular German university and therefore under the regulation of a Western European, liberalized government – is absent; more specifically, disbanded (aufgelöst). This otherness *in absentia* not only arranges Yunes into the immensity of the mass Islamic ornament but also marks the radical retreat of the Muslim organization from the German bureaucratic and social system and concordantly from the façade of integration. That the German university serves as the site of this absence is no accident. As the details of the Hamburg terror cell unfolded after the September 11 attacks, many right-populist political and social critics claimed that Germany's postwar "version of religious tolerance" allowed the Hamburg cell "to flourish" and render "German universities hospitable to radical Islam."[23]

---

20 Siegfried Kracauer, *The Mass Ornament: Weimar Essays*, trans. by Thomas Y. Levin (Cambridge: Harvard University Press, 1995) p. 77.

21 Ibid., p. 76.

22 Ibid., p. 76.

23 Robert S. Leiken, 'Europe's Angry Muslims', *Council on Foreign Relations* (Aug 2005) < http://www.foreignaffairs.com/articles/60829/robert-s-leiken/europes-angry-muslims> [accessed 14 Aug 2008].

Scholar and self-defined liberal Muslim Bassam Tibi claimed that a German "love of foreigners" (Fremdenliebe) in reaction to the National Socialist past enabled German institutions to serve as staging grounds where Islamists and their sleeper-agents could build their "logistics under the misuse of migration and Diaspora" ("wo die Islamisten ihre "Schläfer" und die entsprechende Logistik unter Mißbrauch von Migration und Diaspora aufgebaut haben").[24] Tibi characterized the cultural tolerance fostered at the university as just another example of "blue-eyed multiculturalism" that has shaped Germany into a land of uncontrolled immigration.[25] Furthermore, multiculturalism prevented German do-gooders (Gutmenschen) from recognizing that Islam and the political ideology of Islamism must be strictly differentiated,[26] and hence the Hamburg cell was given free space to organize and radicalize.

While the call for the demarcation between Islam and Islamism is undoubtedly a rational one, the unified constitution of the foreign/friend Yunes figure, the at once integrated Muslim and dangerous Islamist, complicates such a clean demarcation. Indeed, the amorphous distinction between "good" and "bad" Muslim is the very engine of *The Friend.* Any dramatic tension in the film rests upon the unpredictable potential of the Dr. Jekyll / Mr. Hyde-Muslim who could either fall in love or murder for God. Ultimately, the sort of rational differentiation which Tibi calls for is incongruent with the filmic world of *The Friend*, for the narratology of the film is binary. There is no intermediary point charted between Western European secular integration and Islamic fundamentalism. The third necessary point would have to represent peaceful, measured Muslim observance. Dictated by Fischer's use of September 11 as a narrative frame, such a representation simply does not exist in the film.

By way of conclusion, it must be admitted that film theory which only seeks to reveal the ideology lurking behind the camera often produces the unsatisfactory conclusion that, because of the illusory, propagandistic nature of film, the viewer would be better off fleeing the theater and reading a book. Although this political reading of *The Friend* comes close to such a critique, it is nevertheless crucial to put the artistic use of such politically loaded symbols like 9/11 under the microscope. It has been provocatively suggested that we "might be better off forgetting 9/11" due to its terrifying, often misused symbolism and the political abuses thereof.[27] While it now seems obvious

---

24 Bassam Tibi, *Islamische Zuwanderung: Die gescheiterte Integration*, (Stuttgart: Deutsche Verlags-Anstalt, 2002) p. 45.

25 Ibid., p. 10.

26 Ibid., p. 44.

27 Maja Zehfuss, 'Forget September 11', *Third World Quarterly*, 24 (2003), 513-

that 9/11 was politically and strategically used by the American, and to a lesser extent German, governments to implement anti-terror legislation with "unprecedented haste,"[28] the artistic use of 9/11, especially in popular culture, does not always betray such clearly identifiable goals and therefore warrants more scrutiny than ever. 9/11 as image (the WTC in flames) is often used in a right-populist framework, further emphasizing the simple fact that September 11 is ideologically charged, mediated, and therefore not, by any stretch of the imagination, a politically neutral image. Its packaging as art does not divorce it from this distinction.

The over-determined signification granted to *The Friend* by September 11 cannot help but construct the identity of the Muslim figure as the reification of terrorism. The Muslim placed in opposition to the burning towers and the 3000 dead cannot remain a mere Muslim but is forced into the skin of the Islamic terrorist. Yunes as not only the Islamic other but also the integrated foreigner is the nightmare of Western European immigration. He is the amalgamated terrorist formed from the various biographical facts of the Hamburg terror cell and quickly established as a member of the "we" that is the fearful conception of Islamism. The weight of September 11 threatens to restrict interpretation in the film. It contributes to a visual narrative in the form of a non-chronological detective story which places Yunes at once within and outside of German society: as friend and as foreigner. In the end, the terrorist with a human face is merely a redrawing of the Islamist caricature. He may walk amongst us, speaking a language of tolerance, but quietly plans violent martyrdom. With such a filmic representation, suspicion is painted on the face of every brown Muslim in Germany, and thus can a single character come to embody one billion Muslims. And condemn them.

528, p. 515.

[28] Ibid., p. 518.

Bibliography

Adelson, Leslie A., 'Against Between: A Manifesto', *Unpacking Europe*, ed. by Salah and Iftikar Dadi (Rotterdam: NAi Publishers, 2001), 244-255

Brinkbäumer, Klaus et al., 'Attas Truppe', *Der Spiegel*, 6 (2006), 74-85

Butler, Judith, *Giving an Account of Oneself* (New York: Fordham University Press, 2005)

Cziesche, Dominik, 'Allah, die Liebe und der Tod', *Der Spiegel*, 26 (2004), 48-50

Fremder Freund, dir. by Elmar Fischer, on DVD (Naked Eye Produktions, 2003)

Kracauer, Siegfried, *The Mass Ornament: Weimar Essays*, trans. by Thomas Y. Levin (Cambridge: Harvard University Press, 1995)

Leiken, Robert S., 'Europe's Angry Muslims', *Council on Foreign Relations* (Aug 2005) <http://www.foreignaffairs.com/articles/60829/robert-s-leiken/europes-angry-muslims> [accessed 14 Apr 2008]

Mani, B. Venkat, *Cosmopolitical Claims*, (Iowa City: University of Iowa Press, 2007)

Radstone, Susannah, 'The War of the Fathers: Trauma, Fantasy, and September 11', *Signs*, 28 (2002), 457-459

Tibi, Bassam, *Islamische Zuwanderung: Die gescheiterte Intergration* (Stuttgart: Deutsche Verlags-Anstalt, 2002)

Zehfuss, Maja, 'Forget September 11', *Third World Quarterly*, 24 (2003), 513-528

Žižek, Slavoj, *The Universal Exception: Selected Writings,* II. ed. by Rex Butler and Scott Stephens (London: Continuum, 2006)

Ghosts on the Skyline: Chris Marker's France after 9/11

Alison J. Murray Levine

Chris Marker's *Chats Perchés/The Case of the Grinning Cat*, a 58-minute video essay produced for the Franco-German television channel ARTE in 2004, is here understood as a commentary on life in France after 9/11. The commentary is not only present in the political themes of the film; it is also built into its formal composition. An apparently meandering narrative in fact constitutes a tightly woven and meticulously crafted argument about political culture and its primary pillar, that of communication, in the world after the catastrophe. Through a deconstruction of the primary elements of communication—text, sound, and image—Marker advances a profound critique of all forms of mediated exchange, proposing instead the necessity of direct collective dialogue and action. In elaborating this critique, he undermines the authority of the very medium within which he works, that of the documentary video, explicitly demonstrating its ability to transform and distort reality. In this view, *Chats perchés* may be read as Marker's suggestion that the events of September 11th were produced by a hyper-mediated society in which the transformational nature of direct collective action has all but disappeared.

It is one of those few truly sunny days in Paris when the sky glows bright blue and shadows stand out clearly on walls. The white exoskeleton of the Pompidou Center glistens; its lurid green, blue, and red pipes glow in the evening light. High up on an apartment building across the Beaubourg square, a painted yellow cat grins Cheshire-like from the dingy wall opposite the museum. Far below, a crowd of people opening and closing umbrellas walks clockwise around the gigantic golden flowerpot that graces the square. "*Tournons autour du pot,*" they intone. "Let's walk around the pot." The pot, catching the rays and shot from a low angle, rises above the crowd like a giant Cyclops. Its one eye gleams.

A giant flowerpot, a circling crowd, an onlooking cat: such is the scene in an early sequence from Chris Marker's *Chats Perchés/The Case of the Grinning Cat*, a 58-minute video essay produced for the Franco-German television channel ARTE in 2004 on life in France after 9/11.[1] In French, *tourner autour du pot* means to talk around a subject without getting to the point. One might accuse Marker of precisely this rhetorical flaw. Ostensibly, the subject of his video is the yellow cat, the work of a mysterious graffiti artist who paints cats in impossible places all over the city of Paris and beyond. Politics,

1 *Chats perchés/The Case of the Grinning Cat*, dir. by Chris Marker, on DVD (ARTE Video, 2004; First Run/Icarus Films, 2004).

however, appear to explode into the film independently of the filmmaker's intentions, hijacking the thematic direction. He veers off message, off target, off the mark. He starts turning around the pot.

And yet, I would argue, it is this hijacked message, this detour, that is precisely the point. Marker's apparent meanderings in fact constitute a tightly woven and meticulously crafted argument about political culture and its primary pillar, that of communication, in the world after the catastrophe. Through a deconstruction of the primary elements of communication—text, sound, and image—he advances a profound critique of all forms of mediated exchange, proposing instead the necessity of direct collective dialogue and action. In elaborating this critique, he undermines the authority of the very medium within which he works, that of the documentary video, explicitly demonstrating its ability to transform and distort reality. 9/11, Marker suggests, was the result of a hyper-mediated society in which the transformational nature of direct collective action has all but disappeared.

Chris Marker and *Chats perchés*

While well known to art enthusiasts for his resolutely avant-garde and politically engaged writing, films, and video installations, Chris Marker remains a relatively obscure figure on the international stage. One of the most prolific artists of the second half of the twentieth century, the director gained international recognition in the 1950s for two documentary collaborations with Alain Resnais, the blistering denunciation of colonialism that was *Les statues meurent aussi/Statues Also Die* (1953) and the stark portrait of the Holocaust in *Nuit et brouillard/Night and Fog* (1955). He is perhaps best known for the creation of *La Jetée* (1962), the cult classic that he shot mostly with a Pentax still camera and that inspired Terry Gilliam's *Twelve Monkeys*. But many of his other works are little known outside of France. The quirky, retiring artist, who is now 87, is a self-proclaimed "*publiphobe*." He steadfastly refuses to grant photographs or interviews and drives the press to distraction, forcing them to produce titles such as "Rare Marker" or "The Invisible Man." In his work as in life, the man who was born Christian-François Bouche-Villeneuve slips behind an endless stream of pseudonyms. In so doing, he constantly redirects attention back to his work, a prodigious collection of essays, novels, films, video installations, photography, and more recently, digital media productions and videos.[2]

Over the last ten years, the scholarly world has taken a renewed interest in Marker's *oeuvre*. A series of journal articles and special issues came out in the 1990s in France and Germany, and the first comprehensive monographs on the filmmaker followed in Europe.[3] London's Institute of Contemporary Arts organized an exhibition in 2002 entitled "Chris Marker: The Art of Memory." The next year, the first DVD edition of *La Jetée* and *Sans soleil/Sunless* was published in France and in the US. Also in 2003, two special issues of *Film Comment* were devoted to Marker's work. Critical attention in English has followed, with two monographs in the United States and in Britain in 2005 and 2006 respectively, as well as a number of secondary articles.[4] Marker was featured in major exhibitions at MOMA in 2005 and at the Wexner Center for the Arts at The Ohio State University in 2007.[5] Despite making quite a splash in the French press and even securing North American distribution, *Chats perchés* has virtually escaped this recent flurry of scholarly attention.[6] Most responses to it have focused primarily on its surface-level political commentary and not its aesthetic project. And yet, *Chats* represents an important step forward for Marker both in terms of his resistance to the

2 Chris Darke, 'The Invisible Man', *Film Comment,* 39 (2003), 32; Samuel Douhaire and Annick Rivoire, 'Rare Marker', *Libération,* 5 March 2003, p. 1.

3 Birgit Kämper and Thomas Tode, *Chris Marker: Filmessayist* (Munich: CICIM, 1997); Guy Gauthier, *Chris Marker: écrivain multimedia, ou voyage à travers les médias* (Paris: L'Harmattan, 2001); and *Recherches sur Chris Marker*, a special issue of *Théorème* (2002).

4 The two monographs in English are Catherine Lupton, *Chris Marker: Memories of the Future* (London: Reaktion Books, 2005) and Nora Alter, *Chris Marker* (Chicago: University of Illinois Press, 2006).

5 The title of the MOMA exhibition was "Owls at Noon Prelude: The Hollow Man." Bill Horrigan curated the Wexner Center exhibition, which was entitled "Chris Marker: Staring Back" and was accompanied by a sumptuous published catalogue. *Chris Marker: Staring Back,* ed. by Bill Horrigan (Columbus, OH: Wexner Center for the Arts, 2007).

6 For an excellent overview of Marker's engagement with the film essay form, see Alter, pp. 16-20. For responses to *Chats perchés,* see Annick Rivoire, 'Chats discutent: Chris Marker et l'auteur de Monsieur Chat racontent leur rencontre artistique, et leur démarche dans *Libération', Libération,* 4 December 2004, pp. 26-27; Annick Rivoire, 'Chris Marker passe le témoin', *Libération,* 4 December 2004, p. 25; Jay Murphy, 'More of What It Is: Catching up with Chris Marker', *Afterimage* (October 2005), pp. 31-37; Bill Horrigan, 'Some Other Time', in *Chris Marker: Staring Back*, pp. 137-150; Chris Darke, 'First Look: Musique Concrète', *Film Comment,* 41 (2005), p. 14; Manola Dargis, 'Leftist Politics Scampers Through Paris on Playful Paws', *The New York Times,* 20 December 2006, E11. *Chats perchés* is not mentioned in the filmographies of the two monographs that postdate it—Alter and Lupton—this is doubtless due to production deadlines for the manuscripts that predated the release of the program.

aesthetic limitations imposed by a particular medium and his response to a question that for him, post-9/11, is fundamental: "how do people manage to live in such a world?"[7] Because it may be unfamiliar to many readers, a brief synopsis of the work precedes my analysis of its aesthetic and political project.

Chats perchés begins, quite concretely, with a message.[8] Against a black screen, a white text message reads, in French: "You have a message waiting." This message directs the viewer, along with hundreds of other people, to the square in front of the Pompidou Center, where they receive written and aural instructions (via cell phone and flyer) to perform various actions that culminate in the scene of an amused crowd walking around an enormous pot with open umbrellas. "All that under the gaze of a cat," remark the textual intertitles that function as one of the many narrative aliases. From the ground, the camera zooms in on the brightly colored yellow cat painted on the wall high above. "A CAT?" quips the next intertitle. Next, the point of view changes. "FLASH BACK," we read. A high angle shot shows the Parisian skyline as bagpipe music whines incongruously across the rooftops. It is one of those bright, hazy days in Paris when the sun is formless yet present. An inattentive viewer might not even notice the two ghostly towers that appear on the skyline, in semi-transparent juxtaposition, their clouds of billowing smoke chillingly recognizable once they have been identified. They are there and not there, these two towers: a memory, as clear and real to French viewers as to every American who was also not a direct observer. "We are all Americans," wrote Jean-Marie Colombani in *Le Monde* on September 13, 2001.[9]

This ghostly appearance is, to my knowledge, the only direct mention in the film (or indeed in Marker's work more broadly) of the events of 9/11. And yet the film, which begins in November 2001, is clearly an exploration of the aftermath of these events, of this "new era" of which Colombani wrote so eloquently. To begin with, the narrator wanders the streets of Paris in search of more painted yellow cats. Bill Horrigan has written that Marker's "cosmology" views cats and owls as the "presiding deities," so it is perhaps not surprising that the filmmaker decided to pursue these images.[10] When

---

7 Douhaire and Rivoire.

8 This article examines the original French version of the film released on DVD in 2004 by Les Films du Jeudi/Arte video, not the theatrical/DVD version released in 2006 by First Run/Icarus Films with an additional English-language commentary. All quotations are my translations from the French.

9 This editorial, which had an extraordinary impact, was republished in *Le Monde* on 23 May 2007.

10 Horrigan, p. 138.

asked to provide a photograph of himself, Marker has notoriously sent images of owls and cats; he writes social commentaries using the alter-ego of his own cat, Guillaume-en-Egypte; and these animals equipped with large eyes and night vision have often featured prominently in his work. In *Chats perchés,* however, the feline quest soon becomes intertwined with political events. The film advances chronologically, and soon the date is April 21st, 2002, date of a "catastrophe." The viewer might immediately recognize the political resonance of this date, but the filmmaker defers expectations, playfully explaining that the "catastrophe" in question is an injury to a cat's paw. Bolero, the cat that Marker has filmed in the subway, catches his paw in an escalator and requires first aid. The cat will recover, but "as a misfortune never comes alone," the intertitles inform us, another unfortunate event occurs on the same day. In the first round of the French presidential elections, the unthinkable happens. *Le Figaro* titles it "Le séisme." For *Le Parisien,* it is "Le choc." *Liberation*'s headline reads simply, in six-inch letters: "NON." Jean-Marie Le Pen, the candidate for the far-right National Front Party, comes in second, defeating the socialist Lionel Jospin, thus passing through to the second round.[11]

Marker's narrator appears to be diverted from his original purpose as crowds pour into the French streets to protest the possibility of electing Le Pen. This spontaneous outpouring of left-right solidarity, united against the far right, galvanizes the film in a new direction. Other street demonstrations follow, in support of rights for Muslim women and freedom for Tibet, but most particularly against the Iraq war. Cries of "1, 2, 3, 4, we don't want your f-ing war!" overlap with chants of "Napalm, it wasn't Sadaam, it was Uncle Sam." In response to the napalm chant, the intertitles provide a quiet interjection: "And who was it that gassed the Kurds?" In any case, in the streets of Paris, the pro-American solidarity in the immediate aftermath of 9/11 has been transformed into bitterness in response to the war, a bitterness that, as the narrator reminds us, is sometimes expressed in recycled slogans and concepts from the past.

---

11 In French presidential elections, all eligible candidates appear on the ballot in the first round of voting. If no one candidate receives an absolute majority, a run-off election is held between the two candidates receiving the most votes in the first round. Usually, the two candidates who make it to the second round are from the major center-left and center-right parties. In 2002, the far-right candidate (Jean-Marie Le Pen, of the National Front) edged out the center-left (Lionel Jospin, the Socialist), shocking the nation and leaving no left-wing choice in the second round. The entire French Left had to vote for the center-right candidate, Jacques Chirac, who won the second round with 80% of the vote.

Marker's two areas of interest—politics and yellow cats—converge when a news broadcast reveals images of demonstrators carrying placards of Monsieur Chat in their march. It is not immediately clear what the cats mean, but over the course of the investigation, they seem to connect with a diffuse sense of hope—for change, for a better world, for happier times ahead. This sense of hope will never become explicitly defined in the film. Instead, Marker's camera seems to stand in for Marker's own characterization of himself in a rare interview he granted *Libération* in 2003. In this interview, he states that like the Elephant's Child in Kipling's *Just So Stories*, he is a man of insatiable curiosity, and he seeks to understand how people continue living.[12] Like the felines who pop up in odd places and provide a visual refrain for the film, Marker's camera appears and disappears in different times and places to point out overlooked details or to bear witness to instances of collective action. The cats seem to serve as an iconographic reminder that collective action can bring hope to the world. At the end, the intertitles ask a simple question: "what if the cats left us for good?" The cats begin disappearing one by one from the city walls. Implicit, although never explicit, in the narrative is the assumption that in order to preserve the world for future generations, we must, first and foremost, hold onto hope.

The preceding synopsis more or less coincides with what most reviewers have written about *Chats perches* and, indeed, with what Marker himself said in a rare interview he granted to *Libération* in tandem with Monsieur Chat's artist.[13] What has not come out in the existing scholarship, however, are the profound questions this video essay asks about the limits of representation itself. At every turn, *Chats perchés* undermines the supposed authenticity of the documentary form and its component parts: sound, text, and image. The authoritative narrative center that is the hallmark of traditional documentary is split into so many fragments that its "truth" value disappears. The meticulous precision of the editing reinforces this fragmentation, as the following argument will demonstrate. Insofar as it calls into question the fundamental elements of the very medium within which the artist is working, *Chats perchés* is solidly aligned with Marker's previous work, whether in writing, film, photography or digital media. Marker has repeatedly asked his viewer/readers to suspend their understanding of a clear distinction between fiction and non-fiction.[14] Here, however, the question of representation and its

12 Douhaire and Rivoire.

13 Rivoire, 'Chats discutent' and 'Chris Marker passe le témoin'.

14 Marker's work has repeatedly undermined the authoritative nature of documentary, as is evident in pieces as chronologically and formally diverse as *Lettre de Sibérie* (1958), *Sans soleil/Sunless* (1982), and his CD-Rom creation, *Immemory* (1997). *Lettre de Sibérie*, for

limits takes on a new urgency because of its implications in the events of 9/11—an overly mediated world has gone awry.

Deconstructing the documentary form

In order to reflect on the theme of a world gone awry because of distortions through mediated messages, Marker opens his film by drawing the viewer's attention to the message itself. The very first screen after the title is text: white letters on a black background, that quickly invert to black on white, stating, "vous avez un message en attente" (you have a message waiting). Instantly, the viewer is positioned as the recipient of a message, and at the same time alerted to the materiality and to the mediated form of the message. The origin of this message is unclear; it is not a text message, nor a voice-mail; it has an owl logo; perhaps it comes from the internet or from some other unidentifiable (and unreliable) source. As early as the first screen, the filmmaker casts doubts upon the sending and receiving of messages. He asks the viewer to doubt their origin.

From this doubtful message, the film moves to an example of the influence of a message on a crowd. Through a documentary sequence (we assume, although we are not sure), he demonstrates how this message, sent to many people, has led them to come together and to perform ridiculous actions in the Beaubourg Square. It is ridiculous because they open their umbrellas and the sun is shining; it is ridiculous because they are told to sing "let's go around the pot"; but the people themselves are not ridiculous. They are amused, good sports, willing to play along with a creative project they do not quite understand. In retrospect, this sequence has a chilling undertone; it demonstrates how easily a crowd can be assembled and manipulated by a mys-

---

example, contains multiple narratives of the same event, demonstrating the impossibility of objectivity or impartiality. Murphy, p. 32. See also Lupton, p. 57. The multiple narrators in *Sans soleil* force the viewer to "waver between fictional and nonfictional intelligibility," raising questions about the fictional or nonfictional status of the film. Hamid Naficy, *An Accented Cinema: Exilic and Diasporic Filmmaking* (Princeton, NJ: Princeton University Press, 2001), pp. 148-9; see also Allan Casebier, 'A Deconstructive Documentary', *Journal of Film and Video,* 40 (1988), p. 34. *Immemory* constantly oscillates between fictional and non-fictional modes; one section claims to be a "real imaginary museum" in which well-known paintings alternate with photographic images of real people digitally altered to look like paintings. In the "Memory" section of the disc, the narrator introduces the notion of an Uncle Anton who is "real," and assures the viewer that while "I did not hesitate to take liberties with my own memory, [...] everything concerning Uncle Anton is as absolutely truthful as possible."

terious mediated message that has no origin. In the light of the ghostly towers that follow, the viewer cannot help but wonder what influence similar mediations might have played in the unfolding of the events of September 2001.

Throughout *Chats perchés,* the viewer receives many signals to pay attention to various forms of mediated representation. From the opening screen, the editing underscores a process that Hamid Naficy noticed in *Sans soleil,* writing about "dense texts that not only point to referents and other texts but also are themselves pointers to other pointers."[15] This process entails a heightened attention to signifiers, in whatever form they may appear—image, text, and sound. The viewer is forewarned to pay attention to the aspects of "rhetorical fiction" that are inherent to all documentary, including Marker's own.[16] As Michael Renov writes, "documentary [...] employs many of the methods and devices of its fictional counterpart."[17] Marker's work insists on the necessity of doubting the veracity and authenticity of the documentary gesture at every turn.

After the opening sequence, which provides several examples of mediated texts of which the viewer must be suspicious—written text on screen, a mechanical voice reinforcing the instructions given in this text—the viewer of *Chats perchés* is confronted with yet another kind of text, the graphic intertitles that appear as black screens with white letters. Eschewing the voiceover commentary common in expository documentary, Marker engages the viewer in the reading of text, thus underlining the importance of textual mediation in contrast to other forms of communication.[18] At first, these intertitles appear to provide a kind of relief, because the stable narrator has arrived. Quickly, however, it becomes clear that these intertitles constitute only one of the various aliases of the narrator.[19] A second voice intervenes in the intertitles, called the "Morpheye," which appears to allow the narrator various kinds of

15 Naficy, p. 150.

16 Bill Nichols, *Representing Reality: Issues and Concepts in Documentary* (Bloomington, IN: Indiana University Press, 1991), p. 112.

17 Michael Renov, 'The Truth About Non-Fiction', in *Theorizing Documentary,* ed. by Michael Renov (New York: Routledge, 1993), p. 3.

18 Bill Nichols posits a strong authorial voice as a defining characteristic of "expository documentary" in his useful taxonomy of documentary forms, one version of which can be found in Nichols, 'The Voice of Documentary', in *New Challenges for Documentary,* ed. by Alan Rosenthal and John Corner (New York: Manchester University Press, 2005), p. 23.

19 It seems appropriate to use the term "alias" for the narrator of a Marker film because of the director's lifelong propensity for using aliases for himself and for his many narrators. Christian-François Bouche-Villeneuve has called himself, variously, Chris. Marker, Chris Marker, Guillaume-en-Egypte, Sandor Krasna, and many other names that overlap with those of his narrators, who also tend to take multiple forms, genders, and names in his works.

digital distortions of the sound and image that follow. Even in this sober form of non-diegetic narration, therefore, the narrative authority is fragmented, leaving the viewer with no clear central point of identification.

The sound editing in *Chats perchés* provides additional evidence that nothing can be taken for granted as authentic "truth" in this video. Ambient sound in traditional documentaries lends authority to an image, as it gives the viewer the impression of being inside the event. Wind blows, street noise intervenes, and birds chirp to reinforce the feeling that the sound was recorded in a spontaneous documentary fashion along with the image. In *Chats perchés,* the ambient sound that should accompany the on screen image is often split from it, drawing attention to the image as image, and to the sound as sound. One example is the sequence early in the video depicting yellow cats on the chimneys of apartment buildings high above the streets. The ambient sound has been removed from these images, replaced instead by ethereal music that suggests an other-worldly atmosphere. The viewer becomes abruptly aware of the previous absence of ambient sound when a train passes and its accompanying sound fades back in, regrounding the image in a comprehensible soundscape. The French presidential election is presented as a collage of sounds mixed over images that do not correspond to them. Unidentified screams and cries accompany the shocking newspaper headlines; the voices of television announcers mingle with those of left-wing politicians calling on voters to rally around Chirac; and a voice promising the "great surprise" of victory for Jean-Marie Le Pen accompanies images of street demonstrators chanting something that the viewer cannot hear.

This constant splitting of sound from image also works to undermine the authority of the documentary image itself. In *Chats perchés,* images draw attention to themselves as images, raising the question of their framing and interpretation. Early in the film, a tight shot of one painted cat fades briefly as a newspaper picture of the same image, along with headline ("yellow cats invade walls") and story, appears in juxtaposition over the original image. This technique is repeated twice, further underscoring the multilayered process of mediation: Marker's camera frames the image of the newspaper framing the image of the cat. The filmmaker returns to the theme of the image several times, taking a particular interest in images that, like the cats, proclaimed themselves in the urban landscape as images before they were framed for the camera. One extensive sequence, for example, titled "the street museum," consists of a montage of various forms of street art: graffiti, murals, billboards, and images taken from newspaper kiosks. These images have no particular relationship to the broader themes of the film, but rather, they lead the viewer to reflect on the ubiquity—but also the perfidy—of the image in contemporary urban society. Once again, the speculative links to the influences of images on the events of 9/11 are suggested but are not made explicit.

As a logical consequence of this obsessive attention to sound, text, and image, Marker's filmed essay also takes pains to remind the viewer of its status as a film. The graphic intertitles, which appear as white letters on a black screen, are reminiscent of the intertitles that appeared in silent films in the early days of cinema. One title that appears very early in the film, "FLASH BACK," makes a further self-reflexive gesture through the use of the language of cinema. Other uses of the language of cinema recur in the intertitles; the camera meanders through the Paris subway system to the "soundtrack" of the musicians playing there, and later, an erroneous piece of ambient sound attached to an image is labeled as "a little soundtrack error, quickly repaired." Should the viewer have somehow missed the repeated allusions to film, Marker's camera catches a boat passing on the Canal St. Martin, just in front of the Hôtel du Nord, the setting for Marcel Carné's 1938 eponymous film classic. The boat's name is Marcel Carné, and, as if in a passing memory, the voices of Louis Jouvet and Arletty fade in on the soundtrack, speaking the famous "atmosphere" line from the film.

Combined with the ghostly appearance of the burning twin towers on the skyline, these frequent references to film, as well as to the building blocks of the representational process, encourage the viewer to think about mediated messages in general, and particularly the role they may have played in the events of September 11th. Perhaps even more importantly, the film as it unfolds questions the limits of representation itself in the post-9/11 world. Of particular concern in this work is the medium of documentary film/video, which is traditionally associated with other non-fictional systems that Bill Nichols has called "discourses of sobriety" (science, economics, politics, foreign policy, education, religion).[20] Because of its association with these non-fictional discourses, documentary as a genre commands respect as a vehicle of information and education. It is, after all, the opposite of fiction.[21] Documentaries, as both Nichols and Renov have written, speak about *the* world outside of the frame (that is, the "real" world, the one in which we

---

20 Nichols, *Representing Reality,* p. 3.

21 Bill Nichols explains that this is partly because "documentaries offer pleasure and appeal while their own structure remains virtually invisible, their own rhetorical strategies and stylistic choices largely unnoticed." Nichols, *Representing Reality*, p. x. To wit, *Le petit Robert* (2000) defines a documentary as "a didactic film, presenting authentic documents that were not produced for the occasion (as opposed to a fiction film)"; the *Oxford English Dictionary* proposes the following: a documentary film is "factual, realistic; [...] based on real events or circumstances, and intended primarily for instruction or record purposes."

live), while fiction alludes to *a* world (an imaginary one).[22] And yet, according to Marker's critical position in *Chats perchés*, it is these very images of sobriety that have led the modern world astray, perhaps because they catch the viewer off guard, in "belief" mode. As his video essay unfolds, the process of deconstruction of the documentary form, the very medium within which he has chosen to work, becomes even more explicit.

The sequence in which Marker's project becomes evident even to the viewer who might have missed the ghostly towers or the early warning messages about signs and referents is entitled "Genealogy of the Cat." At this point in the film, the narrator parodies another "discourse of sobriety"—genealogy, or the serious search for origins—by launching into an imaginary genealogy of the yellow cat in art history. First, several allusions to well-known cat characters appear: the Cheshire Cat from Alice in Wonderland, and Miyazaki's cartoon cats. Then, an "expert" is convoked to give a lecture on some art-related topic; we cannot understand what he says, because his speech is completely garbled. Dressed in black jeans, black jacket, and white tee-shirt, he looks the part as he appears to provide an analysis of Van Eyck's *Betrothal of the Arnolfini*. But his learned commentary is useless, and the moment is humorous. Meanwhile, the camera moves in on a close-up of the Van Eyck painting, and it discovers that Monsieur Chat is actually hidden in the mirror within the painting. The yellow cat, we subsequently discover, was present in many masterpieces over the centuries: we see him in the Chauvet cave paintings, Roman mosaics, Van Gogh's yellow bedroom, and Picasso's *Demoiselles d'Avignon*. The moment is light, and the viewer can chuckle, because the paintings chosen are so well known that the fakery is obvious.

As this sequence unfolds, however, discomfort and questions begin to unsettle the spectator. Marker's camera (or perhaps I should say, the digital image program on his computer) films (or should I say, creates) a series of images that include the yellow cat. The French post office issues a series of stamps with the yellow cat. This seems plausible—artists and artworks are often featured on stamps—and yet this particular series is pictured on a series of envelopes sent to Chris Marker's production company to the attention of various deceased directors such as Luis Buñuel, Louis Feuillade, and Max Ophuls. The cat appears on illuminated signs in the metro; a viewer not living in Paris might not know whether this was possible. The cat appears in the tabloids. Again, the viewer is left wondering if, once again, Marker has added the image digitally himself or if the tabloids actually did their own story about the yellow cats on the walls of Paris. At every level, it is almost im-

---

[22] Nichols, *Representing Reality*, p. 113; Renov, p. 2.

possible to keep from wondering: is this real? Or did he fake it? Every stage of the reflection is engaged with the question of mediation. The very question "is it real?" means that the viewer must accept without question the first level of mediation—that Marker did not intervene to change the image—but cannot help reflecting on how many other levels of mediation preceded this level. Someone drew the cat, someone else photographed it, someone else decided to place it in an article, and someone else filmed the paper on the rack. The question, therefore, of at which level the mediation was "real" or "true" seems to retreat irretrievably into the distance. The real and the imaginary have become intertwined, or as Deleuze has written, "indiscernible."[23] It is this very indiscernibility that ultimately creates the strength of Marker's project.

When *Chats perchés* ventures onto the Internet looking for the cats, Marker's implicit critique of the role of digital media in undermining truth and authenticity becomes nearly explicit. As if providing further citations for his thesis that the cats are important in contemporary culture, the camera films (creates?) websites that mention the cat. Names such as CNN Interactive, Time, Pictures of the Year, Musexpo, Einstein Archives Online, and Mad make up the list of "citations," and again, the viewer pauses to think about whether it might be possible that the cat became so popular that these sites did stories on the cat. Some are perhaps less plausible than others, but the very mental work that is required in asking these questions foregrounds the act of thinking about digital media with which we are confronted every day. Because of the anarchy that rules the internet, such media must be carefully parsed and evaluated; each modern visitor to the web has her own conscious or unconscious framework for deciding what sites are "trustworthy" sources of information.[24] Despite all the mediation, we still want to know whom we can trust, where the truth lies.

Ironically, it is the genealogical sequence, which should establish and fix origins, that does the most to undo them in this video. The origin of both word and image, narrator and cat, explodes into a million fragments and ultimately disappears. The authority of what follows is, therefore, profoundly suspect. The filmmaker's undermining of authority bleeds into subsequent

---

[23] Gilles Deleuze, *Cinema 2: The Time-Image,* trans. by Hugh Tomlinson and Robert Galeta (New York: Continuum, 2005), p. 7.

[24] When I taught this film in a graduate film seminar, my students admitted running to the Internet after watching the film to find out which sites were "true" and which Marker had invented. I would like to thank these students, and particularly Aline Charles, Katherine Lakin, and Caroline Meyer for the stimulating discussions that sparked some of the ideas for this essay.

representations of political discourse, as, for example, when clips of Tony Blair and George Bush explaining the reasons for the Iraq war intervene. The Iraq war, a direct consequence of the events of 9/11, appears as yet another product of mediated images and representations. In one sequence, a US general attempts to stall a question about the cause of the Iraq war by saying, "That's a great question," and by his head, a cartoon thought-bubble pops up that reads: "gulp!" Reprising the earlier sequence in the Paris subway, when passengers glide along a moving sidewalk to the "soundtrack of the metro," a later subway sequence includes travelers gliding along, oblivious, to the soundtrack of the bombardment of Baghdad. In this video essay, the Iraq war appears as the result of a carefully edited narrative, a discourse of sobriety in its own right, with documentary proof brought to the table as evidence. And yet, based on the deconstruction of documentary forms of argument and proof presented in *Chats perchés*, its fictional underpinnings appear as saliently as does the digital insertion of the yellow cat into *Les Demoiselles d'Avignon* or onto the home page of the White House. When yellow cats appear in an American street demonstration against the war, the viewer understandably wonders if the cats were added digitally, or if in fact, the banners are real. The doubt persists.

In such a climate of uncertainty, the reader of this chapter might well ask if Marker simply wants to leave his viewers with a feeling of doubt and hopelessness. It is my view that this is not the case. The strategies Marker deploys to propose a solution to the vagaries of the media, however, may at first appear to be somewhat ironic, given his forward-looking artistic practice. The political message that ultimately emerges from *Chats perchés* is the old standby of the European Left: collective action is the answer. In this respect, Marker is the left-wing politically engaged filmmaker we have known since the 1950s. He returns to the collective street demonstration in this project as if obsessed. He wanders "from demonstration to demonstration" asking the question: "where are the cats?" "where are the cats?" When he finally discovers the protestors marching with banners proclaiming "Make Cats Not War," the musical soundtrack switches from tentative flutes to a triumphal, organ-like processional, giving the viewer a sense that events are moving in a positive direction.

Marker's video suggests that he is patently aware that these demonstrations are not new, but rather cycle through history, and he intercuts references to the past with those from his cinematic present. It is clear from the profusion of interwoven demonstrations that it is the principle of collective action that interests him rather than the individual issues at hand. On the subject of the Bush/Saddam showdown, one intertitle reads, "One imagines Churchill giving Hitler 48 hours to leave Germany." "Slogans go back in time," one intertitle remarks, as past and present intermingle. "First it was JOHNSON-ASSASSIN-FREE VIETNAM [...] then later, IT'S ONLY A BEGINNING, WE MUST CONTINUE THE FIGHT." These intertitles are intercut with images from the May 1968 street protests and present-day demonstrations. "1-2-3-4, we don't want your f--ing war," is an American protest chant from Vietnam. "That one is straight from the Front Populaire," another intertitle adds, as demonstrators from Force Ouvrière chant a recycled slogan from the short-lived left-wing coalition government that galvanized France in the late 1930s. One set of demonstrators rewrites a 1940s song about the Marshal Pétain, "Maréchal nous voilà," to attack Prime Minister Raffarin. The power of the demonstrations, in this video, is in the enthusiasm of their participants, and also in their sheer number and variety. It is clear that if there is any answer to the fragmentation of modern society, it is through this kind of direct intervention in political events that involves face-to-face contact rather than mediated exchange.

As a sort of coda to the sequence of demonstrations, Marker's camera lingers in slow motion on a mass commemoration of the victims of the AIDS epidemic. Thousands of people, most of them young, lie on the grass of the Champ de Mars. Medium shots gradually give way to longer and longer shots, each completely filled with recumbent forms. Like the earlier towers, this image, also in the shadow of a tower (Eiffel's), triggers another chilling memory for the viewer. When the color drains from the image and the camera is at a sufficient distance that the bodies begin to lose detail, the shots bear a ghastly resemblance to footage from the liberation of the Nazi death camps that Marker and Resnais showed in *Night and Fog*. This sequence passes entirely without comment, but like the ghost towers, reminds the viewer of what can go wrong in modern society.

As counterpoint to these images of social solidarity, Marker's video juxtaposes another kind of crowd behavior. Just after the AIDS demonstration, Marker finds "the people" on the square of Paris' city hall, mesmerized by images on an enormous screen. They are watching "eleven billionaires kicking a ball," the narrator's dismissive characterization of a soccer game in the World Cup. The camera and intertitles go on to point out that the French team, despite the portraits displayed all over Paris "with Stalinian dimensions," (enormous faces on billboards, printed on buses, in the subway), "did not score a single goal." And yet once again, a crowd is in the sway of a mediated image. Less playful here than in the opening sequence on the Beaubourg Square, Marker's political message returns in full force.

As might be expected, the conclusion to *Chats perchés* is enigmatic. Two events draw the filmmaker's attention: the death of Léon Schwartzenberg, the doctor who became involved in defending the rights of illegal immigrants, and the imprisonment of Bertrand Cantat, the lead singer of the music group Noir Désir, accused of having murdered his girlfriend in Vilnius, Lithuania. The cats make a brief reappearance as little circles of paintings in street corners, and the intertitles comment, "thanks cats—we will need you, wherever we are headed." The final text recounts a legend surrounding the founding of Vilnius, in which a wolf is heard howling up on the mountain, and a duke, hearing the sound, decides to found a city whose reputation will be heard all around the world like the wolf's howl. Besides the obvious overtones of death evoked by these and other sequences in the film, the impression left to the viewer is one of a chaotic modern world in which it is easy to lose one's way. The final text appears to reflect on how to make one's voice heard among the chaos. Which is, after all, what Marker is still trying to do, at the age of eighty-five.

Conclusion

Writing about Chris Marker's work is a bit like solving a puzzle. The opening scene, in which the participants receive instructions to perform a strange exercise but do not understand the meaning of it until they have finished, might serve as a metaphor for the analytical process he asks of his readers or viewers. Because of the scarcity of his own pronouncements about his goals and objectives, the viewer is forced to return to the works themselves, hunting for clues that may confirm the correctness of a particular theory. This feeling of embarking on a treasure hunt seems to align with Marker's personality; as he recently admitted to Monsieur Chat in the pages of *Libération*, "I am not averse to mysteries."[25] It is tempting to apply to Chris Marker the catlike description he gives of his uncle Anton in his CD-Rom *Immemory* (1998): "he is reported here and there as people who disappear always are, people whose invisibility confers upon them a ubiquitous presence, richer in details than that of people who are always there and whom no one notices."[26]

In this respect, *Chats perchés* is typical of Marker's earlier works. Its narrative branches and detours appear to strain against the obligatory linearity

---

25 Rivoire, 'Chats discutent'.

26 Chris Marker, *Immemory*, on CD-Rom (Paris: Centre Georges Pompidou, 1998).

of the film medium in general, as well as against the single narrative position of the documentary in particular. Rather than speaking from a stable narrative center, the narrator slips instead among the various subject positions of the camera, the intertitles, the Morpheye, and the editor. Even the sound editor is a narrative alias; the "*tissu sonore*" or "sound fabric" is attributed to "Michel Krasna," a fictional character whose name alludes to Sandor Krasna, the fictional narrator of *Sans soleil,* and also to Anton Krasna, the "uncle Anton" who appears in *Immemory*. Indeed, in *Immemory*, Marker made full use of the possibilities of hyperlinks to create a work that has multiple pathways embedded in its very form.

In *Chats perchés,* Marker returns once again to the linear constraints of film, despite having declared in 1984, "film and video are equally obsolete when you consider the incoming reign of digital images."[27] In a later interview, he repeated his view, that "film won't have a second century. That's all."[28] What has happened, however, post-9/11, is that he returns to the medium in order to deconstruct its very parameters from within, almost as an object lesson in the medium's fragile, flawed, and pretentious nature. He returns to it, I think, because despite its problems, he acknowledges the tremendous impact that it continues to have. And so, he returns in order to reveal its inner workings, its component parts, its fallacious arguments. The everyday "creative interpretation of actuality" that is central to documentary, such as selection of detail, metonymy, and allegory, snaps into sharp focus.[29] Marker's unconventional editing style isolates various narrative elements—sound, text, image—with the precision of a scalpel, thus bringing them to the attention of the viewer. He creates a "documentary" in which the real and the imaginary intermingle, becoming so embedded in each other as to become indiscernible.[30] Separating them is no longer the business of this documenta-

---

[27] Chris Marker, 'Terminal Vertigo: a New-Technology Interview with Chris Marker', *Monthly Film Bulletin,* 51 (1984), p. 196.

[28] Marker quoted in Lupton, p. 178.

[29] This is particularly true in the slow-motion sequences in the video; see in particular the sequence of a woman dancing in a demonstration to free Tibet. The camera deliberately moves lower to include a statue of the French Republic in the frame, as the editing switches to slow motion and ambient sound gives way to non-diegetic music. Through this process, Marker demonstrates the transformation of an image of a woman and a statue into allegories for abstract ideas, thus embodying the "creative interpretation of actuality" that is central to documentary film. John Grierson, to whom the quotation is attributed, is cited in Paul Ward, *Documentary: The Margins of Reality* (New York: Wallflower, 2005), p. 6.

[30] Of neo-realism, Deleuze writes that "it is as if the real and the imaginary were running after each other, as if each was being reflected in the other, around a point of indiscernibility." This comment can be applied to Marker's work, albeit to a very different end. Deleuze, p. 7.

ry, which instead takes on the mission of proclaiming the impossibility of their separation.

If my analysis of this documentary is convincing, then a reader with a logical mind might well ask if this work in fact has anything to say, to reprise Bill Nichols' terminology, about *the* world outside of the frame, as documentaries traditionally should. Specifically, the role of art and the artist in this world appears to have been severely undermined. Has the great social mission of documentary—to educate and inform—disappeared altogether? And yet, paradoxically, this documentary is attempting to achieve a social mission of its own in the world outside the frame. Its broad thematic concerns ask its viewers to pay attention to art and its ability to bring people together. Its political stance asks them to value collective action. Its formal composition makes a further request of them: to question authority and be aware of the mediated forms in which messages arrive. It seems to project a dogged refusal to give up on art, despite the impossibility of creating a faithful transcription of reality.

Since the completion of *Chats perchés*, Marker has continued to explore the limitations and possibilities of various media. In his online virtual museum, fittingly titled "A Farewell to the Movies," the elemental notions inherent to the medium once again become central to his project.[31] Where image, text, and sound were the basic building blocks of *Chats perchés,* here in a three-dimensional environment, Marker adds a further layer of reflection on lines, planes, and dimensions themselves. Multiple frames hang on the walls of what appears to be a circular gallery. In each two-dimensional frame, a three-dimensional moving image advances in time. In one part of the museum, these frames break off from the walls of the gallery, dancing and spinning in a three-dimensional ballet with other frames, as the movie images they contain continue to roll forward in time, obeying their own internal logic. In his farewell to the movies, Marker already seems to be pushing the limits of his new medium and asking his visitors to think through it with him. Indeed, perhaps it is Marker's view that the only thing that makes life possible at all after the catastrophe is the self-reflexive potential contained in the artistic gesture.

---

[31] Chris Marker, *A Farewell to the Movies*, Video tour at Les Inrockuptibles <http://www.lesinrocks.com/index.php?id=38&tx_extract[notule]=207874&cHash=3> [Accessed 15 May 2008]. Portal to access on Second Life: <http://slurl.com/secondlife/Ouvroir/189/64/40>.

Bibliography

Alter, Nora, *Chris Marker* (Chicago: University of Illinois Press, 2006)

Casebier, Allan, 'A Deconstructive Documentary', *Journal of Film and Video,* 40, no.1 (1988), 34-39

Dargis, Manohla, 'Leftist Politics Scampers Through Paris on Playful Paws', *The New York Times,* 20 December 2006, E11

Darke, Chris, 'The Invisible Man', *Film Comment,* 39, no.3 (2003), 48-50

---, 'First Look: Musique Concrète', *Film Comment,* 41 (2005), 14

Deleuze, Gilles, *Cinema 2: The Time-Image,* trans. by Hugh Tomlinson and Robert Galeta (New York: Continuum, 2005) [orig. pub: *Cinéma 2, l'Image-Temps* (Paris: Les Editions de Minuit, 1985)]

Douhaire, Samuel and Annick Rivoire, 'Rare Marker', *Libération* (Paris), 6 November 2003, 1

Gauthier, Guy, *Chris Marker: écrivain multimedia, ou voyage à travers les médias* (Paris: L'Harmattan, 2001)

Horrigan, Bill, 'Some Other Time', in *Chris Marker: Staring Back*, ed. by Bill Horrigan (Columbus, OH: Wexner Center for the Arts, 2007), 137-150

Kämper, Birgit and Thomas Tode, *Chris Marker: Filmessayist* (Munich: CICIM, 1997)

Lupton, Catherine, *Chris Marker: Memories of the Future* (London: Reaktion Books, 2005)

Marker, Chris, dir., *Chats Perchés/The Case of the Grinning Cat*, on DVD (ARTE Vidéo, 2004; First Run/Icarus Films, 2008)

---, *Immemory*, on CD-ROM (Centre Georges Pompidou, 1998)

---, Marker, Chris, *A Farewell to the Movies*, Video tour at Les Inrockuptibles <http://www.lesinrocks.com/index.php?id=38&tx_extract[notule]=207874&cHash=3> [accessed 15 May 2008]. Portal to access on Second Life: <http://slurl.com/secondlife/Ouvroir/189/64/40>.

---, 'Terminal Vertigo: a New-Technology Interview with Chris Marker', *Monthly Film Bulletin,* 51 (1984), 196-7

Murphy, Jay, 'More of What It Is: Catching up with Chris Marker', *Afterimage* (2005), 31-37

Naficy, Hamid, *An Accented Cinema: Exilic and Diasporic Filmmaking* (Princeton, NJ: Princeton University Press, 2001)

Nichols, Bill, *Representing Reality: Issues and Concepts in Documentary* (Bloomington, IN: Indiana University Press, 1991)

---, 'The Voice of Documentary', in *New Challenges for Documentary,* ed. by Alan Rosenthal and John Corner (New York: Manchester University Press, 2005), 1-16

Renov, Michael, ed., *Theorizing Documentary* (New York: Routledge, 1993)

Rivoire, Annick, 'Chats discutent: Chris Marker et l'auteur de Monsieur Chat racontent leur rencontre artistique, et leur démarche dans *Libération*', *Libération* (Paris), 4 December 2004

---. 'Chris Marker passe le témoin', *Libération* (Paris), 4 December 2004

Ward, Paul, *Documentary: The Margins of Reality* (New York: Wallflower, 2005)

Daring to Imagine: Frédéric Beigbeder's *Windows on the World* and Slimane Benaïssa's *La Dernière Nuit d'un damné*

Carolyn A. Durham

In 2003 Frédéric Beigbeder and Slimane Benaïssa were among the first foreign writers to produce original solutions to the representation of 9/11 in literature and to do so in surprising similar ways, given otherwise dramatic differences between the two Francophone novelists and their two works of fiction. Beigbeder's *Windows on the World* and Benaïssa's *La Dernière Nuit d'un damné* directly confront the two events that are most clearly both factually unverifiable and emotionally incomprehensible: how the victims of the terrorist attack died on the upper floors of the World Trade Center and how the suicide bombers came to justify an act of mass murder. In order to speak what is considered unspeakable, both Beigbeder and Benaïssa seek to create a new language and an original form of expression, using key literary strategies of postmodern fiction. Beigbeder combines different genres, texts, tones, languages, places, and times as he alternates between the reflections of a family trapped in the World Trade Center and his own observations as novelist, engaged in the act of inventing the story of the family's final moments. Benaïssa incorporates extensive quotations from the Koran and other religious writings into his fictional narrator's first-person account of the preparation for the terrorist attacks so that the reader is as immersed in the narrator's gradual embracing of Islamic fundamentalism and of jihad as is the character himself.

Writing in 1940, Philip Rahv, co-founder of the *Partisan Review*, the preeminent journal in which the fusion of the political and the literary was first attempted, expressed the hope that the literature of the United States might increasingly be shaped by international rather than national forces.[1] Almost fifty years later, on the eve of the announcement of the winner of the 2008 Nobel Prize for literature, Horace Engdahl's critique of American literature resounded strangely over the distance of half a century. Noting that Europe, in pointed contrast to the United States, remains "the center of the literary world," the secretary of the Nobel Prize jury described American writers as "too sensitive to trends in their own mass culture," "too isolated," "too insular," and, finally, too constrained by their own "ignorance" of foreign-language texts to "participate in the big dialogue of literature."[2] If the announcement ten days later that the 2008 Nobel Prize had been awarded to the French writer J.M.G. (Jean-Marie Gustave) Le Clézio was received in the United States as a surprising and unexpected choice, Le Clézio's selection

---

1 Pankaj Mishra, 'The End of Innocence', *Guardian*, 19 May 2007 http://www.guardian.co.uk/books/2007/may/19/fiction.martinamis/print [accessed 6 August 2008] (para. 9 of 39).

2 Horace Engdahl, 'Associated Press Interview', *Guardian*, 2 October 2008 (p. 27).

clearly honors a writer whose life and work together exemplify a permanent commitment to cross-cultural and multicultural conversations.

Even though the political events that intervened in the fifty years between Rahv's and Engdahl's statements—a world war; a long-term cold war; repeated conflicts in Asia, Europe, and the Middle East—arguably proved unable to further the *Partisan Review*'s long-delayed agenda, the terrorist attacks of September 11, 2001, might well have been expected to do so at long last. In actuality, however, the American novels that deal with 9/11 and its aftermath have been consistently criticized for their exclusive focus on the individual and the domestic consequences of 9/11 for its survivors. As Pankaj Mishra notes in *The Guardian*, "most of the literary fiction that self-consciously addresses 9/ll still seems underpinned by outdated assumptions of national isolation and self-sufficiency."[3] At the same time, another common response to the American literature of 9/11 has questioned the very right of 9/11 novels to exist at all. In the same journal, Anthony Cummins wonders whether novelists can ever "earn the right to anchor fiction to lived horror in so stark a fashion," accusing those who have tried of using the attacks "too cheaply" and to "unearned" emotional ends.[4] In the introduction to *Literature after 9/11*, the first collection of literary criticism to be devoted to what has become a new body of literature in the last seven years, Ann Keniston and Jeanne Follansbee Quinn agree that early journalistic and eyewitness accounts of the terrorist attacks codified a narrow range of acceptable responses to 9/11—heroism, solidarity, transformative change—that at once rendered all other reactions taboo and questioned the very aesthetics of even attempting to portray "an event that seems incommensurable, inaccessible, and incomprehensible," in short, that is, *unrepresentable*.[5]

In this context, perhaps only non-American authors could initially be expected to take up the challenge effectively. Frédéric Beigbeder and Slimane Benaïssa, two writers who by chance share Le Clézio's nationality and bicultural background, were among the first to propose original solutions to the dual problem of the restrictions of an exclusively national perspective and the

3 Mishra, (para. 38 of 39).

4 Anthony Cummins, 'Does Literature Sell 9/11 Short?', *Guardian*, 23 February 2007 <http://blogs.guardian.co.uk/books/2007/02/does_literature_sell_ 911_short.html> [accessed 6 August 2008] (para.2 of 6).

5 Ann Keniston and Jeanne Follansbee Quinn, 'Introduction', in *Literature After 9/11*, ed. by Ann Keniston and Jeanne Follansbee Quinn (New York: Routledge, 2003), 1-15 (p. 5).

limitations of realistic accounts.[6] They do so, moreover, in surprisingly similar ways, given the otherwise dramatic differences between the two novelists and their two works of fiction, both published in 2003. Beigbeder's *Windows on the World* and Benaïssa's *La Dernière Nuit d'un damné* directly confront the two events that are most clearly both factually unverifiable and emotionally incomprehensible: how the victims of the terrorist attack died on the upper floors of the World Trade Center and how the suicide bombers came to justify an act of mass murder. Beigbeder, convinced that the only way of knowing what happened is to invent it, dares to imagine what took place in the restaurant at the top of the North Tower of the World Trade Center between 8:30 a.m., when "tout est encore possible" (everything is still possible), and 10:28 a.m., when the tower collapsed.[7] Benaïssa, haunted by the "terrible question" asked by "l'humanité entière" (every other human being), uses his own Islamic and Arabic culture to "reconstruct" the three years of preparation that preceded the 9/11 terrorist attacks in an attempt to "dire le possible de cet impossible" (to explain the possibility of this impossibility).[8]

In order to speak what is considered unspeakable, both Beigbeder and Benaïssa logically seek to create a new language and an original form in which to express themselves. The general importance of such an act is no doubt heightened by the critical need to counteract the strong belief that 9/11 was a fundamentally visual event such that the endless rebroadcasting of the planes hitting the World Trade Center and the subsequent destruction of the Twin Towers told us everything we would ever want or need to know about that day: "Le rôle des livres," observes Beigbeder, "est d'écrire tout ce qu'on ne peut pas voir à la télévision" (The role of books is to record what cannot be seen on television).[9] Although to some extent *Windows on the World* and *La Dernière Nuit d'un damné* illustrate the distinction within 9/11 literature that Keniston and Follansbee Quinn make between two contrasting patterns

---

6 Le Clézio is of French-Mauritian background and has for some years divided his time between France, Mauritius, and New Mexico; Benaïssa was born in Algeria and sought asylum in France in 1993; Beigbeder, whose grandmother was American, is of Franco-American background.

7 Frédéric Beigbeder, *Windows on the World* (Paris: Gallimard, 2003), p. 71. Unless otherwise indicated, all translations are taken from Frédéric Beigbeder, *Windows on the World*, trans. by Frank Wynn (New York: Hyperion, 2004).

8 Slimane Benaïssa, *La Dernière Nuit d'un damné* (Paris: Plon, 2003), p. 11. Unless otherwise indicated, all translations are taken from Slimane Benaïssa, *The Last Night of a Damned Soul*, trans. by Janice and Daniel Gross (New York: Grove Press, 2004), p. 11.

9 Beigbeder, p. 111. See also Laura Frost, '9/11's Falling Bodies', in *Literature After 9/11*, ed. by Ann Keniston and Jeanne Follansbee Quinn (New York: Routledge, 2008), 180-206 (p. 183).

of innovation and convention, both novels also use key literary strategies of postmodern fiction. These include, most notably, a dependence on intertextuality that engages Beigbeder and Benaïssa in precisely the kind of extended literary dialogue praised by Engdahl.[10] In both cases, moreover, the reader is deeply and personally engaged in the text as he or she is forced to share the experience of the novels' first-person narrators and to do so explicitly as a highly literate and self-conscious reader of texts. Indeed, each novel contains at its exact center a passage that serves as a *mise-en-abyme* for the text as a whole. In *La Dernière Nuit d'un damné*, both Raouf and the reader settle down "pour une longue séance de lecture du Coran" (a long reading session of the Koran).[11] In *Windows on the World*, we visit, in the company of Frédéric Beigbeder, a Paris exposition devoted to representations of historical and modern disasters.[12]

Beigbeder's representative spectator is first shocked by the deliberate eclecticism of an exhibit whose photos and videos explicitly intermingle industrial catastrophes, terrorist attacks, and natural disasters in an internal duplication of the formal structure of Beigbeder's own novel. *Windows on the World* most visibly alternates between the reflections of Carthew, David, and Jerry Yorston, a divorced father and his two young sons who are trapped in the eponymous restaurant, and the observations of Beigbeder himself, engaged in the act of writing the account of the family's final moments from the top of the Montparnasse Tower in Paris. If a number of reviewers were already scandalized by the disjunction of tone and significance that they perceived between the two stories that make up the dominant framework of the novel, Beigbeder's fictional collage is, in fact, much more diverse and complex than it appears at first view.[13] Its curious combination of different genres, texts, tones, languages, places, and times ultimately embraces, like the

---

10 Keniston and Follansbee Quinn interpret the two patterns in terms of a chronological shift: "the first novels about 9/11 featured formal innovations [. . .]. Later novels have tended to be more formally conservative" (p. 4). *Windows on the World* and *La Dernière Nuit d'un damné* both date from 2003.

11 Benaïssa, p. 157.

12 Beigbeder, pp. 160-63.

13 Only Laura Miller's unusually favorable review acknowledges the complexity of the novel: "Frédéric Beigbeder's 'Windows on the World' is the first novel to perfectly capture the bizarre collection of emotional modes we juggled in 2002, just after the first shock of Sept. 11 was beginning to wear off. The book staggers from full-fledged storytelling to barely veiled memoir to essay to random, canny observation. It's a discombobulated, contradictory, work, but it rings true in a way other stabs at the same topic haven't." Laura Miller, '"Windows on the World" by Frédéric Beigbeder', Salon.com, 20 March 2005 <http://dir.salon.com/story/books/review/2005/03/30/beigbeder> [accessed 8 May 2008] (para. 1 of 4).

Paul Virilio exposition, "ce qui arrive" in "notre monde." Indeed, the discomfort that Beigbeder feels in the museum directly echoes the uneasiness he experienced while writing *Windows*: "A-t-on le droit? Est-il normal d'être à ce point fasciné par la destruction" (Does one have the right? Is it normal to be quite so fascinated with destruction)?[14] Similarly, the general public outrage that accompanied the inauguration of the Paris exhibit echoes the initial critical response to the literature of 9/11: "N'est-il pas trop tôt pour esthétiser une telle desolation? . . . Vais-je pouvoir me regarder dans la glace après avoir publié un roman pareil?" (Isn't it too early to make art of such misery? . . .Will I be able to look myself in the eye after publishing this book?).[15] What troubles Beigbeder most is the realization that by virtue of his own gaze he is somehow "implicated" in the horror depicted in the images he is watching.[16] It is, of course, precisely this acknowledgement of the "complicity" involved in a questionable act of reading and writing that allows him—and therefore us—to relive the events of September 11.[17]

One image in particular haunts Beigbeder: the large-screen projection of photos of Ground Zero covered in rubble, mud, and piles of twisted iron: "Les tours lisses et étincelantes se réduisent à un répugnant désordre chaotique" (The smooth glittering towers have been reduced to a hideous, chaotic mess).[18] Like the scaffolding that rose up in the vast empty space left by the destruction of the twin towers in the days following 9/11, the novel that Beigbeder constructs out of the absence of the World Trade Center is of necessity autogenerative and autoreflexive. *Windows on the World* is openly crafted as a tower of words, visually realized in the penultimate section of the novel whose textual narrative of "10h28" is printed in two parallel columns.[19] Just as Beigbeder concludes his account of the Virilio exhibit with a self-referential description of the very sight that is reproduced on the cover of his book—"ce panache blanc dans le bleu du ciel, comme une écharpe de soie, suspendue, entre la terre et la mer" (the white plume against the blue of the sky, like a silk scarf hanging suspended between land and sea)[20]—the title of

---

14 Beigbeder, p. 161.

15 Ibid., pp. 161, 163.

16 Ibid., p. 163.

17 Both Alain Resnais's *Hiroshima, mon amour* and his *Nuit et brouillard*, which Beigbeder cites directly, deal similarly with questions of the complicity of the spectator, the horror and yet the necessity of memory, and the transformation of the site of a disaster into a tourist attraction. In general, the literature of 9/11, like Beigbeder's novel, often references the Holocaust.

18 Beigbeder, p. 161.

19 Ibid., pp. 366-68.

20 Ibid., p. 163.

the novel becomes the original generator of the fiction. To give an English name to a novel written in French no doubt reflects the renown of the restaurant at the top of the World Trade Center, but the title also identifies the bilingual nature of the text for which it serves as a key metaphor. In the course of the novel, Beigbeder not only references a number of direct or indirect associations with the title words, ranging from Microsoft Windows[21] to the lyrics of a Burt Bacharach anti-war song,[22] but he also interrogates language to propose a series of alternate names: End of the World, Windows on the Planes, Windows on the Smoke, Windows on the Crash, Broken Windows.

Two of the most interesting examples explicitly contrast the fragility of buildings to the permanence of art. The first also provides an intriguing illustration of the intertextual density and autogenerativity of Beigbeder's writing. With the destruction of the World Trade Center, Manhattan once again resembles the city in which J.D. Salinger, Beigbeder's favorite author, set *The Catcher in the Rye*. The title that the novelist borrowed from a line in a Robert Burns poem—"If a body meet a body coming through the rye"—is transformed by Salinger's narrator into "If a body catch a body coming through the rye." Holden Caulfield is determined to become this "catcher in the rye" who saves children from falling off a cliff. By association with a line in the Bacharach song about "little children play[ing]," Beigbeder confronts what Laura Frost identifies as the single most important of the images of 9/11: the footage of the falling bodies whose rapid repression and subsequent censorship epitomizes our refusal to confront what happened on the top floors of the World Trade Center.[23] Although Beigbeder will not ultimately save his fictional hero, who jumps to his death at the conclusion of *Windows on the World*, his own redemption as Yorston's alter ego casts the writer in the role of rescuer: "Le plus beau destin possible: les attraper avant qu'ils ne tombent. Moi aussi je voudrais être l'attrapeur à travers les fenêtres. The Catcher in the Windows" (The most perfect of all possible destinies: catching them before they fall. I too would like to be the catcher).[24]

The second example concludes a discussion of the American writers of the Lost Generation. As Beigbeder explores the Paris immortalized in Ernest

---

21 Ibid., p. 22.

22 Ibid., pp. 38-39.

23 Frost, p. 182.

24 Beigbeder, pp. 54-55. When the Yorston family does jump at the end of the novel, Beigbeder transforms the fall into a flight in a pattern that is characteristic of 9/11 literature: "Pendant un court instant, j'ai vraiment cru qu'on s'envolait" (For a split second, I really believed we were flying) (p. 354). Foer uses a visual strategy of reversal to accomplish something similar at the end of *Extremely Loud & Incredibly Close*. See Frost.

Hemingway's *A Moveable Feast*, he notes the disappearance of the apartment building in which the novelist once lived at 113, rue Notre-Dame-des-Champs: "cet immeuble n'existe plus. La seule chose qui en reste, c'est un livre: Paris est un immeuble mobile" (this building no longer exists. All that remains of it is a book: *A Moveable Edifice*).[25] The final title that Beigbeder proposes for his own novel confirms the "moralité" he uncovers in the Hemingway anecdote: "quand les immeubles disparaissent, seuls les livres peuvent s'en souvenir. . . . il [Hemingway] savait que les livres sont plus costauds que les immeubles" (when buildings vanish, only books can remember them. . . . he knew that books are more durable than buildings).[26] Beigbeder, whose text is haunted throughout by his unsuccessful efforts to recover his own childhood memories, ultimately chooses to redefine the "roman autobiographique" (autobiographical novel) as a narrative that documents not self-revelation or self-discovery but rather the author's disappearance into the 9/11 victims whose permanent erasure he has chosen to immortalize in the present of literature.[27] Beigbeder seeks to create a fictional "miroir sans tain" that he extends outward to his readers so that we too may perceive the shadow of our own reflections on the tinted glass windows of the twin towers: "Certains critiques disent du cinéma que c'est une 'fenêtre sur le monde.' D'autres disent cela du roman aussi. L'art serait une Window on the World" (Some critics claim cinema is a 'window on the world.' Others say the novel is. Art is a window on the world).[28]

The "Window on the World" created by Beigbeder consists of a textual collage of references to world literature that at once produces a homage to Manhattan and the World Trade Center as the cosmopolitan global center of the world and challenges conflicts among peoples and countries based on differences of national languages and literatures: "New York: la ville où on parle 80 langues. Les victimes de l'attentat étaient de 62 nationalités différentes" (New York: a city where they speak 80 languages. The victims of the attack were of 62 different nationalities).[29] The international dialogue that Beigbeder interweaves importantly includes such diverse foreign writers as Milan Kundera, Fyodor Dostoevsky, and Franz Kafka, but it also logically privileges a Franco-American cross-cultural conversation in an effort to bridge what quickly became the most visible of misunderstandings to arise in the post-9/11 world. Beigbeder's political intentions are clear—"J'écris ce

---

25 Beigbeder, p. 170.

26 Ibid., p. 171.

27 Ibid., p. 288.

28 Ibid., pp. 287-88.

29 Ibid., p. 213.

livre parce que j'en ai marre de l'anti-américanisme hexagonal" (I am writing this book because I'm sick of French anti-Americanism)[30]—and his book was well received in France where it won the Prix Interallié in 2003. Its reception in the United States, in contrast, turns outs to confirm Beigbeder's critique of American chauvinism: "son isolationnisme culturel, l'absence totale de curiosité des Américains envers les travaux des étrangers" (its cultural isolation, its complete lack of any curiosity about foreign work).[31] The underlying subtext of a series of angry responses by readers of the English-language translation appears to be a strong sense of outrage that a foreigner, and particularly a Frenchman, has somehow dared to appropriate America's national tragedy to his own literary ends.[32] In fact, Beigbeder's purpose is much more broadly global, in keeping with his desire for a world beyond borders: "Je rêve de supprimer les nations. J'aimerais ne pas avoir de pays" (I dream of abolishing nations. I would love not to have a country).[33] *Windows on the World* offers one answer to Rahv's and Mishra's internationalist goals, most recently reiterated in Michael Rothberg's demand for a "global aesthetic" in the wake of 9/11: "September 11 was a global event. It demands a literature that takes risks, speaks in multiple tongues, and dares to move beyond near-sightedness."[34]

Beigbeder tellingly follows the words I have quoted above by citing the lyrics of John Lennon's similar challenge to our imaginations—"Imagine there's no countries."[35] In a methodical eradication of traditional boundaries, characteristic of the novel as a whole, Beigbeder's text indiscriminately juxtaposes allusions to popular and canonic literature, to different literary genres, and to normally distinctive art forms. Before the novel even begins, the writer cites a Walt Whitman poem, an entry from Kurt Cobain's diary, and

---

30 Ibid., p. 29, my translation.

31 Ibid., p. 32.

32 See, for example, the customer reviews of *Windows on the World* at Amazon.com (<http://www.amazon.com/review/product/140135984/ref=cm_cr_pr> [accessed 30 September 2008]) A reader named Dineson finally denounces the "whiff of xenophobia" in the frequent complaints of bad taste, which he believes to be based on Beigbeder's perceived "lack of reverence in dealing with a disaster that directly impacts AMERICANS, for god's sake." The characteristic failure of American readers to understand Beigbeder's use of satire, comedy, and black humor might also attest to longstanding Franco-American cultural differences. American readers are thus particularly upset by an explicit sex scene in Beigbeder's novel.

33 Beigbeder, p. 299.

34 Michael Rothberg, 'Seeing Terror, Feeling Art: Public and Private in Post-9/11 Literature', in *Literature After 9/11*, ed. Ann Keniston and Jeanne Follansbee Quinn (New York: Routledge, 2008), 123-142 (pp. 140-41).

35 Beigbeder, p. 299.

contradictory descriptions of the role of the novelist offered by Tom Wolfe and Marilyn Manson. Subsequently, his textual references include Dorothy Parker, Sinclair Lewis, Joris-Karl Huysmans, Philippe Labro, Charles Baudelaire, J. G. Ballard, Russell Banks, Jean-Paul Sartre, Marguerite Duras, Henry Miller, Louis-Ferdinand Céline, Hunter Thomas, Albert Camus, F. Scott Fitzgerald, Georges Pérec, Alain Robbe-Grillet, René Descartes, Edmund White, and perhaps fifty other writers, without counting the many cinematic and musical allusions. Indeed, early in the novel, Beigbeder's list of his own personal favorites among American artists alone includes 23 writers, sixteen musicians, and fifteen filmmakers.[36] If Beigbeder's strategy is fully in keeping with postmodern literature's general defiance of conventional notions of originality, authority, and referentiality, he also has a far less playful purpose, which, by chance, is also apparent in the full text of the stanza that Beigbeder quotes from Lennon's "Imagine": "Imagine there's no countries / It isn't hard to do / Nothing to kill or die for / And no religion too / Imagine all the people / Living Life in peace."

In the course of *Windows on the World*, Beigbeder repeatedly returns to one reference in particular, the only text he cites progressively and virtually in its entirety. At three different points in the novel, he quotes directly from *Genesis* XI: 1-9, the biblical account of the construction and the destruction of the Tower of Babel. To begin with, he quotes verses 1-3, which do not yet include any mention of what will become his central metaphor for the contemporary global world and for his own novel. Initially, we have only his version of "all the people living in peace": "La terre n'avait alors qu'une seule langue et qu'une même manière de parler" (And the whole earth was of one language and everyone spoke in the same way).[37] Subsequently, Beigbeder cites verse 4, in which the decision to build "une ville et une tour dont le sommet touche le ciel" (a city and a tower, whose top may reach into heaven) in an effort to make "un nom" (a name) for themselves is announced.[38] Interestingly, Beigbeder's unacknowledged ellipsis of the full motivation for the plan ("afin de ne pas être dispersés sur toute la surface de la terre" [lest we be scattered abroad upon the face of the whole earth])[39] eliminates any human responsibility for the punishment God delivers in verses 5-8: "confondons-y tellement leur language, qu'ils ne s'entendent plus les uns les autres. C'est en cette manière que le Seigneur les dispersa de ce lieu dans tous les pays du monde" (there confound their language, that they may not under-

36 Ibid., p. 30.

37 Ibid., pp. 76-77, my translation.

38 Ibid., p. 110.

39 My translation.

stand one another's speech. So the Lord scattered them abroad from thence upon the face of the earth).[40] Ironically, contrary to the very expectations he has carefully set up, Beigbeder never cites the last verse of the passage in which the tower is finally named. It is clearly unnecessary; as in the case of the twin towers themselves, the significance of the *9th* verse of the *11th* chapter of Genesis is highlighted by its very absence.

Beigbeder's claim that he doesn't know why he keeps thinking about this particular book of the bible—"j'ignore pourquoi je pense à la Genèse" (I don't know what makes me think of Genesis)[41]—works similarly to engage the reader in the active construction of the text. It is precisely the act of "genesis" that preoccupies Beigbeder as postmodern novelist: the coming into being of his own novel, generated out of other texts, out of language itself, out of the empty space where another tower once stood. In the context of 9/11, the insistence on oral language in *Windows on the World* is poignantly appropriate as a reminder that the only factual record we have of what happened to people like Carthew Yorston and his children consists of the phone messages left by those trapped on the upper floors of the World Trade Center. To replace the historic language of Babylon, Beigbeder creates an original form of "franglais" spoken by American and French characters alike, "la langue du futur" (the language of the future):

> Il ne faut pas avoir peur des mots anglais. Ils s'intègrent paisiblement à notre idiome, afin de créer la langue mondiale, celle qui désobéit à Dieu: la langue unique de Babel. Les words du world. Le nouveau vocabulaire SMS ('A12C4'), les logos d'internet ☺, l'évolution de l'orthographe kidélirgraphe, la popularisation du verlan, tout cela contribue à fabriquer la novlangue du troisième millénaire.[42]
> (We shouldn't be afraid of English words. They are calmly integrated into our own in order to create a global language, one that defies God: the single language of Babel. Les words du world. The lexicon of text messaging ('CU L8R'). Internet emoticons ☺, the rise of phonetic spelling and slang, all of this contributes to creating the novspeak of the third millennium.)

The novel incorporates lengthy passages of dialogue conceived in what is precisely this new, hybridic language, the most remarkable of which may be the repeated conversations between two Wall Street traders who communicate in a combination of technospeak and advertising slogans. Elsewhere, Beigbeder draws attention to language by repeating snatches of dialogue and song lyrics, creating long enumerative passages, engaging in word play and

40 Beigbeder, pp. 152-53.
41 Ibid., p. 152.
42 Ibid., pp. 175-76.

the creation of neologisms, changing font size and type, and embedding unidentified quotations within the narrative.[43] Unsurprisingly, Beigbeder is far less interested in the history or the mythology of *Babel* than in the etymology of the word: "Le mot Babel désigne Babylone mais évoque la parole (d'où le verbe 'babiller')" (The word Babel represents Babylon, but brings language to mind (hence the verb 'to babble')).[44] The bilingual language and fragmented form of his own novel thus become a textual act of vindication for the divine retribution that cleverly targets not the tower itself but rather the very foundation of language: by severing the essential relationship between words and their referents, God assures that the citizens of the world can no longer communicate with each other. Beigbeder imagines a creative and thoroughly modern solution in *Windows on the World*, which undermines God's intent by metaphorically teaching the contemporary reader a foreign language. In a global universe, mutual understanding will no longer be based on an original common language but rather on international multilingualism and multicultural literacy.[45]

Benaïssa also makes extensive use of spoken language and intertextuality in *La Dernière Nuit d'un damné*, as he too raises significant questions about the nature of the linguistic sign. Initially, in keeping with the fact that in some ways Benaïssa has written a traditional realistic novel of ideas, his direct engagement with what he defines as "une fiction" (fictional), on the grounds that "je ne suis aucun des personnages et qu'aucun d'eux n'est réel" (I am not to be found in any of the characters, nor are they real), takes the form of an "Avant-propos" that precedes the novel itself.[46] From the beginning, Benaïssa inserts his "plaidoyer contre toutes les idéologies de la mort" (plea

---

43 For example, he ponders whether "*atterrir*" or "*immeublir*" best resolves the semantic question of what verb to use to designate the landing of a plane flown into a building: "Préparez-vous à l'attourrissage" (Prepare to skyscrape) (pp. 120-21, my translation). Although Beigbeder frequently identifies an intertextual reference after the literate reader has already recognized it, as in the case of Céline's *Voyage au bout de la nuit* or Sam Mendes's *American Beauty*, I am convinced that one of the most important intertexts of *Windows on the World* is never named. The first section of Paul Auster's *The New York Trilogy* is set in Manhattan, has the suggestive title of "City of Glass," and focuses on the linguistic consequences of the fall of Babel; Auster is widely read in France.

44 Beigbeder, p. 152.

45 Beigbeder playfully speculates that the Tower of Babel once had a twin—"Saviez-vous qu'il y avait deux tours de Babel? Les archéologues sont formels.[. . .] Il était une fois les Twin Towers de Babel... en Irak" (Did you know that there were two towers of Babel?[. . .] There were once Twin Towers of Babel . . . in Iraq)—in what is perhaps an ironic justification of the American government's odd decision to declare war on Iraq in the aftermath of the terrorist attacks of 9/11 (pp. 282-83).

46 Benaïssa, p. 11.

against all ideologies of death) into an international literary tradition, marked by "Le dernier jour d'un condamné" (*The Last Days of a Condemned Man*), Victor Hugo's 1832 condemnation of the death penalty, and *One Day of Ivan Denissovitch*, Alexandre Soljenitsyne's 1962 denunciation of forced labor camps.[47] The novel itself is the first-person story of Raouf, a young American Muslim of Egyptian and Lebanese background and a successful software engineer in Silicon Valley, whose sense of cultural exile and spiritual disillusionment following the death of his father will lead him to embrace 9/11 martyrdom.

Despite the implied subjectivity of the novel's narrative technique, in one important sense Raouf is essentially absent from his own account, which incorporates not only extensive quotations from his friend Athman, his boss Djamel, and the speeches and sermons of various imams but also a number of passages from three different kinds of religious writing: the Koran, the Hadith, and a variety of other prayers and supplications. In the case of Raouf, the ultimate requirement that the future martyrs "organise[ent] une absence en étant toujours là" (make it look like you've disappeared while still being here) has already been largely realized well in advance of the final stage of preparation for the terrorist attacks.[48] At the same time, however, the novel's narrative strategy also gives a strong textual presence to the reader, who is subjected in the same way as is Benaïssa's narrator to the identical discourse the latter hears and reads so that we are ultimately as immersed in and as disturbed by Raouf's gradual embracing of Islamic fundamentalism and of jihad as is the character himself.

In contrast to the powerful rhetoric that characterizes the pages of citations, Raouf's own language seems curiously prosaic for such an otherwise highly literate novel. Indeed, at times he seems to be a textbook example of all that successful fiction writers, enjoined in workshops and how-to manuals to "show, don't tell," should avoid. The introduction of each new character takes the form of an objectively informative biographical portrait, and Raouf's obsession with descriptive detail and factual data is such that we are given exhaustive accounts of daily events from which apparently no element, no matter how obvious or seemingly irrelevant, can be omitted. To use a cinematic analogy, he cannot bring himself to "cut to continuity." But Raouf, of course, is not a professional writer. Indeed, even as he continues to cling to mundane objects and certain daily habits of his former life, he willingly and easily abandons literature at a very early stage of his recruitment: "Depuis

[47] Ibid., p. 9.

[48] Ibid., p. 150.

dix-huit mois, je n'avais plus vu de film ni lu de romans et cela ne me manquait pas" (For eighteen months I hadn't seen a movie or read a novel, and I didn't miss it at all).[49] More importantly, as his prose suggests, he is decidedly literal minded, which is precisely what makes him an ideal audience for those speakers and writers who are skilled in the art of verbal persuasion.

Islam, as presented in *La Dernière Nuit d'un damné*, is explicitly defined as both a written text and one that is fundamentally transparent, tautological, and essentialist. As Anthame explains it, "l'islam est un livre qui s'applique et qui ne se discute pas" (Islam is a book which is applied and not questioned).[50] Unlike Judaism or Christianity, whose sacred religious texts are open to questioning and interpretation by the faithful, Muslims need only read the Koran to understand God's word: "Dans le Coran, il n'y a pas de mystère à éclairer, [. . .] Il n'y a pas de sens caché" (In the Koran, there is no mystery to clarify, [. . .] There is no hidden meaning). Moreover, in direct contrast to the limited scope of other religions, "l'islam est complet, tautologique. L'islam est la religion qui intègre la politique, et la politique qui dit la vérité, c'est de la religion" (Islam is complete, it's tautological. Islam is a religion integrated with politics, and the politics that tell the truth are religion).[51] This immediate illustration of tautology is only one of many in the novel, which also describes a belief system that precludes all ambiguity or complexity: "la solution, c'est la foi. Ou tu l'as ou tu ne l'as pas" (The solution is faith. Either you have it or you don't).[52] The appeal of such simplicity is reinforced in Raouf's case by a particularly strong penchant for submission to authority, in keeping with the Arabic etymologies of *Islam* (submission) and of *Muslim* (one who surrenders).

In this context, Raouf's many conversations with Athmane and their repeated visits to regional mosques, made for the express purpose of exposing Raouf to the sermons of different imams and teaching him to recognize different schools of thought, might well seem contradictory; and certainly Benaïssa's intention is no doubt ironic in part. On the other hand, such interventions are always directly inspired by a religious passage, and in terms of length and detail, they always remain subordinate to actual quotations from the Koran, the Hadith, or another prayer. The commentary functions as a linguistic gloss on certain words or an *explication de texte* of an original piece of writing, which therefore retains its primacy and its centrality. As Raouf's final "guide" explains to him and to the four other would-be martyrs: "Depuis

[49] Ibid., p. 113.
[50] Ibid., p. 114.
[51] Ibid., p. 83.
[52] Ibid., p. 91.

ma première parole aujourd'hui et jusqu'à la dernière le jour de votre départ, je vais distiller pour vous le sens des mots" (From my first word to you today until my last on the day that you leave, I'm going to distill for you the sense of the words).[53] Paradoxically, as such terms as *gloss* and *distiller* suggest, Islam, despite its literalism, is also transcribed in what for most believers is a foreign language, resulting in a highly literate religion that is arguably not only well designed to appeal to the illiterate but which also grants extraordinary power to the imam, who functions of necessity as a translator. The Koran is considered to be the sacred and direct word of God in Arabic alone; once the text is translated into any other language, it becomes only an interpretation of the original. *La Dernière Nuit d'un damné* is thus doubly fictional since Benaïssa has not only positioned religious texts within the framework of a novel, but he has also included his own translations of the original Arabic text.

Still, Benaïssa's reader is better informed than his narrator, who abandons novels only to fill his head with words that by his own admission he doesn't understand very well. We must remember that the one-third or more of the book that consists of quotation is being read or heard by Raouf in the original Arabic, a language in which he reads slowly and in which he is proud to be able to read the Koran at all "vu mon niveau d'arabe" (given my level in Arabic).[54] The first five days of the recruits' final training are devoted to reading the Koran aloud in order to substitute the teachings of "l'université de Dieu" for their American educations and to counteract the influence of American culture. Moreover, beginning with the private lessons in Islamic theology that prepare Raouf to reconfirm his faith and continuing up to the moment he abandons his fellow terrorists on the very day of the planned attack, he memorizes an extraordinary number of texts.[55] The success of the planned jihad depends on preventing independent thought and eradicating fear, largely accomplished by designing the terrorist action to correspond to Islam's five daily prayers and then requiring the jihadists to repeat them over

---

53 Ibid., p. 167.

54 Ibid., p. 233.

55 He does so in part to compensate for what he accepts as his own lack of acculturation into Islamism. On the other hand, Raouf's ultimate failure stems from his refusal to take the drugs that have been prescribed for him out of the belief that an action requiring a practice condemned by Islam cannot finally be Islamic (see pp. 248, 252). Beigbeder, in confronting the same inability to understand that informs Benaïssa's fiction as a whole, also assumes that the terrorists must have been drugged: "Comment ces hommes-là ont été capables d'égorger des hôtesses de l'air avec des cutters [. . .] Etaient-ils drogués, et si oui, à quoi?" (How men like this could slit stewardesses' throats with a craft knife [. . .] Were they on drugs, and if so, what?) (pp. 320-21).

and over.[56] If the following quotation seems long, it nonetheless omits the actual prayers embedded in the text of the novel:

> Pendant ces cinq étapes, vous ne penserez qu'à trois choses: à *Dieu*, à l'*action*, et à vos *suppliques* de chaque instant.
>
> A votre réveil le matin, vous direz la supplique du réveil: [. . .]
>
> Au moment où vous vous habillerez, [. . .] vous direz la supplique de l'habit: [. . .]
>
> Avant de sortir [. . .] dites la supplique qui correspond au sortir de la maison: [. . .]
>
> Quand vous arriverez à l'aéroport, vous direz la supplique du lieu: [. . .]
>
> Dans vos coeurs, et sans que personne ne s'en aperçoive, vous direz [des versets du Coran]: [. . .]
>
> Quand vous serez dans la salle d'embarquement, [. . .] faites semblant de lire tout en récitant dans vos cœurs [des versets du Coran]: [. . .]
>
> Quand vous serez dans l'avion, redites la supplique du voyage:[. . .]
>
> Vous ouvrirez le combat et criant "*Allahou Akbar*." Vous direz à haute voix des versets du Coran pour emplir le coeur des voyageurs d'effroi.[57]
>
> (During these five steps, you will think of only three things : of God, of the *action*, and of your constant *supplications*.
>
> When you rise in the morning, you will say the morning supplication: [. . .]
>
> At the time you get dressed, [. . .] you will say the supplication of clothing: [. . .]
>
> Before going out [. . .] say the supplication for going out of the house [...]
>
> When you arrive at the airport, you will say the supplication of place: [....]
>
> When you reach your departure gate, [. . .] pretend to be reading while reciting in your hearts [verses of the Koran]: [. . .]
>
> When you are in the plane, say the travel supplication again: [. . .]
>
> You will begin the battle crying "*Allabu Akbar*" ("God is Great"). You will say verses of the Koran out loud to fill the passengers' hearts with fear.)

In the final letter that Raouf writes to Djamel before leaving for the airport, it is hardly surprising that the personal metamorphosis occasioned by his belief that Islam has brought him "plus qu'une identité" (more than an identity) actually casts him in the role of a ventriloquist's puppet or a trained parrot: "Moi qui n'arrivais jamais à finir mes phrases, j'ai appris à les terminer grâce à la récitation du Coran car on ne peut laisser les versets de Dieu en suspens" (For someone who never managed to finish a sentence before, I learned to complete each one thanks to my recitation of the Koran, because you can't

---

56 The division of Benaïssa's novel into five chapters imitates this same structure. Similarly, Beigbeder points out the similarity in the time frame between his fiction and the events it recounts: "L'enfer dure une heure trois quarts. Ce livre aussi" (Hell lasts an hour and three quarters. As does this book) (p. 18).

57 Benaïssa, pp. 221-226.

leave the verses of God suspended in midair).[58] Appropriately, once he panics and flees the airport, Raouf discovers that he has metaphorically lost both his literacy and his memory: "Pour retrouver mes esprits, j'ai ouvert le Coran au hasard [. . .]. Plus je lisais, moins j'arrivais à me concentrer... Etaient-ce mes larmes qui troublaient ma lecture?[. . .] j'ai essayé de réciter les versets que j'avais appris. [. . .] Ma mémoire était restée silencieuse... Je ne savais plus" (To get my bearings, I opened the Koran at random [. . .]. The more I read, the less I could concentrate. . . . Was it because my tears were interfering with reading? [. . .] I tried to recite some verses I had learned [. . .] But my memory remained silent. . . . I didn't know how anymore).[59] The same failure is repeated twice more in essentially the same words, first as Raouf contemplates suicide—"Ma mémoire était au silence. Je ne savais plus..." (my memory was silent. . . . I didn't know how anymore. . . .)[60]—and then in the moment immediately prior to his arrest when he finally abandons writing: "Ma mémoire est encore au silence. Je ne sais plus. . . . J'arrête mon écriture ici. Je crois que la police est venue pour m'arrêter...C'est sûr" (My memory is still silent. I don't know anymore. [. . .] I'm stopping my writing here. I think the police have come to arrest me . . . I'm sure of it).[61] Unable to recall the empty verbiage that has replaced his own identity and destroyed his capacity for self-reflection, Raouf, in a particularly appropriate punishment, is reduced to silence.[62] In an equally ironic and equally suitable gesture, Raouf's mother will have the last word in the misogynistic and ultimately exclusively male world of *La dernière nuit d'un damné*. In reflection of the novel's epigraph, addressed to Benaïssa's own mother for her courageous opposition to Islamic martyrdom, the disapproval of Raouf's mother, who denounces her son's acts as mad, absurd, savage, and blasphemous, indirectly

58 Ibid., p. 237.

59 Ibid., pp. 246-48.

60 Ibid., p. 251.

61 Ibid., p. 257.

62 To some extent the same thing is true of *Windows on the World*. As the novel approaches its end, Beigbeder finds it increasingly difficult to describe what is happening, and notations of "paragraphe coupé" (paragraph cut) or "page coupée" (page cut) suddenly begin to appear. Fittingly, his justification for "l'abus d'ellipses" (our misuse of ellipses) is precisely to force his readers to "dare to imagine" in their turn: "J'ai coupé des descriptions insoutenables. . . . Je les ai coupées parce qu'à mon avis, il est encore plus atroce de vous laisser imaginer ce par quoi elles [les victimes] sont passées" (I have cut out the unbearable descriptions. [. . .] I cut them because, in my opinion, it is more appalling still to let you imagine what became of them) (p. 331, my translation).

allows the novelist to end his fiction, as it began, with an explicit condemnation of his narrator.[63]

Brian McHale argues in the conclusion to *Postmodernist Fiction* that just as "tragic or serious texts about death are also, as if inevitably, about texts, about themselves . . . texts about themselves, self-reflective, self-conscious texts, are also, as if inevitably, about death."[64] Certainly this is the case in both *Windows on the World* and *La dernière nuit d'un damné*, in which the transgression of ontological boundaries, on which McHale bases his argument, is accompanied by the crossing of multiple literary, generic, cultural, and linguistic barriers as well.[65] Both novels thus successfully avoid appropriating the tragedy of 9/11, as so many critics, readers, and reviewers fear that fiction will do, precisely by translating it in the sense that Jacques Derrida has used the term. "Translation," the antipode to "appropriation," erases neither our horror at the deaths that occurred in the World Trade Center nor our horror at the ability of the terrorists to plan such deaths. On the contrary, Beigbeder and Benaïssa accomplish acts of "love" or "passion" that leave the events of 9/11 intact, even as, indeed perhaps because, they dare to imagine them.[66] Because *Windows on the World* and *La dernière nuit d'un damné* have now been translated into English and a Franco-American project to translate Beigbeder's text into film is currently underway, we can hope that the two novels will help to enlarge American participation in a long-postponed international literary dialogue engaging crucial human and global concerns.

---

63 Benaïssa, pp. 259-72.

64 Brian McHale, *Postmodernist Fiction* (New York: Routledge, 1957), p. 231.

65 One of the titles that Beigbeder contemplates for his novel is "La Mort: mode d'emploi" (Death: a user's manual), a parodic inversion of George Péréc's *La Vie: mode d'emploi*" (*Life: A User's Manual*). Raouf's guide informs the terrorists that if "le Coran parle autant de la mort, c'est parce que c'est à travers elle que s'établit notre relation à Dieu" (If the Koran speaks so much about death, it's because our relationship with God is established through death) (p. 171).

66 Bliss Cua Lin, 'Remade in Silence: Silvia Kolbowski's *A Film Will be Shown without the Sound*', *Art Journal* (Fall 2007), 85-87.

Bibliography

Beigbeder, Frédéric, *Windows on the World* (Paris: Gallimard, 2003).

---, *Windows on the World*, trans. by Frank Wynne (New York: Hyperion, 2004)

Benaïssa, Slimane, *La Dernière Nuit d'un damné* (Paris: Plon, 2003).

---, *The Last Night of a Damned Soul*, trans. by Janice and Daniel Gross (New York: Grove Press, 2004)

Customer Reviews of *Windows on the World*, Amazon.com, <http://www.amazon.com/review/product/140135984/ref=cm_cr_pr> [accessed 30 September 2008]

Cummins, Anthony 'Does Literature Sell 9/11 Short?', *Guardian*, 23 February 2007 <http://blogs.guardian.co.uk/book/2007/02/does_literature_sell_911_short.html> [accessed 6 August 2008]

Engdahl, Horace, 'Associated Press interview', *Guardian*, 2 October 2008, 27

Foer, Jonathan Safran, *Extremely Loud & Incredibly Close* (New York: Houghton Mifflin, 2005)

Keniston, Ann and Jeanne Follansbee, 'Introduction', *Literature After 9/11*, ed. by Ann Keniston and Jeanne Follansbee (New York: Routledge, 2003), 1-15

Frost, Laura, '9/11's Falling Bodies', *Literature After 9/11*, ed by Ann Keniston and Jeanne Follansbee (New York: Routledge, 2003), 180-206

Lin, Bliss Cua, 'Remade in Silence: Silvia Kolbowski's *A Film Will Be Shown without the Sound*', *Art Journal* (Fall 2007), 85-87

McHale, Brian, *Postmodernist Fiction* (New York: Routledge, 1957)

Miller, Laura, '"Windows on the World" by Frédéric Beigbeder', Salon.com. 20 March 2005< http://dir.salon.com/story/books/review/2005/03/20/beigbeder> [accessed 8 May 2008]

Mishra, Pankaj, ;The End of Innocence' *Guardian* 19 May 2007 <http://www.guardian.co.uk/books/2007/may/19/fiction.martinamis/print> [accessed 6 August 2008]

Rothberg, Michael, 'Seeing Terror, Feeling Art: Public and Private in Post-9/11 Literature', *Literature After 9/11*, ed. by Ann Keniston and Jeanne Follansbee (New York: Routledge, 2003), 123-142

Perspectival Adjustments and Hyper-Reality in *11'09"01*

Silvia Schultermandl

The question as to what is real and in what way contemporary textual responses to 9/11 deal with reality offers the scope for my investigation of the aesthetic and ideological strategies that emanate from contemporary literature and film which seek to offer direct responses to 9/11. I argue in this chapter that Alain Brigand's *11'09"01*, a compilation of eleven short movies, demands two different kinds of perspectival adjustments: those needed for the viewing audience to make sense of the film and those for the movie itself to emphasize its discussion of the international impact of 9/11. I borrow the term "perspectival adjustments" from Julia Watson and Sidonie Smith's assertion that a deconstruction of Western-centric practices of literary autobiography is in place for the sake of more diverse and counter-monolithic forms of narrating selfhood.[1] The perspectival adjustments in *11'09"01* equally deconstruct the monolithic category that 9/11 has become both as an actual event of international repercussions, on the one hand, and as the preoccupation with New York City, on the other. In particular, the movie offers an interesting take on the question of what reality is, for instance, by exposing the hyper-real mechanisms of narration that are needed in order to communicate what 9/11 means in various localized international contexts.

Reality After 9/11

Many critics have argued that 9/11 altered our concept of reality, especially when it comes to the question of what we can imagine to be real. Paul Virilio, for instance, notes such a blurring between real disasters and simulated disasters when he observes the following:

> As the attack on the World Trade Center was being broadcast live, many TV viewers believed they were watching one of those disaster movies which proliferate endlessly on our television screens. It was by switching channels and finding the same pictures on all the stations that they finally understood that "it was true." [2]

This "monstrous dose of reality" that 9/11 brought about in the US resonates in the cultural criticism of reality in contemporary US culture.[3] In the guest

---

1 Sidonie Smith and Julia Watson, 'Introduction: De/Colonization and the Politics of Discourse in Women's Autobiographical Practices', in *De/Colonizing the Subject: The Politics of Gender in Women's Autobiography*, ed. by Sidonie Smith and Julia Watson (Minneapolis: University of Minnesota Press, 1992), xiii-xxxi (p. xvii).

2 Emma Wilson, 'Europe's 9/11', *Paragraph: A Journal of Modern Critical Theory*, 23 (Nov. 2004), 100-12 (p. 101).

3 Susan Sontag, 'The Talk of the Town', *The New Yorker*, 24 September, 2001 <http://www.newyorker.com/archive/2001/09/010924ta_talk_wtc> [accessed 13 November 2008] (para. 29 of 44).

editor's introduction to the special theme issue "Responses to 9/11" of *The Journal of American Culture*, Jane Caputi addresses this notion of continuous disbelief with which people meet the events of 9/11 and the subsequent changes in the New York City skyline by relating the personal reaction one of her sisters had to the events, quoting her as expressing "her instant conviction that a 'schism' has opened up in reality and that a world had disappeared."[4] This sentiment illustrates forcefully the approach that Slavoj Žižek has taken in his attempt to theorize the notion of reality in relation to 9/11.

In *Welcome to the Desert of the Real* (2002), Žižek discusses the interconnectedness between the concepts of *virtual Reality* and *reality*: "Virtual reality is experienced as reality without being so. What happens at the end of this process of virtualization, however, is that we begin to experience 'real reality' itself as a virtual entity."[5] Žižek thus underscores the relationship between real and simulated reality. Žižek's argument further addresses this issue when he observes the "derealization" that emanated from the media coverage of 9/11: "while the number of victims—3.000—is repeated all the time, it is surprising how little of the actual carnage we see—no dismembered bodies, no blood, no desperate faces of dying people."[6] In other words, not only through what was being depicted but through what was not depicted did controlled images of the US in the form of censored images of the attacks themselves get disseminated around the globe. While Žižek does not argue that sensationalist news coverage is in place, he notes that the absence of realistic details is particularly noteworthy because of the stark contrast between the 9/11 news coverage and the more excessive depiction of human suffering in relation to disasters that occur in the Third World. In the systematic omission of graphic details about 9/11, especially in comparison to the prevalence of such details in footage on disasters in the Third World, Žižek sees an indication for a possible ideological manipulation that communicates to Western audiences that "the real horror happens there, not here."[7]

Žižek's notion of reality raises the question of how art can capture this new sense of reality. Several 9/11 novels set in the US, including Don DeLillo's *Falling Man* (2007), Mohsin Hamid's *The Reluctant Fundamentalist* (2007), Jay McInerny's *The Good Life* (2006), Claire Messud's *The Empe-*

---

4 Jane Caputi, 'Guest Editor's Introduction: Of Towers and Twins, Synchronicities and Shadows: Archetypal Meanings in the Imagery of 9/11', *The Journal of American Culture*, 28 (March 2005), 1-10 (p. 2).

5 Slavoj Žižek, *Welcome to the Desert of the Real*, (London and New York: Verso, 2002), p. 11.

6 Ibid., p. 13.

7 Ibid., p. 43.

ror's Children (2006), or Jonathan Safran Foer's *Extremely Loud and Incredibly Close* (2005), depict the attacks on the Twin Towers in New York City as a turning point in American history, one that entirely alters their protagonists' lives. With the exception of Hamid's novel, these texts are all set in downtown Manhattan, offering the protagonists' direct view of the attacks on the World Trade Center or directing them in their searches for meaning in life after the attacks into the lower Manhattan area. What unites all of these literary responses to 9/11 is their emphasis on the iconic meaning that the attack on the World Trade Center Twin Towers in NYC has. All of the above books recall, often in minute detail, the moments when the Towers fell, or the very moments when the true devastation of these events became visible in the forms of streets filled with soot and debris. And these descriptions, probably because they are so well known to many audiences who recognize them from the visual images shown on CNN and other global media, appear real, although the content remains difficult to accept or even make sense of. The feeling that "this can't be real" is indeed what many people felt when they first heard about or saw images of the burning and later collapsing Twin Towers. And perhaps only because these things really did occur does the literary representation of these events make sense to the audience. In other words, because art imitates life, as it were, can such horrific images as depicted in the above texts withstand the skepticism of a doubtful reader who might otherwise easily reject the depiction of such events as too-far fetched and over the top. Thus, especially when it comes to depictions of 9/11, the lines between fact and fiction, between what can be real and what can not, are blurred.

In Frédéric Beigbeder's novel *Windows on the World* (2004), one of the two narrators takes this idea a step further when he argues that only fiction can make sense of reality. In a meta-fictional commentary, this narrator suggests the following:

> Writing this hyperrealist novel is made more difficult by reality itself. Since September 11, 2001, reality has not only outstripped fiction, it's destroying it. It's impossible to write about this subject, and yet impossible to write about anything else. Nothing else touches us.[8]

This reality, so we see throughout Beigbeder's novel, depends upon a specific context from which the attacks on the WTC on September 11, 2001, can be approached. In the case of Beigbeder's narrator, that context is Le Ciel de Paris, a restaurant up top the Tour Montparnasse in Paris, France. In constant

---

8 Frédéric Beigbeder, *Windows on the World*, translated by Frank Wynne (London: Fourth Estate, 2004), p. 8.

meta-fictional commentary throughout the novel, the narrator refers to his storytelling as a way of offering a "hyper-reality," one that needs to include a frame of reference other than the Twin Towers or New York City in order to be able to "relate" the incident.

Perspectival Adjustments in *11'09"01*

My essay takes cues from Beigbeder's idea of hyper-reality and applies it to two short films featured in the critically acclaimed movie *11'09"01* (2002), a project undertaken by French producer Alain Brigand, who invited 11 directors from as many countries to contribute one piece that deals with the events on September 11 in New York City.[9] Each of the eleven shorts offers a different perspective on 9/11, both the actual occurrences in New York and the myth that 9/11 has become in the popular imaginary. None of the depictions of 9/11 that the movie offers resembles much the images of what 9/11 has come to signify in the literary responses to 9/11 set in the US: the planes hitting the North and the South Tower of the World Trade Center, the sense of chaos and turmoil around New York's tallest building, the destitution and alienation in the New York City landscape that the collapsed towers left. While such images became dominant, almost canonical, in the literary responses as well as in the global media coverage of the event, *11'09"01* privileges alternative, even marginal, perspectives on 9/11 by either focusing on narratives connected to 9/11 that are set in countries other than the US, or by portraying 9/11 from a point of view that does not evoke the images that we recognize from the news. By emphasizing the particular international contexts in which these events occurred and by connecting them to a variety of social and material realities that different people deal with, this compilation of eleven shorts puts the 9/11 events in an international dialogue with local events that occurred outside the US. And by putting into perspective the events of 9/11 in the US, the shorts expose and subvert the "American-centric and provincial" assumption that 9/11 carries internationally unprecedented meaning.[10]

Thus, while many literary responses to 9/11 and the global media coverage of 9/11 depict one kind of reality of 9/11, the movie invites the audience

---

9 Alain Brigand, *11'09"01*, on DVD (Galatée Films / Studio Canal, 2002).

10 Marita Sturken, 'Memorializing Absence', *Social Science Research Council*, < http://www.ssrc.org/sept11/essays/sturken.htm > [accessed 2 December 2, 2008] (para. 1 of 15)

to challenge the absolute terms of this reality and to consider various other perspectives on 9/11. The very title of the compilation of eleven shorts offers one such perspectival adjustment: while the American version of the movie is entitled *September 11*, the original title is *11'09"01*, "the date of the attacks as it would appear on the European calendar" as opposed to the American calendar.[11] While 9/11, in the American tradition of indicating time, recalls the 911 emergency call in the US, the 11'09"01 format evokes one of the main structural elements of the film: the fact that each of the 11 shorts is exactly eleven minutes and nine seconds and one frame.

Each of the eleven pieces offers a different story that is related to 9/11, on the one hand, and to specific events in the country the individual directors seem to represent, on the other. While there are multiple conversations going on among the eleven shorts and their intertexts, they can be grouped together along the following thematic strands. The first category deals with different perspectives and modes of aestheticization of the actual events in New York City. For instance, Claude Lelouche's piece (France) depicts the events of 9/11 from the perspective of a deaf-mute French woman and frames the attacks on the Twin Towers with a romantic relationship between the woman and an American tour guide. Alejañdro González Inárritu's piece (Mexico), a collage of audio and video snippets of the actual news coverage of the attacks on the Twin Towers, offers glimpses of several "jumpers," as well as off-voice recordings of cell phone calls from people trapped in the burning towers. And Sean Penn's piece (United States) depicts an old widower whose somber one-bedroom apartment literally in the shadow of the Twin Towers is finally illuminated once the Twin Towers collapse, a fact that makes the old man realize and accept for the first time the absence of his late wife.

A second category depicts various events that Patricia Keeton calls the"other 9/11."[12] There is, for instance, Danis Tanović's piece (Bosnia-Herzegovina) which depicts the efforts of the women of Srebrenica on the 11th day of every month to call for national and international recognition as they are protesting the losses of loved ones by marching silently on the main town square. The "other 9/11," namely the coup d'état on Chilean president Salvador Allende is subject of Ken Loach's piece (United Kingdom), which offers the perspective of a Chilean exile in London who writes a letter on the first anniversary of the events of 9/11 in New York, explicitly creating a

---

11 Stef Craps, 'Conjuring Trauma: The Naudet Brothers' 9/11 Documentary', *Canadian Review of American Studies/Revue canadienne d'études américaines*, 37 (2007), 183-204 (p. 195).

12 Patricia Keeton, 'Reevaluating the "Old" Cold War: A Dialectical Reading of Two 9/11 Narratives', *Cinema Journal*, 43 (Summer 2004), 114-21 (p. 114).

parallel between the two dates but, more importantly, delineating in what ways the CIA and then-US Secretary of State Henry Kissinger participated in the coup d'état which left thirty thousand Chilean citizens murdered and many surviving victims traumatized to this present day.

The third category deals with issues that surfaced in the aftermath of 9/11, such as terrorism and national paranoia. In this category, Samira Makhmalbaf's piece (Iran) depicts a young Iranian teacher's attempt to relate the international ramifications that the attacks on the Twin Towers might entail to children in an Afghani refugee camp in Iran. One such ramification is depicted in Amos Gitaï's piece (Israel) in which a reporter enumerates a list of events that all occurred on September eleven, thus deconstructing the monolithic importance that the events in New York City have instilled into the date September 11. This reporter's initial attempt to cover a local terrorist attack in Tel Aviv gets taken off the air so that exhaustive coverage of the attacks on the Twin Towers in New York can be broadcast. In the same vein, Youssef Chahine's piece (Egypt) starts with the effects that the attacks on the Twin Towers have on an Egyptian director and then shows this director engaged in a conversation with a deceased American Marine on the social relevance of civil resistance and terrorism for Palestinians. Also with a keen eye on the international interconnectedness of terrorism, Idrissa Ouedraogo's piece (Burkina Faso) depicts the attempt of five young boys to capture Osama bin Laden in their home town in hopes of obtaining the ransom that the international police set on him so that they may sponsor medical treatment for malaria and AIDS patients across Africa. The issues of terrorism also overshadow the story line of Mira Nair's piece (India), which, based on a true story, thematizes the extent to which young Muslim males in the US are subject to allegations of terrorism as part of a spreading Islamophobia in the wake of 9/11.

While all of the above categories feature pieces that are set contemporaneously with the events on 9/11 or in their more or less immediate aftermath, the last piece, directed by Shohei Imamura (Japan) predates the actual events in New York City. Imamura's piece depicts a former soldier of the Japanese Imperial Army who, after returning from duty in WWII, prefers to live as a snake rather than as a human being, a fact that leaves his parents and wife both deeply ashamed of and alienated from him. This piece also sticks out for its overtly fantastic elements, such as those evidenced in the last scene of the piece, where a snake seemingly addresses the viewing audience, telling them that there is no holy war. Fantastic elements also appear in some of the other shorts, but to a much lesser degree. With the exception of Alejañdro

González Inárritu's highly experimental piece, they offer overtly realistic depictions.

Together, the eleven shorts are in dialogue with each other about a variety of social and cultural issues both in the US and in the countries the individual directors represent. (In this sense, Mira Nair's piece about the mother of Salman Hamdani, a young Pakistani American who was first accused of being complicit in the attacks on the Twin Towers and later, after his dead body was found in the debris of the collapsed towers, became a national hero on account of the assistance he offered the rescue workers on site, is listed under the country India, Nair's country of origin.) The intertextual dialogues between the various pieces suggest the plurality of responses to 9/11 that the compilation wants to generate; while each piece offers a unique perspective and operates with a unique strategy in order to create different moods and impressions on the audience, the cacophony of voices is indicative of the possibility, even need, of a counter-monolithic approach to 9/11 in order to discuss the plurality of global experience and relevance of the event. One specific detail that emphasizes this notion of multiple voices and perspectives is, of course, the fact that each of the shorts has different protagonists, but more importantly, that six out of the eleven shorts are in languages other than English; one is in sign language. This counter-monolithic depiction of 9/11 in itself is a response to what James F. Tracy calls "America's New Global Imperialism," a type of dominance that takes the form of media productions in "for-profit news and entertainment media" that are "in conformity with the real and practical strategic ambitions of US governmental and corporate policy makers."[13] This counter-monolithic cacophony of responses also deconstructs the hegemonic importance that has been instilled into 9/11 by making the US the subject of international attention. In line with Marita Sturken's assertion that to consider the attacks of September 11, 2001, as an event that marks a turning point in global history is to make a "particularly American-centric and provincial" assumption (online), Brigand's *11'09"01* instead investigates the international connectedness of the events in New York City and other global phenomena that are equally characteristic of the postmodern global world order.

What is remarkable about the film is that despite the attention to minute details of the social and material realities of the pieces' plot and setting, the directors do not frame their pieces as sensationalist counter-views of international events but, rather, emphasize the interconnectedness of 9/11 and the

---

[13] James F. Tracy, 'Bearing Witness to the Unspeakable: 9/11 and America's New Global Imperialism', *The Journal of American Culture*, 28 (March 2005), 85-99 (p. 86).

personal experiences different people have of 9/11 and its aftermath. While all the eleven shorts aestheticize the different contexts in which 9/11 "happened" through different genres and stylistic strategies, in the shorts by Iranian director Samira Makhmalbaf and Israeli director Amos Gitaï, the idea of hyper-reality resonates in a particularly compelling way. In the following section, I offer a discussion of these two shorts and their depictions of this international interconnectedness between 9/11 in New York and events in the local setting of the pieces.

Visual Hyperreality of 9/11

Samira Makhmalbaf's piece, the first one on the compilation of eleven short films, is set in a brick-making factory in an Afghani refugee community in Iran. The piece starts with a close-up shot of several men, wearing kurtas and turbans, one of whom pulls a water bucket suspended on a rope. These scenes are shot with a hand-held camera which, together with the grainy texture of the images, lends a documentary feel to the images. This scene, and the subsequent one where a young girl pours the water onto a mound of clay that a couple of other children are treading with their bare feet, might come as somewhat of a surprise to the audience who expects to see something about 9/11. Instead, the film shows children packing clay into wooden molds and then setting the bricks to dry in the sun, two of them discussing an accident in the camp that left two people dead. The coherence of these scenes then gets disrupted by the appearance of the teacher, who, with confident stride but seemingly preoccupied air, walks across the factory area. Indeed, the thematic link between the local scene and the attacks on the Twin Towers can only be guessed until the young teacher gathers up the children who are working in the factory to their make-shift school in an attempt to teach them about the attacks on the World Trade Center in New York. The implication that this is a difficult task becomes clear both from the fact that the teacher needs to convince the parents to let their children participate in the class, even by refusing to give them books unless their children show up at school, and by the fact that the children are unable to make sense of the information she gives them.

This becomes evident from the responses the teacher gets when she solicits information from the children about whether they know what happened that day. She asks them: "Children, important news. A big incident took place in the world. Who knows anything about it?" When, after a moment of silence and tension, she indicates that it is an event of "major importance," it becomes clear from the children's responses what kind of events truly matter to them: one boy, Esmat, reports that two people fell into the water well and died. Then a girl, Najeebeh, reports that her "Auntie" in Afghanistan was buried in the ground up to her neck and stoned to death. After the teacher prompts the children to think about a "more important global incident," another girl guesses that "a flood came and everyone was killed." These events, which to the children communicate the social conditions of their immediate environment, stand in stark contrast to the event the teacher wants them to care about. The contrast becomes most evident when the teacher tells the children about fallen towers, and later about mobile phones, and people buried in debris, and then, perhaps unsure her message reaches her intended audience, asks the children whether they even know what a tower is.

In order to make the children understand what a tower is, she tells them to look outside. And with the children's gaze, the camera's gaze shifts outside and depicts the smoking tower, the chimney of the brick kiln, against a perfectly clear blue sky. That her attempt to make the children visualize the magnitude of the events in New York by explaining to them what a tower is fails becomes clear when the children refuse to comply with the teacher's request to "keep a minute of silence in honour [sic] of those killed in New York." Because the children cannot relate to the events in New York City, or perhaps anything else that does not occur in their immediate social environment, her final attempt is to make the children stare at the smoke coming out of one of the high chimneys for a minute of silence and reflection. The way the scene is framed creates the impression that the children are staring up toward the top of one of the burning Twin Towers, an image that simulates the possible view from the plaza of the World Trade Center. The vantage point, although different from the one that the actual images of the burning Twin Towers conveyed on the global news coverage of the attacks, evokes a similarity between the Twin Towers and the tower of the chimney kiln, not only as a pedagogical tool with which the teacher tries to reach her pupils, but also as a means of inscribing the imagery that the movie audience associates with 9/11.

And by making the children visualize the concept of a burning tower as they keep a minute of silence, the teacher puts the children in a situation where they create their own memories of the incident in New York City in their own local environments. In this sense, the teacher in Makhmalbaf's piece exposes the children to a process that Lacan defines as *anamorphosis*, "a process whereby a change in the viewer's standpoint causes a visual stimulus to take on a radically different form."[14] With the term anamorphosis, Lacan denotes not only the spatial but also the metaphorical adjustments needed to generate a different perspective. Louis Sass specifies:

> The key element for Lacan is the shift of perspective that occurs when something that had once seemed to be merely a potential *object* of the subject's attentive gaze is suddenly revealed to be itself a *subject*, typically a threatening subject who takes the first subject as its own object.[15]

In Makhmalbaf's piece, such a moment of anamorphosis occurs at the end of movie, when the children look up towards the top of the smoking chimney. And while most of the shots in this final section of the movie either depict the children from the perspective of the teacher or the smoking chimney from the perspective of the children, the final shot offers a tableau taken from a distant angle, one that shows the smoking chimney against the clear blue sky with the teacher and the children standing beneath it, standing on what appears to be a flat roof top. In this scene, the movie proposes a double gaze in that it exposes the act of looking by making the children and the teacher both subject and object of the gaze at the same time.

Such a perspectival adjustment brings about the distinction between what Lacan calls "Reality" and "the Real," which in Makhmalbaf's piece pertains to the children's answers to the teacher's question about the "big global incident." Reality for the children is, among other things, the spatial and cultural setting in an Afghani refugee camp in Iran, or, more concretely, the brick factory where they work. Part of their Reality is also the daily events that occur there, events that the children discuss while making clay bricks at the factory. The aspects of the children's Reality only refer to their immediate surroundings and do not take into consideration in what way they are also participants in the global world. By being forced to confront the global realities, including the attack on the Twin Towers in New York City, incidents that are to a certain extent beyond their comprehension, the children experience what Lacan defines as "the Real." For the children in particular, this move from Reality to the Real also connotes a shift from innocence to experience, thus implying the transformative impact of 9/11 on a localized international level.

The children's shift from innocence to experience is particularly interesting because of the implied contradiction between the teacher's comment that

---

14 Louis Sass, 'Lacan and 9/11', *Raritan: A Quarterly Review*, 23 (Summer 2003), 162-66 (p. 162).

15 Ibid., p. 163.

the children should "keep [their] innocence" and her attempt to make the children understand the global importance of 9/11. Such a shift suggests a coerced maturation process, one that brings into sharper focus the perspectival adjustment that the short thematizes. Given the fact that the teacher attributes more importance to the attacks in New York than to the children's displacement from Afghanistan, the short seems to indicate that the children, who can't begin to comprehend the attacks, are more affected by them than they are by their own displacement and their living conditions in the refugee camp. However, while the children's anamorphosis marks their interconnectedness between their social and material realities and the reality of 9/11, Makhmalbaf's piece also implies a coerced maturation process for the viewers by forcing them to consider the global interconnectedness of the children's social realities and 9/11. And perhaps while the circumstances of the children's immediate lives are already profoundly transformative, the depiction of the social and material realities the children experience in the refugee camp and in the brick factory demands of the viewers an adjustment of their perspective so as to undergo their own sort of transformation and to be less provincial and US-centric. The children's anamorphosis at the end of the short thus not only implies a shift from reality to the Real for the children, but also for the viewing audience who associates with 9/11 only the images of the attacks on New York. The images of 9/11 that the viewing audience has internalized as absolute signifiers of 9/11 are being put into perspective, and they, thus, deconstruct the monolithic meaning that 9/11 has gained in many parts of the world. Because the children are standing in for the viewing audience, the perspectival adjustment that Makhmalbaf's piece demands of its viewers is to consider that the transformative impact that 9/11 might have in their lives is equally as strong as the transformative impact that their dislocation from Afghanistan has on the viewers' lives. Makhmalbaf's piece thus forces its viewers to consider the children in the Afghani refugee camp as part of the Real that becomes tangible in the interconnectedness between the significance of 9/11 in the US and in Iran.

Audible Hyperreality

A similar transition from reality to the Real is central to Amos Gitaï's piece. Whereas Makhmalbaf's piece starts with a visual image that the audience might have difficulty placing in relation to 9/11, Gitaï's pieces starts off with an undefined audible impression, possibly the sound of an explosion. This sound, however, might evoke the sound of a plane crashing into one of the

Twin Towers, until the visual depiction of the bomb squad agent shouting directions in Hebrew indicates that the crime scene is not in the US. And from the information this agent shouts into his walkie-talkie, the audience soon gets the details of the event: two car bombs and a suicide bomber with a backpack. Such information is also conveyed by the dynamics of the scene, the chaotic running around of passers-by, injured people, the bomb squad agents, police officers and paramedics, as well as by the intensive background noise such as screaming people, motor scooters driving by, sirens going off, the bomb squad and the ambulance staff shouting instructions to co-workers. The camera, which seems to be planted in a fixed spot, follows the events by turning the gaze left and right, like an audience at a tennis match, and then zooming in on details. This is, in fact, the position that camera maintains throughout the entire piece, offering one long shot of the events without cuts, with some of the main figures at times stepping out of the frame of vision. In the midst of this turmoil, a television reporter and her crew, who were out to shoot a feature on people doing their holiday shopping for Rosh Hashanah in Jerusalem Street in Tel Aviv, rush to the site in order to cover the event first-hand.

In line with the chaotic and dynamic setting, the news reporter fails at her attempt to offer a coherent news story of the events she witnesses: either she is being cut off by the police and bomb squad who try to usher her away from the site, or she is being interrupted by an eyewitness who continuously steps up to her in hopes of getting on the news, or she interrupts her own description of the site for a brief interview with the police and paramedics. This inability to create a coherent story of the incident seems to be self-generated by the chaos into which the reporter immersed herself. In contrast, the fact that she is not allowed to broadcast her story is a much more strategic decision which was imposed on her by her producers and the editor of her show. She argues with her producer: "The public has a right to know!" thinking that she is live on the air, when actually the editor cut her off, a fact that she only learns after having made several attempts at a coherent news coverage in the midst of the chaotic site. Frustrated by the fact that the editor does not put her on the air, she shouts, "Who gives a shit about New York!" and then reasons, "But we are right in the middle of a terrorist attack in Tel Aviv!"

When she realizes that her story on the local incident is consciously suppressed in favor the coverage of the events in New York City, she starts reciting several incidents throughout world history that also happened on a September 11, including the seizure of Washington by the British in 1777, the seizure of Malakoff by the French in 1855, the meeting between Roosevelt and Churchill to divide Nazi Germany into an American, a British, and a

Russian section in 1944, and finally, the killing of 19 people in India through a strike of lightening in 1997. This litany displays her frantic attempt to reclaim her voice and agency at a moment (or even the beginning of an era) when only the American 9/11 holds some ground in Western collective memory. It is interesting to note that the reporter does not rehearse the dates according to the Jewish calendar, but according to the Gregorian calendar, at least according to the movie's English and French subtitles.

Soon thereafter, she learns for the first time that a plane hit the Twin Towers, immediately concluding that this must be a terrorist attack, just like she assumed that the incident in Tel Aviv was a terrorist attack even before anybody on site confirmed her suspicions. And then, possibly because she sees another chance to finally get on the air, she links together the two potential terrorist attacks by proclaiming: "One terrorist attack for another!" And the logical sequence she displays in her attempted report is noteworthy: she starts out by drawing parallels between the two terrorist attacks, only to emphasize the one in Tel Aviv by underscoring the symbolic importance of Jerusalem Avenue as an indication of the "existence of the Jewish people." This comment can be taken both as a statement in response to the terrorist attack in Tel Aviv as well as in response to the secondariness her story receives from the editor who prioritizes the news story about New York. By emphasizing the importance of the local terrorist attack, the reporter calls attention to the fact that after the terrorist attacks in the US, many other occurrences seem to have become secondary. And while at first her emphasis on "the existence of the Jewish people" evokes a nationalist discourse that seeks primarily to solidify the existence of the state of Israel, the catalogue of international events occurring on September 11 throughout history does not glorify Israeli nationhood but is directed at explicitly undermining the status of global importance that the attacks on the US acquired without privileging any nation state.

The perspectival adjustment that Gitaï's piece demands of its audience becomes apparent at the end of the movie. While the reporter slowly walks away in resignation, telling her crew that she feels sick, an off-voice, which appears to be that of her producer, explains to her why she cannot get on the air. It soon becomes clear that the producer does not actually talk to the reporter at that moment but that his comments are the responses to what the reporter was saying a few moments ago. It almost appears as if the audience finally hears his side of the conversation with a considerable time lag, a fact that emphasizes the lack of communication and understanding between the reporter and her producer. When the producer tempts her by saying "Remember the time and date, 9 in the morning, September 11! No one will ever forget this date," it finally becomes clear what prompted the reporter to rehearse her knowledge of events in world history that all occurred on a September 11. The producer's comment aims at solidifying the hegemonic status of the US by instilling into the events a global meaning of such magnitude which "awards traumatic events in the US more historical weight than those in the rest of the world."[16] And while the producer asks her whether this is "some dumb game show," thus discrediting the importance of all these events that occurred on a September 11 the reporter enumerates, the reporter's rehearsal of these events makes sense for the audience because it is indicative of her refusal to accept the monolithic importance of the events in New York.

Conclusion

Both pieces evoke a clear speaker-audience situation: the teacher's attempt to make her pupils understand the magnitude of 9/11 and the tragedy that this event signifies, and the reporter's attempt to give the local terrorist attack the attention she feels it deserves. The messages that the two speakers, the teacher and the reporter, are trying to communicate paint entirely opposite images of the New York 9/11: one wants to relate the magnitude of the New York attacks and the other one the magnitude of a local event. But by simulating the sender / receiver situation of the communication of 9/11, both pieces expose the mechanisms of the transmission. Both women incessantly try to make sense of the situation—the events in New York and of the immediate situations in which they find themselves—due to their responsibility to relate information. And both of them, as suggested by the fact that it is not clear in Makhmalbaf's piece whether the children also understand the metaphorical meaning of the tower they are staring at and by the fact that the reporter's story does not get broadcasted, only partly succeed in conveying their intended messages.

Yet while the attempted communication the pieces depict only partly succeeds in relating the message that the speakers want to get across, the message that the two shorts want to relate to the viewing audience succeeds precisely because the pieces force the audience to perform the very perspectival adjustments that they depict. By emphasizing the visual and audible adjustments that various characters in these two pieces undertake respectively, the two narratives probe the viewing audience's ability to empathize with the teacher's and the reporter's attempts at relating *their* stories to their intended

16 Sturken, para 1 of 15.

audiences. For instance, when the camera perspective follows the teacher walking towards the make-shift school, depicting her as saying, "You can't stop atomic bombs with these bricks," and "There are three million Afghan refugees living in Iran. Whatever happens to them will happen to you too," it leaves the audience wondering what the piece has to do with 9/11 possibly to the same extent as the children might wonder what 9/11 has to do with them. And by separating the discussion between the reporter and her producer, Gitaï's piece amplifies the lack of consensus between the editor or producer and the reporter as far as their understanding of what deserves to be broadcast as an important event in world history is concerned. Both pieces make the audience participate in the creation of meaning, at the same time as they expose the audience to the global realities that have not acquired the monolithic status that the events in New York have been inscribed with.

Therefore, by making the subject of these two shorts their own attempts to make sense of the situation that 9/11 causes in two international contexts, these pieces underscore the hyper-reality implied in the process of dealing with the reality of 9/11. Both pieces demand of the viewers perspectival adjustments that accommodate the viewers' own social and material realities as well as those depicted in the shorts. These two pieces from *11'09"01* thus follow Judith Butler's imperative that in dealing with the reality of 9/11, "we will need to emerge from the narrative perspective of US unilateralism and, as it were, its defensive structures, to consider the ways in which our lives are profoundly implicated in the lives of others."[17]

---

[17] Butler, Judith, *Precarious Life: The Power of Mourning and Violence*, (London: Verso, 2004), p. 7.

Bibliography

Beigbeder, Frédéric, *Windows on the World*, translated by Frank Wynne (London: Fourth Estate, 2004)

Brigand, Alain, *11'09"01*, on DVD (Galatée Films / Studio Canal, 2002)

Butler, Judith, *Precarious Life: The Power of Mourning and Violence*, (London: Verso, 2004)

Caputi, Jane, 'Guest Editor's Introduction: Of Towers and Twins, Synchronicities and Shadows: Archetypal Meanings in the Imagery of 9/11', *The Journal of American Culture*, 28 (March 2005), 1-10

Craps, Stef, 'Conjuring Trauma: The Naudet Brothers' 9/11 Documentary', *Canadian Review of American Studies/Revue canadienne d'études américaines*, 37 (2007), 183-204

DeLillo, Don, *Falling Man* (New York: Scribner, 2007)

Foer, Jonathan Safran, *Extremely Loud and Incredibly Close* (Boston: Houghton Mifflin, 2005)

Hamid, Mohsin, *The Reluctant Fundamentalist* (Orlando: Hartcourt: 2007)

Keeton, Patricia, 'Reevaluating the "Old" Cold War: A Dialectical Reading of Two 9/11 Narratives', *Cinema Journal*, 43 (Summer 2004), 114-21

McInerney, Jay, *The Good Life* (New York: Vintage Contemporaries, 2006)

Messud, Claire, *The Emperor's Children* (New York: Vintage, 2006)

Sass, Loius, 'Lacan and 9/11', *Raritan: A Quarterly Review*, 23 (Summer 2003), 162-66

Sontag, Susan, 'The Talk of the Town', *The New Yorker*, 24 September, 2001 <http://www.newyorker.com/archive/2001/09/010924ta_talk_wtc> [accessed 13 November 2008]

Sturken, Marita, 'Memorializing Absence', *Social Science Research Council*, < http://www.ssrc.org/sept11/essays/sturken.htm > [accessed 2 December 2008]

Tracy, James F., 'Bearing Witness to the Unspeakable: 9/11 and America's New Global Imperialism', *The Journal of American Culture*, 28 (March 2005), 85-99

Watson, Julia, and Sidonie Smith, 'Introduction: De/Colonization and the Politics of Discourse in Women's Autobiographical Practices', in *De/Colonizing the Subject: The Politics of Gender in Women's Autobiography*, ed. by Sidonie Smith and Julia Watson (Minneapolis: University of Minnesota Press, 1992), pp. xiii-xxxi

Wilson, Emma, 'Europe's 9/11', *Paragraph: A Journal of Modern Critical Theory*, 23 (Nov. 2004), 100-12

Žižek, Slavoj, *Welcome to the Desert of the Real* (London and New York: Verso, 2002)

Manipulative Fictions: Democratic Futures in Pakistan

Cara Cilano

Post-9/11 US militaristic rhetoric and action, with their sweeping domestic and international consequences, have had little truck with the other. In marked contrast, recent Pakistani fictions—a novel and a film—use what Gayatri Spivak refers to as the epistemological breach of 9/11 to construct an ethical moment, a repositioning in which the primary other of the US's "war on terror," the Muslim male, becomes a self. Moreover, these two Pakistani fictions envision possible democratic futures in Pakistan that result less from the US's efforts to ensure democracy's safety through its "war on terror" and more from a nuanced representation of the cultural tensions in Pakistan itself. The two works I focus on are Mohsin Hamid's 2007 novel *The Reluctant Fundamentalist* and Shoaib Mansoor's 2007 film *Khuda Kay Liye* or *In the Name of God.* In both of my examples, some manipulation of the narrative takes place. With the film, the viewer observes the manipulation, aware of who perpetrates it, and, in the novel, the reader herself is subject to the manipulative forces of the narrative through a first-person narrative voice. *Khuda Kay Liye* resolves its manipulations at the level of story; in contrast, *The Reluctant Fundamentalist*, wherein the reader's implication in the narrative manipulation is at its most extreme, offers no neat resolution at all. The presence of manipulation in both the novel and the film functions, first, to mirror the disorientation of the American-based characters as they experience life as Muslim males in the US immediately after 9/11. The manipulation also functions to highlight how US-centric views, as well as radical Islamist ones, contribute to the construction of the Muslim male as the other so that the reader/viewer may both become aware of her presumptions and, potentially, acknowledge the possibility of alternative democratic practices and spaces.

In an interview published in 2003, Jacques Derrida expressed his concerns over what effect the events of 11 September 2001 would have on how people will imagine, know, and live in the future. Of the seemingly pervasive culture of fear—think of those color-coded security warnings at US airports, for instance—brought about by the US's "tough" stance on terror, Derrida comments, "There is traumatism with no possible work of mourning when the evil comes from the possibility to come of the worst [...]. Traumatism is produced by the *future*, [...] by the threat of the worst *to come*, rather than by an aggression that is 'over and done with.'"[1] The apprehension and anxiety that accompany the traumatism of which Derrida speaks bear the potential to alter radically how those living under the threat of another terrorist attack live, regardless of whether another attack takes place. In such circumstances, institutions vulnerable to alteration, in a negative sense, include democracy itself. And, when Derrida contends that the actions and discourses of the "'bin Laden effect'" "*open onto no future*'," he also points toward the frightening similarities between terrorist rhetoric and that of the US as it conducts its

[1] Giovanna Borradori, *Philosophy in a Time of Terror: Dialogues with Jürgen Habermas and Jacques Derrida* (Chicago: University of Chicago Press, 2003), p. 97. Emphasis in original.

"war on terror," especially with respect to democratic practices in the US and elsewhere.[2]

At the same time, however, Derrida's claim that "[…w]e do not *know* what it [the September 11 attack] is and so do not know how to describe, identify, or even name it,"[3] creates a conceptual space to imagine what it means to live in a post-9/11 world. Derrida's recognition of the events of that September day as a threat to "the system of interpretation, the axiomatic, logic, rhetoric, concepts, and evaluations that are supposed to allow one to *comprehend* and to explain precisely something like 'September 11'"[4] can be understood through Gayatri Spivak's understanding of the ethical as "an interruption of the epistemological, which is the attempt to construct the other as an object of knowledge."[5] A breach in an epistemological system, such as that which concerns Derrida, becomes, in Spivak's words, an opportunity "to listen to the other as if it were a self, neither to punish nor acquit."[6]

Post-9/11 US militaristic rhetoric and action, with their sweeping domestic and international consequences, have had little truck with the other. In marked contrast, recent Pakistani fictions—a novel and a film—take up Spivak's contention, as it were, and use the epistemological breach of 9/11 to construct an ethical moment, a repositioning in which the primary other of the US's "war on terror," the Muslim male, becomes a self. Moreover, these two Pakistani fictions envision possible democratic futures in Pakistan that result less from the US's efforts to ensure democracy's safety through its "war on terror" and more from a nuanced representation of the cultural tensions in Pakistan itself.

The two works I focus on are Mohsin Hamid's 2007 novel *The Reluctant Fundamentalist* and Shoaib Mansoor's 2007 film *Khuda Kay Liye* or *In the Name of God*. In both of my examples, some manipulation of the narrative takes place. With the film, the viewer observes the manipulation, aware of who perpetrates it, and, in the novel, the reader herself is subject to the manipulative forces of the narrative through a first-person narrative voice. *Khuda Kay Liye* resolves its manipulations at the level of story; in contrast, *The Reluctant Fundamentalist*, wherein the reader's implication in the narrative manipulation is at its most extreme, offers no neat resolution at all. The presence of manipulation in both the novel and the film functions, first, to mirror the disorientation of the American-based characters as they experience life as

2 Ibid., p. 113. Emphasis in original.
3 Ibid., p. 94. Emphasis in original.
4 Ibid., p. 93. Emphasis in original.
5 Gayatri Spivak, 'Terror: A Speech after 9/11', *boundary 2*, 31 (2004), pp. 81-111 (p. 83).
6 Ibid., p. 83.

Muslim males in the US immediately after 9/11. The manipulation also functions to highlight how US-centric views, as well as radical Islamist ones, contribute to the construction of the Muslim male as the other so that the reader/viewer may both become aware of her presumptions and, potentially, acknowledge the possibility of alternative democratic practices and spaces.

Through his first-person narrative voice, Changez, the narrator of Mohsin Hamid's *The Reluctant Fundamentalist,* tells his unnamed, presumably American interlocutor that he attended Princeton University and remained in the US as an employee at a high-stakes consulting firm. Changez lived a comfortable life in New York City, though his Pakistani roots are more financially (not socially) modest. Changez's intellectual and financial successes in the US carry with them a bit of resentment, a gnawing feeling of never quite fitting in. This marginalized sense gets exacerbated by Changez's failed attempts to secure the love of an American woman he meets at Princeton. Although Changez returns to Pakistan after 11 September 2001, his feelings about the attacks are pronounced and critical. Changez begins to build a life in Lahore by lecturing at a university, where he quickly amasses a following for his outspokenness against the US. The manipulation of the narrative occurs through both the general untrustworthiness of a first person narrator and the mystery that shrouds Changez's presumably American listener, whom Changez addresses in the second person. As Changez notes the American's demeanor—his nervousness, say—and his actions—including hurriedly sending off text messages and reaching into his suit jacket for what could be a weapon—the reader is left wondering whether this listener is indeed a CIA operative sent to kill Changez for the latter's "radical" pronouncements (read: terrorist threats) or this listener is the target for Changez's own premeditated violence.

Like Hamid's novel, Shoaib Mansoor's 2007 film, *Khuda Kay Liye,* features a privileged Pakistani man, Mansoor, who migrates to the US to study music, who lives there through 11 September 2001, and who eventually returns to Pakistan. The film also features two notable plot additions: first, after the attacks, Mansoor is abducted from his Chicago flat, while sleeping beside his American wife, tortured and interrogated, and eventually deported back to Pakistan, mentally incapacitated, after the "authorities" determine he's not actually a terrorist; and, second, the film follows Mansoor's brother, Sarnad, who remains in Pakistan and travels down a divergent path into religious extremism, culminating in his brief association with the Taliban. In effect, the brothers are mirror images, tracing two possible routes available to young, educated, financially-stable men in Pakistan. Just as Mansoor's American experiment fails miserably, so does Sarnad's extremist one. Both sons return to their parents' comfortable life, though in significantly different conditions. There are two types of manipulation working in the film. The first operates at the level of story and involves Sarnad and his British-born cousin, Mary. The other type is structural: the film begins where it ends, opening with a scene set in Chicago wherein Mansoor's American wife, Janie, learns of his mental breakdown; the audience has no idea yet who these characters are or what precipitated the breakdown.

The novel and the film establish recognizable pre-9/11 minority narratives for their migrant characters. Both male characters—Changez and Mansoor—initially enjoy their lives in the US. Changez comments upon the pleasure he takes in talking to Urdu-speaking New York City cabbies with left-leaning politics. With his privilege and education, Changez stands in for a recognizable South Asian migrant story, the sort Susan Koshy refers to as a South Asian "exceptionalism" that splits into two competing explanations for South Asian identity in the US. The explanation that Changez best represents "stresses ethnicity and class" and "emphasizes the anomalous status of South Asian Americans among racial minorities and embraces the rhetoric of a color-blind meritocracy."[7] Changez's reflection that "[he] suspected [his] Pakistaniness was invisible, cloaked by [his] suit, by [his] expense account, and—most of all—by [his work] companions" illustrates this point.[8]

At the same time, given the novel's post-9/11 sensibility, Changez's integration into American privilege does not happen so seamlessly. Even while Changez tries to convince himself of his own exceptionalism, he nonetheless understands how tenuous his inclusion within this white, upper-middle class echelon is. From the moment of his admission to the university, Changez possesses an awareness of his "special" status:

> Looking back now, I see the power of that system, pragmatic and effective, like so much else in America. We international students were sourced from around the globe, sifted not only by well-honed standardized texts but by painstakingly customized evaluations [...] until the best and the brightest of us had been identified. [...] Students like me were given visas and scholarships, complete financial aid, mind you, and invited into the ranks of the meritocracy. In return, we were expected to contribute our talents to your society, the society we were joining. And for the most part, we were happy to do so. I certainly was, at least at first.[9]

---

7 Susan Koshy, 'Category Crisis: South Asian Americans and Questions of Race and Ethnicity', *Diaspora: A Journal of Transnational Studies*, 7 (1998), 285-320 (p. 285).

8 Mohsin Hamid, *The Reluctant Fundamentalist* (Orlando: Harcourt, 2007), p. 71.

9 Ibid., p. 4.

Changez's assessment of the opportunity Princeton affords him mirrors precisely Koshy's definition of South Asian exceptionalism: it's all about competing in the ranks of the American meritocracy. Yet, Changez's comment that he was swept up in the notion, "at least at first," suggests the hollowness of the opportunity. The circumstances of Changez's post-graduation holiday to Greece bear out this suggestion. Changez notes that his fellow Princetonians make the trip "courtesy of gifts from their parents or dividends from their trust funds," while he affords the vacation thanks to his signing bonus at the consulting firm that recruits him at Princeton.[10] In addition to the class distinction, Changez points out that, among this crowd, he was "well-liked as an exotic acquaintance."[11] Changez's exotic appeal complicates the "colorblindness" of an American meritocracy. And, though Changez quietly chafes under this imposed exoticism while at Princeton, he eventually works it to his advantage. Indeed, part of the entire novel's irresoluteness stems from Changez's self-conscious performances of his own otherness, which leave the reader wondering when and if Changez ever asserts his identity ingenuously.

While Mansoor also occupies a privileged position and, thus, also represents Koshy's notion of South Asian exceptionalism, the film goes a step further by aligning Mansoor *culturally* with Americans who occupy nondominant positions, offering another recognizable—though more generalized—minority narrative. The first scene set in Mansoor's music class opens with the camera trained on the instructor, an African American man, who is "singing" a do-wop rhythm a cappella. The performance is his way of introducing the notion of musical fusion, the topic of the class's first assignment. The instructor tells his students that he wants them to "come together with somebody from a completely different culture, completely different musical background [because] you gonna fuse that together. […] Create layers of sound. […] Creat[e] new music."[12] As the instructor explains the assignment, a second camera pans the students, a mix of several white women, longhaired white men, and Mansoor. To close the scene, the instructor calls out, "Can I get a witness on that? Can I get a witness? Can I get an uh-huh? I gotta know that you're with me," to which his students verbalize their consent appropriately.[13]

What's notable about this scene is how Mansoor experiences a sense of community in a group led by a black man who invokes the call-and-response language characteristic of slave spirituals. The exchange the instructor's in-

---

[10] Ibid., p. 17.

[11] Ibid., p. 17.

[12] *Khuda Kay Liye*, dir. by Shoaib Mansoor, on DVD (GEO Films, 2007).

[13] Ibid.

vocation prompts subtly introduces the troubled history of minorities in the US before an audience comprised of Mansoor, the recent immigrant, and the white students, whose status as aspiring artists—along with the men's long hair—can be read as a mark of their "alternative" sensibilities. At the same time, the assignment itself contains a multicultural promise as it calls for an egalitarian blending that maintains through its layered construction the differences each student's cultural and musical backgrounds possess while in the process creating something new. The notion of fusing the various culturally-inflected forms of music promotes the cross-identification of the characters. The point here is that the scene presents such cross-identification as possible, and, as a possibility, it is remarkable in that it asks the privileged to identify with the less privileged (the reverse is less remarkable insofar as dominant culture asks this of non-privileged people all the time).

The minority/multicultural narrative evoked by Mansoor's participation in the music class illustrates an aspect of Lauren Berlant's argument regarding how liberal political discourse in the US posits minority identity. Berlant coins the phrase "national sentimentality" to refer to "a liberal rhetoric of promise" that "operates when relatively privileged citizens are exposed to the suffering of their intimate Others, so that to be virtuous requires feeling the pain of flawed or denied citizenship as their own pain."[14] Insofar as the "relatively privileged" are inclined to feel the pain of the marginalized, the privileged are then also inclined to make it better for the less privileged among them. Or, as Berlant continues, "In the discourse of national sentimentality, identification with pain [...] would thereby lead to structural social change."[15] In return, the less privileged—the "populations emancipated from the pain"—ideally acknowledge and "reauthorize the universalist notions of citizenship in the national utopia," thereby legitimating the nation's "redemptive notion of law as the guardian of public good."[16] Berlant's formulation of liberal political discourse about minorities underscores the preeminence of pain in the articulation of minority identities. In other words, to be a minority is to bear some wound, some hurt—such as the historical pain of slavery and its legacy, to refer to the scene from *Khuda Kay Liye*—the pain of which only the privileged and fully enfranchised can alleviate. National belonging for minorities, in Berlant's understanding, relies upon the centrality of pain in minority identities. And national law, responsive to the demands of the privi-

---

[14] Lauren Berlant, 'The Subject of True Feeling: Pain, Privacy and Politics,' in *Transformations: Thinking through Feminism*, ed. by Sara Ahmed et al (London: Routledge, 2000), 33-47 (pp. 34,35).

[15] Ibid., p. 35.

[16] Ibid., p. 35.

leged, works to free minorities of their burden. Mansoor's sense of belonging in pre-9/11 US, as exemplified by this music class scene, suggests, in Berlant's terms, "that a nation can best be built across fields of social difference through channels of affective identification and empathy."[17]

This entire paradigm of identification premised on pain shifts after the attacks on September the 11th. June Edmunds and Bryan Turner outline what they call a "9/11 Generation," wherein belonging in the US after the attacks requires the declaration of "'primordial' loyalties rather than cultural diversity."[18] But how to make such a declaration, how to renounce "cultural diversity," when one lives in a "marked" body, as both Changez and Mansoor explicitly do? To state what I think is the relevant point in clearer terms, in post-9/11 US, the pain of the majority, of the privileged, now becomes the foundation of identity claims. It is this pain that mandates empathy, not the "pain" of minorities, especially Muslims, as was the case in Berlant's formulation. For Slavoj Žižek, this post-9/11 shift occurs because of the violent disintegration of "the old security" of American inviolability and leads to a "taking refuge in the innocence of a firm ideological identification."[19] The degree to which this ideological identification has been naturalized in the US proves most worrisome to Žižek, for "it is precisely such moments of transparent innocence […] that are, from the standpoint of the critique of ideology, the most obscure—even, in a certain way, obscurity itself."[20] As a measure of how thoroughly this ideological identification obscures constructive critique, one need only note the preponderance of accusations of unpatriotic speech and actions after 9/11 and continuing throughout the US's protracted "war on terror."

The US identity claims based on the pain of the majority have serious consequences for minority discourse, generally, and, most especially, for the articulation of Muslim identities. David Palumbo-Liu sees the formulation of this ideologically-based majority identity as more than a reversion to the jingoism common to pronounced forms of nationalism; rather, Palumbo-Liu recognizes it as "the imbrication of nationalist and civilizational thinking," wherein "[n]ational interests seem indistinguishable from 'a way of life' and national policy seems synonymous with large, civilizational imperatives."[21]

---

17 Ibid., p. 34.

18 June Edmunds and Bryan S. Turner, 'Global Generations: Social Change in the Twentieth Century', *The British Journal of Sociology*, 56 (2005), 559-577 (p. 570).

19 Slavoj Žižek, *Welcome to the Desert of the Real* (London: Verso, 2002), p. 45.

20 Ibid., p. 45.

21 David Palumbo-Liu, 'Multiculturalism Now: Civilization, National Identity, and Difference Before and After September 11th', *boundary 2*, 29 (2002), 109-127 (p. 110).

This sort of "civilizational thinking" heightens and expands the perceived threat as being directed toward "our way of life" even while it encourages a closing of the ranks in nationalist terms. This doubled movement—outward and inward—results in a paradoxical inclusion for US-based minorities, as Deborah Cohler points out: "The tensions between histories of exclusion and wartime advocacy for civic inclusion mobilize liberal discourses of equality," in so far as "our way of life" is universalized by abstraction.[22] At the same time, as Cohler further contends, the inclusion of those Americans whose identities are shaped by "histories of exclusion" "shore[s] up oppositions between East/West, primitive/modern, feminine/masculine, and abject/normative."[23] Thus, post-9/11 US-based discourses realign minority identifications so as to streamline them into the majority-based ones, bracketing off the sorts of histories that would otherwise preclude such a gesture. This realignment posits the new other—the Muslim male—outside "our way of life." As Evelyn Alsultany asserts, "After 9/11, [...] there emerged an ideological moment that [...] defined US citizens as diverse and united in the 'War on Terror,' over and against Arabs and Muslims, who were represented as un-American, terrorists, enemies."[24]

These two Pakistani works animate the consequences for Muslim male identities in the US that come about because of this shift in the paradigm of identification. Mansoor and Changez both experience violence and humiliation due to their exclusion from belonging to the post-9/11 US, illustrating how post-9/11 US domestic policies and practices encourage a paranoia—what Ghassan Hage has called "anthrax culture"[25]—wherein, according to David Simpson, "Friends and enemies are everywhere, and no one can be sure which is which. The role of the state and its spokespersons is thus to simplify the task and to tell us."[26] *Khuda Kay Liye* shows how the promotion of this paranoia results not only in Mansoor's unjust and inhumane treatment but also in the transformation of the US into a self-colonized state wherein citizens become mere subjects. In the film, Mansoor's declaration of "'primordial' loyalties" fails to secure his continued belonging in the US. Even

---

22 Deborah Cohler, 'Keeping the Home Front Burning: Renegotiating Gender and Sexuality in US Mass Media after September 11', *Feminist Media Studies*, 6 (2006): 245-261 (p. 258).

23 Ibid., p. 258.

24 Evelyn Alsultany, 'Selling Americans Diversity and Muslim American Identity through Nonprofit Advertising Post-9/11', *American Quarterly*, 59 (2007), 593-622 (p. 595).

25 Ghassan Hage, *Against Paranoid Nationalism: Searching for Hope in a Shrinking Society* (Annandale: Pluto, 2003), p. 45.

26 David Simpson, *9/11: The Culture of Commemoration* (Chicago: University of Chicago Press, 2006), p. 144.

after his covert abduction by US authorities and their Abu Ghraib-like torturing of him, Mansoor writes on his cell wall, "I Love US," signaling his incomprehension over how he could come to be suspected of terrorism.[27] This plaintive declaration cannot, however, forestall the authorities' predetermined disbelief in Mansoor's innocence and, hence, cannot safeguard Mansoor from his own mental collapse. Mansoor's ordeal showcases through this individualized tragedy the curtailing of civil liberties.

Moreover, the film expands the significance of Mansoor's confinement in order to critique the transformation of the American public sphere from, ideally, a democratic site to an authoritarian one. During Mansoor's incarceration, his American wife, Janie, protests with a handful of others outside a generic downtown Chicago office building. Janie holds a sign that reads "Free Mansoor Now"; other signs read "Stop Racial Profiling," "Release Mansoor: He Is Innocent," and "Islam Means Peace."[28] As the camera circumscribes the protestors, a suited male bureaucrat exits the building and enters the frame. The music track predominates, so viewers see but don't hear his dismissal of the protest. He then turns on his heels to re-enter the building where, presumably, Mansoor is being held. In frustration, Janie throws down her sign.[29] The absence of dialogue in this scene invites several interpretations. The bureaucrat's ability to quash the protest in a matter of moments, for instance, represents a deployment of power with little actual exertion, suggesting arrogance and self-righteousness. The ordinariness of the downtown Chicago location suggests that these gross infringements of rights and displays of power can and do occur anywhere in the US, not just at Guantanamo Bay or other rendition sites around the world. Further, in light of the demonstration's inability to sway the bureaucrat, the signs themselves, which provide the only language in the scene, come off as ineffective, as though the sentiments they espouse are either cant or simply beside the point. To draw such a conclusion about the signs' language is not to discredit entirely the power of language, for, as one of Mansoor's interrogation scenes shows, the presence of certain languages, like the verses written in Arabic that the US authorities find in Mansoor's flat, set off powerful reactions. Additionally, the very fact of Mansoor's detainment exemplifies the power of the "us versus them" rhetoric of post-9/11 US foreign and domestic policies.

All three of these conclusions drawn from the absence of dialogue in the demonstration scene lead to a fourth: the fundamental breakdown of democracy. Not only does this scene show that Janie cannot effectively advocate for

---

27 *Khuda*.

28 Ibid.

29 Ibid.

her husband's release *on a personal level*, but it also shows that her own and other American citizens' interventions *as citizens* are in vain. In Iris Young's assessment of the workings of the post-9/11 US security state, this democratic breakdown is due to a sort of rabid paternalism:

> Through the logic of protection the state demotes members of a democracy to dependents. State officials adopt the stance of masculine protector, telling us to entrust our lives to them, not to question their decisions abut what will keep us safe. Their protector position puts us, the citizens and residents who depend on their strength and vigilance for our security, in the position of women and children under the charge of a male protector.[30]

Janie's act of throwing down her sign after the bureaucrat chastises her—a gesture that, if taken out of context, could be viewed as petulant, appropriate for a spoiled girl smarting from her father's punishment—crystallizes Young's gendered reading of the security state. At the same time, the camera work in the demonstration scene—filmed, one imagines, on a circular track surrounding the actors—creates the sense that the protestors are encircled, contained, watched and recorded from all angles. The demonstration scene thus portrays the post-9/11 US public sphere as, in Elleke Boehmer's words, "a hostage to its own imperialising fortunes, in so far as it implies that terror is everywhere, and hence it must constitute the primary mode of sovereignty of the counter-terroristic state itself."[31] *Khuda Kay Liye* represents the post-9/11 US as a self-colonizing state, replete with the authoritarian and patriarchal power that has historically accompanied Western colonial endeavors.

The US as a self-colonizing state, thus, relies upon the emergence and combination of the very oppositions, already mentioned above, that Cohler identifies: West/East and masculine/feminine. Further, through this gendered self-colonization, the US's anti-terrorist domestic stance perpetuates the notion that the 9/11 attacks emasculated the US, thereby provoking and justifying the superpower's hypermasculinist and militaristic response. Cohler's analysis of a cartoon, posted on the internet, of Osama bin Laden victimized by architectural sodomy (here, the Empire State Building) demonstrates how these gendered dynamics work: the "cartoon reverses the phallic power of the airplanes penetrating and destroying an oddly feminized World Trade Tower and asserts that the US still has enough penetrative phallic power to do violence to bin Laden."[32] The US's virile and virulent phallic power overcompensates, both internationally and domestically, for what it takes to be its gendered and sexualized violation.

---

30 Joan W. Scott, 'Feminist Reverberations', *Differences*, 13 (2002), 1-23 (qtd. p. 10).

31 Elleke Boehmer, 'Postcolonial Writing and Terror', *Wasafiri*, 22 (2007), 4-7 (p. 5).

32 Cohler, p. 255.

As Cohler's example suggests, such a gender-charged discursive context informs representations of the Muslim male other, a phenomena that *The Reluctant Fundamentalist* fully exploits through Changez's complicated reaction to the 9/11 attacks. Changez smarts from his exclusion from post-9/11 US; like Mansoor, but to a lesser degree, Changez also faces the discrimination and humiliation of profiling,[33] which leaves him feeling "uncomfortable in my own face: I was aware of being under suspicion; I felt guilty."[34] His subsequent actions, however, indicate that he's far from incapacitated, as Mansoor is. Changez explains to his American listener that he was in Manila on business when he saw the attacks on the news, as did most of the world: "I stared as one—and then the other—of the twin towers of New York's World Trade Center collapsed. And then I *smiled*. Yes, despicable as it may sound, my initial reaction was to be remarkably pleased."[35] Aware of his reaction's inappropriateness through his use of the word "despicable" and from viewing the reaction of his interlocutor, whose "large hand has […] clenched into a fist,"[36] Changez confesses his own "profound sense of perplexity" over his reaction, but, nonetheless attempts to explain (or justify?) it: "But at that moment, my thoughts were not with the *victims* of the attack […] no, I was caught up in the *symbolism* of it all […]."[37] Even from his own perspective, Changez's aesthetic appreciation of the attacks is deplorable, so far outside of an acceptable response as to be all but unmentionable. Yet, Changez does mention it, leaving both his silent interlocutor and the reader to draw (perhaps reactionary) conclusions about the significance of his impropriety.

The ambiguity surrounding Changez's reaction to the attacks could be clarified, if a reader were so inclined, from the gendered scripts that frame Muslim men as suspicious. Thus, in a way, Changez's post-9/11 visit to his parents in Pakistan potentially compounds his "guilt." While there, he finds his family and compatriots tense, frightened, and frustrated by the impending American invasion of Afghanistan and Pakistan's mounting tensions with India, inflamed as they are by the US military presence once again making itself felt in the subcontinent. Before he returns to the US, Changez grows a beard. US anti-terror discourses code a bearded Muslim man as a threat, a signification both Changez and his co-workers in the US fully understand: "It is remarkable, given its physical insignificance—it is only a hairstyle, after all—the impact a beard worn by a man of my complexion has on your fellow

---

33 Hamid, pp. 75, 117.
34 Ibid., p. 74.
35 Ibid., p. 72.
36 Ibid., p. 72.
37 Ibid., p. 73.

countrymen. [...A]t Underwood Samson I seemed to become overnight a subject of whispers and stares."[38] In effect, Changez's decision to grow his facial hair serves as a gendered response to the humiliation he suffers for being "a man of [his] complexion" in the US. That is, Changez's beard provides the apt counterpoint to the hypermasculinist US rhetoric after the attacks, the respective masculinist assertions supporting what Vaheed Ramazani calls the "manly manichaeism" established by both the US's and the terrorists' public posturing.[39]

At the same time, though, Changez's role as first-person narrator relies upon ambiguity that frustrates a reader's certainty, a manipulation that works on several levels. Hamid's novel thus plays a narrative trick on readers much like Toni Morrison's short story "Recitatif" does; that is, both fictions lay hints and inferences at readers' feet in an effort to see which narrative readers will find more believable. Is Changez really an extremist who incites terrorism with his rhetoric? Or, is Changez being targeted by the CIA simply for standing up for his democratic principles and for telling the truth to power? For those inclined to interpret Changez's beard as a sign of his Islamist fundamentalist sympathies, for instance, Bruce King points out, "[T]he narrator is trained by his American employers to focus only on economic fundamentals. In becoming a possible terrorist leader he has changed sides from one fundamentalism to another."[40] As the narrator, Changez also makes the most of his beard's doubled signifying potential. When one of Changez's coworkers questions him about his beard, Changez responds, "'They are common where I come from.'"[41] Changez's rejoinder shifts the perceptual frame of reference; instead of accepting the transparency or naturalness of the bearded Muslim man as an Islamist fundamentalist or, worse, a terrorist, Changez's answer introduces an alternative normativity. If a bearded man does not necessarily signify a fundamentalist or terrorist in Pakistan, then such a figure must then signify a kind of masculinity that is not the mirror image of the hypermasculinist pose struck by US anti-terror rhetoric. In other words, in a different context, Changez's beard may well point toward a mas-

---

38 Ibid., p. 130.

39 Vaheed Ramazani, 'September 11: Masculinity, Justice, and the Politics of Empathy', *Comparative Studies of South Asia, Africa and the Middle East*, 21 (2001), 118-124 (p. 118).

40 Bruce King, 'The Image of the United States in Three Pakistani Novels', *Totalitarian Movements and Political Religions*, 8.3 (2007) <http://www.informaworld.com/10.1080/14690760701571338> [accessed 1 September 2008].

41 Hamid, p. 130.

culinity not accounted for by the "manly manichaeism" of "war on terror" discourses.

In addition, the doubleness that results from the narrative ambiguity or manipulation expands the possibility of alternative gender normativity to introduce similarly alternative configurations of the public sphere. For instance, Changez points out that, upon his return to Pakistan, his participation "in demonstrations for greater independence in Pakistan's domestic and international affairs" was framed by the international media as "anti-American":[42]

> The first of our protests to receive much attention took place not far from where we are now. Your country's ambassador was in town, and we surrounded the building in which he was speaking, chanting and holding placards. There were thousands of us, of all possible affiliations—communists, capitalists, feminists, religious literalists—and things began to get out of hand. Effigies were burned and stones were thrown, and then we were charged at by large numbers of uniformed and plain-clothed police.[43]

Upon hearing this explanation, his interlocutor, according to Changez, has "adopted a decidedly unfriendly and accusatory tone."[44] In turn, Changez asserts, "I see from your expression that you do not believe me."[45] One wonders if Changez's American interlocutor could have believed him, since the scene, as it "grew to newsworthy size,"[46] provides a visualization of the angry, threatening Muslim masses that US anti-terror rhetoric codes as anti-American. That Changez says this large demonstration, which, admittedly, gets out of control, was the "first of our protests to receive much attention" indicates that Changez and his like-minded compatriots staged other demonstrations that were not deemed newsworthy by the international press. Arguably, it was this specific demonstration's volatility, as well as the presence of the American ambassador, that allowed it to be interpolated so neatly into the familiar anti-terror narrative.

Yet, the novel's narrative voice also allows for an alternative reading of the scene. As much as it is possible for Changez to be unreliable, it is just as likely that he presents an accurate version of the events. Within this possibility, the demonstration presents a vibrant coalition of divergent political interests, coming together to assert Pakistani self-determination. According to Changez's description of his fellow protestors, feminists align, howsoever

---

42 Ibid., p. 179.
43 Ibid., p. 179.
44 Ibid., p. 181.
45 Ibid., p. 181.
46 Ibid., p. 179.

momentarily, with "religious literalists," a conjunction all but unimaginable for non-Muslim consumers of the international media who are, instead, commonly encouraged to believe that women's self-assertion is anathema to Islam. In place of the dangerously paternalistic and self-colonizing public sphere in which Janie and no more than two dozen others stage their feeble protest in *Khuda Kay Liye*, *The Reluctant Fundamentalist* constructs a vision of a Pakistani public sphere that, while vulnerable to a hypermasculinist military crackdown due to the country's US-backed dictatorship, creates a space for a gendered (and class-based) critique. To grant credibility to Changez's version of the demonstration's import, then, also means to acknowledge the possibility of a vitalized and democratic Pakistani public sphere, one that is certainly taken seriously by the country's militaristic regime, standing this scene in stark contrast to the demonstration, discussed above, that *Khuda Kay Liye* depicts.

Khuda Kay Liye also relies on doubleness through the brothers' parallel plotlines, and, similarly, this doubleness points toward a vision of a democratic Pakistani public sphere. While the film's American-based plotline ends bleakly, resolving its structural manipulation—by the end of the film, viewers know why the white woman (Janie) featured in the first scene is crying—its Pakistan-based plotline gestures toward possibilities. In this Pakistan-based plotline, Sarnad, Mansoor's younger brother, disavows his involvement with music, which, in effect, is also a disavowal of Mansoor, for the two brothers accrue some fame as a musical duo. Taliban-inspired religious fundamentalism lures Sarnad away from his family's otherwise very comfortable upper middle-class lifestyle and makes Sarnad an ideal accomplice to his uncle's plans, the other instance of manipulation in the film. This uncle lives in the UK, where he has a university-aged daughter, Mary, by his British wife. Distressed over Mary's romantic attachment to a white British man, this uncle takes Mary on her first trip to Pakistan and conspires with Sarnad's newfound fundamentalist friends to force Mary into marriage and a life with Sarnad in the tribal regions of Pakistan. Eventually, Mary's British mother and boyfriend get the British foreign office involved, who in turn convince the Pakistani Army to provide a helicopter and security detail for Sarnad's father so that he may retrieve Mary. As the elder man and Mary board the helicopter, Sarnad hesitates and then also climbs aboard. Once safely back in Lahore, Mary speaks with her British boyfriend on the phone, telling him that she will make her father and Sarnad pay by taking them to court in Pakistan. In the ensuing courtroom scene, arguably the film's climax, an esteemed, moderate maulana refutes the teachings of the more radical maulana responsible for Sarnad's short-lived dalliance with the Taliban.[47]

Through a series of cuts, the film constructs a parallel between Sarnad's and Mansoor's plotlines during these crucial scenes, though their resolutions point in opposite directions. The former resolves itself gradually, as the film cuts between the events I have just described and US-based scenes. So, for instance, just as Sarnad boards the helicopter, the film cuts to a scene in which Mansoor is released from hanging shackles in his US prison and is then humiliated by a female agent who forces him to strip naked. Also, immediately after the demonstration scene in which Janie throws down her sign in frustration, the film cuts to the courtroom scene in which Mary is vindicated.[48] The resolution of the Mansoor plotline, wherein he is mentally incapacitated and deported, suggests the abortive nature of any effort to connect with things American. Mansoor's family takes him in, though he's entirely incapable of engaging with the outside world. The last the audience sees of Mansoor, he's sitting around a bonfire with his family, wrapped in a blanket and completely out of reach mentally and emotionally. Sarnad is also present in Mansoor's last scene, which features Sarnad singing and playing his guitar for his family's enjoyment. He has re-embraced music. Unlike the hopeless circumstances surrounding Mansoor's return, Sarnad's return to his family presents his "recovery" as both possible and probable.

Indeed, the film's final scene, which immediately follows the bonfire scene I just described, expands on what the courtroom scene suggests: namely, the Pakistani public (and legalistic) sphere bears democratic potential because—not in spite of—its valuing of Islamic ideals. This final scene shows Sarnad approaching a mosque where the radical maulana, seated on the floor, lectures to a group of young men, all traditionally attired. Before the maulana can see Sarnad, he responds to the younger man's greeting. As Sarnad comes into the maulana's field of vision, the maulana sees with visible consternation that Sarnad, who has kept his beard, wears jeans, a polo shirt, and vest, along with a baseball cap. Sarnad strides past the group toward the microphone in order to sing the call to prayer. As he does so, he reverses his baseball cap. Barely containing his outrage, the maulana orders one of his pupils to sing the call. Though this pupil removes the microphone from in front of Sarnad, Sarnad keeps voicing the call. The film cuts to a view of the mosque's dome and minarets, over which fly a flock of birds.[49] This scene demonstrates how Sarnad rediscovers a way to interact with his family *and* to reintegrate his life

---

47 *Khuda*.

48 Ibid.

49 Ibid.

and music with his faith as a moderate Muslim in present-day Pakistan. Where the US leaves neither Mansoor nor Janie with any recourse, legal, emotional, or psychological, the film suggests that Pakistan does provide both Sarnad and Mary with options. After the courtroom scene, in what is, admittedly, a romanticized ending, Mary decides not to return to the UK and instead travels back to Pakistan's tribal regions and opens a school for girls.[50] Further, the binaristic thinking that prevails in Mansoor's plotline shows, in Joan W. Scott's words, how "the good versus evil opposition" "makes it difficult for differences within each side—for the contestation of politics—to be seen or heard."[51] Sarnad's plotline, however, plays out this contestation, literally rendering it both visible and audible, in order to hint at positive, though by no means challenge-free, futures. Thus, just as *The Reluctant Fundamentalist* does, Shoaib's film envisions the possibility of active participation in a Pakistani public sphere that values democracy.

The narrative manipulations of both Hamid's novel and Shoaib's film convey their characters' disorientation brought about, in part, by the upheavals of the world political order after 11 September 2001. At the same time, these manipulations involve readers and viewers in the plotlines, thereby creating a similar disorientation mixed with a frustration over the ambiguity of Changez's narrative and the injustice of Mansoor's plight. Even while *The Reluctant Fundamentalist* frustrates narrative resolution, it invites readers to consider alternative understandings of the volatile events Changez narrates. These alternative possibilities, especially where the workings of democracy in Pakistan are concerned, suggest a way to think constructively about a post-9/11 future in Pakistan. Similarly, the obverse side of Mansoor's plotline in *Khuda Kay Liye* holds out the possibility of Sarnad's reintegration into Pakistani public life and his family's private life through his commitment to the Islamic faith. That is, Shoaib's film frames Mansoor's US-based plotline as bootless, due in large measure to the US's rigid and reductive ideological stance against the Muslim male other, whereas Sarnad's Pakistan-based plotline presents Pakistani society as flexible and tolerant enough to promote an Islamic faith community in the face of extremist pressures. Both of these Pakistani fictions focus on the fragility of democratic practice in times of fear and violence, and both offer a way to imagine how to live in the future.

---

50 Ibid.

51 Scott, p. 7.

Bibliography

Alsultany, Evelyn, 'Selling American Diversity and Muslim American Identity through Nonprofit Advertising Post-9/11', *American Quarterly*, 59 (2007), 593-622

Berlant, Lauren, 'The Subject of True Feeling: Pain, Privacy and Politics', *Transformations: Thinking through Feminism*, ed. by Sara Ahmed et al. (London: Routledge, 2000), 33-47

Boehmer, Elleke, 'Postcolonial Writing and Terror', *Wasafiri*, 22 (2007), 4-7.

Borradori, Giovanna, *Philosophy in a Time of Terror: Dialogues with Jürgen Habermas and Jacques Derrida* (Chicago: University of Chicago Press, 2003)

Cohler, Deborah, 'Keeping the Home Front Burning: Renegotiating Gender and Sexuality in US Mass Media after September 11', *Feminist Media Studies*, 6 (2006), 245-261

Edmunds, June, and Bryan S. Turner, 'Global Generations: Social Change in the Twentieth Century', *The British Journal of Sociology*, 56 (2005), 559-577

Hage, Ghassan, *Against Paranoid Nationalism: Searching for Hope in a Shrinking Society* (Annandale: Pluto, 2003)

Hamid, Mohsin, *The Reluctant Fundamentalist* (Orlando: Harcourt, 2007)

Khuda Kay Liye, dir.by Shoaib Mansoor , on DVD (GEO Films, 2007)

King, Bruce, 'The Image of the United States in Three Pakistani Novels', *Totalitarian Movements and Political Religions*, 8 (2007) < http://www.informaworld.com/10.1080/14690760701571338 > [accessed 1 September 2008]

Koshy, Susan, 'Category Crisis:South Asian Americans and Questions of Race and Ethnicity', *Diaspora: A Journal of Transnational Studies*, 7 (1998), 285-320

Palumbo-Liu, David, 'Multiculturalism Now: Civilization, National Identity, and Difference Before and After September 11th', *boundary 2*, 29 (2002), 109-127

Ramazani, Vaheed, 'September 11: Masculinity, Justice, and the Politics of Empathy', *Comparative Studies of South Asia, Africa and the Middle East*, 21 (2001), 118-124

Scott, Joan W., 'Feminist Reverberations', *Differences*, 13(2002), 1-23.

Simpson, David, *9/11: The Culture of Commemoration* (Chicago: University of Chicago Press, 2006)

Spivak, Gayatri, 'Terror: A Speech after 9/11', *boundary 2*, 31 (2004), 81-111

Žižek, Slavoj, *Welcome to the Desert of the Real* (London: Verso, 2002)

Margaret Atwood's *Oryx and Crake*: Canadian Post-9/11 Worries

Sharon Sutherland and Sarah Swan

In this article, we read Margaret Atwood's *Oryx and Crake* as a post-9/11 text. We consider how Atwood uses the genre and devices of dystopic fiction in order to present a uniquely Canadian perspective on the American response to 9/11.

In March 2001, Canadian author Margaret Atwood began writing a dystopic novel about an individual act of terrorism that almost destroyed the entire human race. On the morning of September 11, 2001, she had completed approximately half of the novel and was seated in the Toronto airport, contemplating the rest of the book, when she learned that she would not be flying that day. Despite the "deeply unsettling" coincidence of writing about a "fictional catastrophe" when a "real one happens," Atwood resumed her story after a few weeks and ultimately published *Oryx and Crake*[1] in 2003.[2] Inevitably, perhaps, 9/11 heavily influenced the finished *Oryx and Crake* and infused it with themes like the problematic nature of predicting perceived and real terrorist threats, the difficulties in balancing individual rights and national security in the face of such threats, and the troubling nature of the emerging discourse in government, law, and the military focusing on the "greater good." While scholars have focused much critical analysis on the issues of genetic engineering and bioethics in *Oryx and Crake*, in this paper we offer a reading of *Oryx and Crake* as a post 9/11 text, rife with fears of bioterrorism, increased government information-collection and surveillance, and a loss of individual freedoms in the face of global threats. Also, we consider the ways in which the novel offers a uniquely Canadian perspective on the aftermath of the attacks.

Just as Atwood was a close observer of the 9/11 terrors, Canada, with its heavy geographic, trade, and cultural links to the US, was uniquely situated to observe America's responses to the terrorist attacks. In fact, many of the measures America adopted in the wake of 9/11 directly affected Canada. Increased border control and security, the wars in Afghanistan and Iraq, and heightened immigration restrictions all impacted Canadians. The close proximity to the United States, and the traditional alliances between the two countries sensitized Canada to the issues America faced, and the loss of civil liber-

---

1 Margaret Atwood, *Oryx and Crake* (New York: Random House, 2003).

2 Margaret Atwood, 'Writing *Oryx and Crake*', in *Writing With Intent: Essays, Reviews, Personal Prose 1983-2005* (New York: Carroll & Graf, 2005), pp. 284-286.

ties in America, cloaked under the argument that it is necessary for Americans to surrender those rights in order to achieve national security, alarmed Canadians.[3] It is not surprising, then, that concerns about America and the consequences of 9/11 would appear in Canadian literary works. As Atwood has stated (in agreement with novelist Alistair MacLeod), "writers write about what worries them," and "the world of *Oryx and Crake* is what worries [her] right now."[4] Atwood expresses her concerns specifically through the lens of a dystopic novel, and we argue that this lens is particularly apt for the expression of Canadian worries: the form allows Atwood to speak through a protagonist whose position in relation to the other characters parallels the position of Canada in relation to the US—an intimate outsider directly affected by the political choices being made, yet largely powerless to impact the decisions. The resulting novel is a truly Canadian comment on an exaggerated and dystopic America, showing the worst excesses of Canadian fears regarding the American response to 9/11. In *Oryx and Crake*, individual rights have succumbed to corporate and state domination, dissenters are executed, and the argument that heinous acts may be committed in the name of the greater good is taken to its extreme.

Oryx and Crake: The Plot

Like many dystopias, *Oryx and Crake* essentially begins at the end: an apocalypse has occurred, and as the story unfolds, we gradually discover how and why. One remaining human being, a man who used to be called Jimmy but who now refers to himself as Snowman, provides the narration. Jimmy describes how he grew up in one of many corporate-owned Compounds, where the families of high-level workers lived in tightly controlled and brutally secured environments. His father, a gene researcher at OrganInc Farms, grew human organs for transplant inside of specially bred pigs. Jimmy's mother, a former microbiologist at that same corporation, eventually became so disturbed by the world she inhabited that she ran away, possibly to join a resistance movement, and left Jimmy behind with his father. Years after her desertion, Compound guards showed Jimmy a video of his mother's execution for acts of terrorism.

3 For a detailed account of the impact of 9/11 on Canadians, see Kent Roach, *September 11: Consequences for Canada* (Quebec: McGill-Queen's Press, 2003).

4 Atwood, 'Writing *Oryx and Crake*', p. 286.

As a boy, Jimmy attended OrganInc's grade school, and met Glen (later nick-named Crake), a gifted genius who quickly became his best friend. Crake was an orphan: his father, we learn, was executed when he threatened to reveal a horrendous corporate secret, and his mother died horrifically, moments after being infected with an unidentified biological agent. Following Jimmy and Crake's graduation, Crake moved to an elite institution of genius students, and Jimmy commenced studies at a decaying liberal arts college. Crake eventually offered Jimmy a job assisting him with his "Paradice Project." Crake's project involved creating a new and improved race of beings, and as we learn near the end of the story, he intended that this race would replace humanity. Crake effected the near total destruction of the human race through worldwide distribution of a virus hidden in a popular pharmaceutical pill. Until the very end of the novel, Jimmy is the only known human survivor of the lethal virus. He begrudgingly acts as the guide to Crake's new race of beings, as they appear poised to take over the world from humans.

Dystopia and Its Devices

The world of *Oryx and Crake* is, like all dystopias, horrific. Dystopias, also called anti-utopias, offer a vision of society that is the opposite of utopic. Most basically, dystopic fictions show society at its worst: they feature "a non-existent society described in considerable detail and normally located in time and space that the author intended a contemporaneous reader to view as considerably worse than the society in which the reader lived."[5] While the dystopic world must be significantly worse than contemporary society, the dystopia must have enough connections to current society to create recognition and fear in the reader. It is through the identifiable similarities with contemporary society that the author anchors her critique of existing social conditions.

As a literary form, the "dystopian narrative is largely the product of the terrors of the twentieth century."[6] Dystopian novels and films of the twentieth century reflect specific problems of that time, such as repression of minorities, gender disparity, state violence, war, genocide, and ecocide. Yet the form is highly adaptable. Dystopic visions shift with the specific concerns of

---

5 Lyman Tower Sargent, 'The Three Faces of Utopianism Revisited', *Utopian Studies*, 5 (1994), 1-37 (p. 9).

6 Tom Moylan, *Scraps of the Untainted Sky: Science Fiction, Utopia, Dystopia* (Boulder: Westview Press, 2000), p. xi.

each era and place, allowing post-9/11 authors such as Atwood to explore new concerns arising in the post-9/11, twenty-first century world.

Before *Oryx and Crake*, Atwood was already a familiar name to readers of dystopic fiction. In 1984 (a notable year for dystopias), Atwood published *The Handmaid's Tale*, a critically-praised and prize winning dystopic novel that explored themes of social control and gender disparity in an America where a pseudo-Christian fundamentalist agenda leads to a totalitarian theocracy.[7] Atwood has always been a scholarly writer, and her immersion in dystopias was accompanied by a familiarity with, and reflection upon, the historical developments of the genre. Atwood has commented on the 20th century seminal dystopic visions presented in George Orwell's *1984* and Aldous Huxley's *Brave New World*:

> The 20th century could be seen as a race between two versions of man-made hell—the jack-booted state totalitarianism of Orwell's *Nineteen Eighty-Four*, and the hedonistic ersatz paradise of *Brave New World*, where absolutely everything is a consumer good and human beings are engineered to be happy. With the fall of the Berlin Wall in 1989, it seemed for a time that *Brave New World* had won—from henceforth, state control would be minimal, and all we would have to do was go shopping and smile a lot, and wallow in pleasures, popping a pill or two when depression set in.[8]

September 11, 2001, stopped the advance of the Brave New World. Instead, a third version of a man-made hell emerged. Since 9/11, dystopic visions have increasingly focused on the dangers of corporations; the possible moral, legal, and political justifications for state-sanctioned surveillance, torture and mistreatment of prisoners; and the consequences of implementing an "ends-justify-the-means" philosophy. Also, the "ticking bomb" scenario has become the basis for debating when the interests of society should take precedence over individual rights and freedoms. Atwood describes this third type of world, which is really a combination of the two distinct options presented in the 20th century dystopic worlds, as follows:

> But with 9/11 [...] it appears we face the prospect of two contradictory dystopias at once—open markets, closed minds—because state surveillance is back again with a vengeance. The torturer's dreaded Room 101 has been with us for millennia. The dungeons of Rome, the Inquisition, the Star Chamber, the Bastille, the proceedings of General Pinochet and of the

---

7 *The Handmaid's Tale* won the 1985 Canadian Governor General's Award and the first Arthur C. Clarke Award in 1987. It was also nominated for the 1986 Nebula Award, the 1986 Booker Prize, and the 1987 Prometheus Award.

8 Margaret Atwood, 'George Orwell: Some Personal Connections', in *Writing with Intent: Essays, Reviews, Personal Prose 1983-2005* (New York: Carroll & Graf, 2005) 287-293 (p. 292).

> junta in Argentina—all have depended on secrecy and on the abuse of power. Lots of countries have had their versions of it—their ways of silencing troublesome dissent.[9]

The dystopia of *Oryx and Crake* is exactly this type of contradictory dystopia.[10] Open markets have led to corporate-controlled Compounds where high-level workers and their families live, work, and play, while the lower classes live and work in the dangerous pleeblands. We learn through the deaths of the central characters' parents that the few dissenters who dare to open their minds and their mouths in opposition to this social stratification and corporate control are efficiently eliminated through executions or carefully staged "suicides." The powers of corporate surveillance in the novel are frightening and unfettered: strip searches, mail openings, random interrogations, computers designed to read minds, torture, and false evidence are all common to the pre-apocalyptic world of the protagonist's childhood and youth. At the same time as these hallmarks of totalitarian power abuses abound, the free and open market thrives: corporate America happily manipulates the world marketplace to sell cures to diseases they themselves have created, and the workers (many of whom appear to be complicit in the corporation's darker activities) blissfully enjoy the pleasures of life within the heavily patrolled walls of their Compounds.

All of these themes–surveillance, control, social stratification, etc.–are prevalent in earlier dystopias: it is the increasing intertwining of the Orwellian Big Brother with the economics of the Brave New World that marks *Oryx and Crake* as a millennial dystopia. What makes *Oryx and Crake* more specifically a post-9/11 dystopia is the central theme of terrorism, in this case biological terrorism, which resonates in conjunction with these other themes. In *Oryx and Crake*, the social failings are so dire and seen as so unsolvable as to invite terrorism aimed at the greater good–eliminating the majority of the human race for the betterment of the earth.

In the same way as *Oryx and Crake* draws on traditional dystopic themes, it also draws upon some of the most common devices of the dystopic genre as a lens for its views on post-9/11 America. In particular, *Oryx and Crake*

---

9 Ibid., p. 292.

10 Atwood has argued that the work is not a classic dystopia. In her words, "Though it has obvious dystopian elements, we don't really get an overview of the structure of the society in it […]. We just see its central characters living their lives within small corners of that society, much as we live ours. What they can grasp of the rest of the world comes to them through television and the Internet, and is thus suspect, because edited." *The Handmaid's Tale* and *Oryx and Crake* in Context', *PMLA*, 119 (2004), 513 – 517 (p. 517). However, we argue that the society is indeed visible enough to justify this classification.

adopts a backstory of apocalypse and a post-apocalyptic setting for its protagonist and explores the forces that led to the destruction of America. Similarly, the novel employs a typically dystopic viewpoint on its narrative. An intimate outsider–a member of the society who is in some ways separate from the more powerful elements of the society and not fully convinced of the society's views–tells the tale. As well, language plays an important role in the novel, as it does in many dystopic fictions that explore social control.

The Dystopic Setting

Many dystopias are set in post-apocalyptic worlds, with barren landscapes, imminent dangers, and general devastation.[11] The barely habitable world of *Oryx and Crake*, with its genetically-altered predators, lack of viable food sources, and painfully strong sun, fits well within this tradition. *Oryx and Crake* is not precisely located but appears to be set on the East Coast of the United States, near Boston, Massachusetts, and New York.[12] Only four paragraphs into the story we are told that Snowman wears a Boston Red Sox cap,[13] and, later, the quick train ride between the HealthWyzer compound and New New York supports the view that they are near Boston.[14]

New York has a special place in the setting of the story. Jimmy's parents' obvious nostalgia for the good old days suggests that pre-9/11 New York was an idyllic time and place:

> Remember when you could drive anywhere? Remember when everyone lived in the pleeblands? Remember when you could fly anywhere in the world, without fear? Remember hamburger chains, always real beef, remember hot dog stands? Remember New York before it was New New York? Remember when voting mattered?[15]

This pre-9/11 New York is a drastic departure from the post-9/11 world presented in the novel. In *Oryx and Crake*, the elite and the educated no longer live in cities, or "pleeblands" as they are termed in the novel (presumably, the

---

11 *Logan's Run* (1976) and *Planet of the Apes* (1968) are examples.

12 J. Brooks Bouson, '"It's Game Over Forever": Atwood's Satiric Vision of a Bioengineered Posthuman Future in Oryx and Crake', *The Journal of Commonwealth Literature*, 39 (2004), 139 – 156 (pp. 140, 154).

13 Atwood, *Oryx and Crake*, p. 346.

14 Earl J. Ingersoll, 'Survival in Margaret Atwood's Novel *Oryx and Crake*', *Extrapolation*, 45 (2004), 162 – 175, (p. 93), however, suggests that they are somewhere on the Southern coast of the United States.

15 Atwood, *Oryx and Crake*, p. 75.

word is meant to mean "Land of the Plebians"). Jimmy recounts his one and only visit to the pleeblands in the novel, but first introduces them as "endless billboards and neon signs and stretches of buildings [...] public security in the pleeblands was leaky [...] not to mention the loose change—the addicts, the muggers, the paupers, the crazies."[16]

Instead of living in these cesspools, the elite live in corporate-owned, tightly secured Compounds. This separation closely resembles "the distributed workplace" and "fear cities" described in post-9/11 social sciences literature:

> The most alarming interpretations of 9-11 portray a dystopia gone wild. Pessimistic accounts see counterterror policies as resulting in a proliferation of "fear cities." The post 9-11 city presents a bleak picture of a metropolis suffused with surveillance devices, concrete barriers, and body searches (Marcuse 2002). Urban life as we know it has ceased to exist, replaced by closed-off spaces, restricted access, and intimidating police.[17]

The distributed workplaces of *Oryx and Crake*, the Compounds, serve as a visual metaphor of the corporation's scope: the new distributed workplaces "encapsulate corporate 'yes' culture in a spatial metaphor of bringing together into one place all those who have 'opted in,' who have internalized the goals, truth, and ethics of the company as their own, and excluding or expelling everything that is threatening to this homeostasis."[18] In order to become part of this corporate culture, its members have sacrificed their freedom, and have instead accepted a rule of constant surveillance, searches, and policing.

The degree to which this sense of fear accompanied by constant surveillance in the Compounds reflects post-9/11 American policies is readily apparent. For example, in 2005, the *New York Times* reported that President Bush had removed the requirement that the National Security Agency (NSA) seek approval of the Foreign Intelligence Surveillance Court (FISC) before wiretapping communications of an American citizen in order to expand intelligence gathering operations: "Under a presidential order signed in 2002, the intelligence agency has monitored the international telephone calls and international e-mail messages of hundreds, perhaps thousands, of people inside the United States without warrants over the past three years in an effort to

---

16 Ibid., p. 33.

17 H.V. Savitch, 'Does 9-11 Portend a New Paradigm for Cities?', *Urban Affairs Review*, 39 (2003), 103-127 (p. 118).

18 Grayson Cooke, 'Technics and the Human at Zero-Hour: Margaret Atwood's *Oryx and Crake*', *Studies in Canadian Literature*, 31 (2006), 105-125 (p. 111).

track possible ‘dirty numbers.’”[19] Similarly, searches have been extended, not just in airports where significantly increased security is readily apparent, but also in the New York City subway system where bags are searched on a random basis. Increased border security, more invasive searches, and increased intelligence-gathering all find their fictional counterpart in *Oryx and Crake*’s security-focused Compounds.

Canada: 9/11’s Intimate Outsider

Like the setting, the selection of perspective is fundamental to dystopic narrative. While the typical utopic novel involves the introduction of an outsider into a society in order to elucidate the many positive features of that society, dystopias more frequently draw on the perspective of a disgruntled insider, someone who is part of the society but is in a position to question its norms, or the intimate outsider, a “representative of a discontented social class or faction, whose value-system defines perfection.”[20] In the emotional and cultural fall-out from the events of 9/11, Canadians have been uniquely placed to view American actions through the lens of that typical dystopian protagonist: Canadians have experienced significant impact from 9/11, share American’s concerns with national security, cannot truly extricate from their geographic and cultural connections with the US, and yet are in no position to impact American policies.

Canada necessarily felt the impact of the terrorist attacks of September 11, 2001, more significantly than other countries outside the US. The impact was immediate: 239 aircraft were diverted to Canadian airports from their American destinations following the attack. Canadians housed and fed over 33,000 passengers stranded in their cities and towns for several days. Most Canadians had friends or family directly impacted by the attacks. While 24 Canadians were killed in the World Trade Centre, thousands more were living in or visiting New York, traveling in other American destinations, or, like Atwood, waiting to board a flight to the US.

Geographic closeness adds to the sense that Canadians are inextricably linked to the fate of the US in the face of such terrorism. While Canada is an

---

19 James Risen and Eric Lichtblau, ‘Bush Lets U.S. Spy on Callers Without Courts’, *The New York Times*, 16 December 2005 <http://www.nytimes.com/2005/12/16/politics/16program.html?_r=1&scp=1&sq=%20bush%20lets%20u.s.%20spy%20on%20callers%20without%20courts&st=cse > [accessed 3 June 2009].

20 Darko Suvin, ‘Utopianism from Orientation to Agency: What Are We Intellectuals Under Post-Fordism To Do?’, *Utopian Studies*, 9 (1998), 162-190 (p. 170).

enormous country and may appear to outsiders as containing vast stretches of land far distant from US borders, Canadians live with the knowledge that approximately 75% of the population lives within 100 miles of the US border.[21] Canadians naturally feel vulnerable to attacks on their neighbor, and also live with the knowledge that while, they may be caught in the fall-out of an attack on the US, they do not have a say in the policies of that country.

Canada's connections to the US are not purely physical. American popular culture has a significant presence in Canada. Television shows written and performed by Americans, and often set in famous American cities like New York City, Los Angeles, and Miami, are shown contemporaneously in Canada. Films, books, magazines, and, of course, internet materials are all readily available to the Canadian public. Yet despite the massive consumption of American popular culture products in Canada, Canadians maintain a sense that Canada is a very different nation, both politically and culturally. Atwood aptly described the special relationship between the two countries in an editorial piece she wrote entitled "Letter to America":

> We've always been close, you and us. History, that old entangler, has twisted us together since the early 17th century. Some of us used to be you; some of us want to be you; some of you used to be us. You are not only our neighbors: In many cases—mine, for instance—you are also our blood relations, our colleagues, and our personal friends. But although we've had a ringside seat, we've never understood you completely, up here north of the forty-ninth parallel. We're like Romanized Gauls—look like Romans, dress like Romans, but aren't Romans—peering over the wall at the real Romans. What are they doing? Why? What are they doing now? Why is the haruspex eyeballing the sheep's liver? Why is the soothsayer wholesaling the Bewares?[22]

As a Canadian, Atwood brings this perspective of intimate outsider to her writing on post-9/11 themes. Her protagonist in *Oryx and Crake*, Jimmy, can be seen to reflect many of the characteristics of a Canadian observer of post-9/11 US politics. Jimmy is close enough to the other characters to be privy to private information and details, yet far enough away to maintain a relatively detached perspective. Jimmy's role as intimate observer allows him to be a relatively unbiased witness to the events he describes. Limited only by his inability to contemporaneously comprehend what will later be revealed to be significant events, Jimmy can report on the steps which led to his status as the last man standing.

---

21 Travel and Cultures: Canada <http://travel.nationalgeographic.com/places/countries/country_canada.html> [accessed 3 June 2009].

22 Atwood, p. 281.

In relation to nearly every significant character in the story, Jimmy is near enough to observe, near enough to potentially be impacted by their actions, but not able to influence. As a child, Jimmy's parents largely ignore him, but he is privy to much more than they suspect. He witnesses their private fights, moods, and secret behaviors, and can detect the nuances of his father's relationship with a female colleague. Jimmy's mother's departure brings Jimmy close to the largely ineffectual resistance: like other dystopic protagonists he has a brush with a group that would change the social structure and address the ethics of continued genetic experimentation. But, Jimmy is too young to be taken into his mother's confidence and so is less influenced than the typical protagonist. Instead, Jimmy remains on the outside of the resistance as well. Later, at the Watson-Crick Institute where Crake works, Jimmy is again an outsider, a "neuro-typical" in a land of geniuses. Jimmy repeats his role as intimate outsider even in the new societal order brought about by the destruction of humanity. He is not one of the Children of Crake, a new people who are both frightened of and intimately connected to him. Jimmy serves as a kind of guardian over them, yet his knowledge of the previous world and the restrictions of his human physicality separate him from them. He has little ability to influence those to whom he is so intimately connected.

Language of the "War on Terror"

From the "doublespeak" of *1984*, through the Russianized Nadsat of *A Clockwork Orange* and the naming practices of *The Handmaid's Tale*, language as a source of political and social power and control has been an important theme of dystopic fiction. In *Oryx and Crake*, Atwood makes her protagonist a person with unusual fondness for language. Jimmy enjoys language: as Snowman, he often indulges in the memory of words that no longer have meaning and will be lost forever when he dies. Snowman's musings about words early in the novel alert the reader to the importance of language throughout. As a mediocre student, Jimmy has little choice about his subjects of study, but he chooses to enter into a program aimed specifically at the manipulation of language as a tool of marketing, persuasion, and obfuscation. His courses at Martha Graham include Applied Logic, Applied Rhetoric, Medical Ethics and Terminology, Applied Semantics, Relativistics and Advanced Mischaracterization, and Comparative Cultural Psychology. Jimmy is trained to sell items that might well be seen as abominations if described accurately; he learns to massage words, and this skill is precisely what makes him valuable to Crake who needs someone he can trust to market his Blyss-

Pluss pills. It is also what makes Jimmy a good reporter of Crake's actions because he recognizes when Crake's rationalizations and flights of rhetoric are "bogus," and does periodically call Crake on it:

> "Immortality," said Crake, "is a concept. If you take 'mortality' as being, not death, but the foreknowledge of it and the fear of it, then 'immortality' is he absence of such fear. Babies are immortal. Edit out the fear, and you'll be ..."
>
> "Sounds like Applied Rhetoric 101," said Jimmy.[23]

Although language has been a theme of dystopias since the early 20th century, the focus on applied rhetoric as a trade resonates more with the post-9/11 era where spin doctors are employed to fashion language that will engage the public on the side of a "War on Terror." A nationwide fear and sense of vulnerability following September 11 was appeased by declaration of a War on Terrorism–a name capturing the communal need for both control and revenge. More importantly, a war justifies the suspension of some human rights, and so the rhetoric of war supports increased surveillance and forms the basis for the loss of other rights and freedoms. The rhetoric suppresses opposition to actions done to fight the war: in regards to the US Patriot Act, the rhetoric of war made it difficult to question the validity of the immensely increased powers of the state to detain and interrogate immigrants suspected of terrorist-related acts, because the Act itself clearly defines these acts as patriotism. Media stories have even focused on the rhetoric adopted by the administration to support continuing American military presence in Iraq. For example, *The Christian Science Monitor* reported in September 2006 that a war of rhetoric was "heating up" over the Iraq war:

> Thursday, President Bush launched a series of speeches aimed at building support for efforts to combat terrorism and for the Iraq war. His address before the American Legion in Salt Lake City followed tough speeches this week by other top administration officials that characterized Iraq war opponents as "defeatists" and "appeasers," likening the threat of Islamic fundamentalist-driven terrorism to "fascism."[24]

The significant focus on rhetoric in post-9/11 America is paralleled by a similar focus in *Oryx and Crake*. That focus in the novel is satirically underscored by Jimmy's largely unreflective participation in training to effectively ma-

---

23 Atwood, *Oryx and Crake*, p. 303.

24 Linda Feldman, 'Bush Escalates War-On-Terror Rhetoric', *The Christian Science Monitor*, 1 September 2006 <http://www.csmonitor.com/2006/0901/p03s03-uspo.html> [accessed 22 February 2009].

nipulate language, and the irony of his eventual solitude as the final repository of most human language.

Theme: For the Greater Good

As is likely clear from the discussion thus far, dystopias are intensely concerned with existing social and political power structures. The themes of dystopias are clearly connected to the concerns of the society creating these fictional works. In the early to mid-twentieth century, for example, the classic dystopias of Orwell and Huxley reflected a fear of rising totalitarianism commensurate with the swells of fascism and totalitarianism then occurring in Europe. In the 1970s and 1980s, as feminism revealed patriarchy and gender biases in Western political and social control systems, dystopias like Atwood's *The Handmaid's Tale* turned their attention to issues of gender-based repression. Following 9/11, dystopic worlds again shifted to voice new anxieties. Most significantly, these dystopias featured the clash between individual rights and the protection of society, and considered the question of whether the government may restrict civil liberties in order to promote national security. The argument that certain unsavoury actions are necessary in order to achieve the greater good of stopping global terrorism is a dominant theme in many post-9/11 dystopias, including *Oryx and Crake*.

Atwood has explicitly stated her concerns regarding the argument that individual rights must give way to the greater interest of national security. In her "Letter to America," she offers a telling criticism of America's responses to 9/11:

> You're gutting the Constitution. Already your home can be entered without your knowledge or permission, you can be snatched away without cause, your mail can be spied on, your private records searched. Why isn't this a recipe for widespread business theft, political intimidation, and fraud? I know you've been told all this is for your own safety and protection, but think about it for a minute. Anyway, when did you get so scared? You didn't use to be so easily frightened. [...]
>
> If you proceed much further down the slippery slope, people around the world will stop admiring the good things about you. They'll decide that your city upon the hill is a slum and your democracy is a sham, and therefore you have no business trying to impose your sullied vision on them. They'll think you've abandoned the rule of law. They'll think you've fouled your own nest.[25]

The argument that civil liberties must be sacrificed for the overall benefit of society has been featured in many of America's post-9/11 works. For in-

---

[25] Atwood, p. 282.

stance, on television, there was a marked shift in the kind of moral dilemmas characters faced. Whereas the late 1980s through 1990s saw an increase in protagonists struggling with morally ambiguous dilemmas and agonizing over their choices, the post-9/11 protagonist had to work out *when* it is morally appropriate to commit heinous acts for the greater good, not *if* it is. The show most often cited as demonstrating this post-9/11 morality is the Fox series *24*. In that show, Counter-Terrorism Unit Lieutenant Jack Bauer often engages in horrific acts of torture, and even murder, in order to thwart an imminent terrorist attack. The show asks its audience to accept these acts as justified, even when they are unauthorized and illegal, because Jack is trying to save thousands or even millions of Americans at the cost of only a few (sometimes clearly innocent) lives.

Atwood described the argument used in America to justify the state's intrusion on civil liberties:

> Democracies have traditionally defined themselves by, among other things—openness and the rule of law. But now it seems that we in the west are tacitly legitimising the methods of the darker human past, upgraded technologically and sanctified to our own uses, of course. For the sake of freedom, freedom must be renounced. To move us towards the improved world—the utopia we're promised—dystopia must first hold sway.[26]

Oryx and Crake is deeply sceptical of the notion that a dystopia can lead to a utopia. Instead, the novel suggests that when a dystopia is offered as a cure to an imperfect society, that cure may be worse than the disease. In the novel, the dystopic restrictions of the pre-apocalyptic world are not a means to an end, but are in fact a precursor of the ultimate end: the total destruction of the human race. While many of the novel's characters tout the dystopic social systems as the necessary means to a better society, in *Oryx and Crake* the freer and less protected pre-9/11 society is presented as a clearly preferable alternative. That world, where people could fly without fear, lived in cities, and where "voting mattered," is an obvious improvement on the state of affairs in the fictional future of the novel. This theme of dystopia leading to utopia is linked to the idea of a *pharmakon*, that which is "both poison and cure."[27] Pharmakons play a profound role in the novel. In addition to the figurative role of a dystopia as that which is supposed to be cure but is in fact poison, the novel presents a physical manifestation of this idea through the BlyssPluss Pill. Crake's pharmaceutical masterpiece is a single pill that purports to protect the user against all forms of sexually transmitted diseases,

---

[26] Ibid., p. 293.

[27] Grayson Cooke, p. 112.

provide an unlimited supply of libido and sexual prowess, and prolong youth. However, as Crake reveals to Jimmy, it also secretly sterilizes its users.[28] And, we later learn, it does even more than that: it is the means through which Crake attempts to exterminate humanity.

The characters often repeat the message that the current dystopia is a necessary means to a better world, that the increased surveillance, enormous police powers, and lack of freedoms are necessary to achieve a greater good. For example, Jimmy's father argues for the current system when his mother, troubled by her loss of personal freedoms and the abuses of power she witnesses, complains to her husband "about the tight security at the HelthWyzer gates—the guards were ruder, they were suspicious of everyone, they liked to strip search people, women especially."[29] Her husband ignores her concerns, dismissing the comparison she draws between herself and a prisoner by telling her she did not adequately understand the necessary evils of society:

> Jimmy's father said she didn't understand the reality of the situation. Didn't she want to be safe, didn't she want her son to be safe?
>
> "So it's for my own good?" she said. She was cutting a piece of French toast into even sided cubes, taking her time.
>
> "For our own good. For us."
>
> "Well, I happen to disagree."[30]

Shortly after this discussion, Jimmy's mother escapes the Compound. The swift response of the Compound guards to this event reveals their power and reach: two women are sent to live with Jimmy in order to extract information from him, Jimmy's father faces a very real possibility of torture, and the guards continue to harass Jimmy about his mother's whereabouts even years later. It is during one of these harassment sessions when we learn what happens to those who disagree with the argument that they must relinquish their individual rights for the greater good of society: the video of Jimmy's mother's execution is shown to him.

Crake's father, another person who did not accept the argument that the ends justify the means, suffers a similar fate. The story of how Crake's father died is revealed slowly throughout the novel. First, Crake discloses that his father was a top researcher over at HelthWyzer West, who somehow met his demise at the bottom of a pleebland overpass. While the general opinion, according to Crake, was that he jumped, Crake does not believe his father's death was a suicide. He describes his father as a man who "believed in con-

---

28 Atwood, *Oryx and Crake*, p. 355.

29 Ibid., p. 62.

30 Ibid., p. 63.

tributing to the improvement of the human lot."[31] Later, Crake reveals the reason his father was killed: his father discovered that HelthWyzer was creating diseases and illnesses in order to sell cures for them. When Jimmy expresses his amazement that the corporation murdered his father, Crake corrects his terminology: "'Executed,' said Crake. 'That's what they'd have called it. They'd have said he was about to destroy an elegant concept. They'd have said they were acting for the general good.'"[32]

It is Crake's horror at the actions being taken in the name of the greater good which, ironically, lead him to impose his own version of the greater good on the world: the "Paradice Project."[33] Etymologically, the word appears to be a play on both "paradise," the innocent and idyllic state of being his project aims at, and "pair of dice," a recognition of the gamble he is undertaking. The version of humanity Crake has personally experienced, including the murder of his father, the terrible death of his mother through infection by a man-made bioform, and the execution of his best friend's mother, is such that he spends his nights screaming in his sleep.[34] Disgusted with humanity, Crake embodies the "for the greater good" argument taken to the extreme: he imposes his own view of the good by ending humanity as we know it and replacing it with a much better adapted humanoid species.

Conclusion

Oryx and Crake does not adopt an entirely new literary form through which to address the events of 9/11. Rather, it relies on a new version of an old form, an updated form of the traditional dystopia which combines the two differing dystopic visions presented in *1984* and *Brave New World*, in order to explore the new threats to civil liberties and freedoms posed by post-9/11 US domestic and foreign policies. Many of the devices associated with dystopia, including a post-apocalyptic setting, the perspective of an outsider, a focus on the language of rhetoric, and the thematic societal concerns of oppressions and social controls are contained in the novel, though each is tailored to be associated with specific meanings in the post-9/11 world. The perspective of the intimate outsider marks the novel as Canadian, the post-apocalyptic setting on the North Eastern coast of the United States connects it directly to New York City, and the theme of whether dystopic social order

31 Ibid., p. 224.

32 Ibid., p. 258.

33 Grayson Cooke, p. 112.

34 Atwood, *Oryx and Crake*, p. 263.

can be justified by the argument that it is meant for the greater good reveal the novel to be a subtle Canadian critique on America's responses to 9/11. *Oryx and Crake* reflects Canadian worries about the loss of civil liberties in American society, the increases in surveillance, and the pervasiveness of the argument that horrific means can be justified by laudable ends. Through the established genre of dystopia, *Oryx and Crake* offers a distinctly Canadian perspective on America in the post-9/11 world.

Bibliography

Atwood, Margaret, 'George Orwell: Some Personal Connections', in *Writing with Intent: Essays, Reviews, Personal Prose 1983-2005* (New York: Carroll & Graf, 2005), 287-293

---, 'Letter to America', in *Writing with Intent: Essays, Reviews, Personal Prose 1983-2005* (New York: Carroll & Graf, 2005), 280-283

---, *Oryx and Crake*, (New York: Random House, 2003)

---, '*The Handmaid's Tale* and *Oryx and Crake* in Context', *PMLA* 119 (2004), 513-517

---, 'Writing *Oryx and Crake'*, in *Writing with Intent: Essays, Reviews, Personal Prose 1983-2005* (New York: Carroll & Graf, 2005), pp. 284-286

Brooks Bouson, J, '"It's Game Over Forever": Atwood's Satiric Vision of a Bioengineered Posthuman Future in *Oryx and Crake'*, *The Journal of Commonwealth Literature* 39 (2004), 139-156

Cooke, Grayson, 'Technics and the Human at Zero-Hour: Margaret Atwood's *Oryx and Crake*', *Studies in Canadian Literature*, 31 (2006), 105-125

Feldman, Linda, 'Bush Escalates War-On-Terror Rhetoric', *The Christian Science Monitor,* 1 September 2006 <http://www.csmonitor.com/2006 /0901/p03s03-uspo.html> [accessed 22 February 2009]

Ingersoll, Earl J, 'Survival in Margaret Atwood's Novel *Oryx and Crake*', *Extrapolation*, 45 (2004), 162-175

Moylan, Tom, *Scraps of the Untainted Sky: Science Fiction, Utopia, Dystopia*, (Boulder: Westview Press, 2000)

Risen, James and Eric Lichtblau, 'Bush Lets U.S. Spy on Callers Without Courts', *The New York Times*, 16 December 2005 <http://www.nytimes. com/2005/12/16/politics/16program.html?_r=1&scp=1&sq=%20bush%20lets%20u.s.%20spy%20on%20callers%20without%20courts&st=cse> [accessed 3 June 2009]

Roach, Kent, *September 11: Consequences for Canada* (Quebec: McGill-Queen's Press, 2003)

Sargent, Lyman Tower, 'The Three Faces of Utopianism Revisited', *Utopian Studies*, 5 (1994), 1-37

Savitch, H.V., 'Does 9-11 Portend a New Paradigm for Cities?', *Urban Affairs Review*, 39 (2003), 103-127

Suvin, Darko, 'Utopianism from Orientation to Agency: What Are We Intellectuals Under Post-Fordism To Do?', *Utopian Studies*, 9 (1998), 162-190

Travel and Cultures: Canada <http://travel.nationalgeographic.com/places/ countries/country_canada.html> [accessed 3 June 2009]

From *Inch'Allah Dimanche* to *Sharia in Canada*: Empire Management, Gender Representations, and Communication Strategies in the Twenty-First Century

William Anselmi and Sheena Wilson

Inch'Allah Dimanche (2001) and *Sharia in Canada* (2006) constitute the objects of this chapter. These films represent a particular space of cultural engagement resonating with gender conflict and militarized strategies of communication. The first, a feature length film, addresses issues of tradition versus modernity and the role of authority within an immigrant woman's displaced context. The second, a documentary, presents the debate about allowing for the cultural practice of Sharia law in Canada. Both resonate with the larger issues of cultural displacement and the ensuing struggles that immigrants from many cultures are confronted with in the process of acculturation. Our comparison illustrates the post-9/11 process by which in the West the Islamic Other has been reduced to simplified rendition of terrorist, anti-feminist, medieval, all of which are contained within the rubric of Islamofascism. We place the issues and events represented into a post-9/11 context and in doing so enter into discourse with other cultural texts that are exemplary of the cultural paradigm shift. Cinema "can" still function as a discursive space that renders public the inherit problematics of international politics as lived reality. There are rare instances, such as these two Canadian and French texts, where resistance is actively portrayed. Analyzing these two films also allows for a comparison of how cultural negations and the related polemics occur differently in two countries where multiculturalism is a lived reality in both but is only constitutionally mandated in one, Canada.

This Briefest Century, Bridging It

A French-Algerian feature length film and a Canadian state-sponsored National Film Board of Canada (NFB) documentary constitute the main objects of this investigation. They have come to represent a particular space of cultural engagement: one where the cultural-political tensions discursively set during the 1990s—pitting imperial visions against peripheral forms of resistance—erupted world-wide after the air attack on America's military and economic symbols, resonating with gender conflict and militarized strategies of communication.

American governmental policies since 2001 have enacted an essentialist paradigm shift toward reducing the complex reality of the Other to a marketed "essence"—terrorist, fundamentalist, Islamofascist, for example—the repercussions of which are visibly manifest throughout the globe. Yet such a specific date would still be limited to an emotional implosion—the "why do they hate us?" refrain[1]—were it not for the formidable recent, but historically grounded, build-up to the twenty-first century as America's century and its manifold representations. Within this necessarily mediatic[2] overview, the First Iraq War (1991) is the rationale for the need to return and complete the mission (weapons of mass destruction notwithstanding) due to the sense of *incompleteness*. What better spiritual instrument of moral justification for America to affirm its system of world management after the fall of the Berlin Wall in1989?

Given these parameters, the multiplication during the 1990s of positions of active engagement is not a surprise, considering the language and narratives generated by a belligerent right as the aggregate of various conservative and religious positions. Neoconservative think-tanks such as Project of the New American Century (PNAC) and American Enterprise Institute (AEI), and mouthpieces such as *National Review*, *The National Interest*, and *Foreign Affairs,* advocated, from different perspectives, what was ultimately seen as the necessity for America to affirm its lead in the world. These pro-active apparatuses and their politically-correct clones combined with official US policies in specific ideological constructions that revolved around two intersecting narratives, spiraling DNA-like into a biopolitical new century[3] to bring to a close the material damage of the 1960s/Vietnam era. Epical narratives, much like a Homerian blinding post-modernity (*siege* mentality, and *return* as a means of completion) reverberating with the triumph of visual culture, this process took the form of Francis Fukuyama's *The Last Man and the End of History* (1992) and Samuel Huntington's *The Clash of Civilizations* (1996). Entwined, these moral stories for a new century were steeped in a culture of religious backlash, a periodic reoccurrence in America's ongoing affirmation of identity.

At once dissipation of human hubris and punishment for multicultural capitalism (i.e. heterogeneous capitalism à la Hardt & Negri), the concrete ma-

---

1 In the days following the attacks, the American domestic media replayed images of disoriented citizens wandering in the streets of New York. One perplexed woman in particular was caught on camera asking why anyone would do this to America. This particular clip was given international airtime and it had widespread resonance.

2 "Mediatic," as we define this term, references the media as the process of a specific constellation of economic, social, and political forces.

3 In this context, the biopolitical new century is a consequence of the contrast, on the one hand, of the awareness of the human body as an agent of change within a political structure, and on the other, as the direct target of institutions in the exercise of power, which brings into question such issues as surveillance, militarization of the urban space, and the construction of identity paradigms. The biopolitical new century refers to the delegitimization of the juridical self.

nifestation of the attacks on the Pentagon[4] and Twin Towers results in a particular form of chastisement: the double combination corresponds to the religious overtones of the Tower(s) of Babel inscribed in a Pentagram. These latent, symbolic forces sustained by factual aspects—the Twin Towers were populated by people of various nationalities and languages under the directives of American neo-liberalism and sustained by military-economic strength—imploded in New York, the new world order, *caput mundi.* As such, this site became the ground zero of multiculturalism. Its destruction implied the obliteration of a fastidious multiplicity so as to turn, by reflection, the (American) world back to its happy frontier simplicity. One of the best indicators of such a shift is the most successful American television program yet, *The Sopranos*, which posits the beginning of the end to the 1950s as the Golden Age of the American Dream.[5]

The rhetoric immediately following the shake-up of America was already at hand as a simplified dichotomy that the media could continuously tune into: "you are either with us or against us."[6] This rhetorical strategy is best exemplified by Pope Benedict XVI and his insistence that the EU constitution be grounded in Christian roots. In America, the fanatical evangelical discourse made sure through its spokespersons (military figures, religious leaders, everyday citizens) that the war was actually a religious war. In Canada, this cultural polarization, as it diffused itself primarily across North America and Europe, brought to a close a programmed dream of state multiculturalism that lasted thirty years and was never realized. The image-aspect of multiculturalism—spectacles of folk-dancing and the consumption of exotic foods—is the mode with which neo-liberalism has been able to recuperate

---

4 An illustrative semiotic analysis that shows the entanglement of the Pentagon with the Twin Towers is provided in detail by Deems D. Morrione in 'When Signifiers Collide: Doubling, Semiotic Black Holes, and the Destructive Remainder of the American Un/real', *Cultural Critique* 63 (2006), pp. 157-73. Also, William Anselmi and Lise Hogan provide an extensive cultural reading of the bind between Pentagon-Twin Towers and the subsequent societal and mediatic fallout in the co-authored article 'Scripturing the 21st Century American Ways to Empire Undone, Over', *College Quarterly*, 7 (2004) <http://www.collegequarterly.ca/2004-vol07-num04-fall/anselmi_hogan.html> [accessed 25 May 2009].

5 The main protagonist of *The Sopranos*, Tony Soprano, is a mafia boss who continuously refers to the 1950s as the apex of the American Dream, and the program is an ironic reading of this cultural fantasy as mythopoiesis.

6 This process parallels the history of the Red Brigades versus the Italian state in the late 1970s. The state embraced the same polarizing rhetorical strategy, though a number of critical Italian intellectuals tried to position themselves according to a *third way* that saw them neither *with the state nor with the Red Brigades* (*né con lo Stato, né con le BR*). It is interesting to note that there was no attempt in the West to create a critical distance to nuance the dichotomy after 9/11.

and propagate the cannibalization of difference as a mechanism of integration.[7] In the end, the actual project of multiculturalism as established by Prime Minister Pierre Eliot Trudeau and the Liberal government in the early 1970s, which can be interpreted as merging into *a sui generis* cosmopolitanism[8]—the integration of differences within a heterogeneous and hierarchical Canadian dream—has been vastly modified, if not ultimately abandoned. Simply put, whatever remained of Trudeau's original vision of multiculturalism was neutralized as a public discourse by the events following September 2001.

The dream of a multicultural Canada is framed by two historically drastic events, one internal and one external: the 1970s October Crisis and 9/11. The October Crisis and the invocation of the War Measures Act in 1970 were followed by the Multiculturalism Policy a year later in October 1971.[9] After 9/11, Canadians at large knew the pragmatic idealism associated with official multiculturalism was over when legislative practices associated with the elimination of civil rights, analogous to the War Measures Act, were implemented in the States and quickly adopted here in the form of Canada's Anti-Terrorism Laws: Bills C22, C35, C36, and C42. The legislated restrictions on civil and human rights were tagged to specific ethno-cultural groups that could be visibly identified as the enemy-other: skin color/garments being the ultimate leitmotivs.

While fighting in Iraq under the guise of implementing democracy and claiming to protect civil liberties around the world, the US government has constructed a spectapolitics[10] "Iraq,"[11] which has been, amongst other things,

---

7 The process of the cannibalization of the Other is entertainingly parodied in Jim Jarmusch's 1995 film *Dead Man*.

8 Of the various aspects of cosmopolitanism, the one that pertains to Canada has to be seen as emanating from the educational process, and this in particular relates to the negotiations between bilingualism and multiculturalism. Sheena Wilson, 'Campus Saint-Jean's Bilingual Writing Centre: A Portal to Multiple Cultures and Cosmopolitan Citizenship', *CWCA Newsletter*, 2 (2009), pp. 9-12.

9 The implementation of the War Measure was the drastic and final answer on the part of the state to the FLQ (Front de libération du Québec) that was a revolutionary movement fighting for an independent Québec, much along the lines of similar anti-colonial insurgencies. Interestingly enough, a year later, the liberal government, under Prime Minister Trudeau attempts a manoeuvre to diffuse the malcontent through the institutionalization of multiculturalism through a bilingual framework, as a way of setting up a hierarchy of belonging.

10 Taking to heart Debord's lesson, what we mean with the term "spectapolitics" is simply the immediate and effective political use to one's advantage of any object and/or cultural text which has undergone a spectacularized process. A perfect example of this would be Italian Premier Berlusconi's political use of his involvement with young would-be starlet/politician Naomi Letizia during the late spring of 2009. This event managed to capture national and in-

a powerful tool in eroding Canadian human rights. The fear component in this spectapolitical strategy has aptly legitimized the covert use on the part of the Canadian government of such things as "security certificates" to indefinitely imprison, in Canada, permanent residents or non-citizens who are targeted as possible terrorists. Strategies of this nature have been marketed as security measures, and they have lead to substantial changes in Canadian legislation: changes that have resulted in the erosion of basic civil rights for all individuals, and it should be noted that there is no ongoing discussion about reinstating these rights. Such processes finally partake of an erasure of modernity by re-establishing a pre-Westphalia vision of the relationship between individuals, society, and the nation, returning the West to a medieval mentality while accusing, ironically, its present target, Muslims, of being the unenlightened masses. Such practices—the erasure of individual participation in society through restrictive state measures—have been investigated by a number of critics. Yet, Italian philosopher Giorgio Agamben in his work addressing the *state of emergency* or *state of exception* provides us, in combination with his work on *homo sacer*, a set of well-honed tools for the analysis presented here, which seeks to respond to the mediatic domestication of differences and the marginalization of the Other. Using Agamben's concepts as points of entry, we provide a cultural and political critique in the comparison of the French-Algerian feature length film *Inch'Allah Dimanche* (2001) by Yamina Benguigui with the National Film Board of Canada documentary *Sharia in Canada* (2006) directed by Dominique Cardona to demonstrate how the changes in the cultural and political sphere brought about by the 9/11 events established a polarization process that has retarded the integration of a multicultural lived reality within the greater rubric of globalization as an eco-

---

ternational interest absconding the general economic crises in Italy during this particular period. In so doing, since Italy was gearing up for European elections, as well as regional and municipal ones, in early June, the voting public was polarized between believing his innocence, or not, all to the detriment of an informed vote based on the actual economic conditions which Berlusconi's government had not adequately addressed.

11 Iraq was constructed as the enemy, paralleling the rhetorical strategies used to conflate the term "Muslim" with that of "terrorist." The result is that the term Muslim now denotes a malleable category that is no longer religious but an ethno-political identity visibly manifest. Iraq, too, now has been rhetorically situated on the map of the enemy Other that posits the greatest threat to Western civilization: America. We base this reflection on a courageous and indispensable work that appeared in 2002 *Collateral Language: A User's Guide to America's New War*, edited by John Collins and Ross Glover. We advocate for the release of an updated version, in order to translate to the public what the eight years of the Bush administration have meant for the manipulation of language. One step in the right direction has been the acknowledgment by the Obama administration that waterboarding is actually torture.

nomic hegemony. The first film addresses issues of displacement, tradition versus modernity, and the role of authority within an immigrant woman's multiple context(s), and her autonomous rebirth. The latter re-presents the debate over allowing the practice of Sharia law in Canada alongside Canada's judicial system. These two films clearly show the changing perspectives on Islam and Islamic citizens' social participation in the West; that is, they reveal the political impact of how social narratives formulate the Other-as-enemy and erase critical paradigms that make it possible for citizens to engage politically as groups and/or as individuals. Though these two films are of different genres—feature length and documentary—they nevertheless partake of a process that reflects the cultural realities of individuals, specifically women, and communities struggling to navigate the social-political tensions and the semantic confusions of the early twenty-first century.

Cinema, no matter what television generally might show to the contrary, *can* still function as a discursive space that renders visible the problematic inherent in national and international politics as lived reality.[12] Television's omnipresence is certainly not undermined by cinema as a viewer's choice, yet the time dedicated to watching a movie has a different disposition than that spent watching television, whose main feature is a constant flow of captivating images, at best. Cinema, which also partakes of informative positioning, is a work produced over a longer period of time, and it allows for cultural reflexivity when it is not in the service of government agenda.[13] Televi-

[12] On the ambiguous relationship between cinema and television, Alberto Abruzzese presents the clearest analysis in his seminal work *Lo splendore della TV*.

[13] The friendship between the American government and Hollywood after 2001 has been well-established and was evidenced by the numerous patriotism-inspiring films produced at the beginning of the twenty-first century. This process was made public in the article by Andrew Gumble that had already appeared in *The Independent* on 12 November 2001, entitled 'Bush Enlists Hollywood to "help the war effort"': "The [then] President's chief political adviser, Karl Rove, has met 40 of Hollywood's top executives [. . .] Their agenda: to discuss ways in which the entertainment industry could help the war effort." Andrew Gumble, 'Bush Enlists Hollywood to "Help the War Effort"', *The Independent*, 12 November 2001 <http://www.independent.co.uk/news/world/americas/bush-enlists-hollywood-to-help-the-war-effort-616694.html> [accessed 25 May 2009]. As well, the role that reality TV was playing was becoming quite evident by 2004. Francine Prose, in March 2004 in *Harper's Magazine*, illustrates the incestuous relationship between the Pentagon and the format of reality TV, specifically in relationship to the network ABC, and the fact that this type of programming is actually a form of indoctrination into the American mythos of the individual who surmounts an array of obstacles to achieve a pecuniary triumph. Francine Prose, 'Voting Democracy off the Island', *Harper's Magazine*, 308 (2004), pp. 58-64. On the one hand, cinema has illustrated the desire for the reconstitution of a community after the emotional disarray of enemy-less-ness after the fall of the Berlin Wall, compounded by the fall of the

sion, in this brief exposure, should be seen as reflecting and producing culture with an immediacy that dissipates history into consumable fragments of the ever-present day: emotive reaction in/of the moment as opposed to reflection on the flow of information. Finally, the fact that American politics has such a powerful impact on world cultures makes it more than difficult for forms of resistance to spread through the social-mediatic sphere. Nevertheless, there are instances, such as the two films up for discussion, where ideas of critical resistance, recuperating the positions of the individual within variegated communities, are actively portrayed with varying degrees of success.

Inch'Allah Dimanche

How do human subjectivities respond to what can be considered the trauma of displacement? Do we seek refuge in the world that we bring with us? Do we dare step out into the new society that surrounds us? And what about our familial connections: how do we settle into this un-familial setting? These are some of the questions that on the surface the film *Inch'Allah Dimanche* addresses quite specifically, and yet there is a deeper investigation into the effects of displacement that considers the relationship between colonized and colonizer. The irony of the film is to envisage this particular one-way relationship within the colonizer's home, so that questions pertaining to agency, empowerment, dialectics, feminism, sex, gender, anti-colonial thought, friendship, domesticity, and nomadism are all rubrics that erupt throughout the movie as a form of identity development in the main character, Zouina, a new Algerian immigrant to France. What is also interesting is the particular temporal setting that allows the director, Yamina Benguigui, to displace postmodern politics within a frame of modernity that permits the viewer to reconsider and reconstitute the filtering of the body-politic through a postmodern lens. Since the movie was released in 2001, questions that pertain to emancipation, the body politic, even displacement, would be considered from the contemporary vantage point as démodé and yet, through the skilful management of image narratives by Benguigui, those very rubrics are resituated in a strategy of the political subject's empowerment. Finally, what transpires in *Inch'Allah Dimanche* is the tension between the modern and the postmodern, as it is resolved through Zouina's character, given her heritage and her

Twin Towers. On the other hand, television, through reality TV, reinstates the myth of the rugged individual. This process shows that cinema and television can be used to resolve the ambiguity of a national ethos constituted by individuals all working toward the common good in contrast to the "evil-doers."

response to her new cosmopolitan space, which allows for the development of multiple identities capable of dialoguing with the precise demands of an evolving society in a global world.

Zouina, an Algerian woman, joins her husband in France by relocating there with her children and mother-in-law. Synoptically, the film is a typical case of displacement as a genre, detailing the effects of migration and the reconstitution of the family unit. What constitutes the *detournement* in this film is the genealogical theme that runs throughout, a potentially subversive element with respect to the patriarchal system that governs colonizing and colonized societies. Being forced to leave her own mother, extended family, and motherland, Zouina sees her genealogy de facto severed.

Throughout the movie the spatial axis works as a substitute for the temporal dimension since it contains the development of character: each time Zouina encounters a new experience delineated by a particular space, she undergoes a transformation that broadens her understanding of her situation in France and informs her sense of self. Zouina is systematically rendered invisible inside the home, yet she is visible and acknowledged in the wider community; such a representation runs counter-intuitively to what is expected as the norm. Not only that, but Zouina also discovers that her differences within the Algerian community in France are not strictly generational but situational and that they relate specifically to how displacement is intertwined with tradition and authority. Displacement, as represented in this film, is not simply a geographical experience but an altering of complex interconnected power-dynamics related to gender, culture, class, and identity.

Spatial Relationships to Power: Family Life

With her arrival in France, Zouina becomes subject to a very restrictive life, cloistered in her home, and controlled by her despotic mother-in-law, who partakes of the patriarchal system in order to access what limited power she can through her association with the male head of the household: her son. In France, the mother-in-law can exercise an acquired authority since the new space allows her to behave according to her relationship with the male body and claim aspects of power normally beyond her reach. It is clear that the mother-in-law and her son, Zouina's husband, are primarily interested in the progeny and that Zouina, as the wife, has little value other than to fulfill her servile role within the family structure. As the only non-blood relative to the husband and mother-in-law, Zouina is treated as Agamben's *homo sacer*, a powerless societal refuse. Upon Zouina's arrival in France, her husband does not acknowledge her, first greeting his mother and then his children instead. Then, once established in the new house, Zouina does not partake of the meals: she stands and serves the family, which is a concrete example of her liminal existence. Her voiceless presence is foregrounded by the interlocutory exchanges that swirl around her. For example, Zouina's husband speaks to their son before leaving the house: he tells him not to let anyone in. Then, the husband speaks to his daughter after she first speaks to him. Throughout, he does not acknowledge his wife. These scenes are highly charged at the symbolic level and are proof that Zouina is, for all intents and purposes, the *homo sacer* whose life can be taken at any moment without consequence.

Navigating Private and Public Spaces

The movie director, Yamina Benguigui, manages a fundamental humanistic narrative[14] aimed at Western audiences in order to frame the genealogical search of an Arabic immigrant woman—the generalized Eastern subject as opposed to the Western individual—who within the new immigrant context loses all access to power and spaces of negotiations of identity[15] because of displacement. The genealogy of power-relations is altered, concretely, by space. The mother-in-law, however, prospers in this new environment since

14 We define "humanistic narrative" to be those texts where the Other has a dialogic relationship to the interlocutor and is posited as an equal participant à la Martin Buber rather than as an enemy. Yamina Benguigui succeeds at all levels in integrating within this story of displacement, which seems to naturally invoke the narrative of the voyage, a western trope that amplifies and makes recognizable to western eyes the materiality of migration. The movie's plot-line reverberates with Dante's *Divine Comedy*, just as the *Divine Comedy* resonates with the resurrection of Christ, and just as the resurrection of Christ resonates with the Bacchus celebration and reconstitution of Dionysius. In short, the movie lends itself also to the type of analysis provided by Joseph Campbell in *The Hero with a Thousand Faces* (Princeton, NJ: Princeton University Press, 1949). Particularly interesting is the numerical symbolism of three and four, which combined equal a full week, and bring us to the seventh day of Sunday: *dimanche*. Number three becomes a multiple signifier (much like in Dante): three attempts to find her "friend, three helpers" (the French feminist, the widow, the bus-driver), three Sundays, three children. When the mother-in-law says that "we waited for you for four hours," it signifies that the cycle is complete: four seasons, four points on the compass, four indicates a complete cycle. Zouina was gone for three Sundays, and four hours the last Sunday, and the fourth hour implies she has resurrected herself: has died and is reborn.

15 According to Richard Jenkin's cutting edge work *Social Identity* (2008), the question of identity is centered on the contested binomial identity/identification, and in this work we address the problematic according to "spaces of negotiations of identity." Richard Jenkins, *Social Identity* (New York: Routledge, 2008).

she actually occupies that space hierarchically and has the keys, literally, to controlling the family allocations of resources. (The keys are to the cabinet where sugar and other valuables are kept.) Within this framing narrative, Zouina is thrice exploited: as a submissive wife, as an Algerian daughter-in-law, and as a colonial subject. In this sense, then, the mother-in-law is the altered past attempting to rescind Zouina's genealogical ties to other women, which echoes the reaction she receives in her unauthorized visit to Malika, the Algerian woman Zouina searches for in her three-Sunday search. The mother-in-law, by becoming the tool of a shared system of patriarchal oppression, French as well as Algerian, constitutes the ironic representation of the bridge between modernity and France's colonial past. In fact, her presence is the ambiguity of modernity that is the simultaneity of colonial and post-colonial reality we seem unable to escape as multicultural communities. Displacement has encouraged the mother-in-law to internalize the oppressive modes she has been subject to in her own life and country, as, for example, in the use of fearful stories to scare potential friends away from her grandchildren. This extends to controlling her daughter-in-law's body and sexuality, discouraging, for example, Zouina's French friend Mademoiselle Briat from introducing make-up or the latest fashions into the household. Control without surveillance would be ineffectual as pragmatics of societal order, so reporting on Zouina for letting a man—a duplicitous vacuum salesman—into the house is simply an exercise in the ordering of the refuse whose visibility is problematic in itself and whose communications must be continuously monitored lest the possibility of identitary and genealogical manifestations occur.

Escaping to her backyard provides no refuge since it becomes an overtly public space: an area of confrontation between her family and the retired French bourgeois gardeners hoping to again win their neighbourhood horticultural prize. The hobby of gardening is a narrative expedient to show that the domestication of nature is, by extension, the domestication of the Other throughout history. Zouina, in an effort to escape the apparent banality of systematic oppression and in order to re-establish her sense of belonging in the world, escapes to nature beyond the backyard; in the film, she stealthily breaks loose from confinement through the back door to run through a field with a definite purpose in mind: finding her country woman, Malika.

Roots Extend Mostly Horizontally, Perhaps like a Rhizome

The extended climax, the recuperation of the genealogical line, which the film evokes from its inception, is presented as a broken promise of sisterhood. Seeking alliance outside the home, Zouina embarks upon a voyage of discovery in three defined stages, hoping to find complicity and companionship in another Algerian woman who she has heard lives in a neighbouring area. Zouina's three (Sun)day[16] search—hence "dimanche" in the title—sees her lost on the first day in the land of the dead, at the cemetery, where she meets with the widow (of a French military man) who then becomes an ally in her quest. On the second (Sun)day, Zouina goes to the French widow's home. Sitting in the widow's library, Zouina is surrounded with the dead military husband's books, which are the repository of Western thought and images. Confronted with Algerian history from an oral French perspective as told by the widow, Zouina is placed in a context where a dialogue for negotiations of identities can begin, negotiations that can potentially reconstitute the losses associated with the severing of her genealogical line. The widow, on the other hand, has now become disengaged from the patriarchal system because of her societal condition: she is now able to empathize with Zouina's quest for agency. The film's narrative implies that in Algeria Zouina would have been able to assert her views without suffering the condemnation she faces from her Algerian family/community in France.

On the third Sunday, Zouina, with the widow's help, finally discovers Malika, the Algerian woman for whom she was searching. As part of the film's strategic narrative, Zouina's attempt to find Malika is the symbolic attempt to re-establish the genealogical line. However, the meeting is a failure, since Malika has internalized the severance of the genealogical line and looks upon her own daughters as blights, maintaining them only until they can fulfill their roles in the homes of their future husbands. Upon meeting, Zouina greets Malika lovingly as a lost-sister.[17] Malika, however, rushes Zouina into the home, looking about the street, before closing the door, to identify if anyone has seen her unexpected visitor's arrival. Malika immediately quizzes Zouina about her husband, seeking to discover whether Zouina has his permission to visit her. As soon as Malika discovers that Zouina is there illicitly, Malika rejects her, throwing Zouina out of the home. Zouina

---

16 Zouina is able to escape the house on Sundays because it is the working man's day off, and the husband is free to take his mother out to prepare for the up-coming holiday of Eid.

17 This is Zouina's first demonstration of love, beyond duty, and the joyful smile she has when meeting Malika (her counterpart in displacement) resonates with the smile of self-cognition she gives the camera in the closing scene of the film.

cries and begs outside the house, putting her fist through the window. This becomes a defining moment of the narrative,[18] since breaking the window is an attempt, an intentionally crude symbolism, at broadening Malika's horizons.[19] At the same time, the shattering of the window leads the viewer to consider the camera as an optic diaphragm between the subject and viewer: a breaking of the Brechtian fourth wall, or a Pirandellian metaphysical urgency for the amalgamation of spectator and performer.

Frozen Displacement: Narcissism and the Phantom Limb

Zouina is also from another generation of immigrants than Malika (despite their similar ages), represented by the fact that Zouina is more receptive to her French environment. This indicates transformations had already taken place in Algeria in the fifteen years between Malika and Zouina's separate migrations.

The drastic generational differences in attitudes and practices concerning women's autonomy frame the very notion of modernity as we apply it in the West; finally the question is "what is modernity?" Tradition dictates that women are confined to the home, which alienates them from the public sphere. Malika has been entrenched in nostalgia for the duration of her life in France: the Algeria of her emigration has been frozen in time within the space of her home. "Negative nostalgia"[20] provides the invisible mirror that

---

18 Displacement risks fomenting oppression when patriarchal values are overdetermined in the new setting both in the relationship to Malika and the mother-in-law. In this case, Zouina, as the immigrant woman, loses the social network that situated her in Algeria and with that any possibility to negotiate her role(s). The traditional Algerian family dynamic, when transplanted to France, becomes much more oppressive because there is an entrenchment of authority and normal societal mediation is eliminated. For Zouina, Malika represents home and sisterhood, but the intended French audience will also recognize Malika as a Biblical Peter-figure when Malika throws Zouina out of the house and Zouina desperately pleads for Malika not to abandon her. When Malika rejects Zouina, it is a betrayal and a denunciation because Zouina is seen as being too westernized already. Despite the fact that Zouina has only been in France a short period of time in contrast to Malika's fifteen-year residence, Zouina has become aware of women's independence in France through her friendships with Mademoiselle Briat and what she hears on the radio regarding sex, love, and relationships.

19 When Zouina breaks the window, it is an attempt to break through Malika's narcissistic circle of affirmation, which freezes development or metamorphosis and confines her to her home, a domestic space that she can control and wherein she can maintain the culture of an imaginary Algeria.

20 The term comes from a conversation between Antonino Mazza and William Anselmi, with regards to Mazza's 'Afterword: Prophecy Versus Memory: Towards a New Pre-History', in

reflects back to Malika the validation she needs to affirm the propriety of her behavior. For Malika, France is a desert of silence. She does not interact with it; the influence of radio or television in her home would infiltrate her control over the nostalgia within which she dwells. On the other hand, Zouina and Malika's daughter establish a complicity of modernity that can encompass the public space of France within which the home is situated and which, in the end, results in a form of transience and growth. There is the insinuation of recognition at a different level, through eye contact, between Zouina and Malika's daughter, who both understand French media and the parlance of feminism and sexuality. Malika's daughter is being forced by her parents' stasis into marriage with her cousin (presumably back in Algeria). The daughter seems to will Zouina to stop speaking to her mother, knowing what the end result will be. She understands that there is no possibility to penetrate the survival shield that her mother has constructed, just as Zouina's own small children later plead with her to stop begging at Malika's door, another liminal stage where sanctuary will not be accorded, and a space indicating the phantom pain of a severed genealogy. What Zouina does not yet recognize at that moment in her development is that the severing of the phantom limb is an absence which can be reconstituted and that this metamorphosis designates procreative transformation. She realizes this shortly thereafter on her symbolic voyage across the city in the bus, wherein she confirms what she already knows to be true: her sense of self as mediated through a form of French feminism can reconnect her to her extended genealogical origins, and she can affirm herself through the printed word (education) and through her connection to future generations (her children, specifically her daughter).

Claiming Space and the Autonomous-Self Assertion of Power

After putting her fist through the window and receiving no response from Malika[21]—although it should be noted that the viewer sees Malika's silent anguish and tearful breast-beating within the confines of her home—Zouina wraps her bleeding hand in the scarf she pulls from her head. She walks past

Pier Paolo Pasolini: Poetry, trans. by Antonio Mazza (Toronto: Exile Editions, 1991), pp. 133-137. Basically, "negative nostalgia" is a direct result of displacement where identity is stultified by an overpositivization of one's past experiences, which turn out to be anti-historical and solely the reconstruction of an entrenched imagination.

21 Malika's inability to escape from the confinement of her death-like existence in a frozen past is an allusion to the mythological figure of Eurydice, who can not be brought out of the confines of the underworld by Orpheus.

the widow who is waiting for her with a taxi; Zouina does not acknowledge her but bypasses her and boards the bus. The framing of how space can be crossed over is given by the two methods of transportation: the taxi is an individualistic enterprise, whereas the bus represents the fluid community. Yet, the bus driver commands all passengers, aside from Zouina and her children, to disembark. After the other passengers descend, the driver tells Zouina to "stay by my side." He becomes her guide across the city, as she returns home to her new self-discovered identity that encompasses the past and the future, through culture.[22] The past is her Algerian tradition; the future, through implied references to the radio and to the women she befriends, is French late-1960s feminism: transmission of knowledge from woman to woman, mother to daughter, hence the inferred meaning of the film's final images.

The last scene is highly symbolic. Zouina's voyage through the urban landscape inscribes her and the children within their new reality. As the bus approaches her reclaimed home, Zouina looks out the windshield and sees her waiting community: the widow, the young French feminist Mademoiselle Briat, the old couple from next door, her mother-in-law Aïcha, and her husband are standing in front of the house forming a familial tableau. The mother-in-law starts shrilly chastising Zouina for making them wait four hours. At this juncture, the husband takes control by shouting at his mother in Zouina's defence: the mother-in-law retreats inside the home. The hierarchy is transformed, and in the final scene the male gaze of the camera is brought to bear upon s/he who gazes because the viewer is imbricated in the husband's reaction to Zouina's final statements. When the camera focuses on Zouina, she ends up reversing the role of the gaze as Laura Mulvey conceived of it: we as viewers become subject to her gaze. In the last scene, Zouina puts her arm around her young daughter and says to her, while looking ahead into her husband's face, "Demain, c'est moi, je vous amène à l'ecole" (Tomorrow, I'm going to take you to school [referring to all three children]). [23] The fact that Zouina sees education as an opportunity and that she reads

---

[22] This is a symbolic reference to Ulysses's odyssey and is evidence that Zouina is claiming belonging for all immigrant women in France. Since Ulysses in the *Odyssey* becomes everyman, he does represent humanity's quest for a hopeful future through a regenerative process. Zouina, as the only woman on the bus, represents all women and the conquest of confined space: the liberation of all immigrant women to move freely in society, physically and metaphorically.

[23] Benguigui artfully plays with viewer expectations based on Hollywood cinema. The look between husband and wife, at first, suggests a romantic marital reconciliation of sorts—a happy ending. The words that follow, however, identify that the happy ending here actually results from a reconfiguration of family power-structures with Zouina looking to the future

and writes inscribes her into the cultural milieu. Because of the pause that follows her statement and the fact that she smiles as the film ends, the viewer understands that the husband has been receptive to this new power-shift. Furthermore, in Zouina's emancipation, she is no longer covering her hair. She has used her headscarf to bandage her bleeding hand that now rests on her daughter's shoulder: the blood signifies the continuity of the genealogy as it has re-written itself over the patterns of the page/scarf. From the traditional perspective, the fact that her hair is publicly displayed *could* symbolize her individual sexual liberation. However, from a Western perspective, the removal of the headscarf *could also* signify the re-appropriation of the body and the reconstitution of a new language to interpret the body: she can now choose whether she wants her hair to signify her sexuality, or not. The hair becomes a free-floating signifier that is no longer predetermined by men's semantics of power. The final scene heals the genealogical caesura that Zouina suffered when she was dragged onto the boat from Algeria to France by her mother-in-law at the beginning of the movie. Genealogy is re-established between Zouina, as mother, and her own daughter, within the context of French urban culture; as an Algerian she becomes integrated within a multicultural society that does not relegate her into a submissive space.

Transitioning to the Twenty-First Century

Inch'Allah Dimanche, released on the cusp of 9/11, indicates a hopeful paradigm for the future that cannot come to fruition based on the interpretation and the media-spin given to September 11, 2001. The dominant rhetoric thereafter fits within a discourse of Clash of Civilizations, supported by the encompassing Western rallying cry: "We are all Americans"/"We are all New Yorkers."[24] This cry functioned as a rhetorical strategy that endeared George W. Bush to the American people and the world, at least temporarily. At the same time, this was part of the polarization of the world into two camps: one constituting civilization and the other as a grouping of monstrous barbarians, as subtly illustrated by the 2007 movie *300*. Finally, it became an issue of the West as a site for the reaffirmation of life and the East as the location of

---

for herself and her children, especially the daughter who appears in the configuration of the last scene.

24 In some European countries the identification was with New York, in other cases with America. Nevertheless, both slogans echoed with the 1985 song "We Are the World," America's music-world contribution to the fight against famine in Africa. Michael Jackson and Lionel Richie, 'We Are the World', USA for Africa, cond. by Quincy Jones (1985).

chaos and death, which is the reversal of the dynamic reflected in *Inch'Allah Dimanche*. This simplistic narrational dichotomy, recounted by the Western media, encapsulates a complex of issues without having to contextualize their meaning.[25] Power is given to a select few reoccurring and echoing images provided in the Western media. Around the time of September 11, these images included the towers collapsing, people crying and asking why anyone would attack benevolent America, and, later, clips of video-game-like night-vision footage of the War in Iraq constantly played on circuit. Over the last decade, the select images have changed, but the quintessential aspect remains the same: images of 9/11 have been consistently used to solidify a state of trauma and mourning that can be used to rally support for the invasion of Eastern countries and the illegal detainment of Muslims in the West,[26] as well as the steadfast erosion of civil liberties in Western nations and the reinforcement of practices against civil liberties in other countries.[27] A surprising element of the erosion of civil liberties throughout the West has been the attempt to implement, through this very same rubric, the notion of Sharia in Canada, specifically in Québec and Ontario. While allowing for Sharia law in Canada—something which apparently had taken place, to some degree, in Ontario, before the documentary was shot—might appear to be a progressive notion, it actually subscribes to conservative capitalist practices of domination over weak constituencies.

---

25 *Inch'Allah Dimanche* is about women, who represent the future and the past. Men, on the other hand, have exhausted their attempts to order life, much like colonialism has consumed itself. The men are metaphorically dead: one male character has long-ago widowed his wife before the beginning of the plot; Zouina's husband himself is a metaphoric zombie; the door-to-door salesman is the trickster of capitalism telling Zouina she has won a vacuum and then setting her up on an unaffordable payment plan; the neighbour man married to the award-winning gardener represents the silent majority; and the bus driver can be interpreted as both a guide away from the underworld and guide to her *new* home.

26 As we finalize this article, in late spring 2009, one of the promised and yet undelivered resolutions of the newly elected American Obama government is to close Guantanamo Bay. However, it was indicated through court proceeding in San Francisco on 9 February 2009, that the legitimacy of extraordinary rendition under the Bush government would be maintained by the Obama Administration, which adopted the same stance on state secret privilege, arguing that releasing evidence against the victims of extraordinary rendition could potentially jeopardize national state security.

27 The outsourcing of torture by Western nations, to countries such as Egypt and Syria, is one example. The feature film *Rendition* (2007) with Meryl Streep and Reese Witherspoon illustrates this process for the viewing public.

Sharia in Canada/ La charia au Canada[28]

Sharia in Canada presents us with a problematic interpretation of the process whereby certain religious leaders tried to tweak the economic agreements between provinces and the US (impacting Canadian multiculturalism) in order to legitimize Sharia mediation courts in Canada. At the time of the film's production there were unofficial mediation courts operating in Ontario, and the film tracks the subsequent debates in Québec and Ontario. The problem with the documentary is that it presents a binary set-up (us versus them), and, informed by secular humanistic principles, it argues against Sharia. In doing so, however, the documentary is unable to nuance and problematize its own position vis-à-vis the complexity of national and international interplay.

Multiculturalism in Canada is not a fixed social category; since even before its inscription into Canada's vision of itself in 1971, multiculturalism was a lived and practiced reality. With the official declaration of multiculturalism, it became even more complex as a rubric, since lived reality was not necessarily integrated into the official bilingual Canadian vision of a multicultural nation. State multiculturalism was based on the pride of one's heritage and the acceptance of specified representations such as the culinary and the performative aspects of heritage cultures.[29] In the end, the term multiculturalism is a contested one, since, throughout the decades, attempts by certain individuals and/or ethno-cultural groups have been made to go beyond the limits imposed by state multiculturalism in order to enter into a dialectic with political power structures, so as to acquire participatory visibility beyond the integrated spaces of performance. This process was undermined by the Meech Lake Accord, which impeded the aspirations of ethno-cultural groups

---

28 This documentary is presented in a non-orthodox format, divided into two episodes that draw on the same interview materials edited with a different communicative strategy and audience in mind. In this article, we concentrate on the first episode entitled "Something to Fear?" because it pertains more specifically to our comparative analysis with *Inch'Allah Dimanche* and its feminist issues in a post-9/11 world. However, the reader should be aware of the existence of the second episode "The Pitfalls of Diversity" that problematizes the multicultural reality in Canada and elsewhere (France and Greece, for example) where Sharia is only one of many different issues that sustain the critical discourse about diversity, assimilation, integration, and social coexistence. The analysis of the two episodes in relationship to one another will constitute the premise for a future investigation.

29 Originally formulated by William Anselmi in 'Italian Canadian as displacement poetics: context, history, and literary production', *Studi Emigrazione/Migration Studies—International Journal of Migration Studies*, XLIV (2007), pp. 369-388. The term was "integrated spaces of performance." The concept was later expanded upon to become "performative multiculturalism" in a co-authored article with Sheena Wilson: 'Performative Radicalism'.

wanting to contribute to a sense of what defines Canadian identity.[30] In other words, identity as a process of negotiation was once again limited by the definition of a bilingual country so that multiculturalism becomes a form of entertainment. What the film demonstrates is how the proponents of Sharia use multiculturalism as a cloaking device to demand Sharia's implementation, and by default the opposition to Sharia ends up fossilizing multiculturalism into its depoliticized spectacular representations. Because a rhetorical binary system has already been established by 9/11, any opposition to Sharia, ironically, reinforces the working script of state multiculturalism that does not permit for any critical engagement about other factors within the lived reality of multiculturalism because any other issues are already pre-established as threatening, hence the title of the episode: "Something to Fear." Despite the documentary's seemingly progressive agenda, it uses a strategy of narration that readily fits the available format in the West for how to deal with the Eastern threat to replace Western civilization with the Caliphate. Ultimately, the film terrorizes the viewer into thinking that Muslim men are the final problem: terrorists in the West, in their own communities, mosques, and families. The semantic laxity regarding the term "Sharia" demonstrates a plurality that ends up confusing, not elucidating, the issues, and as the complexity of Sharia-related issues has not been sufficiently eviscerated, the documentary clarifies nothing and relies on pre-established discourses that are regurgitated as spectacle: i.e. Eastern women to be saved by Canadian society. The viewer is left hanging. Is Sharia something to fear? If so, by whom? Seemingly, it is a problem for Muslim women and, in that scenario, what is the rhetorical goal of the documentary? Is it to spectacularize conflict within Muslim communities or is it to demand neo-colonial intervention on the part of mainstream viewers to save Muslim women? While we, the authors, do *not* think Sharia should be implemented, we also recognize that every manifestation of Muslim expression is a venue for Western siege-mentality, and this is a direct result of 9/11. The rhetorical strategy of the documentary finally capitulates to the maintenance of state multiculturalism that does not permit for any manifestation of multiculturalism beyond its performative mechanisms.

Where the film succeeds is that it does interview several people who expose a number of well-informed arguments against Sharia, while the pro-Sharia proponents undo the rationale of their own argumentation; these inter-

---

[30] For more on how the Meech Lake Accord nullified the participatory claims of ethnic minorities, please see Evelyn Kallen, 'The Meech Lake Accord: Entrenching a Pecking Order of Minority Rights', *Canadian Public Policy/Analyse de Politiques* 14 (1988), pp. 107-120.

viewees provide clues to the viewer about the complexities of the issues surrounding Sharia. But the film fails on two levels: 1) it falls into recognizable tropes that identify Muslim men as a threat, this time to their own communities; and 2) in doing so, it fails to question the role of religion in secular post-9/11 Western societies. Lawyer Renée Côté from the Association nationale, Femmes et droit, Ottawa, bluntly states that religion, per se, is the issue. As a Québécoise who understands the Duplessis[31] reign of power, she argues that it is not Islam but religious institutions in general that subject women to repressive cultural codes, from which contemporary Canadian laws protect them. Sharia cannot function in Canada for the reasons that Sharia itself partakes of multiple interpretations according to different geo-cultural/political spaces, that it is inconsistent with Canada's legal system, and that it disenfranchises Muslim women and presents a threat to other repressed groups. According to Côté and other anti-Sharia advocates in the documentary, integrating Sharia in Canada would result in the erosion of a secular society, and whatever the faith, religious institutions have a historical record of oppressing certain constituencies.

The film, responsibly, tries to present a dialectic on the issue of Sharia, with the aim of presenting an objective purview, but the narrative fails to present a cohesive argument since the anti-Sharia positions are discussed from variegated semantic perspectives: Sharia as a cultural interpretation, Sharia as a legal code, Sharia as a religious issue, and Sharia as a gender power-relation issue. The voice-over does not provide clarification of terminology or an overview of the complex and interrelated issues, so that Sharia ends up being a *passepartout* point of view. As we move away from 9/11, Canada needs to understand how the religious and the cultural have become one and how the failure to differentiate between the two is a direct result of eight years of the Bush Administration and policies, which has had fallout on other national paradigms, Canada's included.

The conflation of religious and cultural spaces is a result of debris authoritarianism[32] in one of its most belligerent manifestations that allows the religious-right to claim authority within the secular world. As such, we would argue that Sharia is an entry point into the dismantling of a post-enlightenment secular society: once a group of women are disenfranchised (regardless of whether they are Muslim), this sets up a process whereby there exists the potential for other factions of society to be exploited and for syner-

---

[31] An interesting reading of Maurice Duplessis's vision of grandeur can be found in Marguerite Paulin, *Maurice Duplessis: le noblet, le petit roi* (Montréal: XYZ, 2002).

[32] By debris authoritarianism we refer to the politically toxic fallout after the 9/11 event that took authoritarian forms and undermined the principles of a democratic society.

gistically coherent ghettos of repression to form. When one religious group oppresses women, then any other religious group can follow suit. Furthermore, allowing a minority group to integrate itself into the secular-legal realities strengthens the attempt throughout North America to institutionalize religious *modus operandi.* This process parallels the dismantling of the welfare state whereby disenfranchised groups cannot rely on the protection of the state but must find solace in charity. The dismantling of the welfare state works in tandem with the erosion of secular society: the argument is that "we" are a community, "we" don't need the government, and the "we" aggregates around religious institutions and is sustained and nurtured by the neo-liberal laissez-faire attitude.

Rhetorical Construction of Sharia in Canada

The discourse of power in the first episode of the film is tied to the hermeneutics of divine text. Throughout this movie, the legitimacy of the printed word is framed by the way words and images have intersected in a post-9/11 world. The opening lines of the documentary are as follows:

> Since September 11, 2001, a new era has begun in the West, one where battles in the name of Islam are being fought in its cities. Muslims here and elsewhere feel besieged on one side by those claiming to dictate their true faith and on the other by people who see their religion as diabolical. In this atmosphere one word strikes fear into people's hearts: Sharia.

This narrative voice-over guides the gaze, but the visual message is a montage of images that stand in contrast to the oral message: the visual and the verbal clash. Whereas the voice seems to present the viewer with a detached analysis, the flow of images elicits particular emotional responses since the images represent people and moments that have threatened Western stability: for example, the first image is of bin Laden holding a machine gun. Since his location is unknown, he is nowhere and everywhere. The next image in the video collage is the collapsing Twin Towers; then British police officers; then what we can assume is the train bombing in Spain; followed by a machine gun mounted on a vehicle traveling through an unidentifiable urban zone; and Eastern[33] police officers—perhaps Pakistani—guarding a contain-

[33] We are aware of the changing political ideologies bound to certain identity-tags. Before 1989 "Eastern" would have dictated East of the Berlin Wall. After 9/11 this designation has shifted locality to the "Middle East," which itself is a free-floating signifier that can encompass any politically contentious region east of Greece, à la *300*.

er; wanted posters presumably representing Muslim terrorists; and, finally, images of people walking and shopping in the streets in what is presumably a Muslim area of town in a large cosmopolitan city. In this shot, some of the women are wearing headscarves, others are not, and the different dress-codes of both men and women suggest a multicultural setting. By the time we see the title "Sharia in Canada. Something to Fear?"[34] superimposed over a downward angled pan-shot scanning elaborately gilded books displayed on a tabletop (visual shopping), the viewer has already been spatially and temporally situated in Canada: Queen's Park, Toronto, 8 September, 2005. The objectivity of the documentary has projected a discursive dichotomy causing tension between the aural and visual messages. It is possible, then, to deconstruct the documentary into a structure whereby the first object of our narrative analysis will be the frame.

Frame

The tone of the documentary, which is comprised of the image and the word, is paradoxical. While the images that introduce the film show moments of terrorism enacted by Muslims, the film narrative goes on to state that Muslims are "besieged on one side by those claiming to dictate their true faith, on the other by people who see their religion as diabolical." This narrative characterizes Muslims as double-victims: victims within their own community and victims within Western society, specifically Canada. This also homogenizes Muslim Canadians: a false representation, since we are not only presented with Muslims living in two different Canadian realities—Québec and Ontario—but also with Muslims from a plethora of cultures, who have different spatial-temporal relationships to Canada.

If the clash between word and image works as a framing device that guides the viewer into the problems that the documentary is trying to present, a number of questions arise: 1) Was the image-word contrast intentional? 2) Did the contrast occur beyond the director's intentions due to the fact that the selected images are context bound and resist inclusion in a discussion that attempts to nuance the problems of multiculturalism for citizens who wish to maintain specific cultural practices that disempower existing Canadian laws? 3) Was the conflation of images and oral narrative a process of intertexuality

---

[34] The name of the French version of the episode is "Qu'est-ce qui fait si peur?" The film is bilingual. The filmmaker interviews people in English and in French, in Ontario and in Québec (namely Toronto and Montréal), and there is both an English and French version of the film; subtitling is provided.

that escaped the consideration of the director and editors of the film, producing its own narrative? The director seems to have used certain images to create a backdrop for this intended message without sufficient awareness that the images are also creating their own narrative, equally or more powerful in the age of the image in which we live, and these two narratives contradict one another at the outset of the film. The contradiction renders the frame unstable. This documentary, therefore, has a certain merit but does not fully address its own potential. Basically, it considers the image as a tool rather than a complete system of communication that has its own grammar and syntax, as well as historical and semiotic relationships to other texts and to culture in general. Taking all of this into consideration, where does the viewer situate him/herself?

Whatever the intentionality of the film, the result is that the choice of images framing the narrative produces an historical representation reduced to a post-9/11 vision of Islam and the Eastern world. This is done to maintain influence over Muslims around the world, including those living in Canada. Within this frame, Sharia is presented as problematic because the film maintains that it is controlled by imams imported from the East to stand guard over Islam in the West, where Islam risks contamination. Imams are also portrayed as agents sent to expand the Islamic sphere of influence in the Western world. According to the documentary, those who have either sought refuge in Canadian laws or those who are enfranchised by them will find themselves again in a perilous situation.

The problematic of the film is that representing the potential threat that Sharia poses in such a polarized manner plays into post-9/11 representations of Islam as an unstable and disruptive rubric. The concern for certain groups, who are at risk of exclusion from the protection of Canadian juridical processes, is valid, yet the argument is faulty and strategically weak because it does not provide the viewer with a nuanced understanding of how women's rights are being undermined and what the far-reaching ramifications could be for any number of Canadian constituencies. The overall process of the documentary succumbs to the spectacle, which bypasses any multicultural problematic and makes only the reductive implication that the real problem is Muslim men. Fear is used here, as in the mainstream media-circuit, and this stultifies the documentary's informative potential. Polarizing an issue, as this narrative does, unifies the political spectrum into reactionary and absolutist statements. Ultimately, in this film, the threat becomes not Muslims, but Muslim men, who abuse their power whether it is in the domestic sphere or the global political arena. Muslim men are equated with fundamentalists who are themselves reduced to the lowest common denominator: *those people, those terrorists*.

Unfortunately, despite the film's critical intentions, it cannot resist the *zeitgeist*, which reduces narratives to authoritarian visions of the world. Viewers fearful of the repercussions of the implementation of Sharia law for Muslim women in Canada, and by extension the progressive erosion of women's rights in general, are encouraged through the construction of the narrative to opt to maintain the status quo (which excludes Sharia). Those motivated by a fear of Islamic fundamentalism will also opt to maintain the status quo: the Canadian legal system. Therefore, in this context, there is only one possible development: no matter what, the maintenance of a right-wing/conservative praxis ensures that neo-liberal ideology remains unchallenged, despite the spectacle created around arguing for or against women's rights. The frame sets up a false history because it narrowly formulates the anti-Sharia argument as simply a feminist problematic without considering the broader implications, which from our point of view would have included the fact that human rights per se are at stake.

Actors

The women interviewed in the film, who represent various Islamic backgrounds—by class, education, and culture—all express their concern about the fact that Sharia mediation would disenfranchise them, because in most Islamic cultures men interpret and apply the Word. While this gendered message comes through, the women's different backgrounds and perspectives, and the information they provide, contribute to the rhetorical failings of the narrative. Upper class educated women represent Sharia as an issue of law, and middle class and working class women provide experiential testimony about the lived reality of patriarchy on the domestic sphere. In so doing, the term Sharia comes to signify a plurality of issues, for which the narrative provides no focus. Therefore, as viewers, we are made to continuously migrate between the public and the private sphere, through the various women, and this is another problem of the post-political [35] world that limits viewers to accepting the authority of television and cinematic rendition of complex issues, as these technologies resonate with authorial voices. In the film, the

[35] Post-political discourse is predominantly a rhetorical strategy that conflates the historical political dialectic, grounding itself instead in the a-historical moment within the fluidity or absence of right/left-political actions. Anselmi & Wilson, 'Performative Radicalism'.

plurality of voices is commendable, yet the plurality of voices also presents different entry points into the "problem" of Sharia – cultural, legal, religious—and the viewer is finally forced to accept the dichotomy at play: Muslim men versus Muslim women. There is no acknowledgement that the erosion of Muslim women's rights will undermine the rights of all Canadians. The debate, for non-Muslims, is a spectacle that will not impact them. No engagement is required on the part of non-Muslim viewers. The film suggests that as a religious-cultural mandate, Muslim women would be obligated to accept Sharia mediation, as opposed to relying on Canada's legal system. Even if both were available to them, community pressure would dictate and there would be no exception from a patriarchal implementation of Sharia. Yet, paradoxically the narrative reinforces a class structure within women's realities, which ultimately alters and consumes genealogical continuity.

Though it claims that all oppressed voices are equal, certain upper class,[36] well-educated women are able to manoeuvre around the dangers of Sharia. One of these women, Fatima Houda-Pepin, is able to inform a political decision.[37] Houda-Pepin is of Moroccan descent, and she represents the uppermost echelon of Québec society, since she is an elected member of the Québec National Assembly. It is, in fact, due to her that Québec passed laws against Sharia, making the province appear to be more pro-active and aware of cultural complexities. Fatima Houda-Pepin is the rational Other who explains the logic of the law. The film, in its representation of this issue, favors Québec as a site of liberalism and secularism.

Amira Elias is a theologian, teacher, artist, and filmmaker from Montreal who represents herself as a religious leader, since she is studying to be a female imam. She is aware of the role that an imam should ideally play in society, and she represents the spiritually aware, socially responsible, not politically motivated leader of the community. This is in contrast to the phantasm of the male religious authority, Syed Mumtaz Ali, who never appears on screen but is represented as an authoritarian imposition on Canadians and specifically Canadian Muslim women.

Nuzhat Jafri is the third woman in this category of actors. She is from the Canadian Council of Muslim Women in Toronto, and as an activist she is particularly concerned with social issues such as *jawaz el mutaa*, marriage of pleasure. She is of Pakistani origin and feels that Canada is one of the best

36 Although class in Canada is not something that is acknowledged in the same way as it is in some countries, it is a condition that is understood in relationship to people's individual (not born) economic strata combined with education and employment status.

37 Québec frames Sharia as a political issue, based on Houda-Pepin's perspective and argument. In Ontario, with no one leading the debate, it becomes more of a social debate.

places to live in the world for Muslim women. Therefore, she is interested in protecting Muslim women's human rights, and she sees Sharia as a threat to that project. Québec lawyer Andrée Côté, who we have already mentioned, represents an intellectual sister and advocate from outside the Muslim community who is able to forge alliances in order to protect the status of all women in Canadian society. The other female characters who appear in the film illustrate by contrast the class hierarchy established through the film's narrative.

One such individual is Mounia,[38] who appears to be from a more working class background. She talks of a Pakistani neighbor who is still confined to an oppressive traditional system, unable to leave the house. Mounia says, "I have a neighbor from Pakistan. The wife never goes outside. I think she's been here 5 years." Mounia is important as a character, both because she has rejected the patriarchal dictate in her own life—she was married at fifteen but is now no longer with her husband and has greater aspirations for her daughter—and because she tries to foster solidarity with other Muslim women who are or have been in such circumstances. For example, she encourages her young Pakistani friend's autonomy. And yet, as we shall see in contrast to the cinematic representation of some of the other women, her visual identity is fully disclosed under the assumption that she will suffer no repercussions, despite the fact that her husband has previously threatened to kill her if she does not send her children to him in Morocco.

Bouchra,[39] whose voice fully represents the oppressed woman, stands as the *homo sacer* body. The camera focuses on a scar on her hand, for example, that illustrates her status as a victim of domestic violence. Bouchra embodies the working class, and she is able to talk about her past abuse directly (not mitigated by a sophisticated analysis) so that her life represents the epidermis of visible oppression. Evidence of her working class status includes the fact that her interview takes place at her kitchen table, the fact that as a young woman (likely in her late thirties) she has already birthed twelve children but seemingly has custody of none (all living with their fathers at this point), and the fact that her understanding of the failings of Sharia mediation, while valid, are drawn from an experiential understanding of law and its applicability to women's daily lives and possibilities for autonomy. Bouchra has been directly affected by the patriarchal vision of Islam promoted by an imam to

---

38 Mounia is one of a number of mothers that echo the narrative voice-over message and legitimize the claims of the narrator and the film.

39 She is a mother (married three times) that has been abused by two former husbands; she came to Canada in 1996. The film's narrator indicates that she has been living in hiding. The implication is that she is in danger.

whom she went for help when separating from her one of her husbands: she lost contact with the two children from that marriage due to the decisions of the imam. Despite the fact that Mounia says she is in hiding, the director still shows her face, as if to say that those who threaten her will not be watching National Film Board of Canada documentaries.

In contrast to the women, the men who appear in the film are not identifiably signified by class, but rather all of them maintain varying degrees of power through their roles and positions. While they promote varying political perspectives and allegiances, they still claim it as their right to speak on behalf of women and their experiences, since power is still male-centered.[40] According to this understanding of social relationships, women have no inherent right to power or autonomy, but rather, power is allocated to them by men. Apart from the lingering phantasm of Syed Mumtaz Ali who instigated the issue of Sharia mediation in Canada but never actually appears in the film, the two major male figures are Mubin Shaikh and Tarek Fatah. The latter is a media personality with his own television show, and he represents a progressive perspective. He is cast in contrast to the zealot trickster Mubin Shaikh, a born-again Muslim by his own definition. In other social circumstances, one could label him an opportunist, a hypocrite, and a would-be radical. He is in favor of Sharia mediation, which he has apparently been conducting with great results (according to his own report) for a number of years in Ontario. He is also an absolutist reader of Sharia and in one public forum argues for the punishment of adultery by stoning, if the population is in favor of such methods of social control.[41]

---

40 Even Tarek Fatah, who is an advocate for Muslim women's rights in relationship to Sharia, still speaks in a way that reveals the patriarchal power that he holds in the mosque, power that he can relinquish to women. Although an advocate, he exposes his deeply engrained sense of gender relations. In the second episode, he says to one of his pro-Sharia adversaries:

> If you wish to put women in the basements, behind barriers then you are free to do it. Don't tell me that I cannot honor my mother, my daughter, my wife. […] I am clear with my prophet and my Allah. I don't expect any imam anywhere to come and dictate to me how to practice my faith. I am asking ordinary Canadians to give me equal rights, where they are in power. In the mosque, where I am in power, I will determine that I will give equal rights to the female gender. If they demand equal rights from Canadians and then in the mosque say "we want equal rights but we don't want to give it to women" they have a sad story ahead of them.

He reveals his belief that he holds the power and can benevolently bestow it on the women in his life.

41 Since the release of the film, Mubin Shaikh has been exposed as a police informant. As part of the "Toronto 18" he was paid $300,000 to report to the RCMP on the activities of his co-

Most obtrusive to the viewer is Shaikh's obvious spectacularized performances honed for his various audiences: people milling about at a public venue (possibly a mosque or a university), debating at universities in Toronto and Montréal, or shouting back and forth with demonstrators in Queen's Park, Toronto, in front of the legislative grounds. Whatever the situation, Shaikh is playing to the camera.[42] His performances are made blatant by his fluctuating dialectal inflections[43] that move from being more or less exotic and Eastern to mainstream Canadian English. His father was born in India and grew up in Britain, and Shaikh himself was born and raised in Canada. From where does the non-descript "Middle Eastern" accent derive? We know from his well-publicized personal history that he lives a life of extremes,[44] and playing the devout Muslim is the most profitable choice of identity for him to adopt at this particular historical juncture. The women in his community who will be subject to the political choices that he advocates, however, do not have the option to fluidly move between identities and lifestyles.

Narrative voice-over, edited dialogues, and visual montage all work together to titillate the viewer with the imminent danger of Sharia. These cinematic techniques contribute to categorize Sharia as a social-legal destabilizer in Canada.[45] Behind this representation we can extrapolate the basic tenant of the post-9/11 world: the civilized enlightened citizen besieged by classical notions of "barbarians at the gate," more contemporarily identified as Islamist[46] or Islamofascist,[47] terms that point to the semantic blurring, which are characteristic of our present political discourses.

---

hort. He later demanded compensation of $2.7 million: $3.0 million minus the $300,000 he had already been paid. Michael Friscolanti, 'The "Toronto 18"—Two Years Later: The Suspects. The Former Suspects. And the Men who Helped Bring Them All Down', *Maclean's* 2 June 2008 <http://www.macleans.ca/article.jsp?content=20080602_121019_7492> [accessed 25 May 2009].

42 We have identified this type of behaviour in a previous article on Irshad Manji. Anselmi and Wilson, 'Performative Radicalism'. We refer to the performer of this behavior as the "optic personage" that is media savvy enough to ultimately bring him/herself to the centre of any debate, thereby manufacturing iconic status for the purpose of economic gain.

43 Here, our term plays on the fact that Shaikh seems to espouse a dialectical process that he feels will be more authentic if he adopts an accented speech.

44 There is biographical information available that tells of his drug-addicted, carousing past lifestyle. He makes mention of it in the film when he points out that he has five tattoos and thirteen self-inflicted cigarette burns, the residue of a wayward life that used to include "girls, drinking, drugs."

45 The second episode demonstrates the "pitfalls" of a multicultural society that is thus destabilized.

46 In the film, Tarek Fatah explains: "The difference between a Muslim and an Islamist is that an Islamist is a Muslim who wishes to impose a political structure that almost borders a

Post-political discourse has become a useful narrative script for politically naïve individuals, and the pro-Sharia debate is framed so as to imply that it becomes not a question of choices in this life, but choices that will impact salvation or damnation. In a 2008 article in *FrontPage Magazine*, Kathy Shaidle reports on the following comments by Syed Mumtaz Ali:

> "As Canadian Muslims, you have a clear choice," wrote the group's president Syed Mumtaz Ali. "Do you want to govern yourself by the personal law of your own religion or do you prefer governance by secular Canadian family law? If you choose the latter, then you cannot claim that you believe in Islam as a religion and a complete code of life actualized by a prophet who you believe to be a mercy to all."[48]

In the article, Shaidle reminds us that "the punishment for apostasy under Sharia law is death." Syed Mumtaz Ali promotes the idea that Muslims must choose between their religious identity and the full rights of Canadian citizenship. He also argues for the implementation of Sharia by claiming that Muslims in Canada deserve sovereignty as is the case for First Nations and Quebecois peoples, but in the same breath he claims that to be Canadian is to be disloyal and to become an apostate to the Islamic faith: in other words, an infidel. The navigation between the uniqueness of Muslim peoples and the expectations formed by the treatment of Others within a multicultural paradigm are conflated so as to become a sense of entitlement without responsibility to one of the constituencies: women. Tarek Fatah points to this fact when he says:

> Mr. Mumtaz Ali would not take aspects of Islamic law that would be liberating, that would allow the woman to pray side-by-side with men, as in the house of God, as in the first mosque of Islam, as in the Kaaba, but he will take invocations from Iran and Saudi Arabia which will throw the women in the back of the bus. So all the things that can be beneficial for the progress of the Muslim world would not be in the Sharia.

This reference to "the back of the bus" implies an apartheid such as was the reality for Rosa Parks in 1955 and was a post-script, in that context, of slav-

---

fascist style of government that excludes everyone, that creates a hierarchy of the chosen and the not chosen. But a Muslim by faith would be someone who believes in the five tenets of Islam."

47 This is a term popularized by the Bush Administration. Cheryl Gay Stolberg, '"Islamo-Fascism" Had Its Moment', *New York Times* 24 September 2006 <http://www.nytimes.com /2006/09/24/weekinreview/24stolberg.html?r=l&emc=etal> [accessed 25 May 2009].

48 Kathy Shaidle, 'Britain's Sharia Courts', *FrontPage Magazine* 17 September 2008 <http://www.frontpagemag.com/Articles/Read.aspx?GUID=A27F7C33-6E33-49D2-BE2F-551AC1893A87> [accessed 25 May 2009].

ery. The limitations imposed by Sharia end up reproducing systems of control of the Other body—slavery, indentured servitude, serfdom—which have been put into practice at particular historical moments, always with the same declination: one group of people oppressing another to create a viable work-force conditioned to accept lesser pay for the work produced, to the benefit of the exploiting class. In the end, human capital is a trope: women are consumed, and imams, according to the film, are paid to collect their dues: i.e. followers.

A Contrast of Visions: Intentionality in Film as a Political Discourse

Sharia in Canada read through the perspective of *Inch'Allah Dimanche* should elicit an understanding of the cultural processes that were at work as semantic paradigms shifted after 9/11. Basically, the shift indicated a passage from the realization of a post-enlightenment political agenda (the entrenchment of civil rights, for example), to the attempts at the erasure of those societal gains through slippages (in the lingual-legalistic sphere) sustained by economic and ideological goals. Movies such as the ones that we have chosen to compare in this article are directly or indirectly informed by these political processes, since they reflect the cultural realities of individuals and communities struggling to navigate the socio-political tensions and contradictions of their respective places/nations/time periods: the cusp of 9/11 (*Inch'Allah Dimanche*) and the subsequent developments by 2006 (*Sharia in Canada*). The analysis encompasses France, the European context, and Canada, as the politics of the individual outside America have become entwined with America's foreign policy after September 11, 2001.

Sharia in Canada fails to present a coherent case because it is subject to the post-9/11 semantic confusion that has altered not only our relationship with language but also how we interpret specific facts through language, another post-political outcome resulting from the erasure of boundaries between public and private realities. As John Collins and Ross Glover state in their introduction to the insightful work *Collateral Language: A User's Guide to America's New War*:

> Just as "collateral damage" describes military damage in addition to the intended targets, "collateral language" refers to the language war as a practice adds to our ongoing lexicon as well as to the additional meaning certain terms acquire during wartime. We call language a terrorist organization to illustrate the real effects of language on citizens, especially in times

> of war. Language, like terrorism, targets civilians and generates fear in order to effect political change.[49]

Taking into consideration the transformative effect that war has on language as well as Agamben's notion of the state of emergency, we then argue that the term "multiculturalism" has been finally voided of any positive potential. Therefore, enacting a multiculturalist point of view encompasses information that pertains to a context broader than national boundaries, in this case Canada's borders, so that when the filmmakers for *Sharia in Canada*, for example, illustrated the pro-Sharia individuals who used multiculturalism to legitimize the practice of Sharia, they needed to be aware that specific historical junctures have reset the semantic space occupied by that word as to avoid their final conclusion, which was that the threat was Muslim men. Therefore, according to the logic of the narrative, the pro-Sharia men who might potentially oppress women in a multicultural setting are de facto terrorists. In the end, multiculturalism is further undermined through this rhetorical process and becomes part of the collateral of debris authoritarianism. In other words, the imperial ambitions of America have their own perspective about what multiculturalism should or should not encompass. These ambitions, therefore, have had direct consequences on Canadian religious, political, and legal concerns. These specific positions have been determined in America; they traverse the multicultural spectrum towards a practice that supersedes any Canadian vision of multiculturalism (therefore destroying it) in the attempt to attain fundmental(ist) political right-wing control, whatever the religion may be. This process toward the integration of religion(s) within the political realm has been sustained by neo-liberalism, ironically, as an expression of individualism and democratic rights. In a nutshell, as neo-liberalism moved through the world, as the actual implementation of the imperialistic aims of the United States, what it has left in its wake is fragmentation and confusion within post-political societies. Countries such as Canada, which espouse a multicultural reality, are impacted by American imperialism, which fosters the most conservative factions of social and political life that end up dominating the media systems—what we earlier referred to as debris authoritarianism. People such as Mubin Shaikh and Syed Mumtaz Ali have taken to this post-political semantic maelstrom as fish to water.

While the film *Sharia in Canada* addresses specific issues relevant in this cultural climate, the documentary fails to negotiate clearly the rhetorical conundrums that conflate civil liberties with the economic tenets of the American

---

49 John Collins and Ross Glover, *Collateral Language: A User's Guide to America's New War* (New York: New York University Press, 2002), pp. 1-2.

Dream and its underlying metaphysical shadow. Where Mumtaz Ali and his followers are able to navigate "political" parlance to recuperate what is most convenient for their interests of domination, the film is unable to de-mask these postmodern *sophists*[50] who thrive in this economic context. In so doing, *Sharia in Canada* represents the reification of ethnicity as a spectacle-commodity.

When we compare and contrast *Sharia in Canada* with *Inch'Allah Dimanche*, precisely because of their different historical contexts, it is possible to envision what has been subtracted from history in terms of progressive developments that were once part of the post-Westphalia vision of a fair and just society. *Inch'Allah* informs us as to the precise limits that are unspoken in the documentary. Zouina's success, finally, is constituted by her ability to navigate different cultural settings, while at the same time she is able to discard that which is an impediment and assume that which emancipates her from oppression. Identities are always in negotiation; without putting undue stress on France's enlightenment formation we must, however, see the results of a society that is able to criticize its own colonial subjugation of others—through postcolonial directors such as Benguigui—and out of these tensions produce critical nuances that are dissipated through the media and people, which allows Zouina to come to terms with her own displaced identity. Her liberation is the one auspicated by such thinkers as Franz Fanon, who would have supported it as a liberation that uses the body-mind as the weapon by which to achieve parity since the struggle for representation is fundamental to the present mediatic climate. *Inch'Allah Dimanche* has, from a certain perspective, a very clear narrative that brings about positive concrete realizations. It is on the cusp of 9/11, thus it can still propose that Zouina, as a displaced Muslim subjectivity, will have a home in France, that she can reformulate her identity to integrate French concepts, and that France too can be a malleable site of interaction and negotiation between immigrants who were until recently the enemy-Other and French-citizens. *Inch'Allah* allows the growth of the individual that encompasses her/his own multiplicity through the positive realizations of displacement.

The comparative analysis of these two films illustrates the semantic confusion that ensues in a post-9/11 world where terms have been altered in order to mute grounded significations and where a polarization of perspectives

---

[50] Here, the sophist is being invoked in its most negative connotation to indicate the rhetorician that Socrates-Plato denounced for the talent to argue anything, beyond even the confines of morality, for monetary reward. What Socrates-Plato could not know was how the media almost two millennia later would allow the sophist exponential resonance without providing any evaluative mechanism.

is used to exercise social control. In other words, certain words have lost their original meaning, and the rhetoric around certain issues is a revision of history caused by a disconnect between words, their etymologies, and the actual context for this loss. The end result can be summed up, once again, by the term post-political, that has come to identify the exact process herein delineated. Powerful images came to signify and encompass the meaning of the 9/11 event. Words have been recuperated by the images associated with specific war-spectacles, creating havoc with the correspondence between the informative aspect of language and sophist practices. The relation between signifier and signified was disconnected and reworked in favor of neo-conservative agendas of the day: changing sometimes daily in relationship to the spectacularization of reality as formulated on television.[51] Alternatively, cinema re-represents television programming within a defined context.[52] The documentary on Sharia reflects on the media and the spectacle surrounding the debate. Yet the film was unable to be critical of those television images that have been naturalized and which have become representative of the polarizing processes, i.e. the enemy Other. Television has become an electronic square for discussion without a critical frame to account for that discourse. The tangible results of this process are television-derived discourses that perform discussion but elude debate.

---

51 Slogans such as "shock and awe" used to identify the war in Iraq became part of an integrated sense of American morality as a pedagogy of submission: "they" were going to be taught a lesson. There was an escalation of the ease with which the spectator was made to disengage from history as it was lived on television. This reaches a pornographic climax, from our perspective, when the term "Shake 'n Bake" is used to define "a mixture of burning white phosphorus and high explosives" used in urban warfare against Fallujah's inhabitants. Darrin Mortenson, 'Violence Subsides for Marines in Fallujah', *North Country Times*, 10 April 2004 <http://www.nctimes.com/articles/2004/04/11/military/iraq/19_30_504_10_04.txt> [accessed 25 May 2009].

52 In reference to this, *Slumdog Millionaire* is quite successful in defining television as a communicative technological apparatus able to create a false sense of community—those individuals congregating in disparate locations and situations to watch the protagonist's rise to fame—whose turmoil can be resolved by an heroic underdog and the celebration around his achievement of capital gain. William Anselmi and Sheena Wilson, 'Slumdogging It: Rebranding the American Dream, New World Orders, and Neo-Colonialism', *Film International* #37, 7 (2009), pp. 44-53 <http://www.atypon-link.com/INT/doi/pdf/10.1386/fiin.7.1.44> [accessed 25 May 2009].

Imagined Communities, Conclusions

The de-colonization process that ensued around the world after the Second World War, together with large migration patterns, resulted in a diversified population demographic in many countries that, if allowed to prosper, would bring to a final crisis national myths of identity and the nation-state, per se. Canada, as a nation, came to define itself in the post-Second World War era but never succeeded to differentiate itself against its American neighbour beyond tropes of mosaic versus melting pot. Multiculturalism as a lived practice in Canada was the fissure weakening the foundation of the wall of the myth of national identity. Canadian Prime Minister Pierre Trudeau attempted, in 1971, to reintegrate the crack in the wall—lived multiculturalism—as an aesthetic attribute by repositioning it through the Multicultural Policy, since the foundation of the Canadian nation-state had shifted. Decades later, the fall of the Berlin Wall[53] echoes the same fears of uneducated masses invading the West, which kick-starts the project of dominance and America's responsibility to govern the world, legitimized by the Fukuyama-Huntington ideological construct. This period of transition existed until 9/11, when the economic and political justification for America's assertion of dominance over the world entered in correspondence with those countries undergoing a crisis of the nation-state to re-compass themselves and reaffirm their hold on the multitudes.[54] The representations of 9/11—through both the dynamic image and the spoken word—allowed for the neutralization of the crisis of the nation-state. No longer concerned about identifying itself as the site of cohabitating ethnocultures, Canada has again become a governable binary. In France, the outcome is governed differently, since the multicultural state fails to materialize and the project of a lived multicultural reality is governed according to

---

53 In the course of contemporary history a loss of critical analysis has occurred whereby the relationship between the two superpowers not only constituted the binary of two system—one "good" and one "evil"—but in this set-up the Soviet Union acted as a space of confinement for the fear of the invasion of the barbarian. With the fall of the Wall, the change in representational strategies of the enemy other shifts from the Rambo Soviets to the Schwarzenegger Arabs (*True Lies*). Furthermore, after 9/11, television and cinema took up the Cold War tropes of the enemy Other and replaced the communist, the KGB, the dark Soviet, with the terrorist, fanatical Muslim, etc. Finally, a possible topic for an analysis of this binary system would have to address the Soviet Union's raison d'être as the West's filter. Obviously, from the position espoused by Roberto Esposito, the Soviet Union as a system of containment is a given, since his work on the biopolitical is grounded in the concept of immunization.

54 Here we use the term "multitudes" in the same capacity as Hardt & Negri, in place of "peoples," "social groups," etc.

two principles: the reactions to ghettoization in the banlieues and Sarkozy's successful image presentation of a unified post-political government that includes members from the left and also "ethnics." What 9/11 evidences and leaves as an unfinished project is the auspicated reality of *Inch'Allah Dimanche* as a lived reality. What the crisis of the nation-state presented was the unwillingness to negotiate a multicultural society in Canada, France, and other countries undergoing the same process that could encompass a lived multicultural reality, a fair and just society where no component would be discriminated against, no matter how large or small. The post-9/11 ideology affirmed the polarization process necessary to the containment of lived multiculturalism. The end of the Bush reign necessarily means that the wall between "us" and "them" (be it metaphorical or literal) is as tenuous as the always-on media circuit that created and fed on it: the multitudes are switching channels. Lived multiculturalism is an ongoing historical and lived reality, and as such it will continue to put pressure on and possibly create cracks in the remaining walls that position us against them.

Bibliography

300, dir. by Zack Snyder, on DVD (Warner Bros. Pictures, 2007)

Abruzzese, Alberto, *Lo splendore della TV–Origini e destino del linguaggio audiovisivo* (Genova: costa&nolan,1995)

Agamben, Giorgio, *Homo sace –Il potere sovrano e la vita nuda* (Torino: Einaudi, 1995)

---, *Stato di eccezione* (Torino: Bollati Boringhieri, 2003)

Anselmi, William, 'Italian Canadian as displacement poetics: context, history, and literary production', *Studi Emigrazione/Migration Studies – International journal of migration studies*, XLIV (2007), 369-388

Anselmi, William, and Lise Hogan, 'Scripturing the 21st Century American Ways to Empire Undone, Over', *College Quarterly.* 7 (2004) <http://www.collegequarterly.ca/2004-vol07-num04-fall/anselmi_hogan.html> [accessed 25 May 2009]

Anselmi, William, and Sheena Wilson, 'Performative Radicalism in contemporary Canadian documentary film', *Film International # 37*, 7 (2009), 44-53 <http://www.atypon-link.com/INT/doi/pdf/10.1386/fiin.7.1.44> [accessed 25 May 2009]

---, 'Slumdogging It: Rebranding the American Dream, New World Orders, and Neo-Colonialism' in *Film International* <http://www.filmint.nu/?q=features> [accessed 25 May 2009]

Campbell, Joseph, *The Hero with a Thousand Faces* (Princeton, NJ: Princeton University Press, 1949)

Collins, John and Ross Glover, *Collateral Language: A User's Guide to America's New War* (New York: New York University Press, 2002

Dead Man, dir. by Jim Jarmusch, on DVD (Pandora Filmproduktion, 1995)

Fanon, Franz, *Les Damnés de la Terre* (Paris: La Découverte, 1961)

Friscolante, Michael, 'The 'Toronto 18'—two years later: The suspects. The former suspects. And the men who helped bring them all down', *Maclean's*, 2 June 2008 <http://www.macleans.ca/article.jsp?content=20080602_121019_7492> [accessed 25 May 2009]

Fukuyama, Francis, *The End of History and the Last Man* (Toronto: Maxwell Macmillan Canada, 1992)

Gumble, Andrew, 'Bush Enlists Hollywood to 'help the war effort'', *The Independent*, 12 November 2001<http://www.independent.co.uk/news/world/americas/bush-enlists-hollywood-to-help-the-war-effort-616694.html> [accessed 25 May 2009]

Hardt, Michael, and Antonio Negri, *Empire* (Cambridge, MA: Harvard University Press, 2000)

Huntington, Samuel P., *The Clash of Civilizations and the Remaking of World Order* (New York: Simon & Schuster, 1996)

Inch'Allah Dimanche, dir. by Yamina Benguigui, on DVD (Mongrel Media: Festival Collection, 2001)

Jackson, Michael, and Lionel Richie. 'We Are the World', USA for Africa, cond. by Quincy Jones (1985)

Jenkins, Richard, *Social Identity* (New York: Routledge, 2008)

Kallen, Evelyn, 'The Meech Lake Accord: Entrenching a Pecking Order of Minority Rights', *Canadian Public Policy / Analyse de Politiques*, 14 (1988), 107-120

Mazza, Antonino, 'Afterword. Prophecy Versus Memory: Towards a New Pre-History', in *Pier Paolo Pasolini: Poetry*, trans. by Antonino Mazza (Toronto: Exile Editions, 1991), 133-137

Morrione, Deems D., 'When Signifiers Collide: Doubling, Semiotic Black Holes, and the Destructive Remainder of the American Un/real', *Culture Critique*, 63 (2006), 157-73

Mortenson, Darrin, 'Violence subsides for Marines in Fallujah', *North Country Times*, 10 April 2004.<http://www.nctimes.com/articles/2004/04/11/military/iraq/19_30_504_10_04.txt> [accessed 25 May 2009]

Mulvey, Laura, 'Visual Pleasure and Narrative Cinema', *Screen* 16 (1975), 6-18

Paulin, Marguerite, *Maurice Duplessis: le noblet, le petit roi* (Montréal: XYZ, 2002)

Prose, Francine, 'Voting Democracy off the Island', *Harper's Magazine*, 308 (2004), 58-64.

Rendition, dir. by Gavin Hood, on DVD (Anonymous Content, 2007)

Shaidle, Kathy, 'Britain's Sharia Courts', *FrontPage Magazine*, 17 September 2008 <http://www.frontpagemag.com/Articles/Read.aspx?GUID=A27F7C33-6E33-49D2-BE2F-551AC1893A87> [accessed 25 May 2009]

Sharia in Canada/ La charia au Canada. Episode 1: "Something to fear? / Qu'est-ce qui fait si peur?" dir. by Dominique Cardona, on DVD (National Film Board of Canada, 2006)

Stolberg, Sheryl Gay, ''Islamo-Fascism' Had Its Moment', *New York Times*, 24 September 2006 <http://www.nytimes.com/2006/09/24/weekinreview/24stolberg.html?_r=1&emc=eta1> [accessed 25 May 2009]

Trevelyan, Laura, 'Shari'a Law In Canada', *BBC News*, 17 August 2004 <http://news.bbc.co.uk/2/hi/programmes/breakfast_with_frost/3574040.stm> [accessed 25 May 2009]

Wilson, Sheena, 'Campus Saint-Jean's Bilingual Writing Centre: A Portal to Multiple Cultures and Cosmopolitanism Citizenship', *CWCA Newsletter*, 2 (2009), 9-12

Within Oceanic Reach:
The Effects of September 11 on a Drought-Stricken Nation

Sofia Ahlberg

As a narrative of ecoliterary imagination, the Australian Peter Carey's *His Illegal Self* (2008) broadens the popular "no blood for oil" slogan with ruminations regarding questions of kinship and commonality. Combining close readings of *His Illegal Self* with recent literary ecocritism, this chapter investigates how the attacks on the World Trade Center authorized Carey to revisit Australia's own repertoire of homeland myths from a transnational perspective. As a response to the attacks of September 11 and what followed, *His Illegal Self* warns against the overmobilization of identity that attacks difference whether in the defense of nature or retaliation against terror.

Central to Peter Carey's most recent novel, *His Illegal Self*, is a preoccupation with the law. Questions concerning legislation and its enforcement propel the plot forward with a fugitive's speed, violating national, ethical, political, and geographical borders in the process. *His Illegal Self* portrays a series of chaotic events in the life of an American, Harvard-educated woman and newly appointed professor of literature, Dial, against the backdrop of the Vietnam War in an enflamed and polarized New York City. When circumstances force her to flee across the ocean, she must acclimate to the lifestyle of a remote hippie community near the towns Nambour and Yandina in southern Queensland, Australia. When in exile, Dial struggles to find common ground between what is deeply personal and what is of communal interest, raising some important questions regarding the role of the progressive intellectual today. Carey's novel allegorizes the state of the global community through the figure of the exiled academic post-9/11 by looking at what happens in the margins of territorial sovereignty from a geo-political perspective. His novel examines "a way of life" and its legal, social, ethical, cultural, environmental, and political dimensions. When holding views that are not in line with the nationalist norm, an obsession with nature becomes paramount to staking out an existence that re-inserts the individual into the nation, no more so than in Australia where environmental concerns often signal opposition to government, countercultural allegiances, and sometimes civic disobedience. When seen through the lens of gender, especially, identification with nature reveals in some cases "complex, ambivalent tendencies toward both violent control and loving repair,"[1] as persuasively argued by Catherine Roach.

Where Carey's novel offers critical insight into the present rather than a retrospective look at subcultures of the past is when it dramatizes those voices from outside society in the act of marginalizing and threatening the sanctity and autonomy of personal space. While the disenfranchised Australians resist Dial's entry into their community and fail to show her solidarity, Dial discovers that her attempt to speak out for the oppressed and the vulnerable backfires. The Australian hippie community attempts to bully Dial into accepting a particular way of life that is not compatible with her values and principles, which are themselves deeply tied up with the university. Dial's intervention on behalf of herself and the boy in her care reproduces the silencing and victimization to which they have been subjected, causing her to reassess her contribution to society. In some ways, *His Illegal Self* is a campus novel out of bounds, one that illustrates a transhemispheric confrontation between the Ivy League and the laws of the Australian jungle. Orbiting the campus in a fearful and frantic way, Dial (short for "dialectic"[2]) amplifies a post-9/11 situation where public debate and contested narratives have been replaced by silence and oppression. In the introduction to *Precarious Life*, Judith Butler writes:

> The foreclosure of critique empties the public domain of debate and democratic contestation itself, so that debate becomes the exchange of views among the like-minded, and criticism, which ought to be central to any democracy, becomes a fugitive and suspect activity.[3]

Without an exchange of arguments and counter-arguments, *His Illegal Self* cautions, the workings of totalitarianism will escape the attention of the otherwise vigilant citizen. Carey's novel signals the urgent need today for more critical freedom that admits varying views. Unable to avail herself of the institutional knowledge she has accumulated over the years, Dial learns to think more widely and deeply about identity and place through first-hand experience of what it means to be exiled. At first, Dial's dismal predicament in Queensland indicates that might is, after all, right. In an early passage in Carey's novel, the contamination of higher education by partisan politics confirms this view. Instead of being a place where views are exchanged and

---

1 Catherine Roach, *Mother/Nature: Popular Culture and Environmental Ethics* (Bloomington & Indianapolis: Indiana University Press, 2003), p. 9.

2 Peter Carey, *His Illegal Self* (New York: Alfred A. Knopf. 2008), p. 180.

3 Judith Butler, *Precarious Life: The Powers of Mourning and Violence* (London & New York: Verso, 2003), p. xx.

conflicts resolved through debate, signs of dissent are met with disapproval and power exercised with impunity. Indeed, it is during the job interview by the chair of the English department at Vassar College that Dial is coerced to accept the suggestion that she call Susan Selkirk, the most radical and infamous founder of the student movement of Harvard to which Dial used to belong. Sensing that reluctance to do so would put her in ill favor with her new employer, Dial has no choice but to once again become an instrument of the movement. Out of a sense of duty mingled with fear, Dial agrees to pick up Susan's young boy Che from his grandmother in order to connect him with his mother who has been in hiding most of his life. Before this happens, however, Che's mother blows herself up while tinkering with a homemade bomb. Dial and the boy are instantly all over the news. Panicking, she turns to the revolutionary underground group who sends her to Australia.

In the company of a young orphaned boy who believes she is his biological mother, Dial's escape from the militaristic anti-war movement is both perilous and lonely. When seeking refuge in the alternative commune in Queensland, Dial lacks the means to emotionally and physically form an attachment to Australia. The absence of an intellectual history in Australia creates a mistrust and contempt of the academic among its white settlers, who pioneered Australia through a struggle with the land. The discomfort Dial feels in the natural environment of Australia excludes her from a sense of kinship with the community. Now resident in New York where he pursues a successful career as a professor in creative writing, Carey alludes to the crucial difference between the US as a settler nation and his native Australia. Whereas the dream of America as the land of new beginnings and abundance is perpetuated in the cultural imagination of many, a journey from the Old World to the Antipodeans has always been perceived as a punishment, even long after Australia ceased to be a convict nation. Its more recent climatic development, including extreme water shortage and rising temperatures, underscores the notion of Australia as a hostile place where human life is under constant threat by the environment on the outskirts of civilization with "places not even on a map."[4] Subject to severe climate change, Australia is vulnerable. Carey historicizes this vulnerability with ruminations regarding settlement and questions of kinship more generally.

Carey explores the notion of Australia as a place where unauthorized legislators measure out forms of penalty, of which the worst is to banish the newcomer to the treacherous jungle on the fringes of its settlement. More durable than bars constructed by humans, the lianas of the jungle shield the

---

4 Carey, p. 21.

commune from the outside as well as quarantine its members from what lies beyond. Its outside text equivalent is found at the heart of the Australian continent where terrorist suspects and refugees are housed in detention centers surrounded by desert. Since the war on terror, these centers have dramatically increased their population as a result of more stringent rules regarding citizenship and residency. In Carey's novel, newcomers Dial and Che are subject to callous and heartless rules and regulations as a way of assessing their right to take up residence. With their poor survival skills, as well as being possessors of a cat who is perceived to pose a threat to the rich birdlife of the forest, Dial and Che score low on the suitability test, and their continued existence in the commune is under threat. Reflecting the socio-political realities of the war on terror, *His Illegal Self* dramatizes oppression in the hands of the oppressed and the formation of second-and third-class citizens. J.M. Coetzee, who has left his native South Africa for a life in South Australia, puts it this way in his recent *Diary of a Bad Year*:

> We are as nature made us. The world is a jungle (the metaphors proliferate), and in the jungle all species are in competition with all other species for space and sustenance. The truth about jungles is that among the nations (the species) of the typical jungle there are no longer winners or losers: the losers became extinct ages ago. A jungle is an ecosystem where the surviving species have attained symbiosis with each other. This achieved state of dynamic stability is what it means to be an ecosystem.[5]

In painting a picture of nature that has evolved more proficiently than the human species because it has learned to survive not in spite of the threats imposed on it but because of them, Coetzee comes close to describing the unlikely marriage of two discourses, nature and terror, that conspire to wage war against the Other. Through the illicit means by which members of the Australian commune attempt to reach an agreement with the American fugitives in the name of preserving a way of life in the remote wilderness, Carey's novel reveals something about nature as terroristic and a group of people who learn to take advantage of endangered nature to subjugate the marginalized and improve their own standard of living. In the geo-political ecosystem that is the "coalition of the willing," the aim is to simultaneously destroy and resuscitate, a paradox that is at the heart of what constitutes political might today, as Inderpal Grewal notes: "it is the interrelation between the sovereign right to kill and the right to rescue that constitutes modes of

---

[5] J.M. Coetzee, *Diary of a Bad Year* (Melbourne: The Text Publishing Company, 2007), pp. 64-65.

modern power."[6] By pursuing and eradicating all roots of terrorism, the US and its allies expect to salvage a way of life unique to the West. In Carey's novel, the persecution against Dial and Che demonstrates the flipside of any such undertaking. In so far as both discourses conjure up a deep sense of loss, fear of losing, and visions of planetary destruction, however, there is hope that a commonality can be located, differences overcome, and challenges met without the alienation of one group over another, a point echoed by Butler who writes, "Loss has made a tenuous 'we' of us all. And if we have lost, then it follows that we have had, that we have desired and loved, that we have struggled to find the conditions for our desire."[7]

By dramatizing a conflict of interest between two traditional allies, Carey's novel draws attention to that which bonds humans and nations. Though speaking the same language, Dial cannot make herself understood in Australia or at home. In one of the last scenes in *His Illegal Self*, Dial is in a telephone booth making a call across the ocean to Che's grandmother in an attempt to set things right. The conversation is fuelled with incriminations and misunderstandings, and Dial's name becomes synonymous with a person waiting for a connecting line. Reflecting the current state of the world in which there is an overload of information and a desperate shortage of communication and dialogue, *His Illegal Self* comments on the state of connectivity between nations and peoples after 9/11.

In her work on planetarity, Gayatri Spivak envisages an alliance more inclusive than globalism. By virtue of rendering our home uncanny, its very abstraction makes the planet an ideal figuration for thinking about collectivity, "referring to an undivided 'natural' space rather than a differentiated political space,"[8] she argues. Spivak's proposal to make our home *unheimlich*[9] is helpful when thinking about international alliances that are too readily assumed on the basis of similarities in culture and language alone. Carey's greatest contribution to post-9/11 discourse, as a diasporic Australian writer, is in opening up the foundations of coalitions and alliances to critical debate. By dramatizing Australian-American cultural conflict, Carey denaturalizes political bonds and returns them to their natural *unheimlichkeit*. The events of 9/11 and its aftermath, his novel implies, occasion the possibility of forging new international coalitions based on ethical responsibility and a shared fate instead of the overmobilization of identity.

---

[6] Inderpal Grewal, *Transnational America: Feminisms, Diasporas, Neoliberalisms* (Durham & London: Duke University Press, 2005), p. 198.

[7] Butler, p. 20.

[8] Gayatri Spivak, *Death of a Discipline* (New York: Columbia University Press, 2003), p. 72.

[9] Ibid., p. 74.

Looking into the Crystal Ball: 9/11 through the Year 1977

With what is known today, what would we have done differently? This is one of the questions that runs through *His Illegal Self* with its chronological cross-currents, narrative ambiguities, near-misses, coincidences, parallel narratives, lack of closure. It is also the question that polemically unites discourses of terror with nature on numerous levels in the collective consciousness of citizens. When terror or nature wreak havoc on humanity, the tragedy is often compounded by the suspicion that something could have been done to prevent the attack. In the case of natural catastrophes, people can be evacuated or forewarned, though sometimes such preventative action tragically fails to take place. There are also concerns that not enough is done in foreign policy and round-table talks to prevent future terrorist attacks from happening. Similarly with regards to climate change, most citizens know that consumption patterns must be radically changed now in order to safeguard the future. To ecocritics such as Katherine Pettus, the task of restoring balance to a severely wounded nature has the potential to call forth the ultimate virtues of citizenship, including patience, commitment, and even love.[10] In Carey's novel the reverse appears to be true.

Members of the Crystal Community, the name of the alternative commune in Northern Australia, protect the fragile ecosystem against the contamination of outside influence, even at the cost of human lives. Showing up uninvited in Dial's hut, Rebecca, one of the commune's members, presents Dial with a bag of maimed birds, threatening, "'You can get rid of this cat or we will get rid of you.'"[11] When Dial objects and mentions that the law is on her side and that she has a right to reside in the commune with the cat in her possession since the owner permitted it at the time of the purchase, Rebecca snorts, "'This is not America, Dial. We don't decide ethical issues with lawyers.'"[12] Phil Warriner, the lawyer in question, is lax about rules, calling himself "an organic lawyer."[13] Making a living on other people's misery is perhaps a standard objection that lawyers face, but Warriner actively pursues areas of conflict where the hand of the law cannot reach: "'You will discover,' he [Warriner] said, still looking down, 'that there are not many rules

---

10 Katherine Pettus, 'Citizenship in Feminism: Identity, Action, and Locale', *Hypatia* 12 (1997), 132-155 (p. 151).

11 Carey, p. 164.

12 Ibid., p. 164.

13 Ibid., p. 116.

on Remus Creek Road and what rules exist have all been broken many times before.'"[14]

Though the geo-political concerns raised in the novel are symptomatic of the time of the novel, year 1972, the corruption of the Crystal Community and the prejudice and hostility of its members reflect a post-9/11 Australia. The following key events from recent Australian history will remind the reader of how Australia's reputation as a decent, helpful and generous people has been severely tarnished. 7 October 2001: In the lead-up to a federal election, the government falsely accused sea-faring asylum seekers of throwing their children overboard in a cynical attempt to secure passage to Australia. The allegations concerning "The Children Overboard Affair" led to stricter border protection to prevent refugees from reaching Australia by boat. 12 October 2002: The Bali Bombings killed 202 people, of which 88 were Australians. The attacks in Bali, a popular holiday resort, fuelled Australians' sense of frailty, and support for Australia's commitment in the so-called Coalition of the Willing rose dramatically. In addition, the failure of the Australian government to prosecute David Hicks, the young Australian Muslim imprisoned by the Americans in Guantanamo Bay in 2001 at home has provoked much criticism in Australia and internationally. Climate change and the government's reluctance to reduce GHG emissions (the largest average per person in the world) caused many to complain about the low level of public debate in Australia.[15] Simultaneous exposure to terror attacks and climate change has congealed into a general fear and dread, as captured by Australian author Richard Flanagan in his recent *The Unknown Terrorist*, a novel in which climate change is part of every news story about terrorism.[16] In addition, Australia's faithful collaboration with the US in Iraq has caused deep injury to the Australian national integrity, not least because its support is often perceived to go unacknowledged by the US.

US foreign policy, sometimes perceived in Australia and elsewhere as severely limited, colors Dial's world view. To Dial and Che, Remus Creek

---

14 Ibid., p. 116.

15 Nicola Henry, 'Individual Income or Wellbeing for All? Overcoming Injustice: Practical and Symbolic Reconciliation for Indigenous Australians', *To Firmer Ground: Restoring Hope in Australia*, ed. by John Langmore (Sydney: New South Wales Press, 2007), 23-53 (p. 26).

16 "A nearby radio ran the same news it always seemed to run and its repetition of distant horror and local mundanity was calmly reassuring. More bombings in Baghdad, more water restrictions and more bushfires; another threat to attack Sydney on another al-Qa'ida website and another sportsman in another sex scandal, a late unconfirmed report that three unexploded bombs had been discovered at Sydney's Homebush Olympic stadium and the heatwave was set to go on, continuing to set record highs [...]" Richard Flanagan, *The Unknown* Terrorist (New York: Grove Press, 2006), p. 12.

Road is beyond comprehension, often likened to something profoundly alien: "The forest around the huts was laced with narrow winding trails, like veins in a creature as yet unnamed."[17] Despite her education, Dial is ignorant of the southern hemisphere, comparing Australia to Albania.[18] When looking for help from the Australian Builders Labourers Federation, Dial betrays her limited view on world politics:

> "The executive will not support this, Dial. It's not like you've dodged the draft and we have to hide you."
> "Draft for what," she asked, watching Che's Coke bubble up and spill across the table. She found the young man glaring at her directly.
> "What?"
> "You're joking!" he said, wiping up the coke himself.
> "Australia is in Vietnam?"
> His cheeks were red, his eyes blue and cold.[19]

A faithful ally of the US, Australia is often perceived to be the underdog, overlooked and undervalued by the dominant player in the war on terror. Dial's reaction to the anti-Americanism that she confronts in Australia reveals something about the unbalanced nature of the alliance: "They hate us. We didn't even know they fucking existed and they've been down here hating us."[20] Carey's novel takes distance from the current war to show that the dynamics of the American-Australian relationship has changed little since last century. In the shadow of the US, Australia is depicted as the Antipodean Mexico, strategically placed as a geographically remote place from the law; "that was its single virtue, to place her up a dirt track at the asshole of the earth,"[21] Dial notes. Australia's debilitating feelings of inferiority towards its ally ooze out of every page of *His Illegal Self*. In lieu of political strength, a macho and bigoted conception of nature secures the nation's place on the world map.

Though nostalgically derivative of the countercultural movements of the 1970s, nature has since become a much more powerful force that, rightly so, has assumed a central role in the political arena. In her introduction to *Shades of the Planet: American Literature as World Literature*, Wai Chee Dimock, echoing Spivak's work on planetarity, stresses the force of the environment in comparison with the nation:

---

17 Carey, p. 139.
18 Ibid., p. 79.
19 Ibid., pp. 79-80.
20 Ibid., p. 103.
21 Ibid., p. 101.

> Territorial sovereignty, we suddenly realize, is no more than a legal fiction, a manmade fiction. This fiction is not honored by religious adherents who have a different vision of the world; nor is it honored by the spin of hurricanes accelerated by the thermodynamics of warming oceans. In each case, the nation is revealed to be what it is: an epiphenomenon, literally a superficial construct, a set of erasable lines on the face of the earth. It is no match for that grounded entity called the planet, which can wipe out those lines at a moment's notice, using weapons of mass destruction more powerful than any homeland defense.[22]

Dimock aligns nature's belligerent force with that of fundamental religious groups "who have a different vision of the world," as if they are not subject to the same manmade fiction that informs and defines territorial sovereignty. Despite increased awareness of the contributing factors to climate change, there is still a belief that the environmental crisis is "out there" and not a crisis within, as Nicola Henry notes in a recent article on Australia and viable solutions to climate change.[23] As such, it rests on the same misapprehensions as does terrorism. One forgets that the best protection against terrorism is to work towards more transnational dialogue and inclusion across the spectrum of political and religious identities, as John Langmore has recently argued.[24] Both terrorism and climate change are issues of social justice, as poverty and despair breed terrorism, and the poorest communities and regions will suffer from climate change the most. Significant not least because it ushers in questions of culture, gender, and identity strangely absent from the environmental debate today, *His Illegal Self* suggests that cultural mobility is both part of the problem and its solution.

---

22 Wai Chee Dimock, introduction, *Shades of the Planet: American Literature as World Literature*, ed. by Wai Chee Dimock and Lawrence Buell (Princeton & Oxford: Princeton University Press, 2007), p. 1.

23 "We must strongly reject the fallacy that we have to choose between environmental prosperity and economic prosperity. Greater collaboration among environmentalists, scientists, policy-makers and economists will help us to do this. Global warming and its consequences should force a revolutionary shift in perceptions about human activity. It is time to view the environmental crisis not as 'out there' in the environment, but as a crisis within." Nicola Henry, 'Turning the Tide: Solutions to Australia's Environmental Crisis', *To Firmer Ground: Restoring Hope in Australia*, ed. by John Langmore (Sydney: New South Wales Press, 2007), 54-86 (p. 86).

24 John Langmore, 'Advancing Global Security and Justice', *To Firmer Ground: Restoring Hope in Australia*, ed. by John Langmore (Sydney: New South Wales Press, 2007), 156-178 (p. 172).

Reading Nature, Writing Terror

Australia's relationship to the US is an old concern of Carey's. Exactly how absurd and incompatible the American dream is to life in rural Australia becomes apparent in an earlier short story "American Dreams," a story about Australians and Americans blinded by artificial constructs of each others' cultures. In *His Illegal Self*, Carey returns to this theme of modes of cultural translation and exegesis. "What an awful place to spend your life,"[25] thinks Dial when confronted with the lack of reading material available in Queensland. Unable to read it, Dial cannot grasp the meaning of Australia:

> She had no idea of what Australia even *was*. She would not have imagined a tomato would grow in Australia, or a cucumber. She could not have named a single work of Australian literature or music. Why would she? It was only temporary.[26]

Though concerned with what she perceives as the fundamental lack of culture in Australia, Dial uses organic comparisons to help visualize this gap. Unless she can imagine a fertile landscape, she is unable to think of examples of Australian creative growth. An understanding (or lack thereof, as the case may be) with a country's geography is bound up with a general expectation of the social and the cultural. In addition, the link between the environmental imagination and nationalism is usually very strong, as Lawrence Buell notes.[27] Certainly this is the case in Australian literature of the past and present.[28] The Australian man Trevor, with whom Dial and Che become dangerously entangled at the Crystal Commune, pronounces his illiteracy as a matter of pride,[29] as if this means that his survival instincts are more developed than those of other people. Without family, Trevor's genealogy and fate are intimately connected with the ecosystem that shelters him from the law, and

---

25 Carey, p. 161.

26 Ibid., p. 78.

27 Lawrence Buell, *The Future of Environmental Criticism: Environmental Crisis and Literary Imagination* (Malden: Blackwell Publishing, 2005), p. 16.

28 Far from discouraging the associations conventionally assumed between environmental hardship and anti-intellectualism, a well-known Australian author, Murray Bail, begs the reader to support the correlation between intellectual and organic growth in his recent novel that also takes the campus as its departure point: "The heat and the distances between objects seem to drain the will to add words to what is already there. What exactly can be added? 'Seeds falling on barren ground' – where do you think that well-polished saying came from?" Murray Bail, *The Pages* (Melbourne: The Text Publishing Company, 2008), p. 78.

29 Carey, p. 26.

his lack of formal education is compensated for by other skills rare in this century and last. The following passage is a point in fact:

> ...he gave off a surprising aura of good health. The raindrops stood on his bare brown skin as if it was a well-oiled coat or healthy vegetable. From his unknotted trouser legs he produced a large papaya, a hand of tiny bananas, the stems still oozing a pale white sap, a huge green zucchini, another papaya, this one with a bright green patch, and a purple eggplant, all of them wet and lustrous.[30]

Apart from the promiscuous coupling of man with nature, a union that results in a strange vision of male fertility, the thing to note about this passage is Trevor's abundance. In view of the scarcity of earth's resources, Trevor's ability to feed himself and others is potent. When Trevor later employs Che to work on his luscious garden in exchange for vegetables and fruit, resulting in the boy spending more time under his questionable influence, Dial's maternal role is radically challenged. The strength of Mother Earth has been sapped as witnessed through the humiliations that Dial must suffer and in its place are muscle and totalitarianism.

Catherine Roach's thesis regarding the perceived notion of Mother Nature as either good or bad in *Mother/Nature*: *Popular Culture and Environmental Ethics* foregrounds the centrality of gender to the post-9/11 representation of terror across cultural, historical, and transoceanic contexts. As conveyed by Dimock in her description of the potent strength of the planet by comparison to any other "weapons of mass destruction," nature's power is usually measured through displays of hurricanes, floods, and other violent environmental disruptions. However, in Australia and other places of severe drought, the true power of nature is measured in its unresponsiveness and refusal to yield crops or irrigation. The Bad Mother, writes Roach, "not only devours but also withholds."[31] As such, Dial's failure as a surrogate mother to Che and her inability to assimilate say something about the dire state of Australian nature and, more obliquely, the uncritical use in Australia of foreign (mainly American) political and economical models that have proven unsustainable from an environmental point of view. The representation of Dial as a temporary, displaced visitor to Australia in the role of Mother Nature reflects the current alienation of Australia vis-à-vis the land. At the pinnacle of recent discourses of terror is a politically charged conversation about what women should be and do. Female suicide bombers and the way women's lives in the Middle East are evoked to justify the current war on terror are some examples of how the configuration of terror and terrorism is gendered for political means.

---

30 Ibid., p. 62.

31 Roach, p. 121.

Carey also correlates gender with terror by suggesting that the ecological breakdown is but one modern form of battle between men and women, a struggle all the more vicious because human survival is at stake. In a climax involving a staged tribunal between Dial and members of the Crystal Community regarding the fate of the cat, Rebecca dismissingly pronounces the verdict, "'You can't even look after the kid.'"[32] Watching Dial's failed attempts to acclimate to a life in the jungle, Che is drawn to Trevor's wealth of useful information and produce, of which he boasts:

> "I've got twenty thousand gallons of water in those tanks. I can have a bloody fountain in the middle of my house. I have fresh veggies, good dope. No one can touch me, man, you understand me. No one knows I even exist. They can't see me with satellites. I am totally a fucking orphan. That's the silver lining."[33]

Out of reach of modernization, including high-tech surveillance systems, Trevor is not so much illiterate as preliterate, enjoying a highly localized and insular lifestyle reminiscent of settler days that valorized independence and freedom over civic engagement. However, his deep intolerance towards others, his propensity towards violence, lawlessness, unpredictable temperament, and general anti-social behavior make him forsake his obligations as a citizen of Australia, let alone the world. His kind is a dire prediction of the anachronistic evolution of mankind in the age of terror post-9/11, insular and fearful, in competition for survival. In the introduction to *Precarious Life: The Powers of Mourning and Violence*, Butler describes the cult of independence as a profoundly anti-global phenomenon:

> I would suggest, however, that both our political and ethical responsibilities are rooted in the recognition that radical forms of self-sufficiency and unbridled sovereignty are, by definition, disrupted by the larger global processes of which they are a part, that no final control can be secured, and that final control is not, cannot be, an ultimate value.[34]

The scarcity of the earth's resources has remobilized issues of civic independence and self-sufficiency as a desirable lifestyle at the cost of intercultural dialogue and cooperation. Carey's novel reveals the extent to which concepts of nature, when interpreted on a localized and individualized level, contribute to a terroristic view of humanity. Questions concerning the environment and terrorism tolerate, in general, very few nuances. President Bush's "you are either with or against us" resonates in the rhetoric of eco-

---

32 Carey, p. 197.

33 Ibid., p. 155.

34 Butler, p. xiii.

logical warfare. As Timothy Morton writes in *Ecology without Nature* with regards to animals and the ecosystem in general, people are forced to come down on the side of ecocentrism or anthropocentrism.[35] There is nothing in between. The myopic perspective of ecocentrism is pointed out by Dial:

> "I'm sorry about the cat," said Dial. "I really am. But you know while we're sitting here arguing about this, Nixon is bombing Cambodia and Laos. Do you want to think what that is doing to the birds? I mean, I just came from a country where my friends are dying trying to end this war."[36]

However, in drawing attention to the frailty of human life *per se*, terrorism and ecology do muster up a global perspective. After all, there is no escape from either climate change or strategically placed units of terror: "Ecology has reminded us that in fact we *are* the world, if only in the negative."[37] The power to conjure up visions of universal death and destruction is rhetorically shared by both, though of course to different ends. Thus, Trevor "could not read or write but he could imagine the end of the world better than a university professor."[38] That which the ecocentrism of the Crystal Community excludes is of course dialogue with the indigenous peoples of Australia, whose knowledge of and attitude toward the earth are desperately needed in the interest of restoring balance to a wounded nature, as argued by Australian activist Patrick Dodson and others.[39] Climate change and terrorism make more urgent the question of identification and domestic belonging vis-à-vis the global. Who do I identify with and how do I move across from one community to the other? Carey grapples with these questions, demonstrating that both problems are cultural at heart in that they challenge individuals and collectivities to debate conceptions of citizenship, ethical responsibilities, attitudes to risk-taking, etc. As trustees of the earth's resources rather than its owners, indigenous peoples of Australia have an extraordinary reservoir of knowledge and ecological humility mostly untapped by the nation's white settlers.

---

35 Timothy Morton, *Ecology without Nature: Rethinking Environmental Aesthetics* (Cambridge, Massachusetts & London: Harvard University Press, 2007), p. 99. Describing forms of left ecological criticism, Timothy Luke considers the possibility of biocentrism as so-called soft anthropocentrism, "which favours the nature-regarding interests of humans." Timothy W. Luke, *Ecocritique: Contesting the Politics of Nature, Economy, and Culture* (Minneapolis & London: University of Minnesota Press, 1997), p. 27.

36 Carey, p. 136.

37 Morton, p. 84.

38 Carey, p. 207.

39 Patrick Dodson, 'Nulungu Lecture', *ANTAR Australians for Native Title and Reconciliation*, 14 October 2008 <http://www.antar.org.au/node/314> [accessed 5 December 2008].

Aboriginal absence, save from the mention of places that go by Aboriginal names, in *His Illegal Self* reflects the lack of national unity in post-9/11 Australia and is a reminder that any attempt to solve global conflicts must begin at home. It might be gratuitous of Australia to condemn acts of terrorism in the context of its recent history of white settlement, but this history also contains confrontations with racism and bigotry and instances of intercultural dialogue that are valuable to recall in the current war on terrorism. The significance of a nation's moral history's confrontation with the present is acknowledged, at least unconsciously, by Dial who brings race into the Crystal Community when reading *Huckleberry Finn* out loud to Che: "...and the air was muggy as Jackson, Mississippi, white ants swarming around the hissing lamp, everybody running for their lives."[40] Bleeding into the pages of *His Illegal Self* is the circum-Atlantic slave-trade that finds transhemispheric resonance within the context of Australia's settlement that saw the systematic eradication of Aboriginal presence. Through this enfolding of history and traumas, Carey demonstrates that the ways in which international coalitions are modelled in the future will decide how humans respond to climate change and terrorism.

Within Oceanic Reach: A Post-9/11 Biosphere

The nudist conveyancing lawyer, Phil Warriner, is sent to the US at Dial's expense in an attempt to set things right between Che's grandmother and herself and to facilitate the transfer of Che, the "property" in question. The spectacular failure of the law to intervene and bring order to chaos and confusion is displayed with tragic-comic effect in Carey's representation of Warriner, for whom Dial can only feel acute "embarrassment."[41] Much is made of Warriner's unsuitability to represent Dial, who knows that eccentricity and difference bar him from membership to an international, elite community: "She should have told him, Take the freaking thing off. Burn it. Where in all the Sunshine Coast would you find a zoot suit? American Negroes wore them, Negroes long since dead."[42] This passage is significant in that it reminds the reader of cultural translations that are unsuccessful and provides proof that the world is far from united, not merely in terms of the wealthy nations' exclusion of others, but also with regards to much needed "effective

40 Carey, p. 141.
41 Ibid., p. 250.
42 Ibid., pp. 250-251.

collective action and mutual support among the less powerful.'"[43] It takes more than fashion to put marginalized peoples and cultures in contact with each other. Above all, the failure of the transfer of Che to his grandmother in Kenoza Lake and the warped communication between Dial and the grandmother remind the reader of the unequal access to voice, wealth, and opportunity, accentuated by post-9/11 restrictions on visas and ethnic prejudices. Being a comfortable citizen of the world is not only contingent on having the right passports and credit cards, but also the right cultural credentials, as Craig Calhoun argues.[44]

After what appears to have been a brief period of distraction by pleasures on offer in New York, involving an encounter with trombonist J.J. Johnson, Warriner is detained and charged with complicity in kidnapping. Shortly thereafter, the Crystal Commune is stormed by the police in pursuit of Che, who has gone underground with Dial and Trevor in anticipation of this hunt. During the violent intrusion by the police, Dial experiences flashbacks to the brutal history suffered by her communist father who was shot during the Greek Civil War. Thinking perhaps that terror and violence are ubiquitous and inescapable, Dial takes the law in her own hands. Driving Trevor's car, Dial regrets her earlier decision to let Che go and snaps him up as he hides in the grass from the police. Fearful that the suspicions against her have become impossible to disprove, Dial has lost all faith in the law. How society addresses post-9/11 security risks will determine the path taken by its citizens and the level of trust they will have towards the authorities.[45] This question is inextricably linked with the equally pressing challenge of how to collectively adapt to climate change. What preventative measures can be taken to protect all citizens against ecological devastation, not just a privileged few, and/or terrorist attacks?

Drawing attention to the question of the law and justice, *His Illegal Self* makes the case that the real challenge of the twenty-first century is to trans-

---

43 Craig Calhoun, 'Social Solidarity as a Problem for Cosmopolitan Democracy', *Identities, Affiliations, and Allegiances*, ed. by Seyla Benhabib, Ian Shapiro, and Danilo Petranovic (Cambridge: Cambridge University Press, 2007), 285-302 (p. 295).

44 Ibid., p. 286.

45 In a discussion regarding risk and terrorism, Inderpal Grewal notes, "If we examine one mode of addressing risk not through insurance but through incarceration, then the synonym for risk is not chance or randomness but danger and 'terror,' and the means for securing the population from this danger is the incarceration of other populations judged by various modes of expertise as dangerous. From the criminal at one level of risk for violence to the 'terrorist' at a higher level representing a risk to the nation, we can see the progressively higher levels of risk associated with particular bodies within specific locations." Grewal, pp. 201-202.

late ethical values into law. Education is crucial to this task. Having opened his eyes to the world beyond Kenoza Lake, a jungle of lawlessness and environmental struggle, Che is initiated into the future through the eyes of a Harvard girl and newly appointed professor in literature, on the one hand, and Trevor who survived the brutality of a Christian orphanage and boasts of an abundance of food and water, on the other.[46] Both options have been shown to be elitist and restrictive; Dial's option is so because she attempts to impose order on her environment despite limited experience of people and cultures, and Trevor's because he has adapted to the disorder by contributing to it. Trevor instructs Che that "'the random pattern is your key to freedom'" and to do "'nothing that could be seen or heard from space.'"[47] He does what Morton outlines as a possibility for survival in the twenty-first century: "Instead of trying to pull the world out of the mud, we could jump down into the mud. [...] We choose this poisoned ground. We will be equal to this senseless actuality."[48]

Detailing the human cost of political violence to its post-9/11 readers, *His Illegal Self* demonstrates the interconnectedness between the individual and his or her environment. Carey's novel makes explicit the desperate need for a broader conception of the ecosystem post-9/11, one that does not segregate or discriminate. Though its protagonist is an eight-year old boy, *His Illegal Self* is anything but diminutive in its outlook. It depicts a world stretched to its limits, an earth flattened, where human activity is monitored in what Buell calls, "multi-scalar terms: local, national, regional, transhemispheric; topographically, historically, culturally."[49] However, crucial to this reconfiguration of the biosphere is the growth of what the narrator in Carey's novel calls "a sort of seed"[50] within each individual, what Che prefers to believe is memory, but what the narrator suggests is something more along the lines of the foundations of the future. The novel ends with Dial scooping him off the ground, producing in Che the sensation that

---

[46] In a revealing passage, Trevor discloses the brutal facts of his upbringing to Che: "'It was a very small room,' Trevor said. 'We knew it well, firstly because we had helped build it. "Man's work with a boy's body" is what they called it. Just off the ship we were divided into gangs to clear brush, dig trenches, lay foundations, gather granite from the quarry, pour barrows full of concrete, burn ourselves with lime. Boys from ten to fourteen. We made the rooms we were beaten in, and worse. And Brother Kiernan now made good use of our Christian labour, mate. As punishment for entering the attic, he had us strip and walk around him naked in a circle and he lashed at us with that bloody cane.'" Carey, p. 167.

[47] Carey, p. 254.

[48] Morton, p. 205.

[49] Buell, p. 96.

[50] Carey, p. 270.

> Something stabbed him, he thought. Even as an adult he would believe that something physical had been left inside him – a small, smooth, not a pearl, more lustrous, luminous, a sort of seed which he would eventually pretend to believe was simply a memory, nothing more, that he would carry along that littered path which would be his own comic and occasionally disastrous life.[51]

The novel's closure, or rather lack thereof, shows that the future is in the making within the individual. In an excerpt from "The Ecology of Freedom," the founder of the social ecology movement, Murray Bookchin alludes to the power within each individual:

> History, in fact, is as important as form or structure. To a large extent, the history of a phenomenon is the phenomenon itself. We are, in a real sense, everything that existed before us, and in turn, we can eventually become vastly more than what we are. Surprisingly, very little in the evolution of life-forms has been lost in natural and social evolution – indeed in our very bodies, as our embryonic development attests. Evolution lies within us (as well as around us) as parts of the very nature of our beings.[52]

In lieu of the survival tactics advocated by Trevor, this view of the self, illicit only insofar as it escapes confinement, suggests potential for a new international coalition based on relational ties and principles with regards to what Butler refers to as a shared fate.[53] By combining discourses of environmentalism and terrorism, Carey's novel brings a uniquely Australian reflection on the attacks of 9/11 and its aftermath, one that emphasizes the need for solidarity networks that extend the boundaries of community within the jurisdiction of self.

---

51 Ibid., p. 270.

52 Janet Biehl, ed., *The Murray Bookchin Reader* (London & Washington: Cassell, 1997), p. 33.

53 "If my fate is not originally or finally separable from yours, then the 'we' is traversed by a relationality that we cannot easily argue against; or, rather, we can argue against it, but we would be denying something fundamental about the social conditions of our very formation." Butler, pp. 22-23.

Bibliography

Bail, Murray, *The Pages* (Melbourne: The Text Publishing Company, 2008)

Biehl, Janet, ed., *The Murray Bookchin Reader* (London & Washington: Cassell, 1997)

Buell, Lawrence, *The Future of Environmental Criticism: Environmental Crisis and Literary Imagination* (Malden: Blackwell Publishing, 2005)

Judith Butler, *Precarious Life: The Powers of Mourning and Violence* (London & New York: Verso, 2003)

Calhoun, Craig, 'Social Solidarity as a Problem for Cosmopolitan Democracy', *Identities, Affiliations, and Allegiances*, ed. by Seyla Benhabib, Ian Shapiro, and Danilo Petranovic (Cambridge: Cambridge University Press, 2007), 285-302

Carey, Peter, *His Illegal Self* (New York: Alfred A. Knopf. 2008)

Coetzee, J.M., *Diary of a Bad Year* (Melbourne: The Text Publishing Company, 2007)

Dimock, Wai Chee, intro, *Shades of the Planet: American Literature as World Literature*, ed. by Wai Chee Dimock, and Lawrence Buell (Princeton & Oxford: Princeton University Press, 2007)

Dodson, Patrick, 'Nulungu Lecture', *ANTAR Australians for Native Title and Reconciliation*, 14 Oct 2008 <http://www.antar.org.au/node/314> [accessed 5 December 2008]

Flanagan, Richard, *The Unknown Terrorist* (New York: Grove Press, 2006

Grewal, Inderpal, *Transnational America: Feminisms, Diasporas, Neoliberalisms* (Durham & London: Duke University Press, 2005)

Henry, Nicola, 'Individual Income or Wellbeing for All? Overcoming Injustice: Practical and Symbolic Reconciliation for Indigenous Australians', *To Firmer Ground: Restoring Hope in Australia*, ed. by John Langmore (Sydney: New South Wales Press, 2007), 23-53

---, 'Turning the Tide: Solutions to Australia's Environmental Crisis', *To Firmer Ground: Restoring Hope in Australia*, ed. by John Langmore (Sydney: New South Wales Press, 2007), 54-86

Langmore, John, 'Advancing Global Security and Justice', *To Firmer Ground: Restoring Hope in Australia*, ed. by John Langmore (Sydney: New South Wales Press, 2007), 156-178

Luke, Timothy W., *Ecocritique: Contesting the Politics of Nature, Economy, and Culture* (Minneapolis & London: University of Minnesota Press, 1997)

Morton, Timothy, *Ecology without Nature: Rethinking Environmental Aesthetics* (Cambridge, Massachusetts & London: Harvard University Press, 2007)

Pettus, Katherine, 'Citizenship in Feminism: Identity, Action, and Locale', *Hypatia* 12.4 (1997), 132-155

Roach, Catherine M., *Mother/Nature*: *Popular Culture and Environmental Ethics* (Bloomington & Indianapolis: Indiana University Press, 2003)

Spivak, Gayatri Chakravorty, *Death of a Discipline* (New York: Columbia University Press, 2003)

Government, Media, and Power: Terrorism in the Australian Novel since 9/11

Nathanael O'Reilly

This chapter examines three Australian novels published since 2001 that address the effects of terrorism on both Australian and Western society: Janette Turner Hospital's *Due Preparations for the Plague* (2003), Andrew McGahan's *Underground* (2006), and Richard Flanagan's *The Unknown Terrorist* (2007). Despite the variety of settings that the novels utilize, they all demonstrate the pervasiveness of terrorism as a dominant political and cultural issue in Australian society since 9/11. Moreover, the novels reveal the relationship between governments and the media, and critique the way that both use terrorism to maintain and expand their power. Turner Hospital's *Due Preparations for the Plague*, set in the United States, France, and Iraq, examines terrorism, Islamic fundamentalism, national security, intelligence failures, government cover-ups, and media manipulation. McGahan and Flanagan both set their novels in Australia after 9/11 and focus on the nation's responses to acts of domestic terrorism seemingly perpetrated by Islamist extremists. Both novels depict governments that have become increasingly totalitarian, ruling societies driven by fear and paranoia. In McGahan's and Flanagan's novels, the government's response to 9/11 and domestic terrorism is to attempt to exert total control over society; however, in the process, the government, rather than terrorism, becomes the primary threat to Western civilization. *Due Preparations for the Plague*, *Underground*, and *The Unknown Terrorist* all expose and interrogate the interdependent relationship between governments, the media, and terrorism, while critiquing the use of terrorism by governments and the media to exert, maintain, and increase power.

Since the terrorist attacks in the United States on September 11, 2001, there has been an explosion in the global media of representations of terrorism, including feature films, documentaries, television programs and both fiction and non-fiction books. At Amazon.com, one can choose from more than sixty thousand books on terrorism published since 9/11. A number of Australian novelists have published fictional engagements with terrorism since 2001, several of which have been published around the world (both in English and in translation) by multinational publishing houses. Given Australia's close political and cultural relationship with the United States, the death of Australian citizens in the 9/11 attacks and the Bali bombings in 2002, Australia's participation in the invasions of Iraq and Afghanistan and the War on Terror, and the Howard government's close relationship with the Bush administration, it was perhaps inevitable that Australian novelists would focus their attention on 9/11 and terrorism more broadly. According to AustLit, the most comprehensive source for bibliographic information on Australian literature, twenty-two Australian adult novels focusing on terrorism have been published since 2001.[1] This chapter focuses on three Australian novels published since 2001 that address the effects of terrorism on both Australian society and the West more generally: Janette Turner Hospital's *Due Preparations for the Plague* (2003), Andrew McGahan's *Underground* (2006), and Richard Flanagan's *The Unknown Terrorist* (2006).

In her review essay, "Histories of the Present," Rachael Weaver argues that contemporary Australian novelists rarely "produce fiction that explicitly and self-consciously deals with the current political climate," and that the publication within the same year of *The Unknown Terrorist* and *Underground*, both written by popular, critically-acclaimed authors, is therefore an unusual and significant event.[2] Turner Hospital's *Due Preparations for the Plague* was published three years earlier, and since it is set before 9/11 and none of the action of the novel takes place in Australia, it does not fit into the category Weaver describes. McGahan and Flanagan both set their novels in Australia after 9/11 and focus on the nation's responses to acts of domestic terrorism seemingly perpetrated by Islamist extremists. Both novels depict governments that have become increasingly totalitarian, ruling societies driven by fear and paranoia. In McGahan's and Flanagan's novels, the government's response to 9/11 and domestic terrorism is to attempt to exert total control over society; however, in the process, the government, rather than terrorism, becomes the primary threat to Western civilization. *Due Preparations for the Plague*, *Underground*, and *The Unknown Terrorist* all expose and interrogate the interdependent relationship between governments, the media, and terrorism, while critiquing the use of terrorism by governments and the media to exert, maintain, and increase power.

Turner Hospital's *Due Preparations for the Plague* was published simultaneously in North America, Europe and Australia.[3] Written by an Australian residing in the United States, the novel examines terrorism, Islamic fundamentalism, national security, intelligence failures, government cover-ups, and media manipulation and complicity. Turner Hospital sets her narrative in the United States, France, and Iraq, and utilizes Australian, American, French, Israeli, and Saudi characters. The novel is concerned with the aftermath of the September 1987 hijacking of an Air France flight from Paris to New York. Turner Hospital utilizes several protagonists, and the action oscillates between events in 1987 and 2000. One of the protagonists is Lowell Haw-

---

1 Twelve of the twenty-two novels are categorized as thrillers, and just seven are by "literary" novelists. Search conducted at http://www.austlit.edu.au/ on 2 Jan., 2009.

2 Rachael Weaver, 'Histories of the Present', *Overland* 187 (2007), 81-85 (p. 81).

3 My discussion of *Due Preparations for the Plague* draws in part on my review of the novel, published in *Antipodes* in 2004.

thorne, whose mother died during the hijacking of Air France flight 64. Lowell's father, a retired CIA operative, dies in Washington under suspicious circumstances during the novel's present. After his father's funeral, Lowell is contacted by his father's psychologist, who delivers an inheritance: a key to locker B-64 at Logan Airport. The locker holds a bag containing ring binders and video tapes. The binders contain files pertaining to secret agents named Salamander and Sirocco. Salamander's identity is unknown, however, Sirocco is described as a Saudi, Iraqi, or Algerian who holds four passports and speaks four languages.

Another protagonist, Samantha Raleigh, one of the twenty children released from the hijacked flight, is convinced that the American government has suppressed the truth about the hijacking and manipulated the media representation of the event. In the year 2000, she is a nineteen-year-old student at Georgetown University. Obsessed with solving the mysteries surrounding the hijacking, Samantha scours previously classified government documents and shares her findings with other members of the Phoenix Club, a support group for survivors. Jacob, another survivor, is convinced that Samantha's quest is treacherous and believes the American government is eliminating survivors. The protagonists of the 1987 sections of the novel are Tristan Charron, a French publisher, and Genevieve Teague, an Australian travel writer. Once lovers, the pair have not seen each other for five years before preparing to board Air France flight 64. Their meeting at Charles de Gaulle airport may or may not be a coincidence; they are detained and questioned by French police on suspicion of espionage, before being allowed to board the flight, which is hijacked soon after take-off.

Lowell reads his father's secret files, which describe plans for the hijacking, and views the video tapes with Samantha, which reveal that Salamander is Lowell's father.[4] The tapes also reveal that the terrorist hijacking was orchestrated by the CIA, with Salamander as the mastermind, in an attempt to eliminate a terrorist cell in Paris. However, the operation took a disastrous turn when Sirocco double-crossed Salamander. In Slavoj Žižek's *Welcome to the Desert of the Real!: Five Essays on September 11 and Related Dates*, he emphasizes the connection between the CIA and terrorism, citing "the fact that Bin Laden and the Taliban emerged as part of the CIA-supported anti-Soviet guerilla movement in Afghanistan."[5] Žižek contends that dominant powers, such as the United States, generate excesses, such as terrorists

---

4 Janette Turner Hospital, *Due Preparations for the Plague* (New York: Norton, 2004), p. 279.

5 Slavoj Žižek, *Welcome to the Desert of the Real!: Five Essays on September 11 and Related Dates* (London: Verso, 2002), p. 27.

trained and funded by the CIA, and that those excesses must be fought and eliminated.[6] However, "the Power" conducts such operations in secret and cannot admit to its activities.[7] *Due Preparations for the Plague* repeatedly critiques the CIA and the American government. Carolyn Bliss argues that Turner Hospital's novel is an indictment of "the insular and paranoid American intelligence establishment and the horrific 'collateral damage' it is willing to accept to accomplish its ends."[8]

In her article on the novel, Dolores Herrero points to the symbiotic relationship between the media and terrorism.[9] Throughout the hijacking, the terrorists are aware that their activities are being filmed and their radio transmissions recorded, and they use the media to their advantage, disseminating fear "to the passengers and to the television audience of the world": "'The world has its eyes on this plane [...] The world is listening to me as I speak,'" states Sirocco.[10] When the hijacked plane lands in Iraq, the terrorists take ten hostages off the plane, including Tristan and Genevieve, then explode the plane, killing the remaining passengers. The surviving hostages are sealed in an underground bunker. Sirocco tells the hostages that they "'will be famous. Whatever happens, your names and your photographs will be in newspapers and on the covers of magazines around the world. We will transmit your passport photographs to CNN. You will achieve immortality.'"[11] The bunker contains video cameras and microphones that transmit the images and sound live, and some of the footage is "made available to global news services [...] [and] broadcast in a dozen countries [...] without censorship."[12] Thus, the terrorists use the media to disseminate fear, while the media use terrorism to boost ratings.

In *The Spirit of Terrorism and Other Essays*, Jean Baudrillard discusses the importance and power of images in relation to terrorism. Baudrillard argues that "the sight of the images" has the most profound impact on the viewers, and that the "impact of the images, and their fascination, are necessarily what [...] [the viewers] retain."[13] In Turner Hospital's novel, the terror-

---

6 Ibid., p. 27.

7 Ibid., p. 27.

8 Carolyn Bliss, rev. of *Due Preparations for the Plague*, by Janette Turner Hospital, *World Literature Today* 78 (2004), 78-9 (p. 79).

9 Delores Herrero, '*Due Preparations for the Plague*: Globalisation, Terror and the Ethics of Alterity', *Kunapipi*, 28 (2006), 25-43 (p. 28).

10 Turner Hospital, p. 161.

11 Ibid., p. 167.

12 Ibid., p. 282.

13 Jean Baudrillard, *The Spirit of Terrorism and Other Essays*, trans. By Chris Turner (New York: Verson, 2003), p. 26.

ists and the CIA agents running the operation are fully aware of the power of the images of the hijacked plane and the hostages, and they use those images as weapons in pursuit of their objectives. Baudrillard addresses the exploitation by terrorists of images, and, by extension, the global media, in his discussion of 9/11. Baudrillard's analysis of the role of images in terrorist attacks applies perfectly to the events in *Due Preparations for the Plague*. He contends that the terrorists "exploited the 'real time' of images, their instantaneous worldwide transmission," and claims that "[t]he role of images is highly ambiguous," since images simultaneously "exalt the event" and "take it hostage."[14] Images, according to Baudrillard, "serve to multiply" an event "to infinity [...]. The image consumes the event, in the sense that it absorbs it and offers it for consumption [...] it gives it unprecedented impact, but impact as image-event."[15]

In Turner Hospital's novel, the images of what Baudrillard terms the "image-event," the hijacked plane exploding and of the hostages in the bunker, are later "*elided* by subsequent editorial construction and slant [...] [their] impact [...] diluted."[16] Thus, the government pressures the media outlets to alter the images and the narrative in order to control the message and the event. Like Baudrillard, Turner Hospital addresses the impact on the viewer of watching images of terrorist attacks. During the hijacking, Samantha's aunt Lou does not turn the television off for four straight days, and later declares, "'It was horrible [...] Just watching and watching, completely helpless.'"[17] The images Lou watches repeatedly during the four days of the hijacking event haunt her throughout the next thirteen years. Samantha and Jacob experience horror first-hand while they are hostages and again after being released: they watch the hijacked plane, containing their parents, explode live on television.[18]

Herrero contends that the novel critiques the "political obfuscation and unacknowledged interference" by an American government engaged in a conflict "that involves consorting with the enemy."[19] The American government refuses to intervene and save the hostages because they do not want to damage their relationship with the Saudi Princes who bankroll Sirocco. To intervene would be to lose power and influence. The government masks its refusal by declaring, "It [intervention] would not be in the interests of nation-

---

14 Ibid., p. 27.

15 Ibid., p. 27.

16 Turner Hospital, p. 282. Emphasis in original.

17 Ibid., pp. 53, 54.

18 Ibid., p. 74.

19 Herrero, p. 25.

al security at this time."[20] The American media report that "[i]ntelligence sources have revealed that the so-called hostage demand was a hoax"[21] without questioning the truth of the false assertion, and, at the State Department's request, the American television networks refrain from broadcasting certain footage. Thus, the government uses its power to control the story, manipulate the public, and avoid accepting responsibility for the death of its citizens.[22]

Samantha and Lowell learn the truth about the hijacking and the relationship between the American government, the terrorists, and the media by viewing the video tapes. Afterwards, they conclude that they must get the tapes out of the country in order to break the story and ensure the survival of the footage.[23] Lou agrees to fly to Paris with the tapes and attempt to disseminate the story through the French newspapers.[24] Although the story is eventually carried by *Liberation* and *Le Monde* in France and *The Guardian* and *The Independent* in Britain, it is met with indifference by the American press, which does not publish any articles on the matter.[25] Lou attributes the American public's lack of interest in the story to a numbness caused by media saturation: "'Horror doesn't reach people anymore. Horror's TV. Horror's special effects.'"[26] Turner Hospital's depiction of the media and the American government, especially the intelligence community and its abuses of power, is a scathing critique of both institutions and the relationship between them.

Andrew McGahan's *Underground*, published three years after Turner Hospital's novel, also critiques the relationship between governments, the media, and terrorism. However, unlike Turner Hospital's novel, *Underground* is set in Australia and takes aim at a specific government and leader, namely the government of John Howard, who was Prime Minister from 1996 to 2007. The novel was published in 2006 and imagines an Australia approximately five years in the future (circa 2011) that has become a police state and is ruled by a Prime Minister, named Bernard James, who is clearly modeled on Howard. The novel is narrated in the first person by the Prime Minister's twin brother, Leo James. McGahan combines elements of both the thriller and satire genres to create a fast-paced, witty, prescient, and disturbing

20 Turner Hospital, p. 286.
21 Ibid., p. 298.
22 Ibid., p. 299.
23 Ibid., p. 375.
24 Ibid., pp. 383-84.
25 Ibid., p. 393.
26 Ibid., p. 394. Zizek and Baudrillard's ideas concerning the relationship between special effects and terrorism are discussed later in this chapter.

novel, which Steven Luebke describes as "a dark, crazy journey."[27] *Underground* depicts a government that uses terrorism as an excuse and tool to expand its powers and reduce the rights of its citizens; moreover, the government effectively uses the media as a weapon to control the public and disseminate fear.

Underground is an extremely serious and political novel, despite the presence of large doses of humor and absurd scenarios. Luebke argues that *Underground* is

> a call to Australians (and Americans) to remember their history, their tradition of democracy [...]. Leo's reflections recall a time when things were different, and McGahan seems to want to leave the reader with the sense that if enough people remember that, the nightmare of a totalitarian world need not come to pass.[28]

Similarly, Anthony Hassall considers *Underground* a "disturbing depiction of the damage that the politically manipulated fear of terrorism is wreaking on Australian society," and describes the novel as "part thriller, part cautionary tale and part futuristic Orwellian nightmare. Its chilling message [is] that the cynically cultivated fear of terrorism could all too easily turn a democracy like Australia into a totalitarian police state."[29] Kerryn Goldsworthy also contends that the ideas informing *Underground* are "chilling," as are the arguments it makes about contemporary Australian society, since "[m]ost of the separate elements of McGahan's dystopian Australia are already in place."[30]

Underground is written as a memoir Leo addresses to the security forces imprisoning him. He repeatedly refers to his captors as "interrogators" and notes that they have forced him to confess "to everything."[31] Leo reveals that he has been repeatedly tortured and wryly comments, "[N]ow that torture is the western way again, you'd be idiots not to use it, right?"[32] The narrative describes the events leading up to Leo's capture, starting with him sheltering in an unfinished resort during a massive cyclone, named "Yusuf" by the Department of Meteorology. Leo speculates that the government deliberately linked the cyclone to Islam, as "a state of emergency decree," because it is

---

27 Steven R. Luebke, 'A *1984* for Our Time', rev. of *Underground*, by Andrew McGahan, *Antipodes* 22 (2008), 75-76 (p. 75).

28 Ibid., p. 76.

29 Anthony J. Hassall, 'The Year's Work in Fiction', *Westerly,* 52 (2007), 187-199 (pp. 190-1).

30 Kerryn Goldsworthy, 'Straight for the Throat', rev. of *Underground*, by Andrew McGahan, *Australian Book Review*, 285 (2006), 25-43 (pp. 8, 9).

31 Andrew McGahan, *Underground* (Crows Nest, NSW: Allen and Unwin, 2006), p. 11.

32 Ibid., p. 82. See also pp. 272, 273-74.

"big and dangerous."[33] During the cyclone, Leo is kidnapped by a home-grown Islamist terrorist group, Great Southern Jihad, which claims to be responsible for detonating a nuclear bomb in Canberra two years earlier.[34] Leo is subsequently "rescued" in a raid by the Australian Federal Police (AFP) and then "rescued" again, along with Aisha, a cell leader of Great Southern Jihad, by a group calling itself the "Oz Underground" and claiming to be a resistance movement.[35] The mission of the Oz Undergound is to save Australia from its own government.[36] Leo spends most of the novel on the run from the federal authorities with Aisha and Harry, an Underground operative. Soon after Leo is rescued by the Underground, the media reports that he was killed during the cyclone and has been declared dead by his brother, even though Bernard knows Leo is alive.[37] Thus, government use of the media to distort the truth and further its agenda is clear from the beginning of the novel. As the narrative progresses, the extent of the government's manipulation of the public via the media becomes clear.

Leo's memoir contains much exposition, and gradually he reveals how Australia was transformed from a liberal democracy into a totalitarian police state. Leo notes that his "current fate [...] is linked to a much wider history. I could go all the way back, ten years and more, to September 11 and the twin towers."[38] However, the most significant event leading to Australia's transformation was not 9/11 but the detonation of a nuclear bomb in Canberra, the national capital. At the time of the attack, Bernard's administration was beset by a plethora of problems, including overseas wars in which Australian troops suffered heavy casualties, car bombs exploding in Australian cities, and economic collapse.[39] Leo was in Canberra when news of the nuclear threat broke: "I switched on the TV and there it was, blazing across the news on every channel. An Islamic terrorist group [...] claimed to have planted an explosive thermonuclear device somewhere in Canberra."[40] While the security forces search for the bomb and the Prime Minister delivers speeches about fighting terrorism, Canberra's residents evacuate.[41] Television camera crews position themselves near Yass, a thirty minute drive north of Canberra,

33 Ibid., p. 3.
34 Ibid., p. 26.
35 Ibid., pp. 47, 63.
36 Ibid., pp. 64-5.
37 Ibid., pp. 41, 61.
38 Ibid., p. 12.
39 Ibid., p. 17.
40 Ibid., p. 27.
41 Ibid., p. 28.

in order to film the nuclear explosion, which Leo notes "was, without question, the most highly rated moment in television history – throughout the world, not just here in Australia."[42] Thus, as is the case in *Due Preparations for the Plague*, the media help stage the event, rather than simply reporting on it.[43] When the nuclear device detonates, billions of viewers watch the cameras zoom in on "an awesome sight, boiling and evil, and an indisputable sign that the world had changed forever, yet again."[44] Baudrillard refers to the attacks on the World Trade Center in New York as "the absolute event, the 'mother' of all events."[45] The nuclear explosion in Canberra in *Underground*, if real, would certainly supersede the 9/11 attacks as "the 'mother' of all events." According to Baudrillard, "the absolute, irrevocable event" constitutes "the spirit of terrorism."[46] Žižek discusses the attacks on the World Trade Center as an event staged by the terrorists and produced by the media, and argues that the terrorists "did not do it primarily to provoke real material damage, but *for the spectacular effect of it*."[47] Like Baudrillard, Žižek emphasizes the importance of images, noting that for "the great majority of the public," the 9/11 attacks "were events on the TV screen."[48] Žižek suggests that the "oft-repeated shot of frightened people running towards the camera ahead of the giant cloud of dust from the collapsing tower" was "reminiscent of spectacular shots in catastrophe movies, a special effect which outdid all others."[49] Baudrillard also makes the connection between the collapse of the twin towers and disaster movies.[50]

In *Underground*, Australian society changes swiftly and fundamentally after the nuclear explosion. Although Australia had been "fighting the war on terror for years" and "had some of the toughest security laws in the world," the government declares a state of emergency, suspends "due process and individual freedoms," instigates martial law, issues a decree effectively outlawing Islam, and forces Muslims into detention centers and "cultural precincts."[51] Parliament grants the Prime Minister the power to "act unilaterally for the duration of the crisis."[52] Baudrillard argues that the increased security

---

42 Ibid., p. 30.

43 I am indebted to Cara Cilano for this point.

44 McGahan, p. 30.

45 Baudrillard, p. 4.

46 Ibid., p. 9.

47 Žižek, p. 11. Emphasis in original.

48 Ibid., p. 11.

49 Ibid., p. 11.

50 Baudrillard, p. 7.

51 McGahan, p. 30.

52 Ibid., pp. 30-1.

measures implemented by Western governments after 9/11 are "merely extensions of terror" and contends that "the real victory of terrorism" is that it has forced "the whole of the West into the obsession with security," creating "a veiled form of perpetual terror."[53] Baudrillard goes so far as to claim that "[t]he spectre of terrorism" forces the West "to terrorize itself," comparing the global police network to "a universal Cold War [...] a fourth world war imprinting itself upon bodies and mores."[54] In McGahan's novel, the state of emergency is initially declared to be temporary, yet it remains in force for two years after the bombing.

After the attack on Canberra, an "endless spate of terrorist attacks" ensues, including car bombings and assaults on oil depots, communications networks, and sporting events.[55] Public figures are kidnapped and assassinated, including the Deputy Prime Minister, whose beheading is "screened across the nation."[56] The increase in terrorism leads to increasingly tougher security responses, including new laws and decrees, and the "massive enlargement" of the AFP (Australian Federal Police), ASIO (Australian Security and Intelligence Organization), and the armed forces.[57] Leo notes that the AFP is backed "by the all-powerful state of emergency laws, and answerable to only one man. The Minister for Freedom. Who happens, of course, to be the Prime Minister."[58] McGahan uses such Orwellian double-speak frequently throughout *Underground*; this rhetorical device is both a satirical convention and a direct allusion to the actual rhetoric of Western governments post-9/11.

In order to maintain and increase power, and to justify increasingly brutal laws and security measures, the government uses the media to spread and incite fear of Muslims, who are inextricably linked to terrorism. While on the run from the federal authorities, Leo is sheltered in the Brunswick ghetto, one of the Muslim "cultural precincts" established by the government after the Canberra bombing.[59] Leo notes that Brunswick contains "something like forty thousand Muslim souls, the vast majority of them forcibly removed from somewhere else."[60] Leo's companion and guide during his time in the ghetto

---

53 Baudrillard, p. 81.
54 Ibid., pp. 81-2.
55 McGahan, p. 31.
56 Ibid., p. 31.
57 Ibid., p. 31.
58 Ibid., p. 40.
59 Ibid., p. 199.
60 Ibid., p. 199.

claims, "'[T]he [news] papers like to pretend we're all animals in here,'"[61] referring to the media's distorted portrayal of Muslims, calculated to inspire fear and hatred amongst "normal" Australians. The Muslim ghetto resident declares: "'Ninety-nine point nine per cent of these people are completely harmless. The government knows that. They could open all the ghettos tomorrow and not a thing would change. It's all just for show.'"[62] However, in order to maintain fear of terrorism amongst the majority non-Muslim population, the government needs the media to run stories about the purported enemy within.

While hiding in Brunswick, Leo, Aisha, and Harry receive information that compels them to travel to Canberra, where they learn the shocking truth that the nuclear explosion was faked. Harry quickly realizes that the bomb "'was the whole excuse'" for all the changes in Australian society: "'The state of emergency. The arrests, the detentions.'"[63] Leo suggests that they inform the media that the nuking of Canberra was faked, but Harry points out that even if they could convince the media, the government has security advisers inside every news organization who must approve every story. These advisers would report the information to their superiors, leading to the swift execution of Harry, Leo, Aisha, and members of the media, and, of course, the suppression of the truth.[64] The fugitives also learn that Aisha's terrorist organization, Great Southern Jihad, was established and orchestrated by the government in order to maintain a state of fear amongst the populace and to justify the constant expansion of government power. As Harry points out, "'This government […] the state of emergency – it only works if there's a constant threat. What better way to keep it all bubbling along than to have some terrorists of your own doing the dirty work?'"[65] Baudrillard suggests that terrorists might dream of an immortal enemy, since the lack of an enemy constitutes the lack of a reason for their existence.[66] Likewise, the Australian government in *Underground* recognizes that the maintenance and expansion of power is only possible if there is a terrorist threat, and thus, when terrorists do not exist, they must be created.

After Leo is captured, an unnamed American intelligence official informs him that the idea to fake a nuclear attack on Canberra in order to be able to use it as a secret administrative base for world governments and multination-

---

[61] Ibid., p. 204.
[62] Ibid., p. 206.
[63] Ibid., p. 245.
[64] Ibid., p. 245.
[65] Ibid., p. 253.
[66] Baudrillard, pp. 55-6.

al corporations was conceived in 2003 during George W. Bush's visit to Canberra, when the Australians ceded control of their capital to the Americans.[67] Goldsworthy argues that Bush's visit to Canberra in October 2003 was the primary inspiration for *Underground*:

> the Americans took over the capital – entry to Parliament House [was] controlled by the president's men; American film crews [were] allowed in where Australian cameras were not – and the Australian government simply rolled over [...]. There is nothing at all imaginary or invented about McGahan's slightly stunned-sounding account of this day.[68]

When Leo asks why a secret base is needed, the intelligence officer explains: "'What it comes down to, Leo, is a kind of double war. On one level it's the official war – the West against the Islamists. But neither the western governments nor the Islamists want that war to end. What they both want is to stay in power, and to keep control over their own people.'"[69] The American goes on to declare that the people "'are the real problem,'" since they do not want the war, but the governments, the terrorists and the "'big media bosses'" do since "'nothing sells papers like the war on terror!'"[70] The official reveals that a real nuclear bomb was used for the fake nuclear explosion, although it was not as big as the government declared and not as radioactive.[71] The bomb was detonated fifteen miles south of Canberra, while the cameras were positioned north of the city: "'They could see the mushroom cloud. But nothing else.'"[72] When Leo asks about images of the ruins of Canberra shown on television, he learns that Hollywood special effects were used, courtesy of Industrial Light and Magic.[73]

Thus, the media enables the government to perpetrate the deception of not just an entire country, but the whole world. The use of Hollywood special effects to fake the nuclear explosion makes the episode a kind of inversion of Žižek's and Baudrillard's claims that the 9/11 attacks were reminiscent of Hollywood catastrophe movies.[74] Rather than a real terrorist attack mimicking a Hollywood movie, Hollywood special effects are used to create the convincing simulacra of a terrorist attack. The staging of the nuclear attack on Canberra is also an excellent example of the kind of event that Baudrillard

---

67 McGahan, p. 261.
68 Goldsworthy, p. 9.
69 McGahan, p. 264.
70 Ibid., p. 264.
71 Ibid., p. 265.
72 Ibid., p. 265.
73 Ibid., p. 265.
74 Žižek, p. 11. Baudrillard, p. 7.

describes in his discussion of what he terms "a negationist society."[75] Baudrillard declares, "No event is 'real' any longer. Terror attacks, trials, wars, corruption, opinion polls – there's nothing now that isn't rigged or undecidable."[76] Baudrillard's argument applies equally well to Richard Flanagan's *The Unknown Terrorist*, which also deals extensively with media manipulation of events.

In *The Unknown Terrorist*, the government and the media both exploit terrorism in order to consolidate and expand their power over the public. Flanagan, like Turner Hospital and McGahan, presents a three-way relationship between the government, the media, and terrorism, in the process critiquing the use of terrorism by both the government and the media. Andrew McCann argues that Flanagan's novel "is largely concerned with the ways in which the government and the media administer popular consciousness in the interests of a xenophobic, anti-democratic agenda."[77] The "anti-democratic agenda" that McCann identifies in *The Unknown Terrorist* is also evident in *Due Preparations for the Plague* and *Underground*; all three novels present governments that trample basic democratic freedoms. In Flanagan's novel, the government is uninterested in government "of the people, by the people, for the people"; rather, the government seeks to create a passive public that can be controlled and manipulated.

The novel is set in Sydney during the present and focuses on two protagonists: a stripper who goes by the names Krystal, the Black Widow, the Russian Doll, and most often, the Doll; and Richard Cody, a television anchorman. The action takes place over just four days, lending the narrative a frenetic pace. The Doll's real name is Gina Davies; she is a twenty-six-year-old who dances at the Chairman's Lounge in Kings Cross, an inner Sydney suburb famous for night clubs, prostitution, and drugs. The event that triggers the novel's action is the discovery of unexploded bombs in Sydney. The news is introduced into the narrative via the media when the Doll hears it on a radio: "More bombings in Baghdad [...] another threat to attack Sydney on another al-Qa'ida website [...] a late unconfirmed report that three unexploded bombs had been discovered at Sydney's Homebush Olympic sta-

---

75 Baudrillard, p. 81.

76 Ibid., p. 81.

77 Andrew McCann, 'Professing the Popular: Political Fiction circa 2006', *New Reckonings: Australian Literature Past, Present, Future. Essays in Honour of Elizabeth Webby*, ed. by Leigh Dale and Brigid Rooney, special issue of *Australian Literary Studies*, 23 (2007), 43-57 (p. 50).

dium."[78] Cody anchors the live television coverage of the bomb scare and finds that the story quickly becomes repetitive,

> then pointless [...]. The crowd was evacuated, the area sealed off [...]. He had continued saying the same thing over and over [...] while a string of so-called experts – mostly consultants wanting a job as an expert in security, terror, politics – commented on each other's remarks, which in turn repeated and elaborated the few brief comments made by the police and government spinners.[79]

Here, Flanagan exposes and critiques the inanity, repetitive nature, and distortion of much media coverage, as well as the close ties between the media and the government.

The media is a ubiquitous presence in *The Unknown Terrorist*, constantly influencing the character's lives through its various manifestations, such as newspapers, television, radio, and magazines. Bruce Bennett contends that Flanagan's "principal target is the Australian media whose journalists and their employers fall too readily for government propaganda and make their ratings-based reputations on vastly exaggerated projections of violent threats."[80] Likewise, Michael Ashby argues that Flanagan vividly depicts the media's role in fuelling "paranoia and prejudice."[81] Flanagan's scathing depiction of the media is achieved not only through the narrator's commentary and the presentation of negative media behavior, but also through statements made by characters who are members of the media. Jerry Mendes, a television network executive, tells Cody, his subordinate, that people do not want the truth, but rather they "'want an exciting illusion [...] Find that sort of story, ginger it up with a few dashes of fear and nastiness, and you've hit gold.'"[82]

Mendes' advice to dispense fear is taken to heart by Cody, who discovers the power of fear in storytelling at a dinner party held at a mansion on Sydney harbor. Holding forth at dinner, Cody argues for the mandatory detention of refugees, inflates stories about "'dangerous Islamic types,'"[83] and speaks passionately "of the atrocities committed in London, at Beslan, in Madrid and

---

78 Richard Flanagan, *The Unknown Terrorist* (New York: Grove Press, 2006), p. 12.

79 Ibid., p. 21.

80 Bruce Bennett, 'Of Spies and Terrorists: Australian Fiction after 9/11', *Asiatic: IIUM Journal of Language and Literature*, 2 (2008), 10-20 (p. 13).

81 Michael Ashby, rev. of *The Unknown Terrorist*, by Richard Flanagan, *Eureka Street*, 16 (2006), 23-24 (p. 23).

82 Flanagan, pp. 26-7.

83 Ibid., pp. 27-8.

Bali."[84] Cody claims torture is necessary and shocks himself "with his opinions and the violence with which he forced them on others."[85] However, he is even more shocked by the manner in which "other people tended to agree meekly with him," not because they share his views, but "because he was stronger, louder, more aggressive."[86] Cody continues to woo his audience with "dark tales of terrible plots foiled, of [...] mass poisonings and bombings and gassings planned and, through vigilance, averted [...] [he] could feel the fear take hold. He sensed the pull of a story, the power of its telling, as the table went quiet."[87] Still seething over his demotion, Cody vows to create "a story [...] that no one would forget."[88]

After the dinner party, Cody goes to the Chairman's Lounge, where he pays the Doll to perform private dances for him. The relationship between the Doll and Cody is purely a financial transaction for her; however, Cody views the Doll (and, by extension, women in general) as a lesser being who exists in order to provide him with pleasure. Although Cody does not know the Doll, she recognizes him immediately: "He was Mr TV, Richard Cody [...] dully reassuring: always the same and telling you what you already knew."[89] After leaving the club, Cody notices the Doll walking ahead of him, and tells her that he will pay well for oral sex. She refuses, and her rejection later partially motivates his campaign against her.[90] After rejecting Cody, the Doll watches the Mardi Gras parade, where she runs into Tariq, whom she met earlier in the day at Bondi beach.[91] After an evening of dancing and drinking, the Doll has sex with Tariq at his apartment.[92] When the Doll awakes, Tariq is gone.[93] Upon leaving Tariq's apartment, the Doll breakfasts at a café across the street; while she is inside, the police search Tariq's building.[94] Unbeknownst to the Doll, she had been filmed entering Tariq's building the night before, and the media are already preparing to transmit images linking her to terrorism.

Flanagan constantly depicts the media as creator of the fear of terrorism, as well as to reveal the Doll's growing recognition of her predicament and

84 Ibid., p. 30.
85 Ibid., p. 30.
86 Ibid., p. 31.
87 Ibid., p. 32.
88 Ibid., p. 33.
89 Ibid., p. 49.
90 Ibid., pp. 54, 105.
91 Ibid., pp. 64, 105.
92 Ibid., p. 67.
93 Ibid., p. 84.
94 Ibid., p. 87.

her fear of the government and her fellow citizens. While shopping on the day after her encounter with Tariq, the Doll notices a large television screen "showing crowds leaving the Homebush Olympic stadium after the previous day's bomb scare. That image gave way to a close-up of a kid's backpack being unzipped to reveal a bomb [...] [before showing] armed police taking up positions around Tariq's apartment block."[95] The images of the raid are followed by "a blurry photograph of a bearded man in Arabic dress [...] beneath which ran a banner saying [...] 'SUSPECTED TERRORIST ELUDES POLICE DRAGNET.'"[96] Later, the Doll watches a news report that names Tariq as a suspected terrorist and contains security camera footage of her and Tariq entering the building: "'It is not yet known,' continued the newsreader, 'who the woman is.'"[97] A few hours later, the Doll sees the same footage playing on television again, this time with an announcer declaring, "'Police are fearful [...] that two terrorists who escaped a midday raid [...] may strike somewhere in Sydney any day.'"[98] In just a few hours, the media transform the Doll from an unknown woman into a suspected terrorist. The recurring images serve to link the Doll to Tariq and the unexploded bombs; moreover, the repetition of the footage creates an escalating level of fear amongst the general public.

When Cody recognizes the Doll on television, he calls his contacts in pursuit of leads and manages to obtain her real name.[99] As Cody gathers information, he begins "rehearsing the story he would present" about Gina Davies' life.[100] Remembering his control of the audience at the dinner party, he desires to repeat the feat, "but this time mesmerizing not a dozen people, but millions."[101] As Cody works on the story, he realizes that "key dramatic elements" are missing.[102] Although Tariq's story is "obvious – a Middle Eastern name and a no-doubt predictable past [...] the pole dancer was different: an Aussie turning on their own – an unknown terrorist."[103] Cody eventually convinces himself that "what at first seemed ludicrous – a pole dancer an Islamic terrorist! – now seemed insidious and disturbing [...] it was up to him [...] to expose what was happening. And what a story it would be! What rat-

---

95 Ibid., p. 91.
96 Ibid., p. 92.
97 Ibid., p. 95.
98 Ibid., p. 97.
99 Ibid., pp. 105-6.
100 Ibid., p. 106.
101 Ibid., p. 106.
102 Ibid., p. 106.
103 Ibid., pp. 106-7.

ings they would get! It had everything – sex, politics, even bombs!"[104] The construction of Cody's narrative about the "unknown terrorist" is explicitly depicted by Flanagan as an artificial process, a combination of disparate elements, a mixture of truth, lies, and speculation. Flanagan engages in such meta-fictional commentary throughout the novel. For Cody, however, whether or not the story is true is irrelevant; all that matters is whether the story will convince the audience.

The media is eager to present stories about terrorism, and thus maintain constant contact with government sources while constructing its narratives. Cody tries persuading his boss to run a special so that he can break the story, and tells Mendes that Channel Six is in a race with the Doll to get the story out first: "her with her bombs or them with a tell-all current affairs special."[105] Mendes gives Cody a half-hour in prime time on the condition that the special has to be about both Tariq and the Doll. Mendes also stipulates that the "big boss […] the chairman of the nation's largest print and electronic media company," must approve the special and clear it with "his Canberra mates."[106] Thus, the media representations of terrorism must be sanctioned by the appropriate government officials to ensure that the interests of all the power-brokers are met. The politicians waste no time in utilizing the media to spread fear and present a strong position on terrorism, appearing on radio talk shows to make statements such as, "'These terrorists are subhuman filth […]. The government needs to be doing more to ensure they are hunted down and eliminated.'"[107] As the media develops the story and receives information from government sources, speculations are presented as facts and possibilities stated as certainties. Flanagan continually depicts the media as unethical, subordinate to the government, and fixated on increasing ratings and market share.

It is through the media that the Doll becomes aware of her predicament: that she is viewed by the government as a suspected terrorist and that she will be hunted down. The Doll views a television announcement stating that Channel Six will air a national exclusive in which Cody will reveal "the true identity of 'the unknown terrorist'"[108] and begins to understand the situation. She considers turning herself in to the police but fears they will not believe her. She also contemplates approaching the media but worries that they will

---

104 Ibid., p. 107.
105 Ibid., p. 113.
106 Ibid., p. 114.
107 Ibid., p. 121.
108 Ibid., p. 139.

set her up.[109] The Doll comes to the conclusion that "[t]o give herself up was madness, for they wanted her as a terrorist [...] they wanted their victim [...] The Doll sensed that no one would tell the truth about her once she was in their power."[110] The Doll realizes that those in power, especially the government and the media, are more interested in pursuing their own agendas than protecting the innocent or telling the truth. Richard Carr argues that the government and "media campaign against the Doll works because the public [...] has a concrete target for their fear. The Doll makes a perfect sacrifice to the terrorist gambit because she *is* a nobody, a person of low status [...] whose arrest and imprisonment will spark no outrage."[111] Although Carr does not mention the Doll's gender, the fact that the she is female, and a stripper, certainly contributes to her status as "a nobody."

The media present the Doll more negatively and sensationally each hour, deliberately conflating the possibility of a terrorist attack in Sydney with previous terrorist attacks in other cities by presenting images in an order that forms a narrative culminating in an attack on Sydney. On one occasion, a "giant screen" displays a "vast image [...] of the Twin Towers burning."[112] The image dissolves into another of a "backpack being unzipped" to reveal a bomb, "before flickering and transforming into giant armed police surrounding Tariq's apartment block."[113] Soon the television news reports are adding new scenes to their catalogue of terror, including

> a murky London tube train moments after it had been bombed; the Sari nightclub burning after the Bali bombing; wounded being taken away from the Madrid train bombing [...] Osama bin Laden [...] Men in robes firing grenade launchers. Great buildings exploding into balloons of fire [...] Hostages about to be beheaded.[114]

As well as forming an over-arching narrative depicting a series of terrorist attacks, each of the images represent a separate narrative, and since each of the images and narratives are familiar to the viewers, there is no need for words. Each image has acquired its power and embedded narrative through repeated exposure. The media distorts and exaggerates the story to such an extent that a number of radio stations begin claiming that the impending at-

---

109 Ibid., p. 141.

110 Ibid., p. 251.

111 Richard Carr, 'More than a Potboiler', rev. of *The Unknown Terrorist*, by Richard Flanagan, *Antipodes* 21 (2007), 184-85 (p. 185). Emphasis in original.

112 Flanagan, p. 148.

113 Ibid., p. 148.

114 Ibid., pp. 159-160.

tack will be in the form of "a dirty nuclear bomb,"[115] despite the lack of *any* evidence. In his discussion of the relationship between the media and terrorism, Baudrillard argues, "There is no 'good' use of the media; the media are part of the event, they are part of the terror, and they work in both directions."[116] Flanagan's depiction of the media in *The Unknown Terrorist* proves Baudrillard's point.

Baudrillard also argues that terrorism runs the risk of "reinforcing the police and security control systems," and contends that such changes have occurred around the world since 9/11.[117] Similarly, Flanagan portrays the government security and intelligence forces as possessing the power to act as they see fit, in secret, and without consequences. Ironically, the power of the security and intelligence forces is based on anti-terrorism laws that have stripped citizens of freedoms and rights. Thus, in the guise of protecting the freedom of citizens, the government reduces freedoms. Moreover, as Ashby argues, Flanagan portrays the police and intelligence agencies as ruthless in their pursuit of rapid results.[118] Although the government and the media work together closely, the media is always subordinate to the government, which holds the ultimate power.

At one point during the construction of his narrative, Cody doubts that he has enough material for a convincing primetime special on "the unknown terrorist"; however, his ASIO contact Siv Harmsen informs him that an anonymous package containing footage "showing a pro-Islamist rally in Cairo in 1989" will soon be delivered to the studio.[119] Moreover, a man named "Bill" is willing to "be filmed as an anonymous security source" and to identify "one of the figures in the footage as an Islamic fundamentalist who happened to be Tariq al-Hakim's uncle."[120] Harmsen also provides Cody with the names of "a former US Special Forces colonel, and [...] a retired senior intelligence analyst who just happened to be in Sydney that afternoon in a hotel close to Six's studios."[121] Addressing a fellow security officer's concern that the Doll may be innocent, Harmsen declares, "'Listen [...] even if you're right [...] you couldn't change any of it. This story, you know, it serves a bigger purpose [...] It's still important that the public know these bastards are

115 Ibid., p. 189.
116 Baudrillard, p. 31.
117 Ibid., p. 55.
118 Ashby, p. 23.
119 Flanagan, p. 255.
120 Ibid., p. 255.
121 Ibid., p. 256.

out there.'"[122] Harmsen claims that "'[u]nless [...] [the public are] terrified, they won't agree with what we do and why we have to do it.'"[123] Here, the maintenance of government power through the manipulation of terrorism and the public, via the media, is abundantly clear.

Žižek argues that the anthrax attacks in the United States in October 2001 gave the West its first post-9/11 experience of a "new 'invisible' warfare in which [...] ordinary citizens [...] are totally dependent on the authorities for information about what is going on: [...][they] see and hear nothing; all [...] [they] know comes from the official media."[124] In *Due Preparations for the Plague*, *Underground*, and *The Unknown Terrorist*, the general public is placed in the very position Žižek describes, relying on the media to provide information regarding both terrorist attacks and the threat of terrorism. However, in all three novels, the vast majority of the population is unaware that the information presented to them has been manipulated by both the government and the media and that the government and the media utilize terrorism and the fear of terrorism in order to maintain and expand power. Thus, rather than being informed and protected by a democratic free press, the public is placed in a state of passivity and ignorance. Steven Lang reads *The Unknown Terrorist* and *Underground* as timely warnings pointing to a dangerous complacency in Australian society regarding politics, and argues that the novels suggest Australian society has "reached a point of disconnect in the workings of [...] democracy" that invites politicians to abuse their power.[125] Lang's points about McGahan's and Flanagan's novels apply equally well to *Due Preparations for the Plague*. The three novels addressed in this chapter all demonstrate the pervasiveness of terrorism as a dominant political and cultural issue in post-9/11 Australian society and present dire warnings about the interdependent relationship between the government, the media, and terrorism.

---

122 Ibid., p. 270-1.

123 Ibid., p. 272.

124 Žižek, p. 37.

125 Steven Lang, 'Slumming It', rev. of *The Unknown Terrorist*, by Richard Flanagan, and *Underground*, by Andrew McGahan, *Overland*, 186 (2007), 18-19 (p. 18).

Bibliography

Ashby, Michael, rev. of *The Unknown Terrorist*, by Richard Flanagan, *Eureka Street*, 16 (2006), 23-24

Baudrillard, Jean, *The Spirit of Terrorism and Other Essays*, trans. by Chris Turner (New York: Verso, 2003)

Bennett, Bruce, 'Of Spies and Terrorists: Australian Fiction after 9/11', *Asiatic: IIUM Journal of English Language and Literature*, 2 (2008), 10-2

Bliss, Carolyn, rev. of *Due Preparations for the Plague*, by Janette Turner Hospital, *World LiteratureToday*, 78 (2004), 78-79

Carr, Richard, 'More than a Potboiler'. rev. of *The Unknown Terrorist*, by Richard Flanagan, *Antipodes*, 21 (2007), 184-185

Flanagan, Richard, *The Unknown Terrorist* (New York: Grove Press, 2006).

Goldsworthy, Kerryn, 'Straight for the Throat', rev. of *Underground*, by Andrew McGahan, *Australian Book Review*, 285 (2006), 8-9

Hassall, Anthony J., 'The Year's Work in Fiction', *Westerly*, 52 (2007), 187-199

Herrero, Dolores, '*Due Preparations for the Plague*: Globalisation, Terror and the Ethics of Alterity', *Kunapipi*, 28 (2006), 25-43

Lang, Steven, 'Slumming It', rev. of *The Unknown Terrorist*, by Richard Flanagan, and *Underground*, by Andrew McGahan, *Overland*, 186 (2007), 18-19

Luebke, Steven R., 'A *1984* for Our Time', rev. of *Underground*, by Andrew McGahan, *Antipodes*, 22 (2008), 75-76

McCann, Andrew, 'Professing the Popular: Political Fiction circa 2006', *New Reckonings: Australian Literature Past, Present, Future. Essays in Honour of Elizabeth Webby*, ed. by Leigh Dale and Brigid Rooney, Special Issue of *Australian Literary Studies*, 23 (2007), 43-57

McGahan, Andrew, *Underground* (Crows Nest, NSW: Allen and Unwin, 2006)

O'Reilly, Nathanael, 'A Timely Tale of Terrorism', rev. of *Due Preparations for the Plague*, by Janette Turner Hospital, *Antipodes*, 18 (2004), 88-89.

Turner Hospital, Janette, *Due Preparations for the Plague* (New York: Norton, 2004)

Weaver, Rachael, 'Histories of the Present', *Overland*, 187 (2007), 81-85.

Žižek, Slavoj, *Welcome to the Desert of the Real!: Five Essays on September 11 and Related Dates* (NewYork: Verso, 2002)

Contributors

Sofia Ahlberg is senior lecturer in the School of Communication, Arts and Critical Enquiry, at La Trobe University, in Bendigo, Victoria, Australia.

William Anselmi is a professor in the department of Modern Languages and Cultural Studies, and Sheena Wilson is an assistant professor at Campus Saint-Jean; both are at the University of Alberta in Canada. Anselmi works on Italian Literature, Italian Canadian Literature and culture. Wilson's research interests involve an interdisciplinary approach to the study of human/civil rights abuses as they are represented in literature, film, and media. Together, Anselmi and Wilson write on issues related to ethno-cultural representations in literature and documentary film. They have previously co-published articles such as "Performative Radicalism in contemporary Canadian documentary film" and "Slumdogging It: Rebranding the American Dream, New World Orders, and Neo-Colonialism." They are currently working on issues related to First Nations Issues and environmental pollution by oil corporations in Canada.

Cara Cilano is an associate professor of English at the University of North Carolina Wilmington in the US. She has published on Indian and Pakistani fiction in journals such as *Ariel* and *The Journal of Commonwealth and Post-colonial Literature*. Her book on fiction about the 1971 Pakistani War is forthcoming from Routledge.

Carolyn A. Durham is Inez Kinney Gaylord Professor of French at the College of Wooster (US) where she also teaches in the Comparative Literature and Film Studies programs. She is a graduate of Wellesley College and received her MA and PhD from the University of Chicago. Her most recent books are *Double Takes: Culture and Gender in French films and Their American Remakes* (1998) and *Literary Globalism: Anglo-American Fiction Set in France* (2005). She is also the author of numerous articles on twentieth and twenty-first century French and American fiction and film.

Margret Grebowicz is an associate professor of Philosophy at Goucher College (US). Her translations from her native Polish have appeared in numerous literary journals, including *Agni*, *Field*, *Third Coast*, *Two Lines*, and *Poetry International*. Her theoretical work has appeared in *Hypatia*, *Philosophy of Science*, *Metascience*, and *The Year's Work in Critical and Cultural Theory*, among other journals. She is the editor of *Gender after Lyotard* and *SciFi in the Mind's Eye: Reading Science through Science Fiction*, and co-author (with Helen Merrick) of the forthcoming *Beyond the Cyborg: Adventures with Haraway*. She lives in Brooklyn, NY.

Gavin Hicks is pursuing a PhD in the Department of Germanic Languages and Literatures at the University of Pittsburgh in the US.

Brandon Kempner is an assistant professor and Director of Undergraduate Studies in the Department of English at New Mexico Highlands University in the US.

Henrike Lehnguth is pursuing a PhD in American Studies at the University of Maryland, College Park, in the US.

Alison J. Murray Levine is an assistant professor in the Department of French Language and Literature at the University of Virginia in the US. She has published in *Cinema Journal* and *Journal of Film and Video*, and has a book on documentary film in interwar France forthcoming from Continuum Press.

Ewa Lipska was born in 1945 and made her poetic debut in 1961. She worked as poetry editor for the publishing house Wydawnictwo Literackie for ten years. In 1975-76, she visited to the University of Iowa as an International Writing Program fellow. She spent 1983 in West Berlin as a fellow of the Deutscher Akademisches Austausch Dienst. Lipska participated in international poetry festivals in Canada (1981), The Netherlands (1985), and Slovenia (1988), and became a founding member of the Polish Society of Writers (Stowarzyszenie Pisarzy Polskich) in 1989. 1991 to 1997 was her longest period away from Poland, during which she lived in Vienna and worked at the Polish embassy as director of the Polish Institute. Since 1997, Lipska has lived in Kraków but travels to Vienna often and is a member of both the Polish and the Austrian PEN Club. She is the recipient of numerous awards, including the PEN Club's Robert Graves award and the award of the city of Kraków, and a two-time nominee for the Nike, Poland's most prestigious award for a volume of poetry.

Ana Cristina Mendes is a researcher at ULICES (University of Lisbon Centre for English Studies) in Portugal. Her interests span postcolonial cultural production and its intersection with the culture industries. Her publications include articles on Indian and British Asian film, and on Indian writing in English. She is currently editing the volume of essays *Salman Rushdie and Visual*

Culture: Celebrating Impurity, Disrupting Borders, and co-editing with Lisa Lau the collection *The Oriental Other Within: Re-Orientalisms and South Asian Identity Politics*.

Magali Cornier Michael is professor and chair of the Department of English at Duquesne University in Pittsburgh, PA, in the US. She is author of *New Visions of Community in Contemporary American Fiction: Tan, Kingsolver, Castillo, Morrison* (2006) and *Feminism and the Postmodern Impulse: Post-World War II Fiction* (1996), as well as several articles and book chapters on contemporary British and American fiction.

Nathanael O'Reilly is an assistant professor of English at the University of Texas at Tyler in the US. He holds a Ph.D. in literature from Western Michigan University, with specializations in Postcolonial literature and theory, British and Irish modernism, and Contemporary Australian literature. His criticism and poetry have been published in North America, Europe, Australia, Asia and the South Pacific.

Silvia Schultermandl holds a PhD in American Literature and Cultural Studies from University of Graz, Austria. She is currently an assistant professor of American Studies at Karl-Franzens-Universität Graz, where she teaches courses in American literature and culture studies. She has published several articles on multi-ethnic American literatures, such as articles on Maxine Hong Kingston and Rebecca Walker, Linda Hogan, Julia Alvarez and Esmeralda Santiago, Nora Ojka Keller, and on motherhood and feminism, such as on Barbara Kingsolver. She recently put together a special issue for the journal *Interactions* on Asian American and British Asian Culture, with a comprehensive critical introduction. She is currently at work on an anthology entitled *Growing Up Transnational* (together with May Freidman, York U, Toronto) and has published a monograph on mother-daughter relationships and transnational feminism in Asian American literature, *Transnational Matrilineage: Mother-Daughter Conflicts in Asian American Literature* (LIT Verlag, 2009).

Susan Sutherland is an assistant professor on the Faculty of Law at the University of British Columbia in Canada, and Sarah Swan is an LL.M candidate at Columbia University in New York City. Together, they have also published on the American television show *Alias*.

Ulrike Tancke earned her PhD in English at Trier University in and is now on faculty in the Department of British Studies at Johannes Gutenberg University in Mainz, Germany.

Index

CPSIA information can be obtained at www.ICGtesting.com
261015BV00001B/14/P

9 789042 027022